D1219167

Taming Globalization

TAMING GLOBALIZATION:

INTERNATIONAL LAW, THE U.S. CONSTITUTION, AND THE NEW WORLD ORDER

Julian Ku

Hofstra University Law School

John Yoo

Berkeley Law School, University of California

OXFORD
UNIVERSITY PRESS

OXFORD
UNIVERSITY PRESS

Oxford University Press, Inc., publishes works that further Oxford University's objective of excellence in research, scholarship, and education.

Oxford   New York
Auckland   Cape Town   Dar es Salaam   Hong Kong   Karachi   Kuala Lumpur
Madrid   Melbourne   Mexico City   Nairobi   New Delhi   Shanghai   Taipei   Toronto

With offices in
Argentina   Austria   Brazil   Chile   Czech Republic   France   Greece   Guatemala   Hungary   Italy
Japan   Poland   Portugal   Singapore   South Korea   Switzerland   Thailand   Turkey   Ukraine
Vietnam

Copyright © 2012 by Julian Ku and John Yoo

Published by Oxford University Press, Inc.
198 Madison Avenue, New York, New York 10016

Oxford is a registered trademark of Oxford University Press
Oxford University Press is a registered trademark of Oxford University Press, Inc.

All rights reserved. No part of this publication may be reproduced, stored in a retrieval system, or transmitted, in any form or by any means, electronic, mechanical, photocopying, recording, or otherwise, without the prior permission of Oxford University Press, Inc.

Library of Congress Cataloging-in-Publication Data

Ku, Julian.
  Taming globalization : international law, the U. S. Constitution, and the new world order / Julian Ku, John Yoo.
    p. cm.
Includes bibliographical references and index.
ISBN 978-0-19-983742-7 (hardback)
  1. International and municipal law—United States. 2. Constitutional law—United States.
3. Globalization and law—United States.
I. Yoo, John. II. Title.
  KF4581.K8 2012
  341.30973—dc23   2011039607

1 2 3 4 5 6 7 8 9
Printed in the United States of America on acid-free paper

Note to Readers
This publication is designed to provide accurate and authoritative information in regard to the subject matter covered. It is based upon sources believed to be accurate and reliable and is intended to be current as of the time it was written. It is sold with the understanding that the publisher is not engaged in rendering legal, accounting, or other professional services. If legal advice or other expert assistance is required, the services of a competent professional person should be sought. Also, to confirm that the information has not been affected or changed by recent developments, traditional legal research techniques should be used, including checking primary sources where appropriate.

(Based on the Declaration of Principles jointly adopted by a Committee of the American Bar Association and a Committee of Publishers and Associations.)

You may order this or any other Oxford University Press publication by visiting the Oxford University Press website at www.oup.com

Table of Contents

vii   Acknowledgments

1   1. Globalization and the Constitution

19   2. Globalization and Sovereignty

51   3. Globalization and Structure

87   4. Non-Self-Execution

113   5. Presidents and Customary International Law

151   6. Globalization and the States

177   7. Globalization and Constitutional Controversy

227   8. Foreign Law and the Constitution

253   Conclusion

259   Index

Acknowledgments

We entertained writing this book together after a chance meeting at Princeton University six years ago. While neither of us had journeyed to New Jersey for globalization, we discovered some shared intuitions about the U.S. Constitution and international affairs. Those common views led us to joint projects in *Supreme Court Review*, *Constitutional Commentary*, and the *William and Mary Law Review*. The journals gave us the chance to try out some of the ideas found here, for which we are grateful, and for granting us permission to reprint some of the work we initially published there.

Julian also thanks the *North Carolina Law Review*, the *Minnesota Law Review*, and the *Yale Law Journal* for permission to reprint some of the work he had originally published with them. John thanks the *Harvard Journal of Law and Public Policy* for permission to reprint some of the work he had originally published with them.

We are grateful for the many friends and colleagues over the years who provided us with valuable advice on this project. We particularly appreciate those who read the manuscript: Jesse Choper, Robert Delahunty, and Sai Prakash. They greatly improved what you read here. We were also fortunate to have received the capable research assistance of Christopher Cella, Janet Galeria, James Phillips, Claire Thompson, and Meng Xi. We could not have completed the project without the good offices of two editors – Michael O'Malley, formerly of Yale University Press, and Kevin Pendergast of Oxford University Press – who provided sage counsel and excellent suggestions for improving the manuscript. Our agent, Lynn Chu, did an outstanding job of helping us not just with the book proposal, but with editing the manuscript. Just because she always goes beyond the call of duty does not make it any more of a surprise each time.

Julian Ku thanks the Maurice A. Deane Law School at Hofstra University for granting generous research support for this project. His former colleagues at Hofstra, Peter Spiro and Mark Movsesian, provided Julian with the mentoring that he needed to begin his academic career. His parents, Sophia and Peter, encouraged him to pursue a career in academia in the first place. His daughter, Lyra-Anne, who arrived in the midst of the project, has been a source of endless delight and inspiration. Julian also could not complete this acknowledgment without thanking his wife, Winnie Chu, whose love, patience and support is the foundation upon which all of his work depends.

John Yoo thanks Dean Christopher Edley Jr. of Boalt Hall for providing the research support that made this book possible. Chris DeMuth, Arthur Brooks, David Gerson, and Dany Pletka of the American Enterprise Institute provided John with a home away from home in Washington, D.C. where he could test these ideas on globalization, constitutionalism, and sovereignty against the practical knowledge inside the Beltway. John would also like to set out his thanks here to two departed colleagues and friends, Phil Frickey and Paul Mishkin, who loved to discuss these ideas in their formative state. They provided the shoulders upon which we stand now. Finally, John wishes to thank his wife, Elsa Arnett, whose wit, smarts, and optimism make him and his work all the better every day.

1 Globalization and the Constitution

That globalization is transforming American society is a truism. As never before, the U.S. economy depends on international trade,[1] the free flow of capital, and integration into the world financial system. International events affect domestic markets and institutions more than ever. Roughly one-third of all American economic activity is related to either imports or exports. Advances in communications, transportation, and the Internet have brought great benefits to the United States. The attacks of September 11, 2001, however, revealed the negative effects of globalization. Counterterrorism, immigration, the environment, drugs, crime, and even mundane issues such as traffic flow depend on the same channels of globalization as the world economy.

Scholars and commentators from diverse fields such as economics, cultural theory, and international relations have weighed in on globalization at great length. But what they have failed to address comprehensively is globalization's effect on the American constitutional and political system. Globalization presents profound challenges because it demands unprecedented levels of international cooperation. To limit carbon emissions, an effective regime must set standards for almost all

---

[1] According to the *Economic Report of the President*, for example, in the first half of 2008 U.S. exports constituted 13 percent of Gross Domestic Product (GDP), the highest proportion ever. *Economic Report of the President*, January 2009, 128 (2009). Until 1970, American exports and imports usually accounted for about one-tenth of the GDP. By 2009, imports and exports of goods and services had jumped to over 30 percent of GDP. *Id.* at 73.

forms of energy use worldwide. To allow for the smooth movement of capital, nations must coordinate their regulatory controls on the financial industry. International organizations have been the handmaidens in the explosion in international legal regimes. Multilateral treaties may ask state parties to delegate lawmaking, law enforcement, or adjudication authority to bureaucracies that are independent of any nation. Globalization sometimes goes beyond national authorities to reach into the domain of U.S. states, which may be the best unit of government to address matters such as crime or drugs.

Efforts at effective international governance create tension with American constitutional rules on the use of government power. Recent examples abound. To what extent do international court judgments have force in American law, invalidating otherwise valid judgments by domestic courts?[2] Can the President and the Senate together sign an international treaty that binds the United States to either legalize or criminalize abortion, or are issues of family law reserved as a matter of American law for the states?[3] Should international and foreign laws be used to interpret the U.S. Constitution?[4] May Congress and the President delegate federal authority to international organizations to regulate domestic conduct, for instance, in arms control or carbon emissions?[5]

While the pressures of globalization may well demand new regulatory regimes, we must consider how global governance will mesh with our existing political and legal systems. The American constitutional system requires that power originate from the bottom up—from the people—and that it be subject to a specific system of federalism and the separation of powers. Globalization, and its consequences for American law, creates serious conflicts with this basic framework. This book will highlight these conflicts and show the way to resolving them.

I. DEFINING GLOBALIZATION

Globalization has drawn enormous interest from scholars in many different academic disciplines. It has also captured the attention of leading public commentators. Yet despite (or perhaps because of) this flood of interest, the term "globalization" has come to represent such a broad array of concepts that the term may have no useful meaning. One influential explanation of the different meanings of globalization, for instance, identifies at least five different usages, ranging from liberalizations of economic regulations to the "deterritorialization" of social space.[6] At least one scholar has dismissed the usefulness of the term "globalization" because it can "mean anything from the Internet to a hamburger."[7]

---

[2] Sanchez-Llamas v. Oregon, 548 U.S. 331 (2006).
[3] The United Nations Convention on the Rights of the Child, Nov. 20, 1989, 28 I.L.M. 1448.
[4] Roper v. Simmons, 543 U.S. 551 (2005).
[5] Natural Res. Def. Council v. EPA, 489 F.3d 1364, 1370–71 (D.C. Cir. 2007).
[6] JAN AART SCHOLTE, GLOBALIZATION: A CRITICAL INTRODUCTION 16 (2000).
[7] SUSAN STRANGE, THE RETREAT OF THE STATE: THE DIFFUSION OF POWER IN THE WORLD ECONOMY xiii (1996).

We certainly do not want to add to the confusion over the definition of globalization. For our purposes, *globalization* refers to the various economic, technological, and social changes that have occurred because of the acceleration of communication, transportation, and information systems across national borders. The processes of globalization have led to (1) the explosive growth in international trade; (2) the swift creation of international markets in goods and services; (3) the easy movement of capital and labor across national borders; (4) the rise of major transnational networks, such as international drug cartels, international crime-fighting regimes, and international terrorism; and (5) the global effects of industrialization on the environment and global commons.

In each instance, these forces have led the United States to seek deeper and more complex forms of international cooperation, often referred to as *global governance*. International cooperation, usually in the form of multilateral treaty regimes, seeks to regulate what had previously been left to independent sovereign states. The complexity of administering international regulatory regimes—which may involve dozens, if not hundreds, of sovereign states—has led to a greater reliance on international institutions to interpret and enforce treaty obligations.

Globalization has also unleashed potentially important new forces in the conduct of international relations: *international organizations* and *nongovernmental organizations* (NGOs). International organizations include the United Nations, the World Trade Organization, and international tribunals such as the International Court of Justice, which can exercise authority with legal force. NGOs can include groups without any formal legal authority and not established pursuant to any treaty—groups such as Amnesty International. Some international relations scholars argue that the rise of international institutions and NGOs has reduced the primacy of nation-states in global affairs. Within the legal academy, a wave of scholarship largely associated with Kal Raustiala and Anne-Marie Slaughter has emphasized the importance of subgovernmental networks in the development of international regulations and norms.[8] Legal scholars and political scientists have focused on the growing network of relationships between national courts of different sovereign states under the rubric of international law.[9]

While some international relations scholars criticize an overemphasis on the role of international institutions and NGOs, we believe that these groups play a critical role in "bringing home" the effects of globalization to the U.S. legal system. NGOs in particular have shown an ability to operate within the domestic U.S. system, influencing the outcomes of governmental decisions in ways that lie outside the competence of international institutions. For example, NGOs have used creative

---

[8] *See, e.g.*, Anne-Marie Slaughter, *Judicial Globalization*, 40 VA. J. INT'L L. 1103 (2000).

[9] *See, e.g.*, Kenneth W. Abbott, Robert O. Keohane, Andrew Moravcsik, Anne-Marie Slaughter, & Duncan Snidal, *The Concept of Legalization*, 54 INT'L ORG. 401 (2000) (focusing on the growing importance of international law in international relations); Laurence Helfer & Anne-Marie Slaughter, *Why States Create International Tribunals: A Response to Professors Posner and Yoo*, 93 CAL. L. REV. 899 (2005); Eric A. Posner & John C. Yoo, *Judicial Independence in International Tribunals*, 93 CAL. L. REV. 1 (2005).

and effective litigation strategies to develop and enforce global governance regimes via the U.S. court system. Such litigation can result, and has resulted, in the adoption of an interpretation of international law over the opposition of the U.S. government's chief foreign policy organ: the executive branch. The ability of NGOs to influence the U.S. government via domestic litigation is one of the most tangible examples of how nonstate actors can create serious and powerful pressure on the U.S. constitutional system.

We believe the consequences of globalization will pose the most direct challenges to the fundamental justification underlying the system of government in the United States: *popular sovereignty.* Unlike other nations, which have located ultimate sovereign power in the nation, in its monarch, or in its national government, the prevailing theory of the U.S. Constitution locates such ultimate sovereign power in the People of the United States.[10] In this view, the various institutions of the U.S. government are merely agents of the People, whose powers are delegated exclusively through the U.S. Constitution. The Constitution provides the exclusive source of sovereign power to the U.S. government.

The theory of popular sovereignty highlights the crucial importance of two fundamental principles underlying the U.S. Constitution's structure: the separation of powers and federalism. *Separation of powers* refers to the system of "checks and balances" between the three branches of the federal government: the Congress, the President, and the courts. As we will explain, globalization's pressure for certain forms of multilateral cooperation could undermine the existing balance of powers between these three branches of the federal government.

Federalism refers to the balance of authority between the national government and the states of the Union. By constitutional design and historical practice, the states exercise a measure of autonomy over certain matters free of interference from the federal government. The federal government, by contrast, has certain express powers over the states in limited, enumerated areas where national intervention provides public goods, or where the states are separately incompetent. Although the growth of the modern federal government has reduced the traditional autonomy of the states, the latter still act as the primary, and in some cases exclusive, lawmaker for many aspects of life. As globalization creates pressure to establish global governance over areas of law currently controlled by the states, federalism becomes a possible casualty.

II. GLOBALIZATION AND CONSTITUTIONAL SCHOLARSHIP

A. Internationalist

Constitutional law scholars have paid little attention to the foreign affairs aspects of constitutional law. Indeed, few discuss the potential for conflict between

---

[10] *See generally* Akhil Amar, *Of Sovereignty and Federalism*, 96 YALE L.J. 1427, 1429–65 (1987); GORDON WOOD, THE CREATION OF THE AMERICAN REPUBLIC 1776–1787 (1969).

American principles of separation of powers and federalism, and the ever more complex conduct of foreign affairs. Constitutional law casebooks and monographs scarcely address the subject.[11] Instead, the relationship between foreign affairs and constitutional law has been left to international law scholars. Until recently, however, many of these scholars have adopted an internationalist approach to questions of international relations and constitutional law. By "internationalist," we refer to a widespread academic view that the decisions of international institutions should subsume, or preempt, the laws of nation-states.

The general internationalist approach to the challenges of globalization and constitutional law supports a series of doctrines that give international law and institutions a powerful role in the American lawmaking system. The internationalist view tends to place few limits on the government's power to make treaties, even on subjects regulated by Congress. These scholars also generally (although not unanimously) assume that foreign affairs can be conducted only by the federal government, even in areas of law traditionally controlled by the states, such as family relations. Treaties such as the Hague Convention on the Civil Aspects of Child Abduction require petitions for action to begin with the U.S. State Department, thereby raising the question of how escalating internationalism will mesh with the original constitutional vision of federalism.

This conception regards treaties as self-executing. In other words, treaties become domestic law immediately with or without congressional implementation. Treaties, which are approved only by the Senate without the participation of the House of Representatives, can thus override earlier statutes passed by Congress. Some internationalists think treaties are equal, or even superior, to other forms of federal law.

The internationalist approach views federal courts as the sole arbiter of the legal effect of treaties and international institutions, with little obligation to defer to the views of the Congress or the President on interpretation. Internationalists also reject constitutional limitations on the delegation of federal authority to international institutions, which, like treaties, can have regulatory power in the United States that is judicially enforced.

Finally, internationalists argue that federal courts have independent authority to incorporate customary international law—international law that is not codified in treaties but is created by the practice of states—unsupervised by the Congress or the President. While customary norms were historically built by long state practice, they have more recently come to reflect public advocacy by nongovernmental organizations and declarations by nation-states with little at stake. In recent years, for example, both international public interest groups and nation-states with small armed forces that rarely engage in armed conflict have sought to play a leading role in changing the laws of war.

---

[11] Indeed, a leading constitutional law casebook devotes a mere 3 out of 1,000 pages to the constitutional law of foreign affairs. See, e.g., Jesse H. Choper, et al., Constitutional Law 125–28 (10th ed. 2006).

In defending these positions, internationalist legal scholars tend to overlook or dismiss separation-of-powers and federalism issues. For instance, the author of the leading monograph in the field, Professor Louis Henkin of Columbia University, typifies the internationalist attitude toward separation of powers and federalism by dismissing them as mere "technicalities."[12] And these scholars can claim some encouragement from the courts. In a well-known case, *United States v. Curtiss-Wright Export Corp.*, the Supreme Court allowed Congress to delegate broad power to the President over foreign affairs in a way that it would not permit in domestic affairs. In another case, *Missouri v. Holland*, the Court held that Congress could pass laws implementing a treaty that would be unconstitutional if enacted solely under Congress's powers to regulate the economy. In both situations, the Court suggested that the Constitution's structural provisions should be read to give the government more flexibility because of the greater demands that international relations place on the nation's interests and security.

B. Transnationalist

Another strand of recent scholarship, often identified as "transnationalist," has taken a more sophisticated and critical look at the effect of globalization on the U.S. constitutional structure. Globalization, transnationalists emphasize, is leading to the disaggregation of the United States as a single nation. Under this view, the state governments and nongovernmental organizations will play a greater role in U.S. public lawmaking. Anne-Marie Slaughter, for example, argues that international relations may be better understood as an interlocking series of governmental and nongovernmental networks rather than as simply relations between unitary nation-states. The rise of transnationalism in the legal academy closely parallels the similar rise of the "global civil society" school in political science and international relations.

The global civil society movement has emphasized the importance of studying nongovernmental social movements as a force for shaping international relations. Legal transnationalism in the United States likewise has focused more on developing the independence of subgovernmental units that interact and "converse" with NGOs and subgovernmental units in other countries. Legal transnationalists believe, for example, that international norms can be formed through a dialogue between the different branches of national governments, or even regional and local bodies, without the mediation of the formal representative of the country (usually the executive branch). An important strand of legal transnationalism has welcomed "court to court" communications between U.S. and foreign and international courts, bypassing the traditional role that the President or Congress plays in regulating cross-border cooperation.

Transnationalists believe that national courts engage in a global lawmaking process that develops a set of broad norms. In this system of informal cooperation,

---

[12] LOUIS HENKIN, FOREIGN AFFAIRS AND THE UNITED STATES CONSTITUTION (2d ed. 1996).

nongovernmental organizations can and should play an active role in presenting such norms to federal courts, just as public interest groups tap the courts to accelerate social change in their preferred direction. As Harold Koh argues, litigation can take part in a "transnational legal process" outside the formal mechanisms of international agreement–making, which is the focus of traditional international law scholars.[13] For obvious reasons, the independence of the federal courts in the interpretation and application of these norms, even against objections by Congress or the President, is an important doctrinal commitment of this strand of scholarship.

Transnationalism's focus on the disaggregation of the state has naturally led to reconsiderations of the U.S. Constitution itself. The leading academic voice in this line of scholarship is Professor Peter Spiro. Not only has Professor Spiro argued that changes in the system of global governance call for reconsideration of certain key constitutional doctrines; he has even suggested that international treaties may be interpreted in the future to override or subsume individual rights guaranteed by the Constitution. The disaggregation of the nation-state, in other words, may eventually lead to the disaggregation of the Constitution.

C. Revisionist

Internationalism and transnationalism dominate the field of international law scholarship. Yet some dissenting academic voices have appeared. Critiques of the internationalist/transnationalist approach to constitutional law, often called "revisionist," generally focus on specific doctrinal issues such as the scope of the treaty power over the states, or the status of customary international law. However, occasionally they also explore historical or functional dimensions of international law.

Revisionism, as the name suggests, has sprung up as a critical movement. Some revisionist scholars have focused on the nature of international law, rather than its domestic effects. Eric Posner, for example, has recently argued in *The Perils of Global Legalism* that international law does not create binding domestic law, but instead represents examples of cooperation and coordination between nations. He criticizes European and academic efforts to transform episodic international cooperation into "legalism, which is a view that loses sight of the social function of law and sees it as an end in itself." International law "thinks of moral and political problems in legal categories and asks lawyers and judges rather than politicians to solve them."[14] Posner challenges the notion that international law is supranational—instead, he contends that it represents the agreements and customs adopted between nations to govern specific subjects.

---

[13] Harold Hongju Koh, *Transnational Legal Process*, 75 Neb. L. Rev. 181 (1996); Harold Hongju Koh, *Why Do Nations Obey International Law?*, 106 Yale L.J. 2599 (1997).

[14] Eric Posner, The Perils of Global Legalism xii (2009).

In a different vein, John McGinnis and Ilya Somin criticize international law because it lacks democratic legitimacy. They argue that international law is made through nondemocratic methods; for example, customary international rules may have been formed by the practice of states at a time when many of them were autocracies. Each nation has an equal "vote" in many international institutions, no matter its population or economic productivity.[15] For McGinnis and Somin, it is not the substance of international law that causes problems so much as the process by which it is developed. But they also believe that compared to the elite-driven process for the creation of certain kinds of international law, U.S. lawmaking is likely to be more democratic and more likely to enhance U.S., and even global, welfare. In some respects, their argument runs counter to that of Posner. Posner's narrow view of international law depends critically on the law's formation by the decision of individual nation-states, but for McGinnis and Somin, this is what robs international law of any claims to democratic legitimacy.

Jeremy Rabkin is one of those rare scholars who grounds his view on a normative defense of national sovereignty over transnationalism.[16] He focuses the bulk of his energy on attacking transnationalism's effort to deemphasize and disaggregate the nation-state as a fundamental building block of international relations. Rabkin argues that constitutional government, at least in the United States, requires a strong conception of national sovereignty. Too much deference to international institutions not only undermines sovereignty but also attacks constitutional government's guarantee of fundamental individual rights. The movements for global governance, reflected in both the internationalist and transnationalist conceptions of constitutional law, present nearly irreconcilable dilemmas for the U.S. constitutional tradition.

For our purposes, it is unnecessary to take a position on whether international law can legitimately make claim to a universality that binds all nations and persons in the world, or whether it is composed of specific agreements between states on particular issues. One of us has published work that criticizes the theoretical foundations of the conventional academic wisdom on international law, specifically in the use-of-force area, because it pursues notions of morality rather than improving general global welfare.[17] For our purposes here, however, we accept as given that international law exists, regardless of its democracy deficit or its nature as a series of inter-state agreements. We assume that the United States wants to abide by it—at least when it is in the national interest to do so.

Our inquiry focuses instead on how the United States should incorporate into domestic law the international law standards that it chooses to follow. Often, scholars who hold a certain view of international law tend to have a complementary vision of

---

[15] John McGinnis & Ilya Somin, *Should International Law Be Part of Our Law?*, 59 STAN. L. REV. 1175 (2007).

[16] JEREMY RABKIN, THE CASE FOR SOVEREIGNTY: WHY THE WORLD SHOULD WELCOME AMERICAN INDEPENDENCE (2004); Jeremy A. Rabkin, *Recalling the Case for Sovereignty*, 5 CHI. J. INT'L L. 435 (2005).

[17] See, e.g., John Yoo, *Using Force*, 71 U. CHI. L. REV. 729 (2004).

the Constitution's requirements for its incorporation. Internationalists, who believe that international law has a supranational force above that of individual nations, tend to see such law as incorporating easily, even swiftly, into American domestic law. Henkin's magisterial *Foreign Affairs and the U.S. Constitution*, for example, takes the view that customary international law—law that is followed out of universal state practice, rather than law that is expressed in treaty form—*automatically* has the status of federal law in court without any need for an intervening act of the President or Congress.[18] Similar approaches, such as Harold Koh's *National Security Constitution* and Michael Glennon's *Constitutional Diplomacy*, share Henkin's view that in the field of foreign relations, the Constitution favors national power over states and the equal participation of Congress and the judiciary in national security decision making. In particular, these authors—and others, such as John Hart Ely and Thomas Franck—argue that the Constitution rejects the idea that judges should stay out of foreign affairs, and do not view such issues as significantly more difficult than others addressed by the federal courts.[19]

In fact, the conventional academic view in answer to the question we pose has long followed Henkin, who believed that gaps and lacunae riddle the Constitution on issues of foreign affairs. Henkin argued in favor of constructing radically different mechanisms for public lawmaking in these areas, usually with the goal of more swiftly incorporating international norms into domestic law. For example, Henkin believed that federalism concerns should not limit treaties in the same manner as domestic statutes, that courts should directly incorporate international law as federal law without an Act of Congress, and that statutes could replace treaties (and their two-thirds requirement for Senate approval) for making international agreements. These results place foreign relations law at odds with the regular process for public lawmaking, which looks to Acts of Congress, passed by both Houses and signed by the President, as the primary means for enforcing norms of domestic conduct. Internationalist and transnationalist scholars, as we have classified them, think there is nothing strange about this, because foreign affairs are different enough to justify unusual procedures.

A different approach is sometimes held out by originalists, who look to the understanding of the Constitution's text at the time of its ratification. Both of us, at times, have written in this vein. One of the leading exponents of this approach is Michael Ramsey. Recently, in *The Constitution's Text in Foreign Affairs*, Ramsey claims that the original understanding requires that federalism apply just as strictly to customary international law as domestic policies, yet he believes that the Framers intended treaties to enjoy a broader power to intrude into areas of state authority. He argues that the President's authority to initiate military hostilities should be governed by

---

[18] Louis Henkin, Foreign Affairs and the Constitution (2d ed. 1997).

[19] *See, e.g.,* John Hart Ely, War and Responsibility: Constitutional Lessons of Vietnam and Its Aftermath (1993); Thomas Franck, Political Questions, Judicial Answers: Does the Rule of Law Apply to Foreign Affairs? (1992); Michael Glennon, Constitutional Diplomacy (1991); Harold Koh, The National Security Constitution: Sharing Power after the Iran-contra Affair (1990).

the same process that applies to regular lawmaking, yet he also thinks that courts should generally play a narrower role in reviewing foreign policy decisions.

Our approach is different from either of these streams of thought. Unlike Ramsey, and unlike in some of our previous work, we do not employ originalism here. While we agree that the Framers of our Constitution established certain basic principles for the making of American law, we do not think that they did, or could have, foreseen many of the legal questions raised by globalization. Instead, we believe that grasping the Constitution's application to the issues raised by globalization depends more on the basic structures of government set out in the Constitution's text, the traditions of American political practice, and even judicial precedents. While this approach might sound reminiscent of the approaches taken by Henkin and today's international and transnational scholars, we disagree with their view that the alien nature of foreign affairs justifies the creation of wholly different governing structures. To us, the Framers' most important decision was to maintain a certain basic structure for the exercise of governmental power at home: lawmaking through congressional bicameralism followed by presentment to the President. At the same time, the Framers believed that foreign affairs demanded a more flexible process that relied more on presidential leadership, given its functional advantages in acting with speed, decision, and dispatch. Thus, our effort is quite the opposite of Henkin's—we believe that the best way to approach globalization is to tame it by subjecting its domestic effects to the same separation-of-powers and federalism rules that apply to any other law. But for conduct and events abroad, we believe that the Constitution frees the government from the straitjacket of the domestic rules of the game, and directs authority to the branch most functionally suited to such quick and momentous decisions: the executive.

III. THE ARGUMENT OF THE BOOK

Unlike the internationalists, we do not view separation of powers or federalism as cumbersome technicalities. Nor do we agree with the more forthright transnationalist case for discarding key constitutional principles in favor of greater global cooperation. On the other hand, while we are sympathetic to the revisionist critique, it has yet to produce a workable framework for reconciling constitutional government and globalization.[20]

In this book we offer such a framework. We believe that the demands of globalization can be *accommodated* while still honoring the fundamental principle of popular sovereignty. Popular sovereignty reflects a basic American commitment to govern by exclusively *constitutional* mechanisms, such as federalism and

---

[20] Nor do we believe that the political process critique espoused by Professors McGinnis and Somin provides a sufficiently comprehensive approach to resolving the dilemmas posed by globalization, because their analysis does not consider conflicts posed by international cooperation and international institutions rather than merely incorporating international law. See McGinnis & Somin, *supra* note 15.

separation of powers, both of which create the political institutions through which the people can exercise power. These constitutional structures may prove burdensome or inefficient, but they enhance accountability and transparency in government—important features of constitutional democracy. Popular sovereignty, therefore, is to be ignored only at one's peril. Globalization poses real challenges to American constitutional law, but the answer is not, as some would have it, abandoning the core principle of the American political system. Popular sovereignty, therefore, is to be ignored only at one's peril.

We believe three doctrines can avoid constitutional problems while still permitting the United States to accrue the benefits of international cooperation in the age of globalization. These are (1) a presumption in favor of "non-self-executing" treaties, (2) recognition of the President's power to terminate international obligations and to interpret international law, and (3) reliance on state implementation of international law and agreements. All of these mechanisms shift basic decisions between the pressures of globalization and the goals of a democratic constitutional government to the executive and legislative branches of the federal and state governments.

Our defense of these doctrines rests on both "functional" and "formal" grounds. Such solutions are supported not only by the text and history of the Constitution and precedent, but also by their functional consequences. While all three doctrinal devices have strong historical and precedential foundations in the U.S. constitutional tradition, one can reasonably disagree about them. In the last few years, scholars have battled to a stalemate on many of them. Previous work, however, has focused on the formal legitimacy of these solutions against others. In contrast, here, rather than try to establish these doctrines as constitutional *requirements*, we argue that these doctrines should be employed because they are *prudent*. To require the political branches of government to fulfill the mandates of international law simply makes sense as a matter of consequences.

From a normative perspective, we also argue that the legislative and executive branches of the federal and state governments are the institutions best positioned to reconcile the pressures of globalization with the U.S. public law system. These institutions are able to mediate the different pressures of globalization and domestic constitutional law because they have the greatest political accountability and functional expertise in the conduct of international relations (in the case of the executive branch) or local public policy (in the case of the state governments).

Conversely, we do not think that the American judiciary should play the kind of autonomous role that internationalists and transnationalists have assigned to it. Although we believe courts should maintain an independent place, we also believe courts should maintain their traditional deference to the executive and the legislative branches in affairs of state, in political questions, in foreign relations, and in war.

A. Non-Self-Execution

The first, most basic, doctrinal device in our approach is the non-self-execution doctrine. This means that treaties and other international agreements are not law in the United States unless or until some other domestic institution (usually Congress) decides to implement it. Under the Supremacy Clause of the U.S. Constitution, treaties are part of the "Law of the Land" and supreme over inconsistent state law. Under the doctrine of non-self-execution, however, courts should refuse to give domestic legal effect to a treaty unless or until some other domestic institution (usually Congress) decides to implement it. Thus, a non-self-executing treaty signed by the President and approved by two-thirds of the Senate would still not have any effect in court absent subsequent legislation implementing the U.S.'s treaty obligations.

Non-self-executing treaties are not without effect. Even without implementation by Congress, non-self-executing treaties create *international* obligations. During the Cold War, arms control agreements with the Soviet Union calling for the limitation or elimination of nuclear weapons entered the U.S. into an international legal obligation. The existence of this obligation did not, however, allow the Soviet Union or any other entity to sue in U.S. courts to require the United States to comply with an arms control treaty, or that U.S. courts are in general authorized to force U.S. compliance. Courts in the United States have held many treaties, including the United Nations Charter, to be non-self-executing. In giving advice and consent to a treaty, the Senate has sometimes conditioned its approval on the understanding that the treaty remains non-self-executing.

Most commonly applied to treaties, the non-self-execution approach also extends to other types of international agreements. The United States is a party to thousands of executive agreements between the President and a foreign country that lack advice or consent from the Senate. These agreements are generally held to have no domestic legal effect absent congressional legislation implementing the agreement's obligations. In some limited circumstances, they may override inconsistent state laws, but only where history supports the exercise of unilateral executive power, as with claims settlements. By contrast, congressional-executive agreements—in which the President submits an international agreement for simple majority approval by both Houses of Congress—are usually self-executing because they contain their own implementing legislation.

Non-self-execution serves important functions. It limits the domestic legal status of treaties and international agreements, requiring something more than the President's signature and the Senate's advice and consent for a treaty or international agreement to have domestic legal effect. The doctrine shifts the decision to more broadly representative institutions. This ensures that the same institution that enacts domestic policy—Congress—will be the one to control the implementation of international agreements within the nation's borders. The treaty, in other words, does not alter the Constitution's allocation of power between the branches of the federal government over domestic policy. The institution in control of implementation is usually the full Congress (House as well as Senate) but, as we will explain further, this power of implementation may sometimes be held by the President or by the individual state governments.

B. Deference to Presidential Interpretations of International Law

Non-self-execution restricts or eliminates the power of U.S. courts to give effect to a treaty or international agreement absent a specific authorizing action by Congress, the President, or the states. Although non-self-execution is perhaps the most important doctrinal foundation of our accommodationist approach, it does not fully resolve the sharp tensions between globalization and constitutional law. Many key aspects of international law remain uncodified in the form of customary international law. In order to maintain the Constitution's normal structure governing public lawmaking, we must develop doctrines that vest the political branches with the control over the integration of unwritten international norms into the domestic legal order. Our accommodating approach relies on the doctrine of presidential control over the termination and interpretation of international law, which includes treaties, executive agreements, and customary international law.

The President is the chief—if not the sole—organ of the U.S. government in the conduct of foreign affairs. Under the Constitution, and ever since George Washington's declaration of neutrality during the French Revolution, the President has borne primary responsibility for managing U.S. policy toward foreign governments. The President not only commands the armed forces, but also nominates and, with the advice and consent of the Senate, appoints ambassadors and other diplomats, and negotiates and makes (with the Senate's cooperation) treaties with other nations. This combination of delegated foreign affairs powers under the Constitution, as well as a long historical practice of presidential control over foreign affairs, has led to the development of a complex and sophisticated foreign affairs bureaucracy supervised by, and responsible to, the President.

The President's role as chief foreign policy organ, buttressed by institutional expertise, supports judicial deference to the President's interpretation and, in some cases, termination of U.S. international law obligations. Under existing doctrine, courts are required to give the President's interpretation of treaties "great weight" when deciding cases governed by treaties and other international agreements. In some cases, the President's interpretation of customary international law receive heavy, if not absolute, judicial deference. The President has also exercised the power to declare U.S. objections to international legal obligations, either by withdrawing from treaties or by challenging the rules of customary international law.

Our understanding of the President's role in the interpretation of international law within the United States is well founded as a matter of historical practice. We recognize that the balance of powers between the judicial and the executive branches over international law remains a topic of substantial academic debate. Our point here is not to revisit these debates, but simply to point out that presidential control over the interpretation of international law can support an accommodationist agenda. In the internationalist or transnationalist conception, the courts are the first and possibly last source of interpretation on the scope and nature of a U.S. obligation under international law. Courts are thus free, especially in the realm of customary law, to adopt broad interpretations whether or not the executive or legislative branches have approved the international law principle.

This court-centered process, while possibly justified by the need to ensure compliance with international norms, nonetheless has drawn the criticism of scholars worried about unelected judges unilaterally imposing international rules on the American people. We believe this is a real and valid concern. The response does not require the abandonment of international law as a tool to build international cooperation. Rather, allowing the President, the most politically accountable and institutionally expert branch of the federal government, to control the interpretation of international law substantially avoids the undemocratic nature of unwritten international law. This approach also permits the United States to continue its participation in the various forms of international cooperation to regulate the forces of globalization.

C. State Autonomy in Compliance with International Law

Our last, and perhaps most radical, proposal envisions a robust role for state governments in the interpretation, incorporation, and implementation of international legal norms. By looking to state governments to take the lead in responding to some of the pressures of globalization, we seek to honor the basic U.S. constitutional commitment to a federal system of government.

The U.S. Constitution generally allocates foreign relations powers to the federal government. Hence, Article I, Section 10 explicitly prohibits states from entering into treaties or international agreements absent congressional approval. Nor can they engage in wars or other traditional forms of international relations. Yet states have long played an important role in the implementation of U.S. obligations under international law and in responding generally to demands of foreign countries when such obligations or demands have implicated matters typically within state control.

Thus, states have often maintained primary control over traditionally local matters involving family law, criminal law, and tax relations with local consular officials. Even in recent years, when such matters increasingly have been the subject of international agreement and international cooperation, states have maintained their central role in maintaining compliance with such international rules. Globalization itself has thrust states into this role, by reaching matters that traditionally have been regulated by state and local government in the American constitutional system. Because it involves knowledge of local conditions and comprehensive enforcement resources—qualities lacking in the federal government—successful adaptation to globalization in areas such as crime, family, and education requires the recognition of the primary role of the states. It is the states, not the federal government, that determine whether the United States can live up to positive rights to education, work, or housing, were it ever to ratify the International Covenant on Economic, Social, and Cultural Rights or the Convention on the Rights of the Child.

Indeed, the federal government itself has expressly relied on states to fulfill U.S. obligations under international agreements. In the process of giving advice and consent to a number of recent treaties, the Senate has made clear that it expects state governments to fulfill all treaty obligations for matters within their traditional control, and expects the national government to provide incentives to ensure state cooperation. A good example is the Vienna Convention's requirement that aliens arrested within the United States must be informed of their right to consult with consular officials. This obligation cannot be fulfilled without the states, which carry out the vast majority of law enforcement in the country. States have become increasingly sophisticated about their independent role in the conduct of foreign relations by developing administrative and bureaucratic capacities to receive and respond to foreign government officials.

A limited but important role for states in the conduct of foreign relations represents a salutary compromise between globalization's necessities and the U.S. Constitution's federalism. Globalization is creating pressure to deepen and expand international cooperation into areas typically controlled by state governments, such as family law, private commercial relations, criminal law, and other areas of social regulation. Nationalization of these areas may actually make the American governmental system less efficient and less responsive to citizens' preferences, which may be better served by the diversity of state policies encouraged by federalism and its competition among jurisdictions. Rather than imposing a uniform rule in response to the needs of globalization, policymakers can seek and have sought ways to preserve primary state control over such areas.

We must tolerate a certain amount of diversity of policy within the U.S. system, but we think it is a price worth paying to maintain state autonomy. If globalization requires a truly national solution, then Congress and the President can act through normal legislation to adopt a national set of rules. But such an action should be the last resort. In our view, accommodation requires working through and with the states before resorting to nationalization. States such as California, Texas, New York, and Florida, after all, have larger populations and economies than many foreign countries.

IV. CONCLUSION

The rest of this book will define globalization and the international regulatory response and describe its effects on the American constitutional system. Chapter 2 examines the process of globalization, rooted in rapid advances in communications, transportation, and technology. The dramatic increase in cross-border transactions and relationships has led to an explosion of international lawmaking and international institutions. The end of the Cold War stalemate encouraged the growth of new multinational institutions that seek to govern more than diplomatic relations between states. International entities write and interpret a new kind of international law that attempts to regulate such traditionally domestic topics as individual rights, criminal punishment, environmental protection, and family relations. New international law has spurred leading scholars and advocates to theorize that a system of global governance has arrived.[21] New international law advances the internationalist framework of greater formal authority for international organizations. It is also consistent with the transnationalist emphasis on a role for nongovernmental organizations in the construction of international cooperation via domestic litigation.

Chapter 3 explains how this complex process places pressure on the U.S. constitutional system. This chapter will introduce and develop the two fundamental structural principles of the U.S. Constitution: separation of powers and federalism. It will examine how globalization erodes these principles. The problem for separation of powers, we argue, is that the new international law transfers the power to control and implement international legal obligations away from the executive and legislative branches. In many cases, this power is being delegated to independent international institutions. In other cases, nongovernmental associations enlist domestic courts to adopt interpretations of international law without the approval or even over the opposition of the elected branches of government.

With respect to federalism, the problem has less to do with international institutions, and more to do with the expanding scope of international regulation. State governments have traditionally controlled much of domestic public policy, including subjects such as domestic relations and criminal law. But the drive to extend the reach of international law threatens state autonomy under the Constitution. We will demonstrate that the movement toward global governance follows the model of regulation introduced in American law by the New Deal, and we predict that left untended, that model will produce similar strains in the constitutional fabric. In some respects, America's evolution toward globalization resembles the Progressive Era's shift toward nationalization from a largely rural, state-centered economy. Advances in transportation, communications, production, and national commerce—and the rise of ideas about the efficacy of centralized state planning—led, early in the twentieth century, to a reconceptualization of the core structure of the Constitution. This took decades of struggle between the political branches and the courts, and it was resolved only with the events of the Great Depression, the New Deal, and FDR's effort to pack the Supreme Court. The judiciary experienced this shift as a wrenching political upheaval, but only because legal thinking did not keep pace with rapid social and economic change. Had constitutional law smoothly adapted to nationalization, rather than overreacting and sparking an eventual crisis, it might have avoided the confrontation of the 1930s.

Chapter 4 introduces the first of our three doctrinal devices for accommodating the forces of globalization within the U.S. constitutional system. Non-self-execution of international agreements has a long-standing historical and precedential foundation. Additionally, and most importantly for our argument here, non-self-execution fits well within our accommodationist approach by allowing the executive and legislative branches to control the domestic effect of treaty obligations. It ensures that

---

[21] The most recent and important work in this genre is ANNE-MARIE SLAUGHTER, A NEW WORLD ORDER (2004).

the activities of the federal government on the international plane do not cause distortions in the public lawmaking process at home.

Chapter 5 offers a defense of the second doctrinal strategy: deference to presidential interpretations of international law. Such deference guarantees that the governmental branch with the most political accountability and institutional expertise controls the level of U.S. cooperation with international institutions and norms.

Chapter 6 examines the limited but important role states can play in the implementation of international legal obligations. Recent doctrinal developments suggest that states have a limited amount of constitutional space to operate independently in the conduct of foreign affairs. We argue that such state activity, supervised by the federal executive and legislative branches, can preserve a role for the states in a world of globalizing regulatory structures.

Chapter 7 examines in detail the encounters between the demands of globalization and the U.S. Constitution by examining recent Supreme Court cases. *Sosa v. Alvarez-Machain*, *Medellín v. Texas*, and *Hamdan v. Rumsfeld* all reflect our accommodationist approach to resolving these challenges. First, we consider the interaction of customary international law with the U.S. court system in the context of lawsuits brought under the Alien Tort Statute. Such lawsuits ask U.S. federal courts to interpret and apply norms of customary international law with almost no guidance or control from Congress or the executive branch. In line with our approach, the Court recognized the dangers of unconstrained judicial incorporation of customary international law although it did not, in our view, sufficiently limit the judicial role.

We also consider the relationship between the United States and the International Court of Justice (ICJ) in the interpretation of the Vienna Convention on Consular Relations. In a series of cases, the ICJ issued judgments requiring U.S. courts to intervene directly in the states' operation of their criminal justice systems. NGOs took up the cause by bringing litigation and filing amicus briefs seeking to force compliance with the ICJ judgments, even absent support from the Congress or the President. As we will detail, key policy makers at both the federal and state levels rejected the internationalist and transnationalist approach. Rather, the ultimate resolution of the ICJ consular relations cases relies on almost all of the accommodationist doctrines we have detailed: non-self-execution, the President's ability to terminate international obligations, and independent state implementation of international obligations with federal executive supervision.

We then consider the role of treaties governing the law of war as a constraint on the President's use of military commissions to try alleged terrorists detained after the September 11, 2001 attacks. In *Hamdan v. Rumsfeld*, the Court was presented with arguments based both on the customary law of war, and a number of non-self-executing treaties. Despite popular perceptions to the contrary, *Hamdan* did not directly impose international law on the operations of the military, but instead looked to Congress's incorporation of it through the Uniform Code of Military Justice. In *Boumediene v. Bush*, we argue, the President and Congress reasserted their authority to interpret and incorporate international law as law of the United States, leading the Court to decide the case on purely constitutional grounds.

Finally, Chapter 8 applies our approach to the Supreme Court's recent practice of looking to foreign and international legal sources to guide interpretation of the Constitution. We can understand the increasing desire to look abroad for law as another feature of globalization. As more social activity crosses national borders, legal systems may reach out to one another to coordinate their regulatory responses. There is certainly dispute over whether foreign law seriously influences the Justices in their understanding of the scope of federalism or individual rights as defined by the Fifth and Fourteenth Amendments. But to the extent that other nations' opinions are determining the outcomes of Supreme Court cases interpreting the U.S. Constitution, our analysis finds that the practice conflicts with the structure of the Constitution and the basic underpinnings of popular sovereignty in our political system. We may be too early in criticizing this trend, as it is still unclear whether the Court's citation of foreign and international law is determining the outcome of cases or playing the role of mere intellectual ornamentation. And certainly the Constitution does not exclude foreign or international norms from our political system. But, in our view, the Constitution does not grant the courts the power of deciding how those norms should affect the Constitution. Rather, as with the other areas under study in this book, the Constitution vests the President, Congress, or the states—not the courts—with the main responsibility to decide how far our laws and politics should go in adopting international standards.

Like nationalization, globalization will inevitably call on us to reconsider fundamental questions: the proper scope of the federal government's regulatory power; the balance of authority between the President and Congress; and the appropriate role of the courts. Legal scholars may only belatedly realize the consequences of economic and social transformation on constitutional doctrine. We seek to explain these issues and chart out some answers. By addressing the problems before crises arise, we may be better prepared to adapt our Constitution to world change than politicians, judges, professors, and lawyers were a century ago.

2 Globalization and Sovereignty

Before we can understand globalization and its effects on the United States, we first must define it. This is not simple. A substantial academic literature surrounds the exact meaning of "globalization." After considering different concepts developed in a variety of academic disciplines, we define globalization as the cluster of processes leading to worldwide economic, social, cultural, and political integration.

The increased intensity of cross-border integration has led many scholars to suggest that globalization is eroding or even eliminating the sovereignty of nation-states. Globalization impacts national sovereignty in three important ways. First, the rise of international trade and capital markets has interfered with the ability of nation-states to control their domestic economies. Second, nation-states have increasingly delegated more authority to independent international organizations. Third, nation-states are facing new limitations in the conduct of their domestic policies because of changes in the nature and scope of international law.

These developments place national sovereignty under pressure. To be sure, the traditional conception of Westphalian sovereignty, where each nation-state exercises absolute and exclusive control over everything that occurs within its territory, has never fully described reality. But unlike the more enthusiastic globalization theorists, we do not think that the decline of national sovereignty is either inevitable or obviously desirable. A system of nation-states maintains the current world order. For the United States and many other countries, sovereignty allows for the protection of democratic decision-making and individual liberties. On the other hand, maintaining a robust respect for national sovereignty does not demand the rejection of globalization or international cooperation. Globalization does not require us to choose between sovereignty and world government.

Our solution is to shift the focus away from Westphalian sovereignty toward "popular sovereignty." By popular sovereignty, we mean the right of the American people to govern themselves through the institutions and processes of decision-making established by the Constitution. Article VI of the U.S. Constitution, known as the Supremacy Clause, has been consistently interpreted to create a hierarchy of federal law that places the Constitution first, followed by "the Laws of the United States which shall be made in pursuance thereof; and all treaties made, or which shall be made, under the authority of the United States." This establishes the supremacy of the Constitution over international laws and norms. As long as the Constitution remains the exclusive and supreme source of legitimate lawmaking authority within the United States, the regulation of globalization must occur through the political and legal system that it creates.

I. WHAT IS GLOBALIZATION?

Few terms are more ubiquitous in public affairs than "globalization." Countless journal articles and publications analyze globalization in the areas of sociology, political science, international relations, and cultural studies.[1] Yet it is striking that, despite the breadth of interest in globalization, there continues to be a substantial lack of consensus on the meaning of the term. As Peter Spiro has observed, "globalization is so broad a phenomenon that comprehensive description now seems almost futile."[2]

In much of the literature, globalization is identified with the reduction of barriers to economic exchange and an accompanying ideological devotion to free markets. In his 1999 best-seller, *The Lexus and the Olive Tree*, *New York Times* columnist Thomas Friedman popularized the concept of the "globalization system" as involving the "inexorable integration of markets, nation-states and technologies to a degree never witnessed before." The system results in the "spread of free market capitalism to virtually every country in the world."[3] Much of the public debate has revolved around the consequences of economic liberalization, the reduction of barriers to the trade of goods and services, and the global integration of capital markets in the post–Cold War era.[4]

---

[1] *See, e.g.,* THE GLOBALIZATION READER (Frank J. Lechner & John Boli, eds., 2004); MICHAEL HARDT & ANTONIO NEGRI, EMPIRE (2000); JAN AART SCHOLTE, GLOBALIZATION: A CRITICAL INTRODUCTION (2000); RICHARD A. FALK, PREDATORY GLOBALIZATION: A CRITIQUE (1999); DAVID HELD, ET AL., GLOBAL TRANSFORMATIONS: POLITICS, ECONOMICS, AND CULTURE (1999); ANDREW LINKLATER, THE TRANSFORMATION OF POLITICAL COMMUNITY: ETHICAL FOUNDATIONS OF THE POST-WESTPHALIAN ERA (1999).

[2] Peter Spiro, *Globalization and the (Foreign Affairs) Constitution*, 63 OHIO ST. L. J. 649, 660 (2002).

[3] THOMAS FRIEDMAN, THE LEXUS AND THE OLIVE TREE 8–9 (1999).

[4] *See, e.g.,* JAGDISH BHAGWATI, IN DEFENSE OF GLOBALIZATION (2004); JOSEPH STIGLITZ, GLOBALIZATION AND ITS DISCONTENTS (2002). *See also* DANIEL W. DREZNER, ALL POLITICS IS GLOBAL: EXPLAINING INTERNATIONAL REGULATORY REGIMES 10 (2007). (defining "globalization as the cluster of technological, economic, and political processes that drastically reduce the barriers to economic exchange across borders").

But globalization has acquired a meaning broader than mere economic liberalization. As Jan Aart Scholte has explained, scholars have used the term in at least five distinct ways. In addition to emphasizing the relationship between globalization and economic liberalization, scholars have also equated globalization with the internationalization of societies and economies, the universalization of a "global culture," the westernization of societies following the Western or American model, and finally the deterritorialization of geography and social space.[5]

These definitions share some basic elements. All refer to acceleration in the levels of cross-border activity between governments, businesses, institutions, and individuals since the end of the Cold War. While the levels of transnational economics have drawn the most attention, the globalization story also includes other forms of cross-border activity, such as the growth of political cooperation, migration, communications, as well as sharp reductions in transportation costs, and the blending of national societies and cultures.[6]

A substantial number of scholars have emphasized the noneconomic aspects of globalization. Many have documented what they see as the rise of a global civil society that reflects noneconomic cross-border relationships. Global civil society, they argue, represents new opportunities for individuals to participate in social and cultural activities that reach beyond the nation. According to this view, the explosion of cross-border interaction has strengthened international institutions and the development of "cosmopolitan" legal obligations.

In our view, globalization refers to the various processes of economic, social, cultural, and political integration across national borders.[7] This definition is drawn from that strand of globalization studies known as "deterritorialism." Deterritorialist theorists emphasize that today's globalization differs from past eras in its effect on physical territory as an organizing principle for social, cultural, economic, or political relations. For example, they argue that an individual in today's globalizing world is just as likely to communicate, interact, or work with someone in another country as they are with someone in their own territorial nation. Physical territory, therefore, becomes less important as a defining characteristic of a modern individual's identity, loyalty, or culture.

While we have some sympathy for this approach to understanding globalization, we do not take a position on a number of related debates. We do not, for instance, take a position in the debate over whether contemporary globalization is fundamentally different from prior periods of world history that were also characterized by high levels of cross-border activity.[8] John Maynard Keynes could write in 1920 that a British man could invest and travel throughout the globe and "could order by

[5] SCHOLTE, *supra* note 1, at 15–16.

[6] *See* JOHN MICKLETHWAIT & ADRIAN WOOLRIDGE, A FUTURE PERFECT (2000).

[7] HELD, *supra* note 1, at 2. In this broader conception, globalization can be conceived as "the widening, deepening and speeding up of worldwide interconnectedness in all aspects of contemporary social life, from the cultural to the criminal, the financial to the spiritual."

[8] For an example of this argument, see PAUL HIRST & GRAHAME THOMPSON, GLOBALIZATION IN QUESTION: THE INTERNATIONAL ECONOMY AND THE POSSIBILITIES OF GOVERNANCE (1996).

telephone, sipping his morning tea in bed, the various products of the whole earth, in such quantity as he might see fit, and reasonably expect their early delivery upon his doorstep."[9] Nor do we consider which of the various forces—technology, economic exchange, or the end of the Cold War—is the root cause of contemporary globalization; we believe that all of these forces have contributed to it.

For our purposes, it does not matter whether or not globalization is truly unprecedented or which force is the primary cause. Even if, as many scholars persuasively argue, the world has undergone periods of globalization prior to the contemporary period, our concern is with the *effects* of today's globalizing world. The *causes* of today's globalization are not central to our analysis, though it is important that the effects are more widespread and the process more accelerated than in the past. It is the *consequences* of globalization for nation-states like the United States, and its system of domestic governance, that is the focus of our analysis.

II. THE CONSEQUENCES OF GLOBALIZATION

Former International Court of Justice President Roslyn Higgins has remarked:

> Globalization represents the reality that we live in a time when the walls of sovereignty are no protection against the movements of capital, labor, information and ideas—nor can they provide effective protection against harm and damage.[10]

Echoing Higgins, most globalization scholarship emphasizes the diminishment of nation-state sovereignty by three phenomena. First, a substantial number of commentators have focused on the impact of the increased levels of economic trade in goods and services accompanied by the rise of globalized financial markets. The integration of the world economies has, in the eyes of some scholars, led to the decline or even the "end" of the nation-state as a meaningful unit of social organization.[11]

Second, globalization has led to an increase in the number and influence of international organizations. These organizations have gained a greater independence from nation-states and now claim the power to exercise sovereign powers themselves.

Third, globalization has produced a fundamental shift in the nature and scope of international law. The "new international law" purports to create universal, binding obligations regulating a nation-state's treatment of its own citizens. Some scholars

---

[9] John Maynard Keynes, The Economic Consequences of the Peace (1920).

[10] *See* Roslyn Higgins, *International Law in a Changing International System*, 58 Cambridge L. J. 78 (1999).

[11] *See, e.g.*, Kenichi Ohmae, The End of the Nation State: The Rise of Regional Economies (1995).

have even suggested that this new form of law should receive a new name: "cosmopolitan law" or "world law."[12] This new form of international law has become an important mechanism for nongovernmental organizations seeking to influence or limit the ability of nation-states to exercise their sovereign powers.

All three of these impacts may be creating what some scholars call a system of "global governance." We consider each aspect of global governance in turn.

A. The Global Economy

Globalization exerts perhaps its most profound effect on the domestic economy. We will not revisit the complex history of economic globalization and the debate over its modern consequences. We focus instead on those prominent elements of economic globalization that constrain nation-state sovereignty.

We can divide economic globalization into two main categories. First, contemporary globalization has followed a sharp reduction of tariffs and other barriers to cross-border trade in goods and services. The lowering of trade barriers between nations has proceeded since the end of World War II and even accelerated in the past two decades. In 1990, the total value of trade in goods was slightly more than 30 percent of global GDP; by 2009, the value of such trade exceeded 40 percent of global GDP.[13] For many developed economies, such as France and Japan, trade in goods now exceeds 40 percent of total national GDP.[14] For much of Europe, the value of trade in goods grew from 40 percent of Europe-wide GDP in 1990 to nearly 60 percent in 2004. For the United States, the overall percentage is much lower. Still, from 1990 to 2004, the value of U.S. trade in goods increased from 15 percent to 20 percent of GDP.

International trade has spread farther and deeper. Since the end of the Cold War, international trade has grown to include a much larger group of nations, while its activity among developed nations has intensified. Developing countries have sharply boosted their participation in the world trading system. For instance, the lowest-income countries have boosted their world merchandise trade activity from about 30 percent of their GDPs in 1990 to nearly 50 percent in 2009.[15]

Although the explosion of cross-border trade in goods and services has drawn substantial attention, economic globalization is even more commonly identified with the cross-border movement of capital. The growth of international capital markets has actually outpaced the level of international trade in goods. Foreign direct investment, for instance, has grown from about $212 billion in 1990 to over

---

[12] See David J. Bederman, Globalization and International Law, 3–54 (2008); Harold J. Berman, *World Law*, 18 Fordham Int'l L. J. 1617 (1995).

[13] World Bank, The Little Data Book 2011, 2 *available at* http://www-wds.worldbank.org/external/default/WDSContentServer/IW3P/IB/2011/08/16/000333037_20110816012153/Rendered/PDF/638470WDI0Exto00Box0361527B0PUBLIC0.pdf

[14] Held, supra note 1, at 180.

[15] World Bank, *supra* note 13, at 9.

1.1 trillion in 2009.[16] Nation-states have facilitated this explosion by reducing national barriers to trade, such as by removing controls on the movement of capital, or by removing tariffs on foreign goods and services. For many commentators, the elimination of national barriers to cross-border economic activity makes nation-states highly vulnerable to global market forces dominated by large multinational banks and corporations. As international trade becomes a larger and more important part of domestic economic output, nation-states can no longer seriously consider imposing significant tariffs or providing large domestic subsidies for fear of retaliation by their trading partners.

Similarly, commentators suggest that nation-states cannot independently determine macroeconomic policies because they cannot comprehensively regulate international capital markets. Nation-states, for example, do not fully control the value of their currencies. Private traders have forced developed nations like the United Kingdom to allow movement in the pound, though more authoritarian nations like China have maintained a tighter grip on their currencies. Currency fluctuation, in turn, has limited the ability of nation-states to pursue expansionary macroeconomic policies. International markets may impose similar constraints on fiscal policy. Because national governments borrow large debts by issuing bonds on the international capital markets, they find their ability to set domestic policy constrained by the value of their securities. The international debt markets may penalize nation-states that run up substantial budget deficits with higher interest rates.[17] In the aftermath of the 2008 financial crisis, Greece adopted serious (and politically unpopular) adjustments to its governmental fiscal policy under pressure from international capital markets, the European Union, and the International Monetary Fund.

The journalist Thomas Friedman provides a colorful account of this phenomenon in describing an imagined conversation with the prime minister of Malaysia.

Globalization isn't a choice. It's a reality. There is just one global market today, and the only way you [Malaysia] can grow at the speed your people want to grow is by tapping into the global stock and bond markets, by seeking out multinationals to invest in your country and by selling into the global trading system what your factories produce. And the most basic truth about globalization is this: *No one is in charge.*[18]

To be sure, this and other accounts of economic globalization can be criticized for overstating the impact on nation-state autonomy. Nation-states, especially those with large domestic economies—like the United States—are far from powerless to set national economic policies.[19] And nation-states are unlikely to "disappear" simply because of economic globalization. But this does not mean that the

---

[16] *Id.* at 2.

[17] HELD, *supra* note 1, at 229–30.

[18] FRIEDMAN, *supra* note 3, at 93.

[19] See DREZNER, *supra* note 4.

economic effects of globalization on nation-states are trivial. Economic globalization has constrained the ability of nation-states to adopt domestic economic policies freely, though the scope of its effects remain contested.

B. The Rise of International Organizations

In addition to cross-border trade and capital movements, globalization has prompted the rise of international organizations (IOs), a new actor in international relations. In contrast to the Westphalian conception of sovereign states, according to one commentator, inter-state relations "are increasingly mediated through rationalized institutional processes."[20] As with the effects of globalization itself, the role of international organizations can be overstated. Nation-states still make the basic decisions of international politics and possess the personnel, budgets, and will to pursue policies with real effects in world affairs.[21] But there is little dispute that institutions, independent of nations, are heavily influencing international rules as never before.

For example, while in the past a border dispute between two nations would have resulted in either a bilateral settlement or a military conflict, global governance regimes might shift the decision to an international body like the International Court of Justice.[22] Similarly, a trade dispute that would have resulted in retaliatory tariffs in the past is now more likely to be resolved by the World Trade Organization.

Although international organizations have existed since at least the nineteenth century, their proliferation and prominence in recent years have led some globalization theorists to hail them as the inevitable successor to the nation-state. As one provocative study describes it, "sovereignty has taken a new form, composed under a series of national and supranational organisms united under a single rule of logic. This new global form of sovereignty is what we call Empire."[23] As we will explain, international organizations have not achieved the level of power and control to justify such characterizations, no matter how colorful. Moreover, such a simplistic discussion suggests either that all international organizations are alike or that they all fit into a single hierarchical system of political control. While some international organizations may pose challenges to national sovereignty, others do not, and many have little impact at all—contrary to the claims of their supporters.

By "international organizations," we refer to legal entities established by more than one nation-state pursuant to an international agreement.[24] This excludes private international organizations like the International Committee for the Red

---

[20] Spiro, *supra* note 2, at 661.

[21] For a skeptical view of international institutions, see John Mearsheimer, *The False Promise of International Institutions*, 19 INT'L SECURITY 5 (1994).

[22] *See, e.g.*, Case Concerning the Land and Maritime Boundary between Cameroon and Nigeria (Cameroon v. Nigeria: Equatorial Guinea Intervening), No. 94 (Oct.10, 2002).

[23] HARDT & NEGRI, *supra* note 1, at xii.

[24] Reparations for Injuries Suffered in the Service of the United Nations, 1949 I.C.J. Reports 174.

Cross or Amnesty International, which are classic examples of nongovernmental organizations (NGOs) established by private parties—much like an interest group in domestic politics. As we explain later in this chapter, such organizations may wield substantial influence, but not in the same way as international organizations (IOs). This definition also excludes entities like a state-owned business, which are under the control of a single state.

Under international law, IOs have a "legal personality," which enables them to act independently. Recognition of this special status represented a significant shift from traditional Westphalian sovereignty. In an important decision, the International Court of Justice considered whether the United Nations could assert diplomatic protection over an individual who had been injured while serving as a United Nations employee. In other words, could the UN, an IO, seek reparations on behalf of its employee against a nation-state? Under previous understandings, only a nation-state could make a claim against another nation-state under international law; thus, only the injured employee's nation could bring a claim on his behalf.[25]

The ICJ ruled that the United Nations has a separate status under international law. It was not simply an agent of the states that created it, but an independent entity able to assert its own legal rights as well as incur its own legal liabilities. The United Nations, the ICJ held, possesses "legal personality" and is an "international person" with the capacity to exercise rights and fulfill duties on the international plane.[26] The ICJ's analysis has been widely accepted by nation-states and applied to other IOs on mundane matters such as property rights and immunity from jurisdiction.

Because an IO can be created by any two nation-states for any purpose, it is not surprising that IOs bear substantial diversity in both form and purpose. This makes it difficult to classify them as a single type of institution based on their structure. Some IOs take the form of international tribunals that resolve disputes between nations. The commission established by the 1795 Jay Treaty to settle claims arising out of the Revolutionary War is an early example.[27] A more modern one is the International Court of Justice, which was established by the United Nations Charter to resolve disputes between members.[28]

Other IOs take the form of agencies designed to administer and implement policies or technical standards arising from an international legal regime. Classic examples are the Universal Postal Union, which administers rules governing international mail or the International Telecommunications Union.[29] Another is the World Customs Organization, which maintains international standards for administering tariffs on goods and services.

---

[25] *Id.*

[26] *Id.* at 183.

[27] Treaty of Amity, Commerce, and Navigation, Nov. 19, 1794, art. V (Jay Treaty).

[28] U.N. Charter, art. 92–96.

[29] Convention on Universal Postal Union, 1939; Constitution of the International Telecommunications Union, 1932.

Still other IOs function as forums for discussion of issues and joint policies. An example is the General Assembly (GA) of the United Nations, which guarantees member states rights to raise and discuss issues of concern. Acting together, the GA may also pass resolutions and recommendations for its member states, but unlike the UN Security Council, it does not have the legal authority to require nations to take action.[30]

IOs pursue a wide variety of purposes. The most basic IO is created by an agreement between two states for a narrow and particular purpose. For instance, the United States and Great Britain formed a series of boundary commissions between 1794 and 1925 to settle and demarcate the boundary between the United States and Canada. The two countries then established a permanent International Boundary Commission in 1925 to inspect and maintain the boundary line. The Boundary Commission, which is composed of one commissioner from each country, has narrowly defined powers and is not authorized to deal generally with overall U.S.-Canadian relations.[31]

At the other end of the power spectrum is the UN Security Council. Formed by all UN member states, it is composed of five permanent members and ten rotating members authorized to take measures to "maintain international peace and security."[32] Its legal mandate authorizes it to act on any matter in the territory of any nation. The veto right of the five permanent members has prevented it from exercising its power often.

Most IOs fall somewhere between the narrow purpose of the Boundary Commission and the broad mandate of the Security Council. Because IOs can be created by as few as two states and as many as 192 states, the diversity in their purposes is not surprising. While the UN system represents the largest network of IOs, other IOs may exist independently of the UN hierarchy. For instance, although many nation-states that are members of the World Trade Organization are also members of the United Nations, the two IOs are essentially independent and only loosely associated as a formal legal matter. The legal structure and administration of the WTO is not related to any UN institutions and vice versa.

As the previous discussion indicates, it is not possible to maintain the view that there is a single "world government" or single IO structure that threatens U.S. sovereignty. The closest attempt to create a single overarching IO, the United Nations, resulted in more of a conglomeration than a single entity. The principal components of the UN system are the General Assembly, the Security Council, the Economic and Social Council, the International Court of Justice, and the Secretariat.

---

[30] U.N. Charter, art. 9–22.

[31] Treaty between the United States and Great Britain in respect of boundary between the United States and Canada, Feb. 24, 1925.

[32] U.N. Charter art. 24, para 1 ("In order to ensure prompt and effective action by the United Nations, its Members confer on the Security Council primary responsibility for the maintenance of international peace and security, and agree that in carrying out its duties under this responsibility the Security Council acts on their behalf").

Each of these principal institutions, however, often operates independently of the others without any single administrator. Myriad agencies associated with the United Nations, such as the World Health Organization or the UN International Children's Fund (UNICEF), also operate on a quasi-independent basis and don't directly answer to a common administrator. Many IOs remain completely outside the UN system.

But the diffuse, diverse, and nonhierarchical nature of IOs does not mean they cannot affect a nation-state's sovereignty. In today's globalizing world, IOs have acquired two characteristics that diminish the sovereignty of nation-states: independence from nation-state control, and heightened powers.

Independence. Because nation-states create IOs, it would seem counterintuitive that the latter could ever limit the sovereignty of the former. From the perspective of principal-agent theory, nation-state principals would generally delegate power to IO agents because they believed the IOs could further the principals' (nation-states') interests.[33] However, IOs could never threaten the sovereignty of nation-states.

This analysis misses a number of key factors behind decisions to create IOs. Nation-states establish IOs in order to resolve interstate disputes, administer or develop technical standards, create forums to discuss policies, or settle various other issues in tandem with other nation-states. In almost all of these circumstances, the IO must reflect the interests of more than one member. Since nation-states tend to have different interests, they have incentives to create an IO that is not completely beholden to any nation-state. Contrary to some of the more spartan theories of international law, such as Goldsmith and Posner's *Limits of International Law*, we theorize that IO independence occurs because it serves as a valuable aid to international cooperation. The willingness of nations to join an IO outside their direct control—one that might issue decisions contrary to their future interests—signals that the nation can be trusted to live up to their international commitments. Nations may suffer some short-term setbacks from an independent IO, but they may still benefit from the longer-term cooperation with other countries.

In other words, member states have incentives to give some measure of independence to an IO in order to prevent that IO from favoring particular members. To be sure, depending on the purpose of the IO, the level of independence will vary. Thus, an IO like the International Court of Justice is often empowered to resolve a border dispute between two nations. It is not surprising that its members receive some measure of independence from both nation-states. Otherwise, the parties could simply negotiate a settlement. On the other hand, the parties to the dispute will establish the range of possible settlements that they will accept before they bring it to the Court, effectively limiting the IO's range of action.

An IO that is mainly focused on offering loans to third-party countries, such as the World Bank, is less likely to need independence from its member states, especially if

---

[33] Darren G. Hawkins, et al., Delegation and Agency in International Organizations 12–17 (2006).

those states are not beneficiaries of the bank's loans. The World Bank should have less independence from its member states than other kinds of IOs since the Bank does not perform the function of settling disputes between nation-states, and instead serves to coordinate actions with respect to nonmember third parties.

IOs can achieve independence from their member states in a number of ways. First and foremost, IOs are usually staffed and led by individuals who are independent from their member states. Such independence is reflected in the appointment and removal of officials. One example of a selection process that should result in a high level of independence is the election of judges on the International Court of Justice. Governments do not appoint members of the Court. Rather, selection requires a vote of the UN General Assembly with subsequent approval by the UN Security Council. This process of selection limits the ability of nation-states to control which of their nationals, if any, will get to serve on the Court.[34] Even more importantly, ICJ judges serve renewable nine-year terms and can be removed only by a unanimous vote of the rest of the members of the Court.[35] There is no provision for removal of an ICJ judge either by her home state or by the General Assembly and Security Council.

These characteristics result in a greater level of independence for the ICJ as an institution. Although there is evidence that the judges of the ICJ vote in a systematic pattern favoring their home states, such bias occurs despite a method of selecting the ICJ judges that secures greater independence. Tellingly, the ICJ has, on a number of occasions, issued decisions against states like the United States with the support of ICJ judges from the United States—demonstrating the efficacy of the ICJ's independent structure.[36]

At the opposite end of the spectrum, representatives to the UN Security Council neither have nor expect independence from their home states. The representatives, usually ambassadors to the United Nations, are appointed and can be removed by their home states for any reason. Such representatives are understood to vote in a manner entirely consistent with the wishes of their home states. The United Nations seems to operate on the principle that each ambassador will represent the interests of his or her own country, and the General Assembly's main achievement is to create a forum where they can air their interests openly.

Of course, even the most independent IO enounters some limits. The ICJ is funded by appropriations from the General Assembly, so member states exercise some financial leverage over the ICJ. By the same token, most dependent IOs, like the UN Security Council (UNSC), can adopt measures that are not supported by some of the member states. While this could not apply to the permanent members because of their veto power, it is possible for the nonpermanent members to be required to do something by the UNSC even if they have voted against it.

---

[34] I.C.J. Statute, art. 17.

[35] I.C.J. Statute, art. 18.

[36] Indeed, the U.S. Judge on the ICJ has voted against the United States in two out of the four cases brought against the United States in that court in the past two decades.

The level of IO independence from nation-states can be located along a spectrum ranging from less independent to more independent. What is clear, however, is that even a somewhat independent IO represents a challenge to nation-state sovereignty. In at least some cases, IOs are authorized to make decisions imposing obligations on nation-states without the states' consent. IO decision-makers are, in some cases, shielded from control by the nation-states they represent. This increases the likelihood of a real conflict between the actions of the IO and the interests of the nation-states that formed them.

Sovereign Powers. Independent IOs might regularly make decisions in defiance of the wishes of their nation-state creators without any threat to sovereignty. Their actions, for example, could carefully avoid infringing on the powers that are held by a nation-state. For this reason, we now focus our attention on IOs that exercise a substantial amount of power previously held by national sovereigns. Unless the IO actually exercises such power, its independence is unlikely to create any serious conflicts with those sovereigns.

Traditionally, IOs did not directly exercise sovereign powers. Instead, the obligations that IOs imposed on nation-states were to be carried out through the latter's domestic law processes. For example, an international arbitral tribunal, such as the U.S.-Mexico Claims Commission, might require a party to pay damages for mistreating citizens of a foreign country.[37] But the nation-state, via its own domestic law processes, had the final word on how and whether to comply with the IO decision. This fits within the traditional Westphalian principle that a state's consent was necessary to any diminution of its sovereignty. In recent years, however, IOs have begun to acquire the sovereign powers previously held exclusively by the nation-states. For example, not only does the European Court of Justice (ECJ) have the power to order a nation-state's compliance with various treaties binding members of the European Union; its judgments also have direct effect within the domestic legal systems of EU members. Its judgments will be given effect notwithstanding contrary domestic laws in member states. Thus, unlike the judgments of traditional IOs like the U.S-Mexican Claims Commission, the ECJ is essentially exercising the sovereign power to interpret and apply treaty obligations within the domestic legal systems of its member nation-states. As the ECJ itself declared,

By creating a Community . . . with real powers stemming from a limitation of sovereignty or a transfer of powers from the States to the Community, the Member States have limited their sovereign rights, albeit within limited fields, and have thus created a body of law that binds both their nationals and themselves. . . . The transfer by the States from their domestic legal system to the Community legal system of the rights and obligations arising under the Treaty carries with it a permanent limitation of their

---

[37] Convention between the United States and Mexico for reciprocal settlement of claims, art. I (Sept. 8, 1923).

sovereign rights, against which a subsequent unilateral act incompatible with the concept of the Community cannot prevail.[38]

In the view of the ECJ, therefore, EU member states have "limited their sovereign rights" and created a body of law that binds both individuals and the EU countries themselves. While there has been some controversy in the domestic courts of the EU member states over whether ECJ judgments would trump constitutional obligations, the basic framework has largely gone unchallenged. The ECJ, as well as other institutions of the European Union, have acquired sovereign powers from member states to override almost all domestic law. The ECJ and other EU institutions have thus acquired the power to bind the nationals of EU countries directly rather than simply imposing obligations on the nation-states.

The ECJ's broad powers constitute the most spectacular example of how modern IOs exercise sovereign powers. The United States has also experimented with the transfer of sovereign powers, albeit on a limited scale, in the dispute settlement process created by the North American Free Trade Agreement (NAFTA). Prior to NAFTA, the Commerce Department had the absolute and exclusive power to impose duties on foreign imports that it believed were either unfairly subsidized or "dumped" on the U.S. market. The power to impose duties and regulations on imports is a classic Westphalian sovereign power and was delegated to Congress under Article I of the U.S. Constitution.

Since the passage of NAFTA in 1994, however, the U.S. government's decision to impose such duties on goods arriving from either Canada or Mexico has been subject to a challenge in a NAFTA binational arbitration panel. The panels are empowered to reverse the U.S. government's decision to impose duties. The only avenue for appeal lies in an extraordinary challenge committee also established by NAFTA. No appeal to a U.S. court or the U.S. government is permitted.[39] Thus, transfer of a sovereign power of the United States (the power to impose customs duties on imports) to an IO (a NAFTA dispute panel) is complete.

IOs can influence and even coerce nation-states without directly exercising sovereign powers. For instance, the World Bank and the International Monetary Fund have required nations that borrow funds to adopt domestic policies such as raising taxes, cutting spending, or lifting controls on financial flows. These directives diminish the freedom of those nation-states, but do so via the exercise of sovereign powers.

It is important not to overstate these developments. We believe that there has been some transfer of national governmental authority to IOs. But these transfers are in

[38] 6/64 Casota v. ENEL (1964) E.C.R. 585, 593–94.

[39] North American Free Trade Agreement, Annex 1904.15 ("The United States shall amend section 516A[g] of the Tariff Act of 1930, as amended, to provide, in accordance with the terms of this Chapter, for binational panel review of antidumping and countervailing duty cases involving Mexican or Canadian merchandise. Such amendment shall provide that if binational panel review is requested such review will be exclusive").

their early stages. The process is furthest along in the European Union, to which the member states have delegated significant authority over a wide variety of matters. But Europe itself may not present the clearest picture, because the European Union may signify the creation of a new regional confederation, or even nation, rather than serving as an example of supranational government. In most areas, IOs still have no direct enforcement resources of their own and depend on nation-states to choose to comply with their decisions. Still, there is an undeniable trend toward IOs with the legal authority to act directly in areas that used to be the province of sovereign nation-states.

In our framework, serious conflicts between an IO and a national sovereign are most likely to occur where that IO both has a meaningful level of independence and exercises sovereign powers. An IO that is independent of a nation-state but does not exercise sovereign powers is not likely to create any serious conflict. An IO that does exercise sovereign powers but remains completely under the control of a particular nation-state is also unlikely to create serious problems.

Figure 2.1 illustrates these categories: the level of an IO's independence from a nation-state is represented on the horizontal axis, and the scope of an IO's sovereign powers is represented on the vertical axis. The four quadrants created thus illustrate the four categories of IOs.

IOs in quadrant B present the least serious threat to sovereignty. These IOs have little independence from nation-states and little sovereign power. IOs that exercise no sovereign powers and have little independence from the U.S. government cannot, in our definition, cause tensions or pressures for the U.S. Constitution.

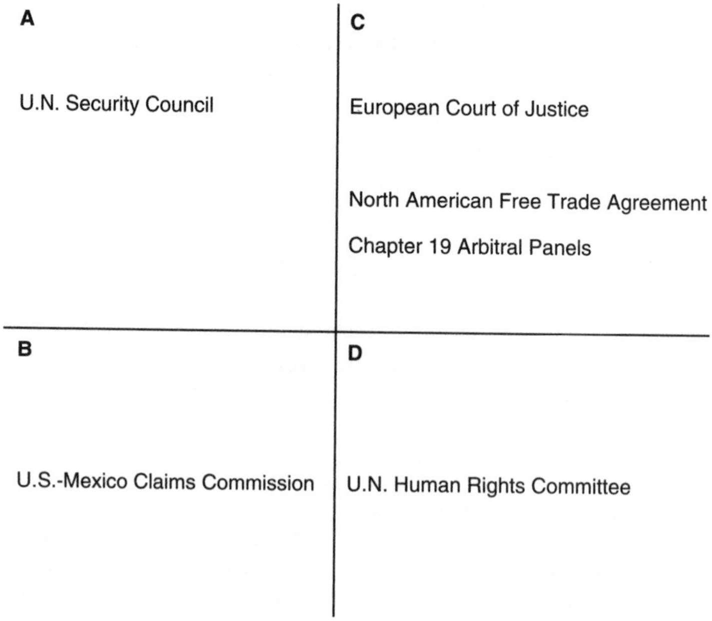

FIGURE 2.1 Independence vs. Exercise of Sovereign Powers

One interesting example of such an IO is the U.S.-Mexico Claims Commission established pursuant to a treaty in 1923. It was authorized to adjudicate all claims by nationals of one country against nationals of the other.[40] Each government appointed one member of the three-member arbitral commission and the two governments jointly appointed the third member.[41] Although the Commission was authorized to resolve all claims submitted to it, all compensation would be paid by the governments, even if the injury had been caused by a national of one of the countries. For instance, if a U.S. citizen won a case claiming injury caused by a Mexican citizen, the Mexican government rather than the Mexican citizen would compensate the plaintiff. The treaty did not authorize the Commission to pay out any money itself or exercise specific sovereign powers.

The IOs in quadrant A have acquired or been delegated an above-average level of sovereign powers but a below-average level of independence from their nation-state creators. One example of such an IO is the UN Security Council. As discussed earlier, the Security Council can exercise nearly unlimited powers to maintain peace and security. Although it has rarely exercised this power, it has in some cases authorized other countries to use military force, ordered countries to turn over wanted war criminals, and acquired governance control over a particular territory. For instance, the Security Council's resolutions were the legal basis for the UN's administration of the territory of Kosovo, even though, prior to its 2008 declaration of independence, Kosovo was recognized as part of the territory of Serbia.

Although the Security Council's powers could seriously infringe on the sovereignty of a nation-state, their existence does not pose a serious sovereignty challenge to a nation like the United States. Under the UN Charter, the United States has a permanent seat on the Security Council, which gives it the right to exercise an unqualified veto over any Council action. Moreover, the United States appoints, and may remove, its permanent representative on the Council, allowing it even more control over Council actions. For this reason, even an IO possessing potentially wide-ranging sovereign powers is unlikely to be a problem for constitutional purposes if it remains under the control of the U.S. government.

---

[40] Convention between the United States and Mexico for reciprocal settlement of claims, art. I. ("All claims (except those arising from acts incident to the recent revolutions) against Mexico of citizens of the United States, whether corporations, companies, associations, partnerships or individuals, for losses or damages suffered by persons or by their properties, and all claims against the United States of America by citizens of Mexico, whether corporations, companies, associations, partnerships or individuals, for losses or damages suffered by persons or by their properties; all claims for losses or damages suffered by citizens of either country by reason of losses or damages suffered by any corporation, company, association or partnership in which such citizens have or have had a substantial and bona fide interest, provided an allotment to the claimant by the corporation, company, association or partnership of his proportion of the loss or damage suffered is presented by the claimant to the Commission hereinafter referred to; and all claims for losses or damages originating from acts of officials or others acting for either Government and resulting in injustice").

[41] *Id.*

Quadrant D represents the opposite situation. IOs in this quadrant are quite independent of the nation-states that created them, but they also lack any meaningful sovereign powers. To the extent that these IOs take positions against their home governments, they lack the authority to enforce or implement those positions domestically. Although these IOs may create potential embarrassment for the foreign policies of their member states, they are unlikely to endanger basic constitutional values in these states.

One example of an IO belonging to this quadrant is the United Nations Human Rights Committee (UNHRC). The UNHRC is authorized to investigate a particular country's compliance with its obligations under the main UN international human rights treaties. Its investigative reports can be extremely critical and often result in recommendations for substantial changes in domestic government policies. The members of such committees are nominated by their home states. But, like members of the ICJ, they cannot be removed by their home governments.[42] Although the UNHCR is highly independent, its lack of any formal sovereign power saves it from causing serious constitutional difficulties. As we discuss below, however, the norms and interpretations advanced by the UNHCR could raise challenges to sovereignty if adopted by domestic courts without authorization from the executive and legislative branches.

The most important category of IOs for our study falls within Quadrant C. This quadrant represents IOs that have a substantial measure of independence *and* can exercise meaningful sovereign power. This combination of independence and sovereignty is most likely to pose difficulties for the United States. Until recently, IOs possessing both characteristics were rare. Even the UN Charter, which many of its founders saw as an opportunity to break with the Westphalian system, rarely establishes entities with such authority. While the UN Security Council may have broad sovereign-like powers, it lacks independence; the UNHRC has the opposite limitation.

Quadrant C, however, is not an empty set. As globalization has led to greater and deeper levels of interstate cooperation, the number of IOs in this category is likely to grow. Some IOs in this category are new creations, while others have lain dormant until recently. We have already discussed two types of independent IOs that exercise substantial powers—the European Court of Justice and the arbitral tribunals established by Chapter 19 of NAFTA. The ECJ poses a greater problem than the NAFTA tribunals. Members of a NAFTA tribunal are selected for a particular dispute by its member countries. Although the member countries cannot later remove tribunal members, their case-by-case service makes it possible for a country to avoid arbitrators who repeatedly rule against them. In contrast, ECJ judges serve six-year renewable terms; and since they are not chosen with a particular dispute in mind, they have substantially more independence from their nominating countries.[43] The ECJ's power

---

[42] International Covenant on Civil and Political Rights, art. 28–31.

[43] Treaty Establishing the European Communities, consolidated text, art. 223, Dec. 24, 2002.

also extends beyond that of the NAFTA tribunals to the many subjects regulated by the European Union agreements. We should make clear, however, that the ECJ has no effect on American sovereignty, but instead serves as a new model of advanced supranational integration that some would like the rest of the world to follow.

Our focus on independence and power does not mean that IOs in the other three quadrants might not raise sovereignty concerns. But we believe our framework clarifies those cases where conflict with nation-state authority is the greatest. It helps to sort through much of the confusion about IOs and their threat to sovereignty. By narrowing our set of problem cases, we can focus on the particular characteristics of contemporary IOs that, in our view, pose a meaningful threat to sovereignty.

The "New" International Law. The system of "global governance" described by many globalization scholars reserves an important place for independent IOs. Parallel to the upward shift of power to supranational organizations is a "downward" shift to subnational governments, nongovernmental organizations, and individuals. A number of scholars have described this phenomenon as the "disaggregation" of the nation-state.[44] As we will detail in chapter 7, much of this downward shift can fit within the U.S. constitutional system. We do identify, however, one aspect of this disaggregation phenomenon that poses more serious constitutional difficulties. NGOs have increasingly used litigation in domestic U.S. courts to build support for transnational and international legal norms. Such litigation creates constitutional difficulties when NGOs attempt to use the U.S. judicial branch to override or depart from the policies set by the legislative or executive branches.

Key to this phenomenon is the development of a new kind of international law, which has two noteworthy qualities. First, international law's emphasis on human rights has increasingly focused on "cosmopolitan" or "universalist" obligations. These values demand greater regulation of a government's treatment of its own citizens, a relationship that had traditionally resided exclusively within the sovereignty of the nation-state. Second, influence over the interpretation of international law, which had relied heavily on the practice of nation-states, has shifted toward independent IOs, nongovernmental organizations, and transnational elites. Indeed, as we will describe, NGOs have seized on the new international law to acquire a certain amount of power.

International law has an ancient pedigree. Used here, "traditional international law" refers to the dominant understanding of international law that existed between the eighteenth century and the establishment of the United Nations in 1945. The classic statement of the traditional approach is found in the *S.S. Lotus* opinion of the Permanent Court of International Justice (PCIJ). "International law governs relations between independent States. The rules of law binding upon States therefore emanate from their own free will as expressed in conventions or by usages generally accepted as expressing principles of law."[45]

---

[44] *See* Spiro, *supra* note 2, at 649.
[45] The S.S. Lotus (Fr. v. Turk.), 1927 P.C.I.J. (ser. A) No. 10, at 18 (Sept. 7).

Traditional international law reflects, in many ways, the basic assumptions of the Westphalian system. Its pillar is the absolute sovereignty of nation-states, or, as the PCIJ put it, their own "free will." International law binds a state only by those rules that a state has voluntarily accepted. A state may express this acceptance either through formal treaty or practice and custom. No central organization enforces rules on states that have not voluntarily accepted them. The nation-state is the only actor because international law applies exclusively to relations between sovereigns. According to one commentator, "the orthodox positivist doctrine has been explicit in the affirmation that only states are subjects of international law."[46]

Private actors are largely excluded from participating in the development or interpretation of international law. Traditional international law rarely had rules regulating private rights or activities. Private parties had no independent rights to assert against sovereign states. Indeed, the unlawful detention of an ambassador doesn't violate her rights as an individual; it violates the sovereign's right to the inviolability of its diplomatic personnel. A private individual seeking vindication of his rights against a nation must convince his own government to seek a diplomatic settlement. The International Court of Justice followed this view as late as 1970 when it rejected the right of individual shareholders to seek remedies under international law against a state.[47]

[W]ithin the limits prescribed by international law, a State may exercise diplomatic protection by whatever means and to whatever extent it thinks fit, for it is its own right that the State is asserting. Should the natural or legal persons on whose behalf it is acting consider that their rights are not adequately protected, they have no remedy in international law.[48]

Because traditional international law focused on developing rules for states in their relations with one another and not between private individuals and states, an individual harmed by another nation or its citizens would have to seek relief through her own court system. Nothing in international law itself, however, forbids a domestic court from using international rules as a source of guidance or persuasive authority. U.S. courts have applied rules of general international law when no other rules of decision, in the form of treaties, statutes, or executive declarations, governed. As the U.S. Supreme Court explained in *The Paquete Habana*, decided at the turn of the last century: "[W]here there is no treaty, and no controlling executive or legislative act or judicial decision, resort must be had to the customs and usages of civilized nations; and as evidence of these, to the works of jurists and commentators."[49]

Traditional international law developed through the absolute sovereignty of nation-states, formal treaties, and custom created by state practice. Private parties

---

[46] Malcolm N. Shaw, International Law 126 (2d ed. 1986) (quoting H. Lauterpacht).

[47] Barcelona Traction, Light, and Power Company, Limited (Belg. v. Spain), 1970 I.C.J. 3, P 78 (Feb. 5).

[48] *Id.*

[49] The Paquete Habana, 175 U.S. 677, 700 (1900).

fell outside international law's purview except to the extent that their activities affected the intercourse between sovereign states. Under this regime, nation-states play the most important role in developing international law through their control of diplomatic and military resources. International agreements affected the development of international law only to the extent that they bound the nation-states to specific (usually bilateral) agreements. The power to make international agreements did not usually lead to rules of general applicability.

More recently, commentators have described the rise of a new kind of international law. They have used different terms such as "world law," "supranational law," or "cosmopolitan law" to distinguish between the new and traditional international law. This chapter will continue to refer to this new law as "international law" because it retains many features of traditional international law.[50] There are two noteworthy features of this new international law that raise serious issues under the U.S. Constitution.

First, the new international law has moved away from its exclusive focus on state-to-state relations and is openly concerned with the relationship between a nation and its own citizens or between citizens of different nations. The *Restatement (Second) of the Foreign Relations Law of the United States*, approved in 1965, did not take a position on whether international law related to any matter other than state-to-state relations. Twenty-five years later, the *Restatement (Third)* unequivocally stated that international law includes rules and principles governing states' "relations with persons, whether natural or juridical."[51] This represents a significant shift from the ICJ's assertion that individuals "have no remedy in international law."[52] Under the *Third Restatement*'s view, the rules of international law will apply to the rights of individuals against states as well as the rights of states against other states.

The most prominent example of international law's shift in focus is in the area of human rights. Modern human rights law's most important innovation is its insistence that human rights are universal. Under the traditional conception of international law, if a wrongdoing state was an injured person's own state, then the individual had no remedy under international law. If France, for example, wanted to deprive its citizens of the right to free speech, that would be of no interest to the United States, which could not claim any harm to its own citizens. International human rights law denies this basic premise. It maintains that a harm of an individual's international human rights, even by her own government, injures other nations.

---

[50] *See* Peter Hay, *Supranational Organizations and United States Constitutional Law*, 6 VA. J. INT'L L. 195, 195–96 (1966) (describing criteria for supranationalism); Patrick Tangney, *The New Internationalism: The Cession of Sovereign Competences to Supranational Organizations and Constitutional Change in the United States and Germany*, 21 YALE J. INT'L L. 395, 399–404 (1996) (describing supranational law and the rise of supranational organizations).

[51] RESTATEMENT (THIRD) OF THE FOREIGN RELATIONS LAW OF THE UNITED STATES § 101, n.1 (1986).

[52] Barcelona Traction, Light, and Power Company, Limited (Belg. v. Spain), 1970 I.C.J. 3, P 78 (Feb. 5).

International human rights law's focus on an individual's relationship with his own state inevitably expands the subject matter of international law. For instance, the International Covenant on Civil and Political Rights, which has been ratified by more than 160 nations, guarantees an individual the rights of free expression, political association, property, life, and procedural justice, among others. Similarly, the International Covenant on Economic and Social Rights guarantees the right to health care, economic well-being, and work. Both agreements operate as a limitation on nations' domestic policies. Together, they encompass many issues that fall within the jurisdiction of the federal government under the U.S. Constitution. During its recent report on its compliance with the ICCPR, for example, the U.S. government responded to concerns raised by the UNHRC about its protection of the right to vote during the 2000 and 2004 presidential elections.[53] NGOs have filed charges with the United Nations alleging widespread violations by the United States of the rights to vote, to a fair trial, to adequate health care, and to adequate housing.[54] Whether or not there is merit to these charges, there is little doubt that the U.S. government's acknowledgment that it has broad international obligations to guarantee rights and protections to its citizens represents a substantial departure from traditional international law's assumption of a state's "absolute and exclusive" sovereignty within its own territory. For now, the United States can resist any legal claims for ICCPR enforcement in its domestic courts because it declared much of the Convention non-self-executing when it was ratified in 1992.

Second, the processes for creating, interpreting, and enforcing international law have changed. Traditionally, the interpretation and application of international law relied heavily on the practice and opinions of nation-states. Customary international law, for instance, rests on the practice of nation-states in their acceptance of a rule as a legal obligation. A nation-state that refused to follow a particular custom or refused to recognize that custom as a legal rule could not be bound. With respect to treaties, a nation-state controlled whether or not it signed, and even after signing, its interpretation of the terms often had substantial weight because it had taken part in the negotiation and drafting. As traditional international law typically governed state-to-state relations, the conduct of the state parties affected interpretations of ambiguous treaty obligations.

Although these interpretive methodologies continue today, the role of state consent in the new international law has become less important because of the combination of jus cogens obligations and international human rights law. Jus cogens consists of those clear and well-established international obligations, such as the prohibitions on genocide, torture, and piracy, that bind nation-states with or without their consent. Although the doctrine of jus cogens is not new, its application to

[53] Consideration of Reports Submitted by States Parties Under Article 40 of the Covenant, Third periodic report of States parties due in 2003, United States of America, para. 397–405.

[54] International Human Rights Law & Hurricane Katrina: ICCPR Violations by the United States Government, United Nations Human Rights Committee Hearings of 17 & July 18, 2006, 87th Session, *available at* http://www.ohchr.english/bodies/hrc/docs/nba.pdf.

international human rights law is changing the method of interpreting and applying international law. Unlike most forms of traditional international law, a state cannot refuse to be bound by a jus cogens norm either by refusing to enter into a treaty or by refusing to treat a jus cogens norm as a legal obligation. Even contrary state practice does not undermine the binding nature of jus cogens norms, which are by definition universal and nonderogable. For obvious reasons, interpretations of jus cogens obligations rarely depend on nation-state consent or practice.

Although jus cogens norms are rare, independent IOs have come to influence the content and scope of many different kinds of international law, shifting the focus away from nation-states. Unchained from traditional international law's rigid focus on nation-states, IOs have become important, and sometimes dominant, actors in the formation, interpretation, and enforcement of new norms of international law. These IOs have taken advantage of an important change in the nature of customary international law. Customary international law (CIL)—that is, unwritten international law—has long been thought to be legally binding because it represented the long-standing, uniform practice of states. But now IOs and some nations look to multilateral treaties as manifestations of CIL, even when they announce a new norm of international law—such as a prohibition on land mines. This "instant" CIL can create universal international norms that theoretically bind even those nations that refused to join the treaty in the first place. IOs outside the control of any nation-state can use this process to effectively impose legal obligations on unwilling nations, further reducing their sovereignty without their consent.

The possibilities of this decentralized or non-state-focused method of developing international law have seized the attention of scholars and advocates. Harold Koh calls for a new method of developing international law; his "transnational legal process" emphasizes the central role that private transnational organizations play in the formation of international law by pursuing a litigation strategy in domestic and international courts.[55] Lawyers working in concert, often through transnational nongovernmental associations, can persuade domestic courts to recognize an international norm without intervention or approval by the political branches of a nation's government. While traditional international law focuses on state practice, the new international law can be shaped first by domestic litigation driven by NGOs. Transnational NGOs have successfully established in U.S. litigation that a ban on torture is a jus cogens international law obligation.[56] Less successfully, NGOs have sought in U.S. litigation to establish international law obligations imposing aiding-and-abetting liability on corporations, the right to organize workers, freedom from capital punishment, freedom from pollution, and freedom from arbitrary detention.[57]

---

[55] See Harold H. Koh, *Transnational Legal Process*, 75 Neb. L. Rev. 181 (1996).

[56] See, e.g., Siderman de Blake v. Argentina, 965 F.2d 699 (9th Cir. 1992).

[57] See, e.g., Sosa v. Alvarez-Machain, 542 U.S. 692 (2004); Flores v. S. Peru Copper Corp., 414 F.3d 233 (2d Cir. 2003); Presbyterian Church of Sudan v. Talisman Energy, Inc., 244 F. Supp. 2d 289 (S.D.N.Y. 2003).

The success, or lack thereof, of these litigation strategies is not as important as their goal. Rather than analyzing state practice or seeking diplomatic opinion, the decentralized lawmaking process allows NGOs to set the international lawmaking agenda and win recognition of new international legal norms. This process also allows IOs without any formal sovereign power, such as the UNHRC, to play a significant role in the interpretation and development of international law. In the view of some commentators, the UNHRC's opinions themselves have achieved substantial and even authoritative influence. These opinions have been invoked, for example, in U.S. domestic litigation in an unsuccessful attempt to block the imposition of a death sentence.[58]

Since the 9/11 terrorist attacks, a combination of transnational NGOs and independent IOs has challenged the legality of various aspects of the U.S. government's war on terrorism.[59] Transnational NGOs, for instance, have participated in domestic litigation to argue that the U.S. government's rendition, detention, interrogation, and trial by military commission of alleged terrorists violate both international human rights law and international humanitarian law. Buttressed by legal opinions from independent IOs like the Council of Europe and the UNHRC, such litigation has had partial success in overturning some U.S. government policies, despite the government's contrary views about the interpretation of the relevant international law norms.[60] This outcome would have been virtually impossible under the traditional conception of international law, which did not permit a nation's actions to be challenged by nongovernmental organizations in its own courts.

III. GLOBALIZATION AND SOVEREIGNTY

The three aspects of globalization discussed above substantially affect the sovereignty of nation-states. In this section, we distinguish between the most widely used conception of sovereignty—"Westphalian sovereignty"—and "popular sovereignty."

A. Westphalian Sovereignty

For most commentators, nation-state sovereignty is synonymous with "Westphalian" sovereignty. It assumes the absolute control of nation-states over all conduct that occurs within their own territories. In the United States, Chief Justice John Marshall described this understanding of sovereignty in an early U.S. Supreme Court decision:

The jurisdiction of the nation within its own territory is necessarily exclusive and absolute. It is susceptible of no limitation not imposed by itself. Any restriction upon it,

---

[58] *See* Domingues v. Nevada, 961 P.2d 1276 (Nev. 1998) (considering the legal interpretation of the ICCPR's limitation of capital punishment issued by the UNHRC).

[59] *See* Julian G. Ku, *The Third Wave: The War on Terrorism and the Alien Tort Statute*, 19 Emory Int'l L. Rev. 105 (2005).

[60] *See, e.g.*, Hamdan v. Rumsfeld, 548 U.S. 557 (2006).

deriving validity from an external source, would imply a diminution of its sovereignty to the extent of the restriction, and an investment of that sovereignty to the same extent in that power which could impose such restriction.[61]

A nation's sovereignty can be diminished or limited, but any such limitations must be "traced up to the consent of the nation itself. They can flow from no other legitimate source." A nation-state might consent to such limitations, for instance, as part of its desire to improve trade relations.

Marshall's statement reveals the two key characteristics of the Westphalian conception of sovereignty.

(1) Within a country's territorial jurisdiction, a nation's sovereignty is "exclusive and absolute."
(2) Any limitation on a nation's sovereignty, such as that arising from international law, can only arise with the "consent" of the sovereign.

To be sure, this definition of sovereignty may not always have prevailed, even among the nation-states themselves.[62] But, as Marshall's statement suggests, absolute state sovereignty was widely accepted as a description of the world's political organization since the time of the Peace of Westphalia in 1648. As Mark Janis writes,

The Peace of Westphalia legitimated the right of sovereigns to govern their peoples free of outside interference, whether any such external claim to interfere was based on political, legal or religious principles. . . . Sovereignty, as a concept, formed the cornerstone of the edifice of international relations that 1648 raised up. Sovereignty was the crucial element in the peace treaties of Westphalia, the international agreements that were intended to end a great war and to promote a coming peace. The treaties of Westphalia enthroned and sanctified sovereigns, gave them powers domestically and independence externally.[63]

Many scholars argue that this version of absolute state sovereignty is being eroded today. As one leading globalization scholar writes, "States can no longer be sovereign in the traditional sense of the word. For both physical and ideational reasons, a state cannot in contemporary globalizing circumstances exercise ultimate, comprehensive, absolute, and singular rule over a country and its foreign relations."[64] Recognizing these trends, some commentators have proclaimed the inevitable end of nation-state sovereignty.

---

[61] Schooner Exchange v. McFaddon, 11 U.S. 116, 136 (1812).
[62] STEPHEN D. KRASNER, SOVEREIGNTY: ORGANIZED HYPOCRISY (1999).
[63] M. S. Janis, *Sovereignty and International Law: Hobbes and Grotius*, in ESSAYS IN HONOUR OF WANG TIEYA 391, 393 (R. St. J. Macdonald ed., 1994).
[64] SCHOLTE, *supra* note 1, at 136.

Table 2.1 Key Differences between Westphalian Sovereignty and Global Governance

	Westphalian Sovereignty	*Global Governance*
A State's Control within Territory	"Absolute and exclusive"	Constrained by market forces, IOs, and NGOs
A State's Exercise of Sovereign Powers	"Absolute and exclusive"	Divided between IOs and national governments
The Binding Effect of International Law on a State	Only on external affairs with state consent	On domestic affairs without state consent in certain instances

This would not be the unalloyed good that some scholars and advocates believe. Even if it was not always respected, the Westphalian system reduced the areas of inter-state conflict, thereby creating more stable inter-state relations. For liberal democracies, Westphalian sovereignty can protect democratic political processes from outside interference. As Jeremy Rabkin has argued, the traditional system of Westphalian sovereignty has resulted in stable and fair governance across many different national systems.[65] Nation-states have exercised their sovereign powers to build and maintain stable, orderly, liberal, and just societies.

All three elements of the system of global governance described above can undermine Westphalian sovereignty.

As described in table 2.1, global governance undermines the main elements of Westphalian sovereignty. In a global governance system, nation-states can no longer assume the absolute and exclusive power to determine domestic policy free of any externally imposed constraints. Rather, market forces, international organizations, and NGOs can pressure nation-states to alter their domestic policies, especially economic ones.

One might believe that our concerns are overwrought. Global governance may be more dream than certainty. Westphalian sovereignty may be merely a shibboleth for neo-isolationists, rather than a value worth protecting. As we readily admit, the institutions of global governance are only now emerging from their infancy. Some, such as the Security Council and the International Court of Justice, have existed since the adoption of the UN Charter in 1945, but have sought to expand their reach only in the last few decades. Proposals for others, such as the World Trade Organization, took a half-century to actualize. A few, such as the International Monetary Fund and the World Bank, have reoriented their missions and become more interventionist in the domestic affairs of nations.

Yet it is undeniable that new species of international cooperation have emerged. New multilateral agreements regulate the internal as well as external conduct of nation-states. Some have existed for some time, and some have been significant

---

[65] Jeremy Rabkin, Law Without Nations?: Why Constitutional Government Requires Sovereign States 15 (2007).

since at least the human rights treaties of the 1960s and 1970s, such as the International Covenant on Civil and Political Rights, or the International Covenant on Economic and Social Rights. But what makes the current round of treaties different is their marriage of sweeping, universal rules with independent institutions of enforcement. The latest version of the General Agreement on Tariffs and Trade, for example, not only requires national treatment for foreign imports; it also creates a rulemaking body (the World Trade Organization) to develop amendments to the treaty, and a court system (the Dispute Settlement Understanding) to resolve trade disputes. The Rome Statute not only outlaws war crimes and crimes against humanity; it also creates a prosecutor's office to investigate and prosecute crimes and a court system to try the defendants. The Law of the Sea Convention both sets out rules for the free navigation of the high seas, and creates an international tribunal for the resolution of disputes. The Chemical Weapons Convention creates a Secretariat that can ban new chemicals and conduct surprise inspections of domestic production sites.

Enforcement mechanisms such as these, as well as the international rules themselves, cause concern among those interested in protecting Westphalian sovereignty. These new forms of multilateral cooperation challenge sovereignty by transferring lawmaking authority from the organs of government established by the Constitution to international bodies. International agreements have yet to prompt the United States to hand over anything really serious, such as assigning the authority to set monetary policy to an international central bank. However, proposals for future climate change plans would be quick to change the status quo, since they call for the creation of an international agency to monitor national energy usage. The effort to create durable institutions with the ability to enforce international norms directly within the American legal system would end Westphalian sovereignty.

Rabkin argues that these developments intrude into the American constitutional system and undermine the capacity of nation-states to pursue their national interest. He sees the world as one in which people form nations. Clothed with full sovereignty, only nations can mobilize their people to defend themselves and to take action outside their borders to prevent the rise of dictatorial powers. Global governance disrupts the relationship between a people and their nation by transferring the locus of legislative and enforcement authority to IOs. National governments will be unable to call on their citizens, who will have divided loyalties, to take action in defense of national interests. Rabkin believes that this will cause a decline in global welfare, because in his view only nation-states retain the strength to stop aggression by authoritarian regimes or to halt human rights catastrophes.

If the organs of global governance were only institutions such as the Security Council or the ICJ, Rabkin's fears would be speculative at best. As a permanent member of the Security Council, the United States maintains a veto, and the Security Council has never issued an order compelling American action directly under U.S. law. So far, the United States has refused to acknowledge that ICJ decisions take direct effect in the domestic legal system, and has even taken the position that such judgments can only be enforced against it under international law by a vote of the Security Council (where it again exercises a veto). For instance, the United States withdrew from the mandatory jurisdiction of the ICJ because of Nicaragua's 1986 suit over the CIA's mining of Managua harbor and the Reagan administration's support of the *contra* guerrillas. More recently, the United States has refused to comply with the ICJ's decisions ordering review and reconsideration of death penalty verdicts against aliens who did not receive their consular notification rights under international treaties.

But critics of global governance can point to more than the UN Charter, the WTO, or the Law of the Sea Convention. They can look to the evolution of the European Community into today's European Union as the future of global governance. Initially, the Communities began as a free-trade area, but over time their member nations delegated increasing legal authority to supranational institutions in an effort to accelerate European integration. The European Union has grown into more than just an agreement for the free movement of goods and services, capital, and people throughout its member nations. Today it is bound together by a Commission that regulates economic, trade, consumer safety, antitrust, and environmental activity throughout the Union; a Council that has its own taxing and spending authority; a Court that exercises judicial review over the legislation of member states; and even a Bank that administers monetary policy through a common currency. These core institutions of pan-European governance do not undergo regular elections; the only instance of popular representation lies in the European Parliament, which does not have the authority to issue the Europe-wide directives that override national legislation. As a result, the European Union has given birth to a large bureaucracy so distant from the usual mechanisms of electorate accountability that criticisms of a "democracy deficit" have regularly arisen.

For those concerned about the threat against sovereignty, it is not just that the ICJ may try to stop the American death penalty in the odd case, but that such moves are precursors to a full-blown, European-style system of global governance. The European Union does not create merely a forum for the resolution of disputes between European nations, as the UN Security Council does for the great powers. Rather, the European Union creates an independent international institution that can act directly upon private individuals and government agencies within its member states. It is not dependent on the nation-states to carry out its will. It has no directly elected legislature or executive branch (though there is a European Parliament with limited powers) that exercise the normal powers of a government. It appears to be governed by bureaucrats and judges in agencies and courts given life by the treaties establishing the Union. It is, in Rabkin's words, a "postmodern construction."[66]

New forms of international cooperation clearly follow the European model as they seek to regulate areas such as pollution, arms control, and trade in services. Just as the European nations sought to create supranational forms of governance that would sublimate the nationalist impulses that had ripped their continent apart in

---

[66] *Id.* at 63 (quoting James A. Caparaso, *The European Union and Forms of State: Westphalian, Regulatory or Postmodern?*, 34 J. COMMON MARKET STUDIES 29 (1996)). Unlike Caparaso, Rabkin does not mean this as a compliment.

two destructive world wars, the new forms of global governance also seek to submerge national interests. A treaty on the prohibition of land mines, for example, does not create a forum for nations to reach accommodation on the use of certain weapons. Rather, it is an effort primarily driven by NGOs and nations that already do not use land mines and do not conduct significant military operations abroad to limit the ways in which all nations may fight. By contrast, the Washington Naval Treaty of 1922, which placed limits on the warships of the United States, Great Britain, Japan, France, and Italy, is an earlier example of an arms control agreement made by the most powerful seafaring nations to serve their interests.

To Rabkin, the International Criminal Court (ICC) represents the Europeanization of international law and politics. The ICC does not serve as a forum to arbitrate disputes between nations, as does the ICJ. Instead, the ICC has its own permanent prosecutors who may initiate cases on their own against the officials of sovereign states and try them before an independent court, which has the further power to sentence and imprison guilty officials. Nations that signed the Treaty of Rome establishing the Court have an obligation to hand over individuals wanted by the ICC, but otherwise the Court does not depend on nations to reach or carry out its decisions. It is true that the Rome Statute allows member states to investigate and prosecute a treaty violation by their own citizens first before the ICC can intervene. But this principle of "complementarity" grants the ICC the decisions of whether a member state has been unwilling to investigate its own citizens in good faith— giving the IO the ultimate say on whether a prosecution will proceed.

These institutions, Rabkin argues, undermine sovereignty by detaching legal and political decisions from the governments that control force within a territory. In other words, "sovereignty appeared as a way of ordering and constraining political life," because "[i]t insisted that law and force must be joined, and that the power to command must be linked with the power to protect."[67] If citizens see international institutions exercising legal authority in their territories, as they do in Europe, they will no longer see their nations as exercising legitimate military force or securing their defense. According to Rabkin, the deterioration of sovereignty will ultimately lead to less rather than more, peace in the world as nations no longer make adequate provision for their own security.

This fundamental change in the nature of international institutions did not evolve naturally, but had been propelled along by expansive academic theories. Contrast Rabkin's critique of global governance with the view of leading international legal scholars, such as Abram and Antonia Chayes, who celebrate the arrival of the "new sovereignty." "New sovereignty" is the power to join international institutions, which alone can solve regional and international problems. The international order is governed not by autonomous nation-states that control all affairs within their borders, but by a "tightly woven fabric of international agreements, organizations, and institutions that shape their relations with one another and penetrate deeply

---

[67] Rabkin, *supra* note 65, at 15.

into their internal economics and politics."[68] The Chayeses argue that if sovereignty refers to a nation's ability to govern activity within its borders, then it must move upward to international organizations because globalization means that no individual state can fully control the people and their activity on their territory.[69]

One way that the "new sovereignty" operates, according to Anne-Marie Slaughter, is through transnational networks of government officials.[70] Finance ministers, for example, meet through organizations like the G-8 and the G-20 to coordinate solutions to international debt crises. Officials of the United States, Canada, and Mexico meet through NAFTA bodies to create a transnational environmental enforcement network. Judges on national courts increasingly cite precedents from other countries and international tribunals, stitching together something like a transnational body of law in discrete areas. These networks share information, build trust between nations, and spread best practices, the combination of which allows them to harmonize and enforce a common set of policies and laws. According to Slaughter, transnational networks will eventually "disaggregate sovereignty" because individual agencies will exercise authority in a nation as part of an international network, rather than as part of a nation-state's government.

In this vision, international institutions and international law reverse the traditional understanding of sovereignty. Sovereignty originally meant that a nation-state was free from any other form of governance in its control of activity within its borders. A nation-state would not be subject to the political claims of a supranational entity, such as the Holy Roman Empire, or a higher authority, such as the Catholic Church. Whether it chose to cooperate with other nations was a matter of its own consent, usually expressed through the form of treaties and long customary practice. According to the theories promulgated by academics and advocates, however, sovereignty is defined not by independence, but by a state's ability to fulfill international obligations. According to Slaughter, "where the defining features of the international system are connection rather than separation, interaction rather than isolation, and institutions rather than free space, sovereignty as autonomy makes no sense."[71] Or, as have written, the new sovereignty is status, membership, "connection to the rest of the world and the political ability to be an actor within it."[72]

According to these academics, sovereignty no longer represents freedom from higher commands, but instead the responsibility to fulfill international obligations. This transformation, though primarily still only in theory, is presaged by the UN Security Council's adoption of the concept of the "responsibility to protect." Initially developed by an international commission led by Canada, the responsibility to

---

[68] ABRAM CHAYES & ANTONIA CHAYES, THE NEW SOVEREIGNTY: COMPLIANCE WITH INTERNATIONAL REGULATORY AGREEMENTS 26 (1997).

[69] See, e.g., Kal Raustiala, Rethinking the Sovereignty Debate in International Economic Law, 6 J. INT'L. ECON. L. 841, 843 (2003).

[70] See generally ANNE-MARIE SLAUGHTER, A NEW WORLD ORDER (2004).

[71] Anne-Marie Slaughter, Sovereignty and Power in a Networked World Order, 40 STAN. J. INT'L L. 283, 286 (2004).

[72] CHAYES & CHAYES, supra note 68, at 26.

protect arose as a legal response to the severe humanitarian crises of the 1990s in places such as the former Yugoslavia, Rwanda, Somalia, and Haiti. Questions arose over whether nations could use force to intervene in the internal affairs of sovereign states that could not or would not stop human rights catastrophes. NATO's intervention in Kosovo was widely thought to intrude into the sovereignty of the former Yugoslavia, and thus to violate the UN Charter's guarantee of the territorial inviolability of every member nation. In response, the concept of the responsibility to protect defines membership in the United Nations as not just "the final symbol of independent sovereign statehood and thus the seal of acceptance into the community of nations."[73] Instead, UN membership also demands conduct as "a responsible member of the community of nations."[74] This includes, most critically, the obligation to respect the human rights of a nation's own citizens. And if a nation did not fulfill this obligation, the "international community," acting through the United Nations, would have the right to intervene.

Rather than honestly acknowledge that this would dilute existing national sovereignty, the commission that developed responsibility to protect claimed that it was only redefining sovereignty. "There is no transfer or dilution of state sovereignty. But there is a necessary re-characterization involved: from sovereignty as control to sovereignty as responsibility in both internal functions and external duties."[75] Sovereignty here takes the path blazed by the European Union. It becomes the duty to comply with international obligations and to transfer certain policy-making authority to supranational institutions. Ultimate authority over whether a government, for example, acts properly toward its own citizens will rest with the "international community" and its interpretation of international human rights law. This narrows the traditional concept of sovereignty: a nation is no longer free to set policy as it wishes within its own territory without external interference. As such, the responsibility to protect represents the movement of international law and institutions, and the underlying concepts of sovereignty, in a European direction.

B. Popular Sovereignty

Broad trends in economic integration and shared global governance are eroding Westphalian sovereignty in powerful ways. But the erosion of Westphalian sovereignty does not mean that nation-states cannot maintain other forms of sovereignty or that nation-states will necessarily wither away. We ask what, if any, elements of the nation-state will remain "sovereign" amid these forces of global governance?

---

[73] International Commission on Intervention and State Sovereignty, The Responsibility to Protect para 2.11 (2001).

[74] *Id.* at para 2.14.

[75] *Id.*

We believe that the American concept of popular sovereignty can help sort out these dilemmas. By "popular sovereignty," we refer to the prevailing theory of sovereignty expressed in the U.S. Constitution. Under this framework, the ultimate sovereign power in the United States is not in the nation's government, but in its people. Through the Constitution, the people delegate limited powers to the government.

This idea was at the ideological heart of the American Revolution. Rejecting the concept that sovereignty was vested in the Crown or in the government, the revolutionaries believed that governments "deriv[ed] their just Powers from the Consent of the Governed," and that when a government abused these powers, "it is the Right of the People to alter or to abolish it, and to institute new Government."[76] Although the true sovereign, according to the political theory of the day, had to possess unlimited, indivisible, and final authority, the American people believed that they could delegate power to different government officials. These officials, however, were not the sovereign themselves but agents of the people, who possessed the ultimate power in society. The Massachusetts Constitution of 1780, which served as a model for the Federal Constitution of 1787, expressed this understanding: "All power residing originally in the people, and being derived from them, the several magistrates and officers of government vested with authority, whether legislative, executive, or judicial, are the substitutes and agents, and are at all times accountable to them."[77]

As James Madison wrote in *Federalist No. 46*, "[t]he federal and state governments are in fact but different agents and trustees of the people, instituted with different powers, and designated for different purposes."[78] Madison reminded critics of the proposed Constitution "that the ultimate authority, wherever the derivative may be found, resides in the people alone."[79] The government can exercise only the power that the people have delegated to it. Any law that conflicts with the written Constitution is illegal, because it goes beyond the delegation of power from the people to the government.

The U.S. Supreme Court has generally followed this theory. In an 1889 decision, for instance, the Court considered the origins of the federal power to exclude aliens. It explained that such a power belongs to the federal government because it is

a part of those sovereign powers delegated by the Constitution, the right to its exercise at any time when, in the judgment of the government, the interests of the country require it, cannot be granted away or restrained on behalf of any one. The powers of government are delegated in trust to the United States, and are incapable of transfer to any other parties. They cannot be abandoned or surrendered. Nor can their exercise be hampered, when needed for the public good, by any considerations of private interest.[80]

---

[76] DECLARATION OF INDEPENDENCE (U.S. 1776).

[77] MASS. DECLARATION OF RIGHTS, art. V (1780).

[78] THE FEDERALIST No. 46, at 239 (James Madison) (Max Beloff ed., 1987).

[79] *Id.*

[80] Chae Chan Ping v. United States (The Chinese Exclusion Case), 130 U.S. 581, 609 (1889).

This analysis comports with the original understanding of the U.S. government's sovereign powers as being "delegated by the Constitution" and "in trust." Because the government serves as trustee, therefore, such powers cannot be transferred to any other institutions or governments.

To be sure, the Court has not always accepted the exclusivity of popular sovereignty as a source for the government's powers. In *United States v. Curtiss-Wright*, for instance, the Court suggested that the U.S. government might possess powers, at least with respect to foreign relations, which arise out of America's status as a nation.[81] *Curtiss-Wright* can be understood as an expression of Westphalian sovereignty, but it remains unclear whether it accurately describes the transfer of authority from the people to the government through the Constitution. This aspect of *Curtiss-Wright* has not been developed by subsequent decisions, which continue to see the Constitution as the sole fount of U.S. sovereign powers.

Focusing on popular sovereignty rather than Westphalian sovereignty has a number of consequences for globalization. First, analysis of popular sovereignty can draw on U.S. domestic precedent and experience in allocating constitutional powers within the U.S. domestic system. This form of analysis can aid in understanding America's relationships with foreign and international institutions.

Second, popular sovereignty can provide a more flexible baseline for maintaining national sovereignty than Westphalian sovereignty. Because of the absolutist claims of Westphalian sovereignty, almost any incursion or limitation on nation-states can be deemed a diminution. By contrast, as we will argue, popular sovereignty already assumes that sovereign powers can be shared, divided, and limited without giving up on the entire system. In other words, popular sovereignty can coexist with elements of global governance in ways that Westphalian sovereignty cannot.

Popular sovereignty is both more and less restrictive than Westphalian sovereignty, as Table 2.2 indicates. If global capital markets restrict the U.S.'s ability to maintain the value of the dollar, this could very well constitute a diminution of Westphalian sovereignty because it violates the absolute and exclusive power of a nation to manage activities within its territory. But such a restriction would not create problems for popular sovereignty, because it does not undermine the Constitution's allocation of powers or its guarantees of individual rights. Indeed, popular sovereignty already assumes that the U.S. government operates under substantial and fundamental constraints within its territory. The difference is that the United States cannot fully control external constraints on its sovereignty generated by the international capital markets, but it can restrict legal limits on its sovereignty by IOs and multilateral treaties by withholding its consent to international regimes.

On the other hand, if the U.S. government were barred by international agreement or international law from controlling the value of its currency, the allocation

---

[81] *See* United States v. Curtiss-Wright Export Corp., 299 U.S. 304, 315 (1936) (arguing that "the powers of external sovereignty did not depend upon the affirmative grants of the Constitution").

Table 2.2 Sovereignty, Popular Sovereignty, and Global Governance

	Westphalian Sovereignty	*Popular Sovereignty*	*Global Governance*
Control within Territory	"Absolute and exclusive"	Constrained by Constitution	Constrained by market forces
Exercise of Sovereign Powers	Control by nation is "absolute and exclusive"	Delegated by people to government through Constitution	Divided between IOs and national governments
Binding Effect of International Law	Only with state consent	Only pursuant to constitutional mechanisms	Without state consent in certain instances

of governmental powers set forth by the Constitution could potentially be undermined. For this reason, we focus our attention on legal limitations placed on nation-states that arise out of globalization. Such *legal* limitations are typically conceptualized as part of the new "global governance" regime (see table 2.2).

IV. CONCLUSION

Globalization is a sprawling concept with a wide range of definitions. Our goal in this chapter has been to isolate a workable definition of globalization and develop an analytical framework for examining its impact on the popular sovereignty of the United States. Relying on a broad definition of globalization that encompasses both its economic and noneconomic impact, we identify those aspects of globalization that could create conflicts with the popular sovereignty of the United States as reflected in the U.S. Constitution. In this next chapter, we elaborate on the structural framework of the U.S. Constitution to understand exactly how these conflicts occur.

3 Globalization and Structure

As we observed in chapter 2, sovereignty in the United States is uniquely intertwined with its founding document. An important part of the Constitution is the definition and protection of individual rights, itself a sign of the authority and responsibility of the government for the nation's people. A more important aspect of sovereignty, however, rests in the Constitution's creation of the national government, the definition of its powers, and the limits thereon. It does this through two primary doctrines: the separation of powers (the organization of authority within the national government) and federalism (the distribution of power between the national government and the states). One need not subscribe to Justice Sutherland's theory in *Curtiss-Wright*[1]—that the federal government must possess all sovereign powers available to any nation-state—to agree that the Constitution grants to the federal government many powers traditionally associated with national sovereignty. These powers include the power to enact and enforce domestic laws, make war, reach international agreements, and regulate international commerce. The Constitution

---

[1] United States v. Curtiss-Wright Export Corp., 299 U.S. 304 (1936). For classic criticism of Justice Sutherland's opinion, see David M. Levitan, *The Foreign Relations Power: An Analysis of Mr. Justice Sutherland's Theory*, 55 YALE L.J. 467 (1946); Charles A. Lofgren, *United States v. Curtiss-Wright Export Corporation: An Historical Reassessment*, 83 YALE L.J. 1 (1973). For more recent discussion, see Bradford R. Clark, *Federal Common Law: A Structural Reinterpretation*, 144 U. PA. L. REV. 1245 (1996); Sarah H. Cleveland, *Powers Inherent in Sovereignty: Indians, Aliens, Territories, and the Nineteenth Century Origins of Plenary Power over Foreign Affairs*, 81 TEX. L. REV. 1 (2002); Michael D. Ramsey, *The Myth of Extraconstitutional Foreign Affairs Power*, 42 WM. & MARY L. REV. 379 (2000).

often addresses these powers through the structures of the separation of powers and federalism. With respect to the separation of powers, for example, the power to make war is divided between Congress and the President, while the power to make treaties is shared between the Executive and the Senate. As a matter of federalism, the Constitution prohibits the states from making war and treaties and from regulating international commerce.[2]

Globalization does not directly pressure these structures. A nation could respond to the growing interconnectedness of the international economy by doing nothing, and its constitutional structures would go unaffected. But it is the natural, and perhaps inevitable, reflex of nations to try to regulate the effects of globalization. It is this attempt to expand the administrative state's regulatory reach in response to globalization that creates distortions in the constitutional structure and, in turn, poses challenges to American sovereignty.

Chapter 2 showed that increased cross-border human activity has led to more international cooperation. Take pollution, for example. Pollution crosses national boundaries, contaminates global commons such as the seas, and may lead to a global rise in temperatures. A single nation cannot undertake unilateral action to regulate pollution of this kind successfully, yet international cooperation would suffer from free-riders: nations that benefit from the reduction in pollution, but refuse to contribute resources or bear any costs to improve the environment. Similar problems are faced by efforts to combat international terrorist groups, control the international drug trade, or stop the spread of nuclear, chemical, or biological weapons technologies.

To reap the benefits of collective action, international cooperation is likely to take forms that resemble those of the American administrative state. An international regulatory regime generally will need to reach all activity, regardless of any individual nation's internal hierarchy of authority. In order to regulate global warming successfully, for example, the Kyoto accords must be able to reach all forms of energy use that produce carbon emissions. Similarly, the Chemical Weapons Convention formally regulates all chemicals in all countries, no matter what their use, source, or location. This sweeping reach usually combines with a permanent IO that is empowered to settle disputes over the agreement between interested nations. It will often issue regulations that adapt the regime to new circumstances or exercise a delegation of authority. Under the UN Charter, for example, the Security Council can call on member states to use any necessary means, including the use of force, against a threat to international peace and security. The WTO agreement establishes a dispute settlement body that hears claims by one nation against another's alleged trade violations. The International Criminal Court brings prosecutions for human rights violations that member states cannot or will not properly investigate on their own. We do not exaggerate the extent of global governance currently with us. Nations still control the levers of world politics, but emerging forms of international

[2] U.S. Const. art I, § 8 (congressional power to declare war); *id.* art. I, § 10 (prohibition on state warmaking).

cooperation are setting the outlines of the new international organizations and laws that are to come.[3]

While relatively young on the international level, these new forms and orders should sound a familiar note to students of the American administrative state. Just as innovative international regimes seek more pervasive regulation of garden-variety conduct, so too did the New Deal seek national control over private economic decisions that had once rested within the control of the states. The Kyoto accords had their counterpart in the federal government's efforts to control the production of every bushel of wheat on every American farm in *Wickard v. Filburn*.[4] The new international courts and entities have their counterparts in the New Deal's commissions and independent bodies, created to remove politics from administration in favor of technical expertise. These international bodies, to remain neutral, must have officials who are free from the control of any individual nation. Similarly, the New Deal witnessed the creation of a slew of alphabet agencies whose officials could not be removed by the President. The New Deal's stretching of constitutional doctrine sparked a confrontation between FDR and the Supreme Court, which kept to a narrower and less flexible vision of federal power and the role of administrative agencies during FDR's first term. Similarly, in the absence of a theory that allows for an accommodation of international policy demands with the U.S. constitutional system, these new forms of international cooperation may well produce an analogous collision with constitutional law.

I. THE STRUCTURAL CONSTITUTION

It is useful to begin by setting out the baseline for the regulation of normal domestic affairs. The Constitution relies on two main structures to regulate and limit the exercise of governmental power: federalism and the separation of powers. Federalism includes two interlinked domestic institutions: a national government that exercises limited, enumerated powers, and states that retain sovereignty over the great mass of everyday affairs. By contrast, the separation of powers allocates authority within the national government over the powers delegated to it by the Constitution.

A. Federalism and the Separation of Powers

Although the Constitution mentions neither federalism nor the separation of powers in its text, it has been understood from the start that both principles lie at the very core of the American government. The *Federalist Papers* extensively described the

---

[3] *See* Julian Ku, *The Delegation of Federal Power to International Organizations: New Problems with Old Solutions*, 85 MINN. L. REV. 71 (2000); John Yoo, *The New Sovereignty and the Old Constitution: The Chemical Weapons Convention and the Appointments Clause*, 15 CONST. COMMENTARY 87 (1998).

[4] Wickard v. Filburn, 317 U.S. 111 (1942).

various provisions of the Constitution that followed both structures. It pointed, for example, to Article I, Section 8 of the Constitution to show that the federal government's powers would be limited, though obviously broader in scope than those of the Articles of Confederation. Opponents urged Americans against ratification in part by arguing that the Constitution did not contain even more forceful protections for federalism and the separation of powers. In defending the Constitution, James Madison argued that the government was "neither wholly *national*, nor wholly *federal*," but a mixture. "In its foundation, it is federal, not national"—in other words, the Constitution required the consent of the states. "In the sources from which the ordinary powers of the Government are drawn, it is partly federal and partly national"—that is, the House of Representatives represented the majority of the American people as a whole, but the Senate gave the states equal representation, while the Electoral College made the President a product of the two. "In the operation of those powers, it is national, not federal"—indeed, the Constitution's powers directly regulate individuals, and not the states. "In the extent of them again, it is federal, not national"—finally, supremacy over some subjects rests with the national government, and some with the states.[5]

If federalism refers to a political system that allocates authority between governmental bodies that coexist within the same territory, then the question of federalism was one the British Empire and its colonies had struggled with for some time. The American Revolution did not truly solve the challenge of distributing power between the national and state governments, and it was the delegates to the Philadelphia Convention who finally attempted to solve the problem. The proposed Constitution that resulted from the Convention, however, is notable not just for its enumeration of new national powers, but also for its rejection of efforts to reduce the role of the states in the national political system.[6]

The Constitution vested Congress with numerous powers that it lacked under the Articles of Confederation. The national government now could impose taxes and duties, borrow and spend money, regulate interstate and international commerce, conduct foreign relations, establish a military, control naturalization and bankruptcy, grant patents and copyrights, and create the lower federal courts and the post office. Congress had the power to govern the territories and admit new states into the Union, and it had an important role in amending the Constitution. The Constitution prohibited the states from interfering in matters of foreign relations, war, and interstate commerce. The Federalists also succeeded in creating a federal government that could act directly upon individuals, without relying on the intervention of the states. As Alexander Hamilton argued in *Federalist No. 15*, "the great and radical vice" of the Articles lies "in the principle of Legislation for states or governments in their corporate or collective capacities, and as contradistinguished from

---

[5] THE FEDERALIST No. 39, at 257 (James Madison) (Jacob E. Cooke ed., 1961).
[6] For discussion of federalism and the Framing, see JACK N. RAKOVE, ORIGINAL MEANINGS: POLITICS AND IDEAS IN THE MAKING OF THE CONSTITUTION (1996).

the individuals of which they consist."[7] With the creation of an independent executive and judicial branch, and the elimination of any state veto over legislation, the national government would be able to enact, execute, and adjudicate its laws independently and directly. With the authority to enact laws "necessary and proper" to the execution of the government's powers, Congress could claim a certain breadth of implied powers as well. After the Civil War, the Reconstruction Amendments expanded Congress's powers to enforce constitutional guarantees of antislavery, equal protection and due process, and voting rights against the states.

The new government, however, would be neither a consolidated nation nor a confederation of sovereign nations. Instead, it would constitute, in Madison's classic phrase, a "compound republic," partly federal and partly national. "The proposed Constitution therefore is in strictness neither a national nor a federal constitution; but a composition of both," Madison wrote.[8] Despite Article I, Section 8's enumeration of new national powers vested in Congress, and Article I, Section 10's prohibitions on state action, the Constitution clearly accommodated the independent sovereignty of the states over most affairs in everyday life. In *Federalist No. 39*, Madison declared that the federal government's "jurisdiction extends to certain enumerated objects only," while the states continued to possess "a residuary and inviolable sovereignty over all other objects."[9] Aside from the written exceptions to their powers in the Constitution, the states emerged from the Philadelphia Convention with their sovereignty intact and protected by the mechanisms of both the Senate and judicial review that were built into the national government.[10]

American federalism, as enshrined in the Constitution's structure, makes the federal government one of limited, enumerated powers. All powers that are not encompassed in the Constitution's grants to the national government are left to the states and the people. As Madison wrote in *Federalist No. 45*, "The powers delegated by the proposed Constitution to the Federal Government, are few and defined. Those which are to remain in the State Governments are numerous and indefinite."[11] This proposition is clearly articulated in Article I, Section 1 of the Constitution, which gives to Congress only the "Legislative powers herein granted," and the Tenth Amendment, which declares that "the powers not delegated to the United States by the Constitution, nor prohibited by it to the States, are reserved to the States respectively, or to the people." Only states may exercise a "police power," the general legislative authority to regulate on any subject not expressly prohibited by the federal Constitution. At the Philadelphia Convention, the Framers rejected an early

---

[7] THE FEDERALIST No. 15, at 93 (Alexander Hamilton) (Jacob E. Cooke ed., 1961).

[8] THE FEDERALIST No. 39, at 257 (James Madison) (Jacob E. Cooke ed., 1961).

[9] *Id.* at 256.

[10] On the importance of the Senate as the representative of the states in federal lawmaking, see BRADFORD A. CLARK, *Separation of Powers as a Safeguard of Federalism*, 79 TEX. L. REV. 1321 (2001).

[11] THE FEDERALIST No. 45, at 313 (James Madison) (Jacob E. Cooke ed., 1961).

proposal to give Congress a broader, unenumerated legislative power to make law in matters where the states were "incompetent."[12]

Changing times, particularly the expansion of the national economy and the growth of the size and tax revenues of the federal government, have historically allowed the national government to expand its reach. During the New Deal the Supreme Court read the Commerce Clause so broadly as to allow the federal government to control not just the national economy, in terms of wages and hours, but also social issues related to the economy, such as racial discrimination in employment. Using its Spending Clause powers, Congress offers the states large sums to follow national standards in education, health care, and other issues that lie beyond its power of direct regulation. According to the Supreme Court, Congress cannot use its spending power to force states to violate the Constitution or to withhold so much money for relatively small conditions that its dictates become "coercive."[13] Nonetheless, the states still retain control over most areas of daily life. States enforce their own criminal laws, subject to the Due Process and Equal Protection Clauses, and set the rules of property, contract, torts, and family law, among many other areas. State government far outnumbers the size and abilities of the federal government to enforce its regulations.

The separation of powers deals with the horizontal, rather than the vertical, allocation of authority. Like federalism, the separation of powers was in practice an American innovation. At the time of the Revolution, Great Britain was governed by an unwritten "mixed" constitution that shared power among different social classes—the Commons representing the people, the Lords representing the aristocracy, and the Crown representing the King. The separation of powers in its pure form existed primarily in the minds of Locke and Montesquieu. Locke defined the legislative power as the power to establish rules of conduct, while the Executive was a "power always in being" who was responsible for executing the laws. Foreign affairs such as war and peace, according to Locke, constituted a separate, "federative" power. Although distinct, the federative power was almost always vested in the Executive, because foreign affairs "are much less capable of being directed by antecedent, standing, positive laws." Montesquieu agreed that legislation ought to determine the rules of conduct that citizens owe to one another or to speak in the "voice of the nation," while foreign affairs would fall to "the executive in respect to things dependant on the law of nations." Although it was Montesquieu's argument that tyranny would begin when the executive, legislative, and judicial powers did not remain distinct that would inspire the Framers, he was writing about an imaginary constitution and not the British constitution as it truly existed. Nonetheless, Blackstone maintained this distinction between the powers over war and peace, which were vested in the Crown, and the regulation of domestic conduct, which was within the sole authority of Parliament.

---

[12] For discussion of this change, see Donald H. Regan, *How to Think About the Federal Commerce Power and Incidentally Rewrite United States v. Lopez*, 94 MICH. L. REV. 554 (1995) (arguing that the enumeration of Congress's powers was meant merely to comprehend all of the situations where states were incompetent).

[13] South Dakota v. Dole, 483 U.S. 203 (1987).

It was not until the American Constitution that the separation of powers was attempted in practice. Like federalism, the separation of powers does not appear by name in any specific clause of the Constitution, though it is inferred from the Constitution's basic structure. The fundamental principle is that there are three types of governmental power—executive, legislative, and judicial—and that those functions should be exclusively assigned to the President, Congress, and the judiciary, respectively. The Constitution makes this clear in the first clauses of Articles I, II, and III establishing the federal government, which vest the legislative power in Congress, the executive power in the President, and the judicial power in the federal courts. These articles follow a general principle of separation of powers: Congress receives all of the federal power to legislate the rules of domestic conduct; the President executes the laws and enjoys a large role in foreign and military affairs; the courts only decide federal cases and controversies.

Opponents of ratification claimed that the new Constitution violated "the political maxim, that the legislative, executive and judiciary departments ought to be separate and distinct," a principle they received from "the celebrated Montesquieu." In response, Federalists claimed fealty to the separation of powers. "The accumulation of all powers legislative, executive and judiciary in the same hands," Madison wrote in *Federalist No. 47*, "whether of one, a few or many, and whether hereditary, self-appointed, or elective, may justly be pronounced the very definition of tyranny." Madison, however, argued that the separation of powers did not require a strict separation of the legislative, executive, and judicial powers from each other, but instead allows for some branches to have a hand in the operations of another. Montesquieu "did not mean that these departments ought to have no *partial agency* in, or no *controul* over the acts of each other." Rather, Montesquieu meant "that where the *whole* power of one department is exercised by the same hands which possess the *whole* power of another department, the fundamental principles of a free constitution, are subverted." Thus, according to Madison, the Constitution could allow the President a qualified veto, or the Senate to sit as a court of impeachment, or the Senate to approve treaties and nominees for executive office, without violating the separation of powers.[14]

The Constitution, therefore, does not embody a pure separation of powers along the lines envisioned by Montesquieu or John Locke, or what would have been suggested by the vesting clauses standing alone. In specific areas, the Constitution inserts checks and balances into the basic plan. The war power, for example, had rested solely in the hands of the Crown and was considered part of the executive powers by Locke and Montesquieu. The Constitution divides it up between Congress, which has the power to raise and fund armies and declare war, and the President, who is Commander-in-Chief. Article II's appointments and treaties clauses give the Senate the right to reject presidential nominations or proposals, while Article I grants Presidents a conditional veto over legislation. On the other hand, the vesting clauses of Articles II and III—in contrast to the specific,

---

[14] THE FEDERALIST NO. 47, at 325–26 (James Madison) (Jacob E. Cooke ed., 1961).

enumerated limits on Congress—have been understood to give the President and the federal courts powers of an executive or judicial nature that are not specifically enumerated. Thus, the Supreme Court has interpreted the President's executive power to include the authority to remove subordinate U.S. officers, except in highly unusual cases of public need for independence. The Court's own right of judicial review is nowhere specifically granted in the constitutional text but has been inferred from Article III.

This structure of separate and independent branches of government, overlaid with checks and balances, can be violated in several ways. A branch can try to aggrandize its own power beyond its constitutional limits; a branch can interfere with another's ability to perform its core constitutional functions; or two branches can collude to expand their powers or those of another branch. Congress, for example, would violate the separation of powers if it promulgated laws that actually decide cases between parties in court or reopened final judgments. Under the separation of powers, however, the three branches of government are coordinate and independent, in that one cannot prevent another from performing its constitutionally assigned functions. Thus, the President cannot exercise lawmaking authority without the delegation or approval of Congress, and the courts cannot decide hypothetical cases that allow it to review law enforcement policies.

The interaction of the independent branches, as mediated through the Constitution's specific power-sharing provisions, has produced some enduring principles. One of the earliest and most profound is that of judicial review, articulated by the Supreme Court in the famous case of *Marbury v. Madison*.[15] Judicial review sprung from the basic structural principle that the Constitution represents higher law, superior to any act of the federal government. The agents of the people could not use their delegated powers to supersede the original terms of the founding document. No branch of government, therefore, could act in a manner inconsistent with the Constitution, even if that meant that a federal court had to refuse to obey an act of Congress that violated the Constitution's terms. The separation of powers requires that the courts even refuse a congressional effort to expand their jurisdiction, because it exceeds the maximum limits set out by the Constitution. It also prohibits Congress from transferring certain federal cases from the jurisdiction of the courts to administrative agencies, lest judicial independence be threatened. Judicial independence, as clarified in other cases, also prohibits Congress from reviewing or reopening final judgments or asking judges to perform a nonjudicial function.

The Constitution's definition of the lawmaking process places further restrictions on Congress. Article I, Section 7's bicameralism and presentment requirement prohibit Congress from regulating the rights and duties of private citizens or other branches of government except through the enactment of legislation. In *INS v. Chadha*, the Court read this structure to prevent Congress from reversing a decision by an administrative agency through the exercise of a veto that passed in the House but did not go to the President for signature.[16] In *Clinton v. New York*, Article I,

---

[15] 5 U.S. (1 Cranch) 137 (1803).
[16] 462 U.S. 919 (1983).

Section 7 prohibited the President from exercising a line-item veto, which had allowed the President to delete individual line items before a new statute could take effect.[17] It is important to recognize that these cases do not just prevent the self-interested expansion of Congress's powers. In the line-item veto case, for example, Congress improperly attempted to transfer power from itself to the President.

Congress's limitation to the enactment of legislation, combined with Article II's vesting of the power to execute the laws in the President, concentrates control over law enforcement in the executive branch—much of which relies on the powers of appointment and removal. The Appointments Clause gives the nomination of important federal officers to the President, with the advice and consent of the Senate and of inferior officers to the President, cabinet officers, or the courts. It does not explain how officers of the United States may be removed, but ever since the first Congress of 1789, the removal power has generally been understood to rest with the President.[18] All three branches have believed that power over the removal of inferior officers gives the President control over the executive branch to ensure that he can impose a uniform execution of federal law. The flip side of this understanding is that the Appointments Clause also precludes the other branches from appointing or removing important executive branch personnel, because to do so would interfere with law enforcement by the President. In *Buckley v. Valeo*, for example, the Court prohibited Congress from appointing members of the Federal Elections Commission, because it would have given Congress control over officers who would enforce federal law.[19] In *Bowsher v. Synar*, the Court struck down a budget reduction act because it gave the Comptroller General, an officer subject to removal by Congress, a role in deciding on spending cuts.[20]

The courts have, however, allowed Congress to place conditions on the President's freedom to remove inferior officers if there is an important public reason to clothe them in independence. Chief Justice Taft had explained the basic rule in *Myers v. United States*: the removal of federal officers must reside with the President so he could control the execution of federal law.[21] But in *Humphrey's Executor v. United States*, the Court upheld restrictions on the removal of the chairman of the Federal Trade Commission because it performed "quasi-legislative" and "quasi-judicial" functions that were not wholly executive in nature.[22] Independent regulatory agencies, apparently, could function outside the President's direct control. In *Morrison v. Olson*, the Court extended the concept of independence to the special counsel statute even though prosecution had long been considered a core executive power. The Court upheld restrictions on the counsel's removal because they did not "impede the President's ability to perform his constitutional duty" and the need

[17] 524 U.S. 417 (1998).

[18] *See generally* Steven Calabresi & Saikrishna Prakash, *The President's Power to Execute the Laws*, 104 Yale L.J. 541 (1994).

[19] 424 U.S. 1 (1976).

[20] 478 U.S. 714 (1986).

[21] 272 U.S. 52 (1926).

[22] 295 U.S. 602 (1935).

for independence when investigating the White House and cabinet officers was sufficiently important.[23]

Discussion of the appointment and removal powers shows that while the Framers erected three independent branches of government, they did not create "a hermetic division between the Branches."[24] In general, the vesting of the legislative, executive, and judicial powers to Congress, the President, and the courts followed a separation of powers model, but the Constitution left those terms undefined, thereby allowing for a certain amount of pragmatic evolution in the forms of government.

B. Nationalization, Globalization, and the Constitution

The greatest strain on this framework, one in which these flexible components of the Constitution were pressed beyond the breaking point, occurred during the New Deal. In response to the Great Depression, the Roosevelt administration and a large Democratic majority in Congress wrought sweeping changes in the structure of the Constitution. Constitutional law of the day was unprepared for the national focus of economic regulation and the creation of a powerful and independent administrative state. It had still kept to the forms and orders of a relatively decentralized system of government that was unprepared for the demands for national regulation created by the New Deal. Before examining how globalization is producing a similar strain on our governmental structures today, we must first understand how nationalization caused one of the most significant constitutional conflicts in American history.

Nationalization of the American economy began in earnest at the end of the Civil War. War had spurred the spread of a nationwide transportation network, with the transcontinental railroad completed in 1869 and the number of railroad tracks jumping from 30,000 in 1860 to 193,000 in 1900. Faster speeds and sharp reductions in the cost of transportation throughout the country laid the foundations for a national market in goods. Railroads became the nation's largest corporations and the biggest investors (in other industries) and gave form to great national trusts.[25] A nationwide communications system had come a little earlier, with the first transcontinental telegraph link in 1861, and the first transatlantic cable in 1866. After Alexander Graham Bell's invention of the telephone in 1875, AT&T installed over a million telephones by 1900. Electricity networks spread in the 1870s, allowing for more efficient lighting and power generation. The invention of steel led to demand for the mining of coal, the development of oil, and greater industrial production.

Nationalization of the economy prompted two responses, one by the private sector and one by the public sector. Railroads accelerated the growth not just of transportation, but of the modern corporate form, which quickly spread to other industries. Limited liability for investors in common stock allowed corporate leaders to tap large amounts of capital for expensive projects. Industrial corporations began

---

[23] 487 U.S. 654, 691 (1988).

[24] Mistretta v. United States, 488 U.S. 361, 381 (1989) (quoting Buckley v. Valeo, 424 U.S. 1 (1976)).

[25] *See* 2 ALAN BRINKLEY, THE UNFINISHED NATION: A CONCISE HISTORY OF THE AMERICAN PEOPLE 524 (3d ed. 2000).

to pursue horizontal and vertical integration of their industries. By the end of the nineteenth century, large trusts had gained monopoly control over different sectors of the economy. The first great trust, John D. Rockefeller's Standard Oil, was founded in 1870, and by the turn of the century it controlled about 90 percent of all oil in the nation. U.S. Steel, created by J. P. Morgan in 1901, produced about two-thirds of all steel in the country.[26] Thus, the private sphere responded to industrialization and nationalization by concentrating economic power.

The U.S. government began to address these developments with national regulation. In 1887, Congress enacted the Interstate Commerce Act to regulate national railroad rates, and in 1890 the Sherman Antitrust Act prohibited anticompetitive monopolies. Neither law, however, saw much enforcement until the presidency of Theodore Roosevelt in 1901. In the following decades, Congress attempted to create the rudiments of administration to regulate the national economy. It enacted more national regulation of the markets, such as a ban on child labor and quality standards for foods and drugs. Efforts to regulate hours and wages, the securities markets, and old age and disability stalled in Congress, however. Under Woodrow Wilson, the Federal Reserve Act of 1913 established the first national banking system since Andrew Jackson had destroyed the Second Bank of the United States. The Wilson administration also bulked up the government's resources to attack monopolies through the Federal Trade Commission and the Clayton Antitrust Act.

These efforts, which culminated in the New Deal, followed two institutional patterns. First, the reach of regulation had to be national in scope. Corporations could escape state regulations simply by relocating their headquarters or operations to other states with more lenient standards. New Deal legislation, for example, set employment hours and wages throughout the nation to ensure uniformity and to discourage states from a destructive "race to the bottom." National regulations could avoid the profound (and sometimes unforeseeable) effects of uncoordinated, conflicting local regulation. The 1938 Agricultural Adjustment Act, for example, allowed the Agriculture Department to set production quotas for all wheat grown in the nation, no matter how small a farm. If all small farms were exempt from the statute, they could produce enough wheat in the aggregate to undermine the federal effort to regulate the quantity available on the national market. When markets were more fragmented, economic activity in one state or region might not have such an immediate impact. The communications and transportation revolutions allowed the decisions of even small producers or buyers to have national effects. As the scope of economic activity had become national, effective government regulation had to extend its reach to keep pace.[27]

---

[26] *Id.* at 523–37. *See also* ALFRED D. CHANDLER, JR., THE VISIBLE HAND: THE MANAGERIAL REVOLUTION IN AMERICAN BUSINESS (1977); ROBERT WIEBE, THE SEARCH FOR ORDER, 1877–1920 (1968).

[27] For discussion of the constitutional dimensions of the New Deal, see WILLIAM LEUCHTENBURG, THE SUPREME COURT REBORN: THE CONSTITUTIONAL REVOLUTION IN THE AGE OF ROOSEVELT (1995); JOHN YOO, CRISIS AND COMMAND: A HISTORY OF EXECUTIVE POWER FROM GEORGE WASHINGTON TO GEORGE W. BUSH 259–88 (2010).

Second, government institutions had to change in order to come to grips with the complexity and speed of the new markets. Instead of enacting extensive schedules of regulations itself, Congress delegated broad swaths of authority to the executive branch. Grants of power to the administrative state often came with few standards for its exercise. The Interstate Commerce Act, for example, gave the Interstate Commerce Commission the task of setting "reasonable and just" railroad rates. The Sherman Antitrust Act declared as illegal "every contract, combination in the form of trust or otherwise, or conspiracy" that was "in restraint of trade or commerce." Political scientists have identified several reasons for such broad delegations. One is transaction costs. As an elected body of 535 representatives and senators, Congress suffers from severe difficulties in deliberating, negotiating, and reaching agreement because of its large size. Second is technical expertise. Congress does not have the resources to develop the knowledge and judgment to solve difficult policy problems in technical and scientific areas. Third is uncertainty. Congress will delegate policy choices in areas of unpredictability and high stakes, such as foreign affairs and war, because individual legislators do not want to be blamed for making the wrong policy choice. Fourth is political accountability. Members of Congress who are primarily interested in reelection, will not risk taking stands on controversial issues where political opposition will result no matter which option is chosen. Reelection will be less difficult if an agency makes the trade-offs between gas mileage and traffic fatalities, or if courts decide abortion policy.[28]

Independence accompanied these broad delegations of authority. Presidents had once seen agencies such as the post office primarily as a source of patronage, which buttressed the decentralized, party-based nature of American politics. Agencies under these new national regulatory statutes served a different objective—they were to take partisan politics out of government action. It was understandable that Congress would be reluctant to delegate broad rulemaking authority to agencies that were under the direct control of its constitutional rival, the President. A constitutional mechanism that provided the agencies with independence from executive control would increase Congress's ability to influence rulemaking decisions. But Presidents since George Washington had exercised direct policy control over the executive branch agencies through their power to replace subordinate officials with ones who would carry out their wishes. In *Myers v. United States*, the Supreme Court had affirmed that Congress could not place limitations on the President's authority to remove executive branch officers (in that case, a postmaster).[29] Congress sought to insulate the new commissions and boards from political influence by restricting the ability of the President to remove their officers except for "good cause," which usually meant a violation of federal law or serious malfeasance in office.

We should be clear that we take no normative position here on whether the New Deal's reworking of the administrative state was desirable. As a matter of

---

[28] *See generally* WILLIAM HOWELL, POWER WITHOUT PERSUASION: THE POLITICS OF DIRECT PRESIDENTIAL ACTION (2003).

[29] 272 U.S. 52 (1926).

consequences, economic historians generally believe that rearmament in the lead-up to World War II, rather than New Deal programs, ended the Great Depression. Nonetheless, our point is not whether the New Deal was effective at bringing the United States out of the worst economic slump in its history, but whether it effectively responded to the nationalization of the economy and society with regulation of similar scope. It seems apparent that it did. The New Deal established federal regulation of the national economy in many areas, which expanded after World War II to cover civil rights, the environment, and health care. In order to regulate an economy of such scope and complexity effectively, Congress delegated broad authority to independent agencies that stressed technical expertise over partisan politics.

The parallels with the move toward international regulation are striking. Globalization has produced an impact on the economy and society that is just as remarkable today as nationalization was more than a century ago. Just as progress in transportation and communication welded states and regions together into a single national market in the nineteenth century, shipping advances, jet air transport, and the Internet have created a global market in many goods and services. Billions in dollars move instantaneously between national stock markets, and the events and policies in one developed country can quickly influence the economy of another—witness the speed with which the recent American credit crisis spread to the financial markets of the other developed economies. Problems like pollution, disease, terrorism, and crime have also become global, moving through the same fast channels of transportation and communications as international trade and capital.

International efforts to regulate the effects of globalization, both the good and the bad, similarly resemble the New Deal's twin characteristics—the breadth of regulation and the delegation to independent regulators. As with nationalization, effective solutions need to be global. Efforts to coordinate government policies on global warming, through the Kyoto accords, provide a good example. Imposing industrial emission standards to lower pollution, for example, will have limited effect if companies can relocate to jurisdictions with less stringent requirements. A truly global solution would require regulation of the carbon-based pollution of every country on the planet. Whether in the form of quotas or taxes or credits, government standards would have to press beyond the limits of the national government's powers to regulate the market to reach conduct that tends to be private or noncommercial. Setting emissions targets for large industrial enterprises may capture a large portion of energy use, but to regulate its output effectively a nation would have to regulate home activity, such as heating, cooking, and transportation, as well.

International cooperation has also adopted the forms of domestic regulations in the establishment of regulatory institutions. Multilateral treaties have created institutions, independent of any nation, to verify compliance with agreements, resolve disputes, and develop proposals for their own extensions. These institutions usually do not depend on any state parties for their decisions, though they could call on third-party nations for help. As broad multilateral agreements have spread, independent international organizations have grown with them. IOs address the likelihood that some treaty parties will not obey an agreement or will interfere with verification, and can help overcome what social scientists call "the prisoners' dilemma": the temptation to cheat for short-term advantage, ruining the greater long-term benefits of cooperation. An IO can also help build trust between state parties by vesting implementation in a neutral, impartial entity that is not beholden to any single nation or alliance.

The Chemical Weapons Convention (CWC) illustrates these developments in the structure of international agreements and organizations. Unlike other arms control agreements, which place numerical caps on arsenals or limit the use of weapons in combat, the Convention seeks to ban the development, production, and stockpiling of an entire class of weapons. If the treaty only regulated weapons arsenals, it would not raise any innovative questions of arms control agreement design. The problem with chemical weapons, and indeed with other forms of weapons of mass destruction, is that the chemicals and the facilities used to produce them are "dual use." Chemicals that have civilian uses, such as pesticides, plastics, and manufacturing, can have military uses as well. A nation that seeks to build a covert chemical weapons capability or arsenal can easily disguise its activities behind a civilian-use front.

To be fully effective, the CWC must regulate not just national stockpiles of chemical weapons, but also the private chemical industry that produces "toxic chemicals" or their "precursors."[30] Thus, industrial chemical facilities, as well as the public weapons arsenals of state signatories to the treaty, fall within the Convention's scope. Chemicals that have been used as weapons are banned. Facilities that produce chemicals that are toxic or are immediate precursors to weapons, but also are used for commercial purposes, are subject to on-site verification and monitoring. States are to enact regulations and criminal penalties for anyone who violates the ban on the possession or production of the most dangerous chemicals. To provide full coverage, the CWC needs to go even further than regulation of major industrial chemical facilities. A laboratory of no more than 1,600 square feet in size can manufacture 100 tons of chemical weapons in one year. Successfully regulating chemical weapons requires that the treaty reach all sites that use and produce civilian chemicals, in addition to the usual military and defense contractor sites that are the subject of most arms control agreements. According to the Office of Technology Assessment, the United States alone has potentially 10,000 sites that qualify for inspection under the treaty.[31]

In order to advance compliance, the treaty regime relies on the second pillar of modern regulation—the creation of an independent institution. In order to verify compliance, the CWC requires that state parties allow surprise "challenge" inspections of any location on their territory by personnel of the treaty organization. The CWC creates an international organization, the Organization for the Prohibition of Chemical Weapons, which has a Technical Secretariat in charge of identifying targets and conducting challenge inspections. Under the treaty, the Secretariat has the right to enter a nation and receive unimpeded access to the site, its personnel, and its records. The Secretariat's decisions are not reviewable by any domestic

---

[30] Convention on the Prohibition of the Development, Production, Stockpiling and Use of Chemical Weapons and on Their Destruction arts. II, VI, Sept. 3, 1992, 1974 U.N.T.S. 45.

[31] *See generally,* John Yoo, *The New Sovereignty and the Old Constitution: The Chemical Weapons Convention and the Appointments Clause,* 15 CONST. COMMENTARY 87 (1998).

governmental body. This independence is critical to the CWC's ability to monitor compliance, particularly by states that might be conducting illicit chemical weapons activity. It builds trust between the state parties by vesting the authority over verification in a neutral entity outside the control of any single nation. Agreeing to enforcement by an independent organization may even be a way for nations to signal their trustworthiness in complying with the agreement in the future. The independence of the organization from national control or influence thus becomes crucial for a nation to bind itself in a meaningful way.

II. REGULATION AND GLOBALIZATION

History suggests that the movement toward international regulation will place stresses on the Constitution's structural frameworks. New Deal innovations placed similar stresses on the existing constitutional law of the day, which produced one of the sharpest constitutional conflicts between the President, the Congress, and the Supreme Court in American history. Only after the President imposed extreme political pressure on the courts did they alter constitutional law doctrines on federalism and the separation of powers to accommodate the New Deal's expanded administrative state. Constitutional law had not come to grips with the effects of nationalization and the government's efforts to regulate them. Unless we have a better grasp of the current and potential effects of globalization on constitutional law, a similar fate might be in store.

To understand the tension between globalization and constitutional law, it is worthwhile to examine the confrontation that occurred in response to nationalization. In the period between Reconstruction and the New Deal, the Supreme Court developed several doctrines that limited the government's ability to regulate private business conduct. First, the Court limited the national government's power to regulate interstate commerce, which is today's great fount of federal authority. In response to the Progressive Era's effort to regulate business, the Court held that Congress's Commerce Clause powers could not reach manufacturing or agriculture within a state. These matters, according to the Court's theory of dual federalism, were reserved for state control. In the 1895 *United States v. E. C. Knight*, the Court blocked the Justice Department's attempt to use the antitrust laws to break up a trust that controlled virtually all sugar refineries in the country.[32] The majority reasoned that sugar refining occurred wholly within the borders of individual states and so did not constitute interstate commerce, which meant it was subject to the "police powers" of the states. In 1918, the Court, in *Hammer v. Dagenhart*, struck down a federal law that prohibited the interstate transportation of goods made with child labor. Even though the federal ban applied only when the product moved across state lines, the Court declared that "the production of articles, intended for interstate commerce, is a matter of local regulation."[33]

[32] 156 U.S. 1 (1895).
[33] 247 U.S. 251, 272 (1918).

The Court enforced its distinction between commerce, which could be regulated by the national government, and manufacturing and production, which remained within the authority of the states and beyond the reach of the Commerce Clause. After *Hammer v. Dagenhart*, Congress attacked child labor by imposing a 10 percent excise tax on all such goods. The Court struck down the law, even though it was enacted by a different power, on the ground that Congress could not use a tax to achieve a prohibited end.[34] The Court imposed parallel limits on Congress's power to tax and spend and its regulatory powers under the Commerce Clause.

The Court matched its limits on federal authority to regulate the economy with similar restrictions on the states. Though the states enjoyed the police power to regulate anything not touched by the Constitution's grants of power to the national government, the federal courts had read the Due Process Clause of the Fourteenth Amendment to place limits on the states. These limits also applied to the federal government because of the Fifth Amendment's Due Process Clause. *Lochner v. New York* (1905), the most well-known example of these limits, struck down a state law that limited the hours that bakers could work. Over the memorable dissent of Justice Holmes, the majority concluded that the Constitution protected the individual right of the bakers to contract to work as much as they liked.[35] Government could not redistribute income within an industry, which was the effect of the law, nor infringe the right of free labor.

A third doctrine posed a threat to the administrative state itself. Under the non-delegation doctrine, the Court had held that Congress could not delegate "legislative power" to the administrative agencies. In *Field v. Clark*, the Court in 1892 had upheld a trade law that allowed the President to restore tariffs if a foreign nation did not provide reciprocal reductions for American imports. The Court declared that the fact that "Congress cannot delegate legislative power to the president" is "universally recognized as vital to the integrity and maintenance of the system of government ordained by the constitution."[36] In *Field*, the Court found that no unconstitutional delegation had occurred because the statute specified when the President could restore tariff rates. "He was the mere agent of the lawmaking department to ascertain and declare the event upon which its expressed will was to take effect." In other words, the nondelegation doctrine would be satisfied if Congress specified factual circumstances in which the executive branch could exercise delegated authority, but would bar open-ended provisions that granted power without any standards as to its use. In *Field v. Clark*, the Court did not invalidate the federal law, but it made clear that the legislature could delegate power to the agencies only to apply Congress's principles to specific cases, not to make the policies themselves.

FDR's efforts to impose regulation on the national economy came into direct conflict with standard constitutional doctrine as it existed in 1932. The National Industrial Recovery Act (NIRA) did not just ban a single product or manufacturing

---

[34] Bailey v. Drexel Furniture Co., 259 U.S. 20 (1922).

[35] 198 U.S. 45 (1905).

[36] Marshall Field & Co. v. Clark, 143 U.S. 649, 692–93 (1892).

process; it placed all industrial production in the nation under federal regulation. The Agricultural Adjustment Act (AAA) did the same with farms; a third act concerned the coal industry. The second wave of New Deal laws, such as the National Labor Relations Act and the Public Utility Holding Company Act, set uniform rules on the activities of unions and utilities, while the Social Security Act created a nationwide system of unemployment compensation and pensions. New Deal lawyers believed that the Interstate Commerce Clause should be interpreted to include almost all economic activity in the nation because almost all goods produced in a state traveled through the channels of interstate commerce. They reasoned that the states were powerless to effectively reverse the collapse of the national economy of the Great Depression.

But constitutional law doctrine did not provide enough space for national regulation of this sort. In 1935, in its first case examining a New Deal law, the Court invalidated the NRA's "hot oil" provision, which allowed the prohibition of petroleum produced in excess of quotas. Chief Justice Hughes wrote for an 8–1 majority that the law unconstitutionally delegated legislative power to the President because it gave the President the wide discretion to make the violations of quotas illegal based on circumstances he deemed proper.[37] That was only a prelude to *Schechter Poultry v. United States*, decided later in 1935, in which the owners of a chicken slaughterhouse were prosecuted for violating industrial codes of conduct (here, the "live poultry code") issued pursuant to the NRA.[38] The NRA purported to reach all industrial production in the country, even the selling of poultry by local dealers, and it allowed the executive branch to delegate the development of industrial codes to trade associations or groups representing the industries themselves. The *Schechter Poultry* Court found the NRA codes unconstitutional in a direct attack on the foundations of the new administrative state. First, it held that Congress had engaged in unconstitutional delegation by allowing the President to decide how whole industries should operate, limited only by what he thought was beneficial for the economy. Congress then compounded this problem by allowing trade groups to develop administrative rules. "Such a delegation of legislative power is unknown to our law, and is utterly inconsistent with the constitutional prerogatives and duties of Congress," Chief Justice Hughes wrote for the Court.[39] This ruling threatened the New Deal laws that vested significant lawmaking authority in the executive branch and the independent agencies.

Schechter Poultry also attacked the other principle of the administrative state: that its regulations had to have nationwide scope. The Court held that the NRA violated the Constitution's limits on the reach of federal economic power, even though 96 percent of the chickens that were bought and sold in New York City, where Schechter Poultry operated, came from out of state. The owners of the slaughterhouse bought their goods from interstate wholesalers, but they only sold their chickens to a local market,

---

[37] Panama Refining Co. v. Ryan, 293 U.S. 388 (1935).

[38] 295 U.S. 495 (1935).

[39] *Id.* at 537.

which did not directly impact interstate commerce. Their activity could not fall within Congress's reach because they had not brought the chickens across state lines themselves, and their only purpose was to sell the poultry to local buyers. If the Court kept to its precedent that intrastate manufacturing and agriculture lie outside of federal authority, more pillars of the New Deal—perhaps even the whole program itself—might have collapsed. In pointed language, the Court specifically rejected the Roosevelt administration's overarching approach to the Great Depression: "Extraordinary conditions do not create or enlarge constitutional power."[40]

In the spring of 1936, the Court declared unconstitutional more elements of the New Deal. In *United States v. Butler*, the Court held unconstitutional the AAA's use of taxes and grants to regulate agricultural production.[41] The majority declared that Congress could not use taxes and spending to regulate intrastate agriculture because it lay within the reserved powers of the states. *Butler* implicated the Social Security Act, which used a combination of taxes and spending to provide relief and pensions to the unemployed and elderly. In *Carter v. Carter Coal Co.*, a 5–4 majority struck down a 1935 law that set prices, wages, hours, and collective bargaining rules for the coal industry.[42] The Court found that the production of coal did not amount to interstate commerce and also fell within the reserved powers of the states. "[T]he effect of the labor provisions. . . primarily falls upon production and not upon commerce," Justice Sutherland wrote for the majority. "Production is a purely local activity." *Carter* made clear that the sick chicken case was not a fluke; any federal regulation of in-state industrial production or agriculture was now in constitutional doubt. In *Jones v. SEC*, the Justices attacked the proceedings of the Securities and Exchange Commission as "odious" and "pernicious" and compared them to the "intolerable abuses of the Star Chamber."[43] In *Morehead v. Tipaldo*, the Court found that New York's minimum wage law violated the Due Process Clause, just as it had earlier found that such laws interfered with the right to contract.[44] As the Court had already found a federal minimum wage in the District of Columbia unconstitutional in the 1920s, the Court had made the regulation of wages, in FDR's words, a "no-man's land"—forbidden to both the federal and state governments.

After his 1936 reelection, FDR proposed a restructuring of the Court that would eliminate it as an opponent of the New Deal. On February 5, 1937, FDR sent Congress a judiciary "reform" bill that would add a new Justice to the Court for every member over the age of seventy. Because of the advanced age of several Justices, Roosevelt's proposal would have allowed him to appoint six new Court members. Rather than criticize the Court for its opposition to the New Deal, Roosevelt disingenuously claimed that the elderly Justices were delaying the efficient administration of justice.[45] Only indirectly did FDR imply a link between the advanced age of

---

[40] *Id.* at 528.

[41] 297 U.S. 1 (1936).

[42] 298 U.S. 238 (1936).

[43] 298 U.S. 1 (1936).

[44] 298 U.S. 587 (1936).

[45] 81 Cong. Rec. 878 (1937) (reprinting FDR's message to Congress).

the Justices and their opposition to the New Deal. "Modern complexities call also for a constant infusion of new blood in the courts," FDR wrote. "A lowered mental or physical vigor leads men to avoid an examination of complicated and changed conditions. Little by little, new facts become blurred through old glasses fitted, as it were, for the needs of another generation." FDR declared that the remedy would bring a "constant and systematic addition of younger blood" that would "vitalize the courts and better equip them to recognize and apply the essential concepts of justice in the light of the needs and the facts of an ever-changing world."[46]

Despite his electoral success, FDR's court-packing plan—the first domestic initiative of his second term—went down to a humiliating defeat, never coming up for a full vote on the floor of Congress. Historians and political scientists have argued ever since whether FDR still won the war. Immediately in the midst of the struggle in Congress, the Justices made a sharp turn. In March 1937, the Court handed down a 5–4 decision upholding a Washington minimum wage law for women. In *West Coast Hotel v. Parrish*, the lineup of votes for and against New York's minimum wage, which had been struck down in *Tipaldo* the year before, remained the same—except for Justice Roberts, who switched sides to uphold the law.[47] In April 1937, the Court upheld the National Labor Relations Act, which had been challenged on the same grounds raised in the sick chicken and *Carter* cases.[48] This time, in *NLRB v. Jones & Laughlin Steel Corp.*, Chief Justice Hughes led a 5–4 majority in rejecting the doctrine that manufacturing did not constitute interstate commerce. *Jones & Laughlin Steel* was the fourth largest steel company in the nation, with operations in multiple states. As the Court observed, "the stoppage of those operations by industrial strife would have a most serious effect upon interstate commerce." "It is obvious," the Court found, that the effect "would be immediate and might be catastrophic." Henceforth the Court would allow federal regulation of the economy, even of wholly intrastate activity, because of the interconnectedness of the national market. To do otherwise would be to "shut our eyes to the plainest facts of our national life" and to judge questions of interstate commerce "in an intellectual vacuum."[49]

While FDR lost in Congress, he had won his larger objective. The Supreme Court would not strike down another federal law that regulated interstate commerce until 1995. Journalists and political scientists immediately attributed the "switch in time that saved nine" to FDR's threat to pack the Court.[50] Even today, creative scholars defend the sweeping constitutional changes of the New Deal—which, unlike

---

[46] *Id.*

[47] West Coast Hotel Co. v. Parrish, 300 U.S. 379 (1937).

[48] NLRB v. Jones & Laughlin Steel Corp., 301 U.S. 1 (1937); NLRB v. Fruehauf Trailer Co., 301 U.S. 49 (1937); NLRB v. Friedman-Harry Marks Clothing Co., 301 U.S. 58 (1937); Associated Press v. NLRB, 301 U.S. 103 (1937); Washington, Virginia & Maryland Coach Co. v. NLRB, 301 U.S. 142 (1937).

[49] 301 U.S. 1, 41 (1937).

[50] *See, e.g.,* Joseph Alsop & Turner Catledge, The 168 Days (1938); Merlo Pusey, The Supreme Court Crisis (1937).

Reconstruction, was never written into a constitutional amendment—by citing the 1936 electoral landslide and the attack on the Court.[51] More recent work argues that the Court's Commerce Clause doctrine was evolving in a more generous direction toward federal power anyway.[52] For our purposes, identifying the precipitating cause of the "switch in time that saved nine" is not as important as its context. The political branches and the judiciary reached a confrontation over the Constitution because existing doctrine could not grapple with the effects of economic and social nationalization. In cases like *Hammer v. Dagenhart*, the Court's view of the economy ignored the advances in transportation and communications that had knitted the states and regions into a national market. Its view that manufacturing and production were distinct and separate from interstate commerce placed strict limits on the national government's ability to regulate the economy during the Great Depression. In cases such as *Schechter Poultry*, the Court placed limits on the structure of the administrative state that grew in response to the nationalization of the economy. Constitutional law had failed to keep up with the demands of the twentieth century. The results were a destructive confrontation between the President and the Court, in which both arguably lost in the short term, and a constitutional law that lifted almost all restraint on the regulatory powers of the administrative state.

III. GLOBALIZATION AND CONSTITUTIONAL ACCOMMODATION

If history provides any guidance, we might expect a confrontation again among the branches of government unless constitutional law adapts to globalization. On one side of the equation, globalization has prompted government responses similar in form to those that arose with nationalization. While national economic and social activity comfortably falls within the federal government's regulatory grasp, existing constitutional law doctrines cannot easily accommodate the broader demands of international regulation. The political branches and the courts have not thought through how best to adapt the U.S. legal system to mediate between its constitutional structure and global governance. In this part, we describe how the tension between international regulation and the Constitution both resembles the confrontation of the New Deal and also, in important respects, exceeds it.

Multilateral efforts to regulate globalized activity mirror the administrative state's efforts to extend into both public and private conduct. For example, the Chemical Weapons Convention attempts to regulate all possession and production of specified chemicals. A global warming agreement would reach most, if not all, forms of energy production and use in the United States. This reach, however, conflicts with the Supreme Court's recent efforts to identify limits on Congress's Commerce Clause powers. As interpreted by the courts, the Clause gives Congress broad authority to

---

[51] 1 Bruce Ackerman, We the People: Foundations 105–30 (1991).

[52] *See generally* Barry Cushman, Rethinking the New Deal Court: The Structure of a Constitutional Revolution (1998).

regulate the movement of goods, people, services, and intangible goods. Congress can prohibit certain articles in interstate commerce, even if its true motive is to regulate the intrastate activities that resulted in their production. Congress can even regulate activities that substantially affect interstate commerce, even if those activities are wholly intrastate and even if their individual impact is trivial, as long as Congress has a rational basis for concluding that their consequences are substantial in the aggregate.[53]

Under Commerce Clause doctrine as it had existed prior to 1995, the broad sweep of treaty regimes like the CWC would not have given courts much pause. After the New Deal revolution, the Supreme Court had not found any federal law to exceed the limits of the Clause, and Congress not surprisingly resorted to this power to regulate a wide variety of subjects, including discrimination, individual rights, crime, the environment, and food and drug safety. But beginning in 1995, the Rehnquist Court imposed limitations on what had become the most sweeping aspect of the Commerce Clause: its application to conduct that has "substantial effects" on interstate commerce. In *United States v. Lopez*, the Court held unconstitutional a federal law that banned handguns near school zones because the conduct lacked an essentially economic character and the guns had not traveled through interstate commerce.[54] First, the handgun law was "a criminal statute that by its terms has nothing to do with 'commerce' or any sort of economic enterprise," the Court concluded.[55] A second important point for the Court was that the link between handgun possession and interstate commerce was too attenuated to justify federal regulation. If the Court allowed regulation of handgun possession because handguns caused violence that harmed economic productivity, it would be "hard-pressed to posit any activity by an individual that Congress is without power to regulate."

In *United States v. Morrison*, the Court held that Congress could not provide a civil remedy for gender-motivated violence that occurred wholly within one state.[56] It reasoned again that the activity had no commercial character, did not involve the crossing of state borders, and could not be considered to affect interstate commerce in the aggregate. This recent case law, however, explicitly reaffirmed and left wholly unqualified the other two "broad categories of activity that Congress may regulate under its commerce power": the "channels" and the "instrumentalities" of interstate commerce. Since neither *Lopez* nor *Morrison* involved a statute that included a jurisdictional element (or "jurisdictional nexus" in which the subject of federal policy is, has been, or perhaps will be in the "channels" of interstate commerce), the Court has given no indication of how elastic this category might be to insulate similar legislation from constitutional invalidation.

---

[53] *See, e.g.*, Heart of Atlanta Motel v. United States, 379 U.S. 241 (1964); Wickard v. Filburn, 317 U.S. 111 (1942); United States v. Darby, 312 U.S. 100 (1941).

[54] United States v. Lopez, 514 U.S. 549 (1995).

[55] *Id.* at 561.

[56] Morrison v. United States, 529 U.S. 598 (2000).

Still, the lines drawn by *Lopez* and *Morrison* would seem to exclude some activities from international regulation when pursued by the federal government through the Commerce Clause. For example, if the regulation of marriage is considered non-economic conduct, then it would not benefit from the aggregation principle of *Wickard v. Filburn*. Although the Court did not draw a bright line in *Morrison* against aggregation in such cases, it observed that the aggregation principle has only been held to operate in areas of a commercial character. In other words, Congress could not add up all of the individual economic effects that a regulated conduct may have on interstate commerce to justify national regulation of intrastate activity. This principle would not be disturbed by the Court's recent decision in *Gonzales v. Raich*, which upheld regulation of a purely intrastate activity even though the Court conceded that it was not "commercial." The Justices held that the federal prohibition of intrastate cultivation and use of marijuana, even when permitted by state law for medicinal purposes, was subject to the aggregation approach because Congress had a rational basis for the effective regulation of the interstate market and traffic in illicit drugs, a quintessentially economic activity.[57]

Another important limitation on Congress's regulation of intrastate activity arises when the conduct falls within an area of "traditional state concern." First raised in Justice Kennedy's concurrence in *Lopez* and then incorporated into the majority opinion in *Morrison*, this concept precludes Commerce Clause regulation in areas historically considered to be subject to state regulation. The underlying offense in both *Lopez* and *Morrison* was criminal in nature, which came within the state's police power. This incursion prompted Justice Kennedy to worry that "[w]ere the Federal Government to take over the regulation of entire areas of traditional state concern, areas having nothing to do with the regulation of commercial activities, the boundaries between the spheres of federal and state authority would blur."[58] In *Lopez* and *Morrison*, the majority identified specific areas—"family law (including marriage, divorce, and child custody)," "criminal law enforcement," and "education"—"where States historically have been sovereign." In both opinions, Chief Justice Rehnquist expressed the concern that "if we were to accept the Government's arguments [to sustain congressional power], we are hard pressed to posit any activity by an individual that Congress is without power to regulate."[59]

Modern international cooperation will run into these limits on federal power because it requires comprehensive regulation of all public and private conduct in a certain category of activity. Much domestic conduct falls within federal regulation, but significant portions do not. In the case of chemicals, for example, Congress could implement the CWC's prohibition with regard to industries and businesses

---

[57] Gonzales v. Raich, 545 U.S. 1 (2005).

[58] Lopez, 514 U.S. at 577 (Kennedy, J., concurring). Justice Kennedy contended that if the line of demarcation between the federal government and the states were blurred, "political responsibility would become illusory" and "[t]he resultant inability to hold either branch of the government answerable to the citizens . . . [would be] more dangerous even than devolving too much authority to the remote central power." *Id.* (Kennedy, J., concurring).

[59] Morrison, 529 U.S. at 613.

operating in interstate commerce. The more difficult question is whether federal power could reach chemicals produced or possessed by private individuals who themselves are not operating in the national markets and cause no "substantial effect" on interstate commerce. *Gonzales v. Raich*, which upheld the Controlled Substances Act's prohibition on marijuana possession, suggests that Congress might have the power in the case of chemicals. "Congress can regulate purely intrastate activity that is not in itself 'commercial,'" the Court declared, "if it concludes that failure to regulate that class of activity would undercut the regulation of the interstate market in that commodity."[60] It could be argued that the regulation of chemicals held by individuals with no intention of sale or transportation across state borders would still fall within federal power because it substantially affects the relevant national market.

Congress's power to regulate interstate commerce, however, might not extend to other types of international cooperation. Energy use, in contrast to chemicals, is neither fully regulated by the national government nor significantly produced within private homes for a national market. It is doubtful, for example, that federal regulation could extend to home production or consumption of energy that occurs off the electric grid, such as wood-burning fireplaces and home generators. Accepting federal power over home energy use would truly test the principle in *Morrison* and *Lopez* that the courts cannot allow the Commerce Clause to reach every form of human conduct. An international treaty regulating gun possession, to which the United States has objected on Second Amendment grounds, would raise similar problems. If such a treaty were to require the criminalization of the possession of certain weapons, the legislation would involve the same doubts that caused the Court to strike down the federal handgun law in *Lopez*. Human rights treaties, which seek to establish rights that go beyond those required by the Constitution's Bill of Rights, involve the same difficulties. It would be difficult to conclude that expanded individual rights would involve interstate commerce or commercial activity. Indeed, they would resemble most closely the type of law invalidated in *Morrison*, which sought to expand federal protections against gender-motivated violence.

Even if the Commerce Clause might accommodate the broad scope of international regulatory treaties, their demands could still cause federalism problems of a second sort. In areas clearly within federal power, Congress cannot impose standards that violate the reserved powers or rights of states as independent political entities within the federal system. In *New York v. United States* and *Printz v. United States*, for example, the Court invalidated federal laws that sought to "commandeer" state officers into performing federal legislative or executive functions.[61] The federal government, for example, can regulate nuclear waste, but it cannot force states to enact legislation adopting its preferred regulations. Congress can require background checks before the purchase of a handgun, but it cannot require state officials to carry out the checks. These principles effectively prevent the federal government

[60] 545 U.S. 1, 18 (2005).
[61] New York v. United States, 505 U.S. 144 (1992); Printz v. United States, 521 U.S. 898 (1997).

from shifting the financial and political costs of carrying out its programs to the states and localities. The same would apply, it seems, for treaties as well. The national government could not require state officials to implement treaty requirements, such as conducting searches of chemical facilities, or passing state legislation to enforce a treaty.

The Agreement on Trade-Related Aspects of Intellectual Property Rights (TRIPs)[62] provides an illustration of the conflict between international regimes and the sovereignty of American states. Under TRIPs, which itself is part of the WTO agreement, state parties agreed to establish minimum substantive protections for intellectual property and to provide for judicial remedies, including compensatory relief, against infringers. The Supreme Court's recent expansion of the protections for states against private lawsuits for damages would prevent full remedies when state governments have violated intellectual property rights. Under *Seminole Tribe v. Florida*, for example, Congress may not provide a remedy in federal court for damages against a state, and under *Alden v. Maine*, the same is true in state court.[63] Even when Congress has used its Section 5 powers under the Fourteenth Amendment, rather than its Commerce Clause power under Article I, to protect an individual's intellectual property, the Court has invalidated comprehensive federal statutes without a showing of systematic state violations of that right.[64] These decisions appear to place the United States in violation of TRIPs by eliminating judicial remedies for violations of intellectual property rights against a class of potential infringers.[65] We will discuss in future chapters how constitutional law can resolve these conflicts between states' sovereignty, national power, and international cooperation; for our present purposes we only want to identify where these tensions exist.

International regimes create equally difficult problems with the separation of powers. Multilateral treaties and their delegation of authority to new organizations raise the issue of delegation in much the same way that the New Deal did. Vesting authority in the CWC, for example, to prohibit the production or possession of specific chemicals raises the same issue as the delegation of similar authority to federal agencies. Under current doctrine, Congress may transfer rulemaking power to the agencies, so long as it has stated an objective, prescribed method to achieve it and articulated intelligible standards to guide administrative discretion.[66] These standards prohibit Congress from delegating its legislative power and provide courts with a loose way to evaluate whether the agencies have exercised their authority legally. They keep Congress involved in the formulation of policy and accountable

---

[62] Agreement on Trade-Related Aspects of Intellectual Property Rights, Apr. 15, 1994, Annex 1C, 33 I.L.M. 81 (1994).

[63] Alden v. Maine, 527 U.S. 706 (1999); Seminole Tribe v. Florida, 517 U.S. 44 (1996).

[64] Florida Prepaid Postsecondary Education Expense Board v. College Savings Bank, 527 U.S. 627 (1999).

[65] *See* Peter S. Menell, *Economic Implications of State Sovereign Immunity from Infringement of Federal Intellectual Property Rights*, 33 LOYOLA L.A. L. REV. 1399 (2000).

[66] Whitman v. American Trucking Assn's, Inc. 531 U.S. 457 (2001); Yakus v. United States, 321 U.S. 414 (1944).

to the electorate for its choices. Although the Court has not invalidated a congressional delegation since *Carter v. Carter Coal Co.*, it still continues to observe that Congress cannot transfer lawmaking without meaningful standards.

At first glance, delegation of rulemaking authority to international organizations would seem to be consistent with these principles. Multilateral treaties usually focus on discrete areas, and the rulemaking authority of international institutions is usually circumscribed with standards that are narrower than those used in the American administrative state. There is an important twist, however, created by the need to vest rulemaking authority in neutral, independent international institutions. In the case of international organizations, the delegation runs not from Congress to the executive branch, but from the United States to an institution that does not fall within the national or state governments. This creates serious problems for the underlying mechanisms that police delegations. Congress cannot enforce its standards through the usual legal or political methods when the recipient of the delegated power is not responsible to Congress, the President, or any other federal authority. Congress has no ready means of monitoring and influencing the performance of international officials, or of measuring their conduct against intelligible standards. Delegation to international organizations also might allow Congress to sidestep the checks on its own lawmaking authority. Bicameralism and presentment promote transparency and accountability in the exercise of legislative authority. Even when legislative authority is transferred to agencies, executive branch officers remain creatures of the national government and subject to the discipline of the political process. Delegation to private parties, the Court held in the 1930s, undermines the public nature of federal power and risks the capture of government policy by private interests.[67]

International regimes may also raise a second type of delegation problem. We have discussed the case when Congress delegates its authority to another domestic governmental actor, the source of most academic commentary on delegation. A second case occurs when Congress attempts to transfer authority from one of the other branches to a different entity. The independent counsel law presents a good case of this type of delegation. There, Congress vested in the independent counsel the authority to investigate and prosecute federal crimes allegedly committed by high-ranking members of the cabinet agencies and the White House, and protected the counsel from removal by the President except "for cause." In *Morrison v. Olson*, the Court upheld the delegation because the counsel was an inferior officer who remained subject to the direction of the Attorney General, even if he or she could not be removed at will. But in cases where Congress transfers law execution authority to

---

[67] On international delegations, see Curtis Bradley & Judith Kelley, *The Concept of International Delegation*, 71 Law & Contemp. Problems 1 (2008) (introduction to symposium on international delegation); Curtis Bradley, *International Delegations, the Structural Constitution, and Non-Self-Execution*, 55 Stan. L. Rev. 1557 (2003) (delegation to international organizations threatens structural constitutional principles). But see Andrew Guzman & Jennifer Landsidle, *The Myth of International Delegation*, 96 Cal. L. Rev. 1693 (2008) (arguing that little delegation to international organizations occurs).

agents completely outside the control of the executive branch, as occurred in *Bowsher v. Synar*, the Supreme Court has found the delegation unconstitutional.

As we have seen, the Appointments Clause has become the battleground for struggles between the President and Congress over the power to enforce federal law. Delegations to international institutions, however, raise a different problem, addressed only by *Buckley v. Valeo*'s discussion of the clause. *Buckley* found unconstitutional the Federal Elections Commission, created by Congress in 1974 to enforce the campaign finance laws, because Congress selected four commissioners. According to the Court, commissioners exercised power under federal law and thus were considered officers of the United States. All officers, the Court held, fall within the Appointments Clause, which gives the President the authority to nominate and appoint officers subject to the advice and consent of the Senate. For an inferior officer, the clause allows Congress to vest appointment in the President alone, department heads, or the courts. *Buckley* described the clause as "a deliberate change made by the framers with the intent to deny Congress any authority itself to appoint those who were 'Officers of the United States.'"[68] In subsequent cases, the Court has emphasized that the Appointments Clause "is among the significant structural safeguards of the constitutional scheme" because it "prevents congressional encroachment upon the Executive and Judicial Branches."[69] In the words of the Court: "[The clause] preserves another aspect of the Constitution's structural integrity by preventing the diffusion of the appointment power."[70] The Clause makes the appointments process public to prevent the diversion of power to individuals not accountable to the political branches and, ultimately, the electorate. "The structural interests protected by the Appointments Clause are not those of any one branch of Government but of the entire Republic," the Court has said, and therefore "[n]either Congress nor the Executive can agree to waive this structural protection."[71]

Placing the enforcement of multilateral treaties in the hands of international organizations will run afoul of these structural limitations. The Chemical Weapons Convention, for example, grants the power to search American chemical facilities to officials of the CWC Technical Secretariat. They are not selected under the Appointments Clause, they are not members of the executive branch, and they are not accountable to the President (or to Congress). Yet they may potentially exercise public authority by choosing the location for searches and carrying them out, while federal law prohibits private citizens from interfering. If the federal government were to conduct similar searches, those who carried them out would have to be officers of the United States chosen under the Appointments Clause, and they would have to operate according to the Fourth Amendment, which itself is enforced by the courts. CWC officials, by contrast, are not responsible to any American officials and are not accountable for their actions to the national government. Indeed, their very

---

[68] Buckley v. Valeo, 424 U.S. 1, 129 (1976).
[69] Edmond v. United States, 520 U.S. 651, 658 (1997).
[70] Ryder v. United States, 515 U.S. 177, 182 (1995).
[71] Freytag v. Commissioner of Internal Revenue, 501 U.S. 868, 880 (1991).

reason for being is to enforce the CWC free from the influence of any single nation. While necessary to create a multilateral inspection regime, the independence of the CWC organization raises delegation problems that compound those that arose for the New Deal agencies.

A third variant of the delegation issue centers on the judiciary. Congress can violate the separation of powers by vesting the authority to decide cases in tribunals located in the executive branch or in independent agencies rather than the federal courts. The Court has allowed some vesting of adjudicatory authority in non–Article III courts, but only if they do not undermine the constitutional role of the federal judiciary.[72] With the administrative state, this problem has arisen when Congress has created rights under new statutory schemes, such as the review of the denial of welfare benefits, or when Congress transfers causes of action from the jurisdiction of federal courts to those of the administrative agencies. Scholars regularly observe that the Court's jurisprudence on this question is unclear. Congress cannot transfer the authority to hear questions of constitutional law or private rights from the Article III courts to an administrative tribunal. It can, however, vest some adjudicative authority in the agencies (today, such courts handle takings, tax, and bankruptcy claims, for example), and has done so from the beginning of the Republic.[73] Again, as with the delegation of legislative authority, even when Congress vests the adjudicative function outside the branch originally given that authority under the Constitution (here the judiciary), that function still rests within the national government.

The spread of international tribunals and jurisdiction over private claims places stress on this framework. A leading example comes from NAFTA, which creates arbitral panels to hear disputes over dumping (the export of goods at prices below cost). Before NAFTA, private parties could bring cases claiming dumping by a competitor to the Secretary of Commerce and the International Trade Commission, whose decisions were reviewable in the Court of International Trade, an Article III court subject to the Court of Appeals for the Federal Circuit and the U.S. Supreme Court. Under NAFTA, a private party can appeal a decision of the ITC or the Secretary of Commerce only to a NAFTA tribunal, not to the federal courts.[74] NAFTA thus transfers claims under federal law that were once heard in federal court to non-U.S. courts. The International Criminal Court, which the United States has yet to join, requires member nations to turn over suspects for trial for war crimes. In the context of the Vienna Convention on Consular Relations and the death penalty, foreign nations no doubt believe that the International Court of Justice will extend greater neutrality regarding whether a foreign defendant's rights under international treaty have been respected than the courts of Texas or Oklahoma will.

---

[72] *See, e.g.,* Commodity Futures Trading Comm'n v. Schor, 478 U.S. 833 (1986).

[73] Richard Fallon, *Of Legislative Courts, Administrative Agencies, and Article III*, 101 Harv. L. Rev. 915 (1988).

[74] Ku, *supra* note 3, at 111; *see also* Jim C. Chen, *Appointments with Disaster: The Unconstitutionality of Binational Arbitral Review Under the United States-Canada Free Trade Agreement*, 49 Wash. & Lee L. Rev. 1455 (1992).

Vesting adjudicative authority in international tribunals can, under certain circumstances, promote international cooperation. International tribunals can identify whether a state party has violated the terms of an international agreement and measure possible remedies without any bias that could be associated with domestic courts.[75] But these tribunals' very independence and neutrality cause problems with Article III of the Constitution. As with the other delegations studied here, the international dimension only compounds the nature of the problem. Even if a cause of action can be moved outside the cognizance of the Article III courts, it is still heard within the American governmental system in a specialized Article I court or an administrative agency. Those two types of tribunals will still be accountable for their decisions to the administrative agency, the executive branch, or ultimately Congress. They will generally be subject in their procedures to the requirements of the Due Process Clause. An international tribunal, however, is not accountable to the U.S. government and need not follow constitutional norms of fair process in their proceedings. Like the Appointments Clause, Article III displays a strong suspicion of congressional efforts to transfer power away from another branch. Shifting adjudicative authority to international courts creates tensions with this principle, and then adds the additional difficulty that the power is moved wholly outside the national government.

IV. SOVEREIGNTY AND GLOBALIZATION

Globalization has sparked two different schools of thought about the Constitution and sovereignty. One approach, best expressed by Louis Henkin and Anne-Marie Slaughter and probably supported by the majority of international law scholars, welcomes the integration of the U.S. legal and political system into a new world order by eliminating barriers to the delegation of authority to international law and organizations. Another school of thought, promoted most visibly by John Bolton and Jeremy Rabkin, rejects the subordination of American interests and freedom of action to international bodies and rules. We agree that globalization is spurring a growth of power in international organizations and law, with serious problems of political accountability and legitimacy. We believe, however, that reinvigorating the Constitution's formal structures of the separation of powers and federalism can address these problems and place American efforts to cooperate internationally on a sounder footing.

A. Accountability

The first way to shore up the nation's response to globalization is to ensure that our actions promote the Constitution's commitment to political accountability. The Constitution reflects a concern for political accountability in two ways. First, it requires members of Congress and the President to undergo regularly scheduled

---

[75] Eric Posner & John Yoo, *Judicial Independence in International Adjudication*, 93 CAL. L. REV. 1 (2005).

elections where they can be subjected to the will of the electorate. Second, the Constitution appears to require these elected officials to take responsibility for the policies implemented by the government, thereby ensuring that the electorate can use their voting power effectively to control policy-making. The Appointments Clause also serves to ensure that the President can be held responsible for the execution of the laws. Alexander Hamilton argued that the requirement of senatorial approval for the President's nominees also encourages accountability for official action. "[T]he circumstances attending an appointment . . . would naturally become matters of notoriety; and the public would be at no loss to determine what part had been performed by the different actors." By contrast, Hamilton noted, the contemporaneous New York State appointments process allowed the legislature to shroud appointments in secrecy, with the result that "all idea of responsibility is lost."[76]

Similarly, the Constitution's vesting of Congress with the sole power to legislate, and its bicameralism requirement for passing legislation, strengthen the government's accountability for the laws. Bicameralism ensures that legislation is the product of a high level of consensus. Congress can be held responsible for the results of its legislation. If Congress can transfer the power to legislate, however, the electorate can impose its will on Congress without any effect on the actual legislation. While there has been some criticism of the electoral process for not maintaining enough democratic accountability, the majority of commentary has focused on the manner by which responsibility for policy is shifted away from politically accountable actors. Thus, commentators arguing against congressional authority to delegate executive powers away from the President and commentators criticizing delegation of legislative powers to administrative agencies have both relied heavily on the detrimental effects on political accountability. They have used public choice analysis to explain why politicians have incentives to shift responsibility for policy-making in order to concentrate directly on reelection. For the most part, these commentators have advocated returning to a formal reading of the Constitution's structure, asserting that the formal structure of the Constitution will ensure greater political accountability for policy-making.[77]

Judicial doctrine has reflected this concern for accountability in two types of cases. First, the Court has noted that delegations from Congress to administrative agencies could weaken the accountability of legislators for their political decisions.[78] Second, in the federalism context, the Court has expressed concern that Congress can avoid political accountability for its policies by using states to carry out its policies.[79]

---

[76] THE FEDERALIST No. 77, at 517–18 (Alexander Hamilton) (Jacob E. Cooke ed., 1961).

[77] *See, e.g.,* JOHN H. ELY, DEMOCRACY AND DISTRUST 131–34 (1980) (arguing that delegation weakens democracy); THEODORE J. LOWI, THE END OF LIBERALISM 93 (2d ed. 1979) (same); DAVID H. SCHOENBROD, POWER WITHOUT RESPONSIBILITY 99–106 (1993) (same).

[78] *See* Indus. Union Dep't v. Am. Petroleum Inst., 448 U.S. 607, 685 (1980) (Rehnquist, J., concurring) (nondelegation doctrine ensures that "important choices of social policy are made by Congress, the branch of our Government most responsive to the popular will"); Arizona v. California, 373 U.S. 546, 626 (1963) (Harlan, J., dissenting in part) (same).

[79] *See* New York v. United States, 505 U.S. 144, 169 (1992) (describing how the federal government can order states to act, and then "remain insulated from the electoral ramifications of their

In both sets of cases, the concern is the same: by shifting, even voluntarily, the constitutional allocation of political powers, Congress muddies the lines of authority for policy-making and makes it harder for the electorate to hold a particular government player responsible for a particular policy. As Justice O'Connor explained in *New York v. United States*:

[W]here the Federal Government compels States to regulate, the accountability of both state and federal officials is diminished. . . . [W]here the Federal Government directs the States to regulate, it may be state officials who will bear the brunt of public disapproval, while the federal officials who devised the regulatory program may remain insulated from the electoral ramifications of their decision.[80]

However, the Court has rarely found analogous delegations to state and private parties to be unconstitutional, despite their deleterious effects on political accountability. It has permitted wide-ranging delegations of both executive and legislative power to states, Indian tribes, and private parties. *Printz v. United States* observed that Congress could enlist state executives and judges to enforce federal law,[81] while the courts have long recognized tribal autonomy to make and enforce law on many civil and criminal matters on reservations. The government has successfully delegated its power to bring lawsuits—a key aspect of the power to enforce the law—to private parties to root out government fraud in what are called "qui tam" actions.[82]

There are at least three good reasons, however, for the Constitution to treat accountability problems created by delegations to international organizations differently. First, because IOs wield powers transferred from different parts of the federal government, and sometimes implement their own will through the federal government, the lines of authority are blurred to an even greater degree than was found unacceptable in *New York v. United States*. A voter would have a hard time determining which government actor is actually responsible for the actions of an international organization.

If, for example, the Court had ordered Virginia to halt its execution of a Paraguayan national convicted of murder in order to comply with a decision of the International Court of Justice, a Virginia voter would have had to untangle a complicated web of political responsibility. The state's Governor would say that he was simply following the dictates of the Supreme Court, whose Justices could claim that they were bound to honor the treaty with the International Court of Justice (ICJ). The Senate and the President, however, would also shirk responsibility because they can validly claim that they did not directly authorize the ICJ's provisional order to stop the execution. Thus, the buck passes from Virginia to the different branches of the federal government, but the only actually responsible actor is the one least accountable to the Virginia voter.

decision"); Printz v. United States, 521 U.S. 898, 920 (1997) ("The Constitution thus contemplates that a State's government will represent and remain accountable to its own citizens").

[80] 505 U.S. at 167–69.

[81] 531 U.S. 898 (1997).

[82] False Claims Act, 31 U.S.C. § 3729 et seq.

Like the federal officials in *New York v. United States*, the ICJ "remain[s] insulated from the electoral ramifications of [its] decision[s]"[83] even though it is effectively legislating a self-executing treaty through its use of the provisional measures authority.

Second, international organizations are less accountable than states or private parties because they are far less likely to be subjected to effective executive oversight. Indeed, one of the main goals of creating more effective IOs is to limit their control by member states. Thus, the WTO allocates the power to issue interpretations to three-fourths of its membership. Similarly, the CWC regime specifically prevents the executive branch from blocking a surprise challenge inspection.

Third, in contrast to most domestic delegations to states or private parties, the scope of an international organization's authority is rarely limited to the constituencies affected by its rules. A state or private organization that is delegated powers by the federal government often has an independent interest to apply the rules in a limited manner because it is responsible to the narrow group affected by the delegated powers. For instance, many federal delegations to private organizations involve the creation of industry-wide rules that apply to the industry alone.[84] NAFTA or WTO tribunal judgments, by contrast, can impose rules that involve virtually all sectors of the economy, or at least all those that affect foreign investment or the export and import of goods and services.

Under the traditional view of international law, an international organization's authority extended only to nation-states. This understanding limits domestic accountability concerns because the organization's reach does not extend beyond its narrow constituency of member states. In contrast, relatively narrow constituencies may still influence a modern international organization (member states, multinationals, and nongovernmental organizations), yet its goal is to create rules of broad applicability that may directly affect private party rights. For instance, in theory a WTO panel is limited to making decisions affecting the member states involved in the dispute. In practice, however, its decisions may require adjustments in the creation or application of domestic law affecting private party interests. But these panels are, in formal terms, completely *unaccountable* to private interests.

The peculiar characteristics that make the new breed of international organizations more effective also make them uniquely unaccountable entities within the U.S. constitutional system. The Founders' concern with maintaining lines of political responsibility, and the continued emphasis by courts and commentators on the dangers of unaccountability, suggest that the delegation of federal power to international organizations creates substantial constitutional stress. At the very least, a formalist approach to international delegations would more likely preserve the traditional lines of political accountability than one that sees little problem at all.

---

[83] 505 U.S. at 169.

[84] *See* Harold J. Krent, *Fragmenting the Unitary Executive: Congressional Delegations of Administrative Authority Outside the Federal Government*, 85 Nw. U. L. Rev. 62, 102 (1990) (discussing external checks on delegations to non-federal entities including a private group's "need to satisfy their own constituencies").

B. Legitimacy

Legitimacy is the second core constitutional problem afflicting new international law and organizations. In the political context, legitimacy refers to the justification of a government's authority to rule over its people. Like many phrases of political theory, its precise meaning is contested. Nevertheless, Robert Dahl's formulation captures the key elements of political legitimacy. "[A] government is said to be 'legitimate' if the people to whom its orders are directed believe that the structure, procedures, acts, decisions, policies, officials, or leaders of government possess the quality of 'rightness,' propriety, or moral goodness—the right, in short, to make binding rules."[85] Whether an entity has legitimacy matters from both a normative and positive perspective. On one hand, the entity's effectiveness is likely to be related to its success at making its normative case for a particular rule or decision. In other words, predicting the normative results of an international organization's decision will depend in part on its positive ability to implement its goals. On the other hand, the very fact that an organization is successful, from a positive perspective, does not necessarily mean that legitimacy questions are settled. Therefore, any analysis of international organizations should confront the "legitimacy" question.

The delegation of federal powers to international organizations raises two problems of political legitimacy. First, to the extent that an IO gains the right to make binding rules over American citizens via international delegation, it must point to some source of legitimacy authorizing its actions. Its effectiveness in implementing its rules will depend in part on its legitimacy.

An international organization can bring its own source of legitimacy to buttress its authority. Alternatively, it can seek to acquire legitimacy from the federal government. But when an IO acquires the power to govern U.S. citizens directly, it has very little independent legitimacy. Even worse, because the federal government's political legitimacy is closely linked to its adherence to formal structural arrangements, international delegations actually reduce the overall legitimacy of the federal government, ultimately weakening the legitimacy of both entities.

International law commentators have recognized that IOs are vulnerable to charges of illegitimacy, with the European Union often held out as suffering from a "democratic deficit."[86] The United States does not belong to any organization that is nearly as ambitious as the EU. Indeed, none of the international organizations of which the United States is a member has an independent source of legitimacy, or has mechanisms making them directly responsible to the populations of its member

---

[85] ROBERT A. DAHL, MODERN POLITICAL ANALYSIS 41 (2d ed. 1970). For a lengthy discussion and citation to various definitions of legitimacy, see Daniel Bodansky, *The Legitimacy of International Governance: A Coming Challenge to International Environmental Law?*, 93 AM J. INT'L L. 596, 601 n. 29 (1999).

[86] *See, e.g.*, Peter L. Lindseth, *Democratic Legitimacy and the Administrative Character of Supranationalism: The Example of the European Community*, 99 COLUM. L. REV. 628, 734–38 (1999) (concluding that even a more democratic EU would suffer from serious legitimacy deficit); *see also* BODANSKY, *supra* note 86, at 597–98 n. 10 (citing "burgeoning literature on 'democratic deficit'").

countries. Rather, these international organizations, more than the EU, depend on the legitimacy provided by state consent to membership. Thus, international delegations in the United States essentially depend on the legitimacy of the government's consent to the delegation. They do not have an independent source of legitimacy.

Because the legitimacy of the U.S. government's consent to such delegations is highly contestable, however, international organizations cannot rely on such consent as a source of meaningful legitimacy. Stephen Carter has eloquently argued that the political legitimacy of the U.S. government, and of the Supreme Court in particular, rests on its adherence to the formal structural requirements of the Constitution.

The constitutional vision of *demos*, then, supposes that our government is the one that the Founders handed down. The interpreter who is guided by the popular imagination must select an interpretive method that exerts pressure . . . on the federal government to confine itself to a set of institutional arrangements substantially continuous with the original design of the Founders whom the popular imagination extols.[87]

Rightly or wrongly, the American people believe that the U.S. government's authority flows from the formal requirements of the Constitution's text. As a consequence, to the extent that the Court allows the other branches to depart from these formal requirements, the political legitimacy of the Court and the federal government as a whole suffers.

New international delegations depart significantly from the Founders' formal structure. The delegation of Appointments Clause powers to the CWC regime, the delegation of the treatymaking power to the ICJ, and the transfer of judicial review to the NAFTA panels all rest on shaky formalist, as well as textualist, foundations. None of these innovative institutional arrangements appear to conform with the structure designed by the Founders as reflected in the Constitution's text and history. While the current Court's case law suggests it would uphold some of these international delegations, the international organizations receiving them cannot draw from the special legitimacy conferred by the Founders' powerful narrative mythos because these delegations do not comply with the Founders' formalist requirements.

By contrast, the state governments, Indian tribes, and private industry groups that have received delegations in the domestic context all claim separate, independent sources of legitimacy. State governments have their own electorates, and Indian tribal governments are responsible to the tribe's members. Even the private organizations with delegated federal power are responsible to their narrow constituencies. Thus, despite not complying with the Constitution's formal requirements, each of these domestic delegations draws on a separate source of legitimacy independent from the Constitution. None of these nonfederal entities acquired broad powers to affect the general population. Rather, the delegations, however open-ended, remain

---

[87] Stephen L. Carter, *Constitutional Improprieties: Reflections on Mistretta, Morrison, and Administrative Government*, 57 U. Chi. L. Rev. 357, 371 (1990).

limited because they affect only the constituencies from which the delegated entity has acquired independent legitimacy.

The inability of international organizations to provide legitimacy commensurate with the scope of their delegated authority—when combined with the serious strains that their delegations place on the federal government's own legitimacy—weigh strongly in favor of adopting a formalist reading of the Constitution. A formalist approach would confer the greatest possible level of political and popular acceptance because any consent to IO authority would then occur with the full extent of the Constitution's legitimating force. Such an approach might require rejecting some delegations, but it would at least ensure the full measure of domestic political legitimacy to support those that survive.

V. CONCLUSION

We should not be misread as attacking the movement toward international cooperation. Rather, our goal here has been to show that the forms of the new international law raise deep structural problems for our constitutional system of government. In some cases, the comprehensive sweep of international regulatory regimes pushes the reach of federal power beyond the limits of the Commerce Clause or into the reserved powers of the states. In other cases, international cooperation may require the delegation of rulemaking, enforcement, and adjudication functions to independent international organizations that create tensions with the Constitution's protections for the separation of powers.

These questions are not wholly new. They have occurred before, when the President and Congress enacted the sweeping laws of the New Deal. In response to the Great Depression, Congress transferred broad legislative authority to the executive branch and independent agencies. The new administrative state ran into a head-on conflict with the Supreme Court's formalist doctrines on both federalism and the separation of powers. Because constitutional law had not kept pace with the changes wrought by the nationalization of the American economy and society, the political branches and the courts collided. Constitutional law gave way, but at a high cost in legitimacy for the President and the Supreme Court. A better understanding of the ways in which law can mediate between the similar demands of globalization and international regulation, on the one hand, and the Constitution, on the other, may help prevent a similar conflict in the near future.

Before finishing with our discussion of the tension between globalization and the Constitution's structural provisions, we should make a normative point. At the beginning of this chapter, we sought to define federalism and the separation of powers in the Constitution, and in the latter half, we identified the problems created by globalization for its structure. If the American people, however, decided to amend the Constitution to alter these fundamental constitutional principles, these conflicts would begin to disappear. One question that concerns us is that these choices should be made not gradually by the courts, but rather through constitutional mechanisms that grant the decisions on accommodating globalization to the elected branches of government, and ultimately the people. But it is always possible that the American people, as in Europe, could decide to weaken different aspects of the Constitution to make international cooperation easier. They could amend the founding document, for example, to allow for the explicit delegation of judicial power to international tribunals such as the International Criminal Court.

We openly confess our view, however, that any fundamental change in the Constitution's structures would be a terrible mistake. Putting aside their historical pedigrees, we think that federalism and the separation of powers today guarantee a number of normative benefits for the United States. Federalism, for example, creates policy competition among states; citizens can maximize their preferences by choosing to live in states with policies that they prefer. States such as California can provide high levels of environmental protection at the cost of lower rates of industrial growth; individuals who enjoy the outdoors over high-paying manufacturing jobs or lower taxes can move there. Federalism encourages innovation in government policy—states serve as fifty "laboratories of democracy" which conduct experiments at solving social problems—that will lead to more effective national solutions. Federalism allows for the more effective provision of public goods—or certain benefits, such as schools, roads, regional transportation systems, parks, and law enforcement—that affect smaller geographic units rather than the nation as a whole. Federalism has significant advantages above and beyond its historical presence in the Constitution.

The separation of powers also provides significant benefits beyond the happy accident of its inclusion in the Constitution. Dividing legislative power between two houses of Congress and the President demands that a high level of consensus exist before the government enacts new domestic legislation. As the level of consensus increases, the law is more likely to express the will of the majority and to represent the better judgment on the right trade-offs for society. Multiple hurdles for the legislative process reduce the chances that special interest groups will use domestic regulation to capture benefits for themselves at the public's expense. At the same time, the separation of powers encourages the vigorous exercise of national powers at the right moment. For example, the President can lead the nation into war, protect the national security, or conduct foreign affairs with "decision, activity, secrecy, and dispatch," in the words of Alexander Hamilton in *Federalist No. 70*.[88] By openly allocating power to the branch best suited for its exercise, the separation of powers encourages accountability to the electorate, which knows which political actors are responsible for success or failures on the field. The separation of powers provides a safeguard for liberty by making it difficult for any one party or group to take over the controls of government altogether, and by giving each of the branches the means to frustrate the plans of the others.

Scholars argue over whether the Constitution's structures have produced the political stability critical to the nation's success. We tend to think that they have. America's decentralized government, both between the national and state governments and

---

[88] THE FEDERALIST NO. 70, at 472 (Alexander Hamilton) (Jacob E. Cooke ed. 1961).

between the executive, legislative, and judicial branches, discourages a rush into radical reforms or sweeping alterations of the basic rules of the political system. The American Constitution may allow grievous injustices—such as slavery and segregation—to persist for long periods of time, but it also creates a risk-averse political system that prevents the United States from swinging wildly in one direction or another. Altering federalism and the separation of powers to allow for greater international cooperation may seem desirable now, but the long-term benefits may not exceed the costs, if those costs weaken the Constitution's governing principles in domestic affairs. Instead, as we show in the following chapters, the American system can accommodate the demands of globalization within existing doctrines of the separation of powers and federalism, though with some difficulty. But we think that accommodation, even with the higher transaction costs of congressional action or less centralization over policy, is worth the price to preserve the constitutional principles that have served the nation so well, for so long.

4 Non-Self-Execution

Perhaps the most effective way for the Constitution to mediate the demands of globalization with popular sovereignty is through a once-obscure doctrine known as non-self-execution. Globalization creates opportunities and problems that require cooperation between states for effective solutions. International agreements remain the primary vehicle for collaboration between states. As we have argued, however, the new forms of international cooperation sparked by globalization can run afoul of basic American constitutional norms involving the separation of powers and federalism. Non-self-execution ensures that decisions involving the design of government, regulatory authority, and individual liberties stay in the hands of those most directly accountable to the American people. In this chapter, we argue—against the trend of academic and some judicial opinion—that courts should presume a treaty is non-self-executing unless the treaty contains a clear statement to the contrary.[1]

Globalization demands some mechanism to mediate between international and domestic law. Legal matters that were once purely domestic now impact many nations simultaneously, and conduct that once occurred solely within the boundaries of a single state can now have significant effects beyond borders. Airborne pollution,

---

[1] *See* Medellín v. Texas, 552 U.S. 491 (2008) (finding Vienna Convention on Consular Relations non-self-executing); Beharry v. Reno, 183 F.Supp.2d 584, 593 (E.D.N.Y. 2002) (finding that treaties are presumptively self-executing); David J. Bederman, *Medellín's New Paradigm for Treaty Interpretation*, 102 Am. J. Int'l L. 529 (2008) (scholarly exchange on doctrine of self-executing treaties).

for example, results from private activity within a nation, but emissions also cross borders easily, and the cumulative effect may be global in scale. Thus, the scope of international agreements has broadened into areas, such as crime, the environment, and human rights, that were once the sole province of national or regional governments. Meanwhile, nationalization of the American economy and society has expanded Congress's powers well beyond interstate commerce to include the same objects of regulation. The expansion of both powers has led to an inevitable clash: either international regulation in the form of treaties or the regular American lawmaking system will set the standards in the age of globalization.[2]

Non-self-execution can play a crucial role because it separates international law from the domestic legal system and then guarantees that the lawmaking method most consistent with popular sovereignty is used to incorporate international law. Under the doctrine, the terms of an international agreement have no effect within the domestic legal system unless Congress or, sometimes, the President implements them. To take the most recent example from the U.S. Supreme Court, *Medellín v. Texas*, the United States agreed in the Vienna Convention on Consular Relations (VCCR) to inform any aliens, upon their arrest, of their right to consult with the diplomatic officials of their country.[3] The International Court of Justice (ICJ) declared that the United States had violated the treaty in the course of arrests in Texas and Oklahoma and ordered "review and reconsideration" of the aliens' convictions, regardless of state procedural default rules.[4] Nonetheless, the Supreme Court held that the treaties granting the ICJ jurisdiction to issue binding judgments interpreting the VCCR were without domestic effect, so the convictions and sentences of the arrested aliens need not be overturned. Only an act of Congress could give those treaties effect in domestic courts and preempt the state criminal justice system. Even the President could not order states to comply with ICJ judgments by reconsidering convictions, because the executive authority did not extend so far over domestic matters.[5]

Medellín shows the doctrine of non-self-execution at work. If the treaties granting jurisdiction to the ICJ had automatic effect in the United States, the ICJ's judgments would have overridden state laws on the arrest, trial, and conviction of criminals,

---

[2] For examples of the domestic subject matter of contemporary treaties, see International Covenant on Civil and Political Rights, opened for signature Dec. 19, 1966, 999 U.N.T.S. 171 (human rights); International Covenant on Economic, Social and Cultural Rights, opened for signature Jan. 3., 1976, 993 U.N.T.S. 3 (human rights); Rio Declaration on the Environment and Development, 31 I.L.M. 874 (environment); Framework Convention on Climate Change, 31 I.L.M. 849; Convention on Biological Diversity, 31 I.L.M. 818 (environment).

[3] Medellín v. Texas, 552 U.S. 491 (2008), construing the Vienna Convention on Consular Relations, Apr. 24, 1963, [1970] 21 U.S.T. 77, T.I.A.S. No. 6820 (Vienna Convention or Convention).

[4] Case Concerning Avena and Other Mexican Nationals (Mex. v. U.S.), 2004 I.C.J. 12 (Judgment of Mar. 31).

[5] Medellín v. Texas, 128 S. Ct. 1346 (2008). For two recent articles taking very different views of the case, see John McGinnis, *Medellín and the Future of International Delegation*, 118 YALE L.J. 1712 (2009) (defending Medellín); Carlos Manuel Vazquez, *Treaties as Law of the Land: The Supremacy Clause and the Judicial Enforcement of Treaties*, 122 HARV. L. REV. 599 (2008) (criticizing Medellín).

creating separation-of-powers problems. The President and two-thirds of the Senate, exercising the executive treaty power, would have authorized an international organization to set rules regulating domestic matters that are typically set only by the House, Senate, and President. Self-execution in this case would also have raised federalism problems because the Constitution generally leaves the operation of the criminal justice system up to individual states, as conditioned by the requirements of the Bill of Rights and the Reconstruction Amendments. By finding the treaty to be non-self-executing, the Supreme Court ensured that the entire Congress would participate in deciding the rules that govern domestic conduct, just as it would if no treaty had existed.

Non-self-execution not only applies to treaties, but can also be seen as a constraint on the other main form of international law: customary international law (CIL). Historically, many rules of international law were drawn from the customary practice of states, which took the form of unwritten rules consistently followed based on a sense of obligation. The tension between CIL and domestic law has become more acute in the last few decades. As we and others have observed, recent years have witnessed an explosion in nontreaty forms of international law, including UN General Assembly resolutions, unratified treaties, the decisions of international and domestic tribunals, NGO reports, and the opinions of international law scholars.[6] Globalization has expanded the power and ambitions of NGOs in particular, many of which have explicitly sought to influence the development of CIL norms through litigation and public advocacy. At the same time, the subjects that CIL allegedly regulates have expanded. If the American legal system presumes that most treaties are non-self-executing, for the reasons we will explain below, it would seem that a similar filter must apply to unwritten international law that has not undergone the lawmaking processes for either treaties or normal legislation. We will elaborate further on the status of CIL in the U.S. system in chapter 5.

Applying a presumption of non-self-execution to treaties carries a final benefit: it protects the appropriate balance between federal and state powers. Scholars refer to this as the *Missouri v. Holland* problem. In *Missouri v. Holland,* decided in 1920, the Supreme Court suggested that the Tenth Amendment, which declares that the powers not delegated to the federal government remain with the states or the people, does not act to constrain the treaty power.[7] According to the majority opinion by Justice Oliver Wendell Holmes, "It is obvious that there may be matters of the sharpest exigency for the national well being that an act of Congress could not deal with but that a treaty followed by such an act could." Unlike Congress's Article I, Section 8 authorities, Holmes observed, no "invisible radiation from the general

---

[6] *See, e.g.,* Curtis Bradley & Jack Goldsmith, *Customary International Law as Federal Common Law: A Critique of the Modern Position,* 110 Harv. L. Rev. 815 (1997); William Dodge, *The Constitutionality of the Alien Tort Statute: Some Observations on Text and Context,* 42 Va. J. Int'l L. 687 (2002); Patrick Kelly, *The Twilight of Customary International Law,* 40 Va. J. Int'l L. 449 (2000).

[7] 252 U.S. 416, 433–35 (1920).

terms of the Tenth Amendment" limits the Treaty Power.[8] In *Missouri*, Congress had passed a statute protecting migratory birds, but the Court struck down the law because it fell within an area controlled by the states and was thus beyond the reach of the Commerce Clause. After the Court's decision, the United States and Canada signed a treaty to protect the same birds, and Congress then enacted new legislation implementing the treaty. In *Missouri*, Justice Holmes's majority upheld the new statute. Many scholars since have declared as "clear and indisputable" the proposition that anything the treaty power can touch is, by definition, not subject to federalism limitations on the national government.[9] Recently, Curtis Bradley, David Golove, Edward Swaine, and Nick Rosenkranz have engaged in important debates about whether *Missouri* remains good law—today the Commerce Clause would encompass migratory birds, so there would be no need to reach the treaty question in that case—but the Court has never reexamined the issue.[10]

In *Missouri* itself, Congress had passed implementing legislation, as we recommend, so the presumption against self-execution would not have made a difference. It would have had a powerful effect, however, in the other great case on the limits of the Treaty Clause: *Reid v. Covert*. In *Reid*, the U.S. government tried, by court-martial rather than a regular criminal proceeding in federal court, a civilian wife for murdering her serviceman spouse.[11] The defendant petitioned for a writ of habeas corpus because the court-martial deprived her of various Bill of Rights protections, such as trial by a jury. The government claimed that the Constitution did not apply extraterritorially, an executive agreement with Great Britain gave the United States the right to try dependents of servicemen by court-martial, and the Uniform Code of Military Justice (UCMJ) made provision for military jurisdiction over civilian dependents. Justice Black, for a four-Justice plurality, rejected these claims on the ground that no treaty could deprive American citizens of their constitutional rights when abroad. But had the courts followed a presumption against self-execution, it could have more easily disposed of the controversy—and with a majority opinion—because Congress had enacted no legislation specifically implementing the agreement. Non-self-execution can prevent the dilution of individual liberties by requiring Congress to approve of any reduction of rights that normally apply to American citizens at home or abroad.

But without a presumption of non-self-execution, the broader scope of treaties threatens to give them an almost unlimited power to legislate on any subject. This outcome is the result of two different developments. First is the expansion of the definition of treaties to include any agreement between two nations under international law, regardless of subject. At one point, some (including Chief Justice

---

[8] *Id.* at 433–34.

[9] Louis Henkin, Foreign Affairs and the United States Constitution 191 (2d ed. 1997).

[10] *See, e.g.*, Curtis A. Bradley, *The Treaty Power and American Federalism*, 97 Mich. L. Rev. 390, 394 (1998); David Golove, *Treaty-Making and the Nation: The Historical Foundations of the Nationalist Conception of the Treaty Power*, 98 Mich. L. Rev. 1075 (2000); Nicholas Q. Rosenkranz, *Executing the Treaty Power*, 118 Harv. L. Rev. 1867 (2005); Edward T. Swaine, *Does Federalism Constrain the Treaty Power?*, 103 Colum. L. Rev. 403 (2003).

[11] Reid v. Covert, 354 U.S. 1 (1957).

Charles Evans Hughes) had attempted to solve the problem of the limits on treaties by arguing that they extended only to matters of "international concern."[12] That effort failed, in part, because of the second trend—an explosion in the number of treaties in all kinds of subjects. Treaties now reach matters that could conceivably extend beyond the regular powers of the federal government. A future global warming treaty, for example, could reach intrastate, noncommercial energy use, such as heating the home, which would be difficult to regulate on Commerce Clause grounds alone. Current human rights treaties might be read to narrow the death penalty or prohibit hate speech that would otherwise be protected by the First Amendment. A principle of non-self-execution that prevented international agreements from exercising direct domestic effect can ensure that the most democratic process—enactment of a statute—approves any significant change in the balance of authorities between the federal and state governments.

Modern treaties create such problems for federalism because the treaty power does not seem to be subject to the same limits that apply to the federal government's other authorities. The Constitution vests the treaty power in Article II, which lies outside the limits that Article I places on Congress. Indeed, one vexing problem that remains is what limits apply to the treaty power at all. Some scholars, such as Henkin even argue that any subject on which two nations have agreed is a valid subject for the treaty power. In this book, we do not take a position on this issue, though one of us has observed that the treaty power must reach beyond Congress's power because of its placement in the Constitution's catalog of executive powers and based on the history of the Jay Treaty of 1795.[13]

Non-self-execution heads off the collision. If treaties do not automatically create domestic law, their effect will depend on whether the President or Congress choose to implement them using their existing constitutional powers. The elected branches would not be taking any action that exceeds their normal constitutional bounds. Maintaining a sharp distinction between international agreements and domestic implementation ensures that the balance of power between the federal and state governments under the Constitution remains intact.

We should register three important caveats. First, we do not argue that non-self-execution must extend to all treaties. We accept that some agreements may take direct effect within the United States. Rather, we defend the use of the non-self-execution doctrine by treatymakers and courts against claims that *all* treaties *must* be self-executing. We further argue that courts should presume a treaty has no domestic legal effect absent a clear statement in the text to the contrary. Second, applying non-self-execution expresses no view on whether treaty provisions might

---

[12] Proceedings of the American Society of International Law at its Twenty-third Annual Meeting 194 (1929) (reporting remarks by Charles Evans Hughes); *see also* RESTATEMENT (Third) of the Foreign Relations Law of the United States § 302, reporters' note 2 (1986) ("It had sometimes been suggested that a treaty or other international agreement must deal with 'a matter of international concern.' That suggestion derived from a statement by Charles Evans Hughes").

[13] *See* John Yoo, *Globalism and the Constitution: Treaties, Non-Self-Execution, and the Original Understanding*, 99 COLUM. L. REV. 1955, 2074–91 (1999).

make for good policy. Treaties such as the VCCR guaranteeing the right to meet with consular officials, or the ICCPR's commitment to fair trials in criminal cases, are without doubt good ideas. They may benefit Americans traveling abroad just as much as foreign nationals living in the United States. Our concern is not the substance of the policy, but the process of deciding whether it will reign supreme within the United States. Non-self-execution ensures that the same process required by the Constitution to regulate Americans domestically is used to enact rules that come from abroad. Third, we do not address the issue of compliance on the international plane. It may well be that non-self-execution causes the United States to renege on an international obligation. In the *Medellín* case, for example, the United States conceded that the failure by state police to warn aliens of their right to consulate notification violated the VCCR. Even if the treaty has no domestic legal effect, the United States might still owe a remedy to another nation for violating the treaty. But whether and how to compensate treaty partners for violations would be up to the political judgment of the President and Congress.

We believe that the treatymakers and courts already respect these principles with many, if not most, of the important treaties adopted in recent years. When ratifying treaties that might have intrusive domestic effects, the President and Senate have almost always included a package of reservations, understandings, and declarations (known as "RUDs"). RUDs attached to human rights treaties, such as the ICCPR, often contain a statement that the treaty is non-self-executing, that the United States is already in compliance without the need for any new legislation, and that the treaty does not affect the balance of authority between the federal and state governments. Although RUDs are controversial among many legal scholars, U.S. courts have accepted them with little difficulty.[14] This is not surprising, as RUDs reflect the understanding of the President and Senate that important questions regarding individual rights and the appropriate levels of government regulation should remain in the hands of the branch designated by the Constitution: Congress.

I. NON-SELF-EXECUTION AS DOCTRINE

Before discussing how non-self-execution preserves popular sovereignty in the area of international law, we must first describe the doctrine itself. The practice goes back to the very beginnings of the Republic. At the time of the Framing, the basic understanding in Anglo-American law was that treaties represented a contract made by the executive branch with another sovereign. Chief Justice Marshall, for example, observed that "[a] treaty is in its nature a contract between two nations, not

---

[14] *Compare* Louis Henkin, *U.S. Ratification of Human Rights Conventions: The Ghost of Senator Bricker*, 89 Am. J. Int'l L. 341 (1995), *and* Stefan A. Riesenfeld & Frederick M. Abbott, *The Scope of U.S. Senate Control over the Conclusion and Operation of Treaties*, 67 Chi.-Kent L. Rev. 571 (1991), *with* Curtis A. Bradley & Jack L. Goldsmith, *Treaties, Human Rights, and Conditional Consent*, 149 U. Pa. L. Rev. 399 (2000).

a legislative act."[15] Marshall considered this "contract between two nations" in foreign affairs as distinct from the legislative power, which governed the government's regulation of domestic conduct by private parties. While Article VI of the new Constitution places treaties on the same plane as the Constitution and federal laws in their supremacy over state law, it does not specify the process for making international law enforceable in domestic law—indeed, portions of the Constitution itself, such as Article III's grant of jurisdiction to the federal courts, are not self-executing, but instead rely on legislative implementation. Although some treaties were given immediate domestic effect, important members of the Founding generation, including James Madison, argued that at least some treaties required an additional legislative act by Congress.[16]

The Supreme Court first recognized that treaties did not always take automatic effect as domestic law in the 1829 case, *Foster v. Neilson. Foster* involved an 1819 treaty that sought to preserve Spanish land grants made before the cessation of West Florida to the United States. Writing for the Court, Chief Justice Marshall refused to enforce a land grant because Congress had not yet enacted legislation implementing the agreement. He distinguished between a treaty that "operates of itself, without the aid of any legislative provision," and a treaty that promises future action by the sovereign parties.[17] Courts could enforce the former, but not the latter. With the latter, "the legislature must execute the contract before it can become a rule for the court." This runs counter to the Supremacy Clause of the Constitution, which declares: "all Treaties made, or which shall be made, under the Authority of the United States, shall be the supreme Law of the Land."

But there were two reasons why the Supremacy Clause did not require automatic enforcement. First, Marshall believed that the courts should defer to the political branches on a question of treaty interpretation. Validity of the Spanish land grants rested on the assumption that the land belonged to Spain. It had been the position of the United States that Florida had actually been conveyed as part of the retrocession of Louisiana from Spain to France (France had lost the territory to Spain at the end of the Seven Years' War). The United States had acquired Florida through the Louisiana Purchase, not the Adams-Onis Treaty, which had settled Andrew Jackson's invasion and conquest of Florida in the First Seminole War against the Spanish. According to Marshall, the "judiciary is not that department of the government, to which the assertion of . . . [the nation's] interests against foreign powers is confided."[18] Instead, the Court's duty is "to decide upon individual rights, according to those principles which the political departments of the nation have established." Here, Marshall was declaring that the judiciary should defer to the President and Congress

---

[15] Foster v. Neilson, 27 U.S. (2 Pet.) 253, 314 (1829).

[16] For a review of the history, see Yoo, *supra* note 13. For a critical view, see Martin S. Flaherty, *History Right?: Historical Scholarship, Original Understanding, and Treaties as "Supreme Law of the Land,"* 99 COLUM. L. REV. 2095 (1999); Carlos Vazquez, *Laughing at Treaties*, 99 COLUM. L. REV. 2154 (1999).

[17] Foster v. Neilson, 27 U.S. (2 Pet.) 253, 314 (1829).

[18] *Id.* at 307.

in determining the meaning and operation of international agreements, and ulti- mately the management of foreign relations. "In a controversy between two nations concerning national boundary," he wrote, "it is scarcely possible that the courts of either should refuse to abide by the measures adopted by its own government."[19]

Second, according to Marshall, the political departments of the government had not created any individual rights based on the treaty. The treaty's text had declared that land grants by Spain "shall be ratified and confirmed to the persons in posses- sion of the lands." Marshall rejected the idea that this provision of the treaty—which promised future action—should take immediate effect in American law. The provi- sion did not "act directly on the grants," but instead "pledge[d] the faith of the United States to pass acts which shall ratify and confirm them."[20] Marshall analo- gized treaties to a contract. With promises of future action, "the legislature must execute the contract, before it can become a rule for the court." When a treaty promises to engage in future conduct, it "addresses itself to the political, not the judicial department."[21]

If, however, a treaty created an individual right and did not require future action by the government, Marshall implied that the courts would enforce it. This actually occurred five years later with the very same 1819 treaty between the United States and Spain. This time, the Supreme Court found that the Spanish text of the agree- ment did not "stipulate for some future legislative action," but instead declared that the land grants "shall remain ratified and confirmed." Convinced by the new trans- lation of the treaty, and by congressional enactments in the interim, Marshall held the same provision of the treaty now self-executing.[22] *United States v. Percheman* shows that the separation-of-power concerns that animate our approach to global- ization are somewhat different from the reasons behind Chief Justice Marshall's support for non-self-execution. Marshall distinguished between treaties that con- templated future actions, which required legislative action, and treaties that required no further implementation.

Marshall could have cited a third reason to support the non-self-execution doctrine: not every provision of federal law is "self-executing." Important provi- sions of the nation's highest law, for example, do not take effect automatically. Much of Article III is non-self-executing, which leaves to Congress the decision to create the lower federal courts and to define their jurisdiction.[23] In the Judiciary Act of 1789, the first Congress did not provide for federal jurisdiction over all of the cases or controversies possible under Article III.[24] For much of our nation's history, general federal question jurisdiction did not exist, and even today the courts cannot

---

[19] *Id.*

[20] *Id.* at 314.

[21] *Id.*

[22] United States v. Percheman, 32 U.S. (7 Pet.) 51 (1833).

[23] For discussion of this question, see Akhil Reed Amar, *The Two-Tiered Structure of the Judiciary Act of 1789*, 138 U. PA. L. REV. 1499 (1990).

[24] RICHARD FALLON ET AL., HART & WECHSLER'S THE FEDERAL COURTS AND THE FEDERAL SYSTEM 32–33 (4th ed. 1996).

hear all diversity cases. If something as vital to the constitutional system as the organization and jurisdiction of the judiciary is non-self-executing, it is difficult to understand why the Supremacy Clause would require that all treaties have a superior status as self-executing federal law. This is also the case with many provisions of federal statutory law, where the courts generally refuse to recognize claims brought by private individuals unless Congress has clearly created a private right of action.

Subsequent judicial developments drew a much sharper distinction between international politics and domestic affairs. If Congress chose not to enforce a treaty, or even took affirmative measures to violate international agreements, the only remedy would have to come from nation-to-nation negotiations. The last place to turn would be the courts. In the *Head Money Cases*, the Court upheld an act of Congress that imposed a fifty-cent tax on each immigrant, in violation of a treaty with Russia. Echoing Chief Justice Marshall, the Court declared in 1884 that a "treaty is primarily a compact between independent nations," and as such, "it depends for the enforcement of its provisions on the interest and the honor of the governments which are parties to it."[25] If a nation violates the treaty, "its infraction becomes the subject of international negotiations and reclamations," going so far as "actual war." With politics providing the remedy, it "is obvious that with all this the judicial courts have nothing to do and can give no redress." Four years later, the Court again made clear that implementation and compliance with a treaty were largely decisions for the political branches, not the courts. "If the country with which the treaty is made is dissatisfied with the action of the legislative department, it may present its complaint to the executive head of the government, and take such other measures as it may deem essential for the protection of its interests."[26] One place foreign nations could not go for redress, however, was the judiciary. "The courts can afford no redress. Whether the complaining nation has just cause of complaint, or our country was justified in its legislation, are not matters for judicial cognizance."

These nineteenth-century cases, which arose as the United States began to assume a place among the ranks of the Great Powers, took the first steps toward an understanding of the relationship between treaties and domestic laws. There are two important understandings to register here. First, these cases did not involve non-self-execution; rather, they addressed the related question of a conflict between treaties and subsequent statutes. They involve what is known as the "last-in-time" rule, which states that treaties and statutes may overrule each other and that the one adopted last is the one that governs.[27] Nonetheless, both cases express a presumption in favor of the mechanisms of popular sovereignty as a means to control the influence of international law in the American domestic order. If international agreements were not subject to such control, then theoretically, they should not be subject to abrogation by an act of Congress, which undergoes a different process

---

[25] Eyde v. Robertson (Head Money Cases), 112 U.S. 580, 598 (1884).

[26] Whitney v. Robinson, 124 U.S. 190, 194 (1888).

[27] For discussion, see Julian Ku, *Treaties as Laws: A Defense of the Last in Time Rule for Treaties and Federal Statutes*, 80 IND. L.J. 319 (2005).

than treaties and is created by Article I, Section 8 (and not Article II, Section 2). Second, even in the nineteenth century, the judiciary continued to accept Chief Justice Marshall's notion that treaties conferring individual rights "are capable of enforcement as between private parties in the courts of the country."[28] So even though the Supreme Court was coming to view the resolution of any conflict between international and domestic law by relying on the nonenforceability of the former, it still reserved a place in federal court jurisdiction for treaties that created private rights of action.

In the twentieth century, the political branches took the lead in resolving the conflict between the broad demands of certain treaties and domestic law. Their involvement was prompted by the burst of international agreement–making at the end of World War II. Some lawmakers feared that the United Nations and other international organizations would have the legal authority to compel the United States to comply with their decisions. Others were concerned that broad human rights treaties would require revolutionary changes in domestic society—it should not go unacknowledged that an important part of this impulse was to prevent international agreements from requiring a change in segregation in the South. In the 1950s, Ohio Senator John Bricker, who saw within the United Nations and other international organizations a movement toward world government, pressed for a constitutional amendment to block the domestic effect of treaties.[29] The Bricker amendment, as it was known, required that all treaties receive legislative implementation, and allowed treaties to run only as far as the scope of Congress's preexisting powers.[30] This would have effectively made all treaties non-self-executing, and it would have put to rest the idea that treaties could regulate matters beyond the normal competence of the federal government. President Eisenhower opposed the amendment because he believed it infringed on the President's ability to conduct foreign policy. He succeeded in stalling the amendment, which failed in the Senate by only one vote, after promising to refrain from further U.S. involvement in new human rights treaties.[31] In other words, the political branches had reached an accommodation that the United States would not accept self-executing treaties that made direct changes in the domestic legal system without the approval of the House of Representatives.

It was not until the 1970s that the political branches devised a process allowing the United States to move beyond the Bricker controversy and enter into human rights agreements. They agreed on RUDs that effectively rendered such treaties non-self-executing within the domestic legal system.[32] For example, in 1992, the United States

---

[28] Head Money Cases, 112 U.S. 580, 598 (1884).

[29] *See generally* DUANE TANANBAUM, THE BRICKER AMENDMENT CONTROVERSY (1988).

[30] S.J. Res. 1, 83d Cong., 1st Sess. (1953); S.J. Res.130, 82d Cong., 2d Sess. (1952); S.J. Res. 102, 82d Cong., 1st Sess. (1951).

[31] TANANBAUM, *supra* note 29, at 175–90.

[32] Congressional Research Service, *Treaties and Other International Agreements: The Role of the United States Senate*, S. Prt. 106–71, 106th Cong., 2d Sess. 39, at 125 (2001); SAMUEL B. CRANDALL, TREATIES, THEIR MAKING AND ENFORCEMENT 70 (1904).

ratified the International Covenant on Civil and Political Rights, which protects a series of individual liberties ranging from the right to life and privacy, to freedom of religion and speech (except for hate speech), to criminal procedural guarantees. The Senate conditioned its advice and consent on several RUDs, with specific reservations making clear that the Constitution's right to free speech took precedence. This arrangement included a "federalism" understanding, which stated that the federal government would be obliged to implement only those treaty provisions that fall within the areas of the federal government's constitutional competence, leaving to state and local officials the task of fulfilling the ICCPR's other terms. It also included a declaration that all of the ICCPR's substantive provisions were "not self-executing" and that nothing in the treaty required or authorized legislation that would violate the Constitution.[33] It seems clear that the purpose of these RUDs was to prevent a treaty made by the President and Senate from causing any change in domestic society. Any actions necessary to reach the standards set out in the ICCPR, for example, would have to undergo the Constitution's regular processes for domestic lawmaking.[34] The presence of a treaty does not change the balance of power between the federal and state governments, nor does it alter the way that those governments regulate participation of the popularly elected House for federal action, and of state legislatures for state and local action.[35]

Prominent scholars have attacked this practice as hypocritical and even "anti-Constitutional." But involving the House of Representatives in the domestic implementation of treaties dates back to the eighteenth century.[36] In 1796, the Washington administration resolved outstanding Revolutionary War issues with Great Britain in the Jay Treaty. The agreement recognized British rights to recover its prewar loans to Americans in exchange for the British evacuation of forts in the Northwest Territory and the restoration of American trading rights in the Caribbean.[37] While the Senate approved the treaty by exactly the two-thirds vote required, the House demanded a role through its right to enact legislation to pay the British debts and to alter the trade laws. Jeffersonians, who held a majority in the House, hoped to use Congress's authority to block implementation and thereby sink the treaty. Washington, by contrast, argued that the Constitution granted the House no discretion to refuse to implement the Jay Treaty because it was already the law of the land.

---

[33] For criticism of the Senate's practice, see Henkin, *supra* note 14; Riesenfeld & Abbott, *supra* note 14. For a defense, see Bradley & Goldsmith, *supra* note 14.

[34] *See* 138 Cong. Rec. S4781-01 (Daily ed., Apr. 2, 1992) (reservations declaring treaty to be non-self-executing and not authorizing or requiring any legislation).

[35] *Id.* (reservation that "the United States understands that this Covenant shall be implemented by the Federal Government to the extent that it exercises legislative and judicial jurisdiction over the matters covered therein, and otherwise by the state and local governments; to the extent that state and local governments exercise jurisdiction over such matters, the Federal Government shall take measures appropriate to the Federal system to the end that the competent authorities of the state or local governments may take appropriate measures for the fulfillment of the Covenant").

[36] *See* Henkin, *supra* note 9, at 202.

[37] The Jay Treaty is reviewed in Yoo, *supra* note 13, at 2080–86.

In support of the administration, Alexander Hamilton argued in the anonymous "Defence" that "each house of Congress collectively as well as the members of it separately are under a constitutional obligation to observe the injunctions of a [treaty] and to give it effect."[38] Leading the Jeffersonians, James Madison and Albert Gallatin argued that no treaty could regulate a matter within Congress's enumerated powers without new legislation. The Constitution, Madison declared in Congress, "left with the President and Senate the power of making Treaties, but required at the same time the Legislative sanction and cooperation, in those cases where the Constitution had given express and specific powers to the Legislature."[39] The House adopted a resolution that treaties could not touch upon matters within congressional competence without legislation, and then proceeded to enact the necessary laws due to the favorable terms of the Jay Treaty.[40]

RUDs are the progeny of those early debates. By ensuring that treaties do not directly regulate matters under the constitutional jurisdiction of Congress, they have allowed treaties that have sat long and lonely on the Senate's executive calendar to move forward. President Truman signed the Genocide Convention, for example, in 1949, but it was only in 1984 that President Reagan could agree on a package of RUDs with the Senate to achieve ratification in 1989.[41] This had led critics to claim that the United States is acting hypocritically, appearing to adhere to international agreements while, in effect, doing nothing to change its actual conduct.[42] Ratification of the ICCPR and other human rights instruments allows the United States to assume representation on various treaty commissions or tribunals, but without bringing its own practices into compliance. RUDs, however, ensure that the same democratically accountable bodies that enact laws continue to do so; treaties cannot alter the basic pathways of American public lawmaking. Professor Henkin, however, does not accept the democracy argument. He declares: "That argument, of course, impugns the democratic character of every treaty made or that will be made by the President with the consent of the Senate."[43] Yet it is unclear how far the democratic nature of treaties extends. The President negotiates and makes treaties, and two-thirds of the Senate, which represents the states, must consent—but this process excludes the House entirely. We believe, as we will explain in the next section, that a general presumption of non-self-execution is the best way to reconcile treatymaking with the processes of public lawmaking established by the text and structure of the Constitution.

---

[38] The Defence No. 36, N.Y. Herald, Jan. 2, 1796, reprinted in 20 PAPERS OF ALEXANDER HAMILTON 4 (HAROLD C. SYRETT ed. 1962).

[39] 5 ANNALS OF CONG. 493 (1849).

[40] See STANLEY ELKINS & ERIC MCKITRICK, THE AGE OF FEDERALISM 441–47 (1993).

[41] See Bradley & Goldsmith, supra note 14, at 412–16.

[42] Henkin, supra note 14, at 344.

[43] Id. at 346.

II. NON-SELF-EXECUTION AND CONSTITUTIONAL STRUCTURE

Critics of non-self-execution believe either that treaties automatically can make law on any subject or that the Constitution grants a separate authority to implement treaties that goes beyond Congress's regular powers. These arguments can trace their pedigree to Alexander Hamilton, who first argued that the Constitution required Congress to implement the Jay Treaty—which settled outstanding issues with Great Britain stemming from the Revolutionary War. Hamilton argued that because the Supremacy Clause made treaties, along with the Constitution and Acts of Congress, the "law of the land," the House and Senate had the authority and obligation to carry out the pacts. To make treaties dependent on legislative execution, Hamilton argued, would make the treaty power a hollow one. "[T]here is scarcely any species of treaty which would not clash, in some particular," with a power of Congress, Hamilton argued. If dependent on legislative implementation, he continued, the power to make treaties—which had been "granted in such comprehensive and indefinite terms and guarded with so much precaution"—would "become essentially nugatory."[44]

Today's critics of non-self-execution have followed Hamilton's example. Scholars such as Carlos Vazquez make the straightforward argument that the Supremacy Clause compels courts to enforce treaties without further implementation.[45] Article VI of the Constitution declares that three types of federal law—the Constitution, "Laws of the United States," and "all Treaties made, or which shall be made, under the Authority of the United States"—are "the supreme Law of the Land." These supporters of self-execution argue that the inclusion of treaties in the Supremacy Clause would be superfluous if they depended on an Act of Congress to take domestic effect. Treaties, at the same time, also expand the federal government's powers. Article I, Section 8's Necessary and Proper Clause gives the legislature the authority to "carry[] into Execution ... all other Powers vested ... in the Government of the United States, or in any Department or Office thereof." Thus, the argument goes, a treaty could expand the reach of the federal government through the Necessary and Proper Clause, even if its subject fell outside Congress's enumerated powers in domestic affairs.

The text of the Supremacy Clause, however, only declares that treaties, like the Constitution and federal statutes, are superior to state law. Article VI does not address how they are to be made supreme, nor does it require that the Constitution, treaties, and federal statutes always be heard in court. This section will argue that other textual and structural elements in the Constitution, particularly the separation of the executive from the legislative power and the animating principle of

---

[44] The Defence No. 36, N.Y. Herald, Jan. 2, 1796, reprinted in 20 PAPERS OF ALEXANDER HAMILTON 4, 18–22 (HAROLD C. SYRETT ed. 1962).

[45] For prominent examples, see Vazquez, *supra* note 5, at 559; HENKIN, *supra* note 9, at 201; Vazquez, *supra* note 16; Jordan Paust, *Self-Executing Treaties*, 82 AM. J. INT'L L. 760 (1988).

popular sovereignty, allow the three branches to defer execution of international law until the President and Congress have determined whether to implement it. Non-self-execution also brings the different provisions of the Constitution into harmony and respects the constitutional goal of a national government of limited powers. Most importantly, it ensures that lawmaking authority remains within the paths set out by the Constitution rather than moving to international fora.

Following a doctrine of presumptive or even mandatory self-execution would create severe distortions in the constitutional fabric that could only be cured by keeping international and domestic law separate. Perhaps the most important role played by a strong rule of non-self-execution is that it would prevent the executive power from intruding into the domain of the legislative. Article II, Section 1 of the Constitution vests all of "the executive power" that resides in the federal government in the President. It establishes the treatymaking power in Article II, Section 2, which also grants the Commander-in-Chief pardon and appointment powers. By its placement in Article II, and following traditional Anglo-American constitutional understandings, treatymaking is clearly an executive power. That does not mean that the President can exclusively exercise all of Article II's executive powers. The Framers gave the Senate a share of the treaty and appointment powers in an effort to dilute the unitary nature of the executive branch. But inclusion of the Senate did not transform the treaty power into a legislative power, just as vesting the President with the veto power (in Article I of the Constitution, with the rest of Congress's powers) did not render the enactment of statutes executive in nature.

The Constitution takes a very specific approach to the enactment of legislation. Bills must undergo approval by the House, which represents the people; the Senate, which represents the states; and the President. Article I creates a finely tuned, demanding process in order to make the exercise of legislative authority difficult and to protect the states and the people from unwarranted exercises of national power.[46] As the Supreme Court has observed, the "choices we discern as having been made in the Constitutional Convention impose burdens on governmental processes that often seem clumsy, inefficient, even unworkable, but those hard choices were consciously made by men who had lived under a form of government that permitted arbitrary governmental acts to go unchecked."[47] Executive power, by contrast, exists not to regulate domestic society, but to marshal the power of the government to carry out the laws, manage the government establishment, conduct relations with foreign nations, and act quickly in times of emergency and crisis. Alexander Hamilton defined the executive power in *The Federalist* as "the execution of the laws and employment of the common strength," which, he believed, "seem to comprise all the functions of the executive magistrate."[48] Allowing treaties to set the rules of domestic society would allow an executive power—though one shared between the

---

[46] *See* Bradford A. Clark, *Putting the Safeguards Back into the Political Safeguards of Federalism,* 80 Tex. L. Rev. 327 (2001).

[47] INS v. Chadha, 462 U.S. 919, 959 (1983).

[48] Federalist No. 75, at 504 (Alexander Hamilton) (Jacob E. Cooke ed. 1961).

President and Senate—to enjoy legislative effect without undergoing the process required for statutes.

Non-self-execution prevents the expansion of an executive power into the lawmaking authority of Congress. Several scholars have argued that the President and Senate may make a treaty on any subject, so long as it is, in the words of the *Restatement (Third) of the Foreign Relations Law of the United States*, "an agreement between two or more states or international organizations that is intended to be legally binding and is governed by international law."[49] If treaties were to take automatic effect without implementing legislation by Congress, they could presumably regulate any matter within Congress's enumerated powers. A self-executing treaty, for example, could set the rules of interstate commerce, define federal crimes, or establish environmental standards, even though all of these powers are currently vested in Congress. As the United States forges multilateral agreements that address matters once purely domestic in scope, treaties will regulate the same issues as domestic legislation.

Recognizing this problem, conventional academic wisdom admits that some exceptions to automatic self-execution must exist. If legislation is "constitutionally required," in the words of the *Restatement*, a treaty cannot be self-executing.[50] For example, most scholars agree that treaties cannot enact criminal sanctions, tax or spend, or declare war without subsequent legislation.[51] Yet defenders of self-execution cannot provide any principle explaining why these authorities are off-limits, but Congress's other powers over interstate commerce or intellectual property rights are not. Madison voiced this same criticism in the Jay Treaty debates: "if the Treaty-power alone could perform any one act for which the authority of Congress is required by the Constitution, it may perform every act for which the authority of that part of the Government is required."[52]

A general presumption of non-self-execution ensures that the basic decisions reserved to the legislature in a democratic form of government stay with the legislature. Setting criminal penalties and making decisions on taxing and spending have long constituted the very core of the legislative power. Indeed, the root of Parliament's ability to gain its independence after the revolutions of the 1600s was through its power of the purse. Our Constitution further defined the federal legislative authority to include the regulation of interstate commerce, which has formed the legal foundations for rulemaking on civil rights, the environment, education, and most of the modern administrative state. The Constitution itself provides no reason to think that these latter decisions can be made through a different process—between the President and two-thirds of the Senate—while the former cannot.

---

[49] RESTATEMENT (THIRD) OF THE FOREIGN RELATIONS LAW OF THE UNITED STATES § 301 (1987).

[50] *Id.* at § 111(4).

[51] *See, e.g., id.* § 111 cmt. i & reporters' note 6; HENKIN, *supra* note 9, at 203.

[52] James Madison, *Jay's Treaty* (Mar. 10, 1796), in 16 PAPERS OF JAMES MADISON 258 (Robert A. Rutland et al., eds., 1977).

Article I, Section 8 allocates all of these decisions to Congress. Non-self-execution ensures that Congress will continue to set policies in all of these areas, regardless of whether or not there is an international imperative behind them.

Non-self-execution also prevents the national government's power to regulate from exceeding the normal limits on Congress's Article I powers. There is a textual logic to the counterargument—if treaties are set out in Article II, they ought not be subject to the limits set out in Article I. This would create, however, a broader power to legislate than that intended by the Framers. Many of the Framers' conscious efforts to limit the legislative power came through specific limitations on Congress. Article I, Section 9's prohibition on bills of attainder, for example, seems to apply only to Congress, as do several of the provisions in the Bill of Rights. If the treaty power allows an alternative route for domestic lawmaking, it would create a way for the national government to regulate free of these textual limits. As Madison said again during the Jay Treaty debates, "if the legislative powers specifically vested in Congress, are to be no limitation or check on the Treaty power, it was evident that the exceptions to those powers, could be no limitation or check to the Treaty power."[53]

Keeping international law and domestic law separate also advances the norms courts have inferred from the Constitution's structures. Chief among these is the separation of powers. The Constitution not only restricts the legislative power to an enumerated list of authorities, but also protects the integrity of the other branches from congressional intrusion. The Supreme Court has read Article II of the Constitution, for example, to place all law enforcement in the hands of officers of the United States chosen through the Appointments Clause.[54] Similarly, it has held that the resolution of cases and controversies arising under federal law must occur through the federal courts.[55] Non-self-execution guarantees that treaties, when they exercise a lawmaking function, obey these and similar structural rules. Otherwise, a treaty could delegate to an international organization powers that normally rest with the executive branch, such as law enforcement or rulemaking. Or a treaty could transfer authority from Congress to the executive branch or to an international organization, or move jurisdiction over treaty cases from Article III federal courts to international tribunals.

These are not idle imaginings. Some treaties, as interpreted by leading scholars, already purport to delegate authority in ways that the Constitution does not permit. Some argue, for example, that the UN Charter transfers the power to declare war from Congress to the President in cases where the Security Council has authorized hostilities.[56] President Truman, for example, claimed that he needed no congressional approval for the Korean War because the UN Security Council had already provided authorization, and Thomas Franck made a similar argument to justify the

---

[53] *Id.* at 259.

[54] *See, e.g.*, Bowsher v. Synar, 478 U.S. 714 (1986) (invalidating deficit reduction act).

[55] Plaut v. Spendthrift Farm, Inc., 514 U.S. 211 (1995).

[56] Thomas M. Franck & Faiza Patel, *UN Police Action in Lieu of War: "The Old Order Changeth,"* 85 Am. J. Int'l L. 63 (1991).

1991 Persian Gulf War.[57] The North American Free Trade Agreement, through a congressional-executive agreement, gives a panel of arbitrators from the United States, Canada, and Mexico the authority to decide issues under federal trade law that once lay exclusively within the jurisdiction of a federal court. Keeping international law and domestic law separate through non-self-execution reduces any distortions of the separation of powers by the demands of international cooperation. The institutions that regulate domestic activity will play the identical role even when the matters are the subject of treaties, and regardless of whether international politics and legal considerations are present.

Of course the United States can still fulfill its obligations, but it must continue to use the regular processes of government decision-making. Thus, if the UN Security Council issues a resolution authorizing the use of force, the United States can still send troops—as it has in the Persian Gulf, Somalia, and Haiti—but it will make that choice using the regular process for deciding on war.[58] If the WTO Dispute Resolution Body orders the United States to comply with trade agreements, it is up to Congress or the President to decide how and whether to revise U.S. law to comply.[59] NAFTA is a good example. Our presumption does not preclude the United States from entering into novel international arrangements, such as the use of arbitrators in the place of federal judges for hearing trade complaints. Indeed, as a congressional-executive agreement, NAFTA received majority support in both the Senate and the House. Our presumption just ensures that before the United States undertakes a significant change in the nature of its international commitments, it uses the regular means of domestic policy-making to reach a decision.

Keeping international law and domestic law separate ensures that fundamental decisions are not transferred from our national institutions, which are elected or chosen through democratic constitutional processes, to independent but also unaccountable international institutions. A critic might respond that our modern administrative state already relies heavily on the delegation of authority from Congress to bureaucracies that are deliberately insulated from the political process. It is true that the legislature has transferred broad swaths of power to agencies that are unelected and whose independence is designed to allow them to exercise impartial expert judgment. At the same time, however, they are still part of the American

---

[57] *Id.*

[58] *See, e.g.*, Michael J. Glennon & Allison R. Hayward, *Collective Security and the Constitution: Can the Commander-in-Chief Power Be Delegated to the United Nations?*, 82 GEO. L. J. 1573 (1994).

[59] For instance, the U.S. has been repeatedly ordered by the WTO Dispute Settlement Body to revise its laws banning internet gambling. See Panel Report, Recourse to Article 21.5 of the DSU by Antigua and Barbuda, United States—Measures Affecting the Cross-Border Supply of Gambling and Betting Services, WT/DS285/RW (March 30, 2007) (finding that new U.S. legislation had not complied with earlier decision requiring nondiscriminatory treatment of internet gambling services). To date, it has not done so, giving Antigua and Barbuda the right to impose limited retaliatory measures. See Decision by Arbitrator, Recourse to Arbitration by the United States Under Article 22.6 of the DSU, United States—Measures Affecting The Cross-Border Supply Of Gambling And Betting Services, WT/DS285/ARB (December 21, 2007) (allowing Antigua and Barbuda to withhold $21 million in trade concessions in retaliation). See also CONGRESSIONAL RESEARCH SERVICE, WTO DISPUTE SETTLEMENT: STATUS OF U.S. COMPLIANCE IN PENDING CASES 37–43 (August 14, 2007).

political process. While the President, Congress, and the courts may struggle for control over the administrative state, the agencies remain under the control of some or all of these American governmental institutions. If the President disagrees with an agency decision, he can block a proposed regulation or remove an agency head; if Congress disagrees, Congress can change legislation, reduce funding, and hold oversight hearings; the courts can reverse agency decisions. None of these options are available if a treaty delegates American lawmaking or law enforcement authority to an international institution, which is free from the political control of any individual state. Non-self-execution prevents decision-making authority from being transferred outside the American lawmaking process altogether.

III. NON-SELF-EXECUTION AND GLOBALIZATION

Maintaining the distinction between international agreements and American public lawmaking will enhance, rather than constrict, the workings of democracy. By democracy, we mean a system that advances a cluster of values, including popular representation, accountability, transparency, and deliberation, among others.[60] Core to these values is the idea that when the government makes rules to regulate the conduct of private citizens, those rules should be made by officials who have been directly elected by the people. Non-self-execution achieves this in two broad ways. First, it includes the most popular legislative body, the House of Representatives, in the basic decisions on treaty implementation. Second, it removes from the least popular branch, the federal courts, the right to make policy decisions on treaty implementation and returns this right to the political branches. Neither of these effects gives the House of Representatives or Congress the dominant role over treaties. Of course, there would be no occasion for any implementation at all without the initiative of the President and Senate to make a treaty in the first place. Instead of aggrandizing Congress, inclusion of the House provides a legislative check on the executive treatymaking power.

As John McGinnis and Ilya Somin have observed, the process of making international law does not fulfill most expectations for a democratic lawmaking process.[61] Each country has an equal vote, regardless of population, economic size, or political regime. In one of the typical forums for international lawmaking—the UN General Assembly—each nation, no matter how small or autocratic, has a seat. Multilateral treaties are usually made by consensus rather than by majority vote, because the latter can give authoritarian governments the ability to exert an outsized influence.[62] The most important international institution, the UN Security Council, has five

---

[60] *See, e.g.,* Adrian Vermeule, Mechanisms of Democracy: Institutional Design Writ Small (2007).

[61] John McGinnis & Ilya Somin, *Should International Law Be Part of Our Law?*, 59 Stan. L. Rev. 1175 (2007).

[62] *Id.* at 1205 (explaining that multilateral treaties are the outcome of a nondemocratic consensus since 103 of the world's 193 nations are either "not free" or only "partly free").

permanent members, only three of which are Western democracies, and any one of which can exercise an absolute veto.[63] Moreover, international agreements are often not made in open, transparent fora. They are sometimes the product of extensive negotiations that have occured far from the public gaze, where nongovernmental organizations often have greater sway than many countries.[64] No democratically elected or accountable institutions perform continuing oversight. Usually, treaties create an institution charged with monitoring and implementation, but not with gathering feedback and adjusting the law.[65]

Contrast this with the elements of the American public lawmaking process. Several different theories exist about the enactment of legislation. A long-held view describes Congress as a forum for deals reached between interest groups. While public choice scholars believe interest groups use legislation to capture rents at the public's expense, pluralists believe they facilitate stability, moderation, and satisfaction with the political system.[66] Congress may also involve more committees and groups who will bring to bear greater legislative and policy expertise, produce more information on choices, and foster communication between political players.[67] Along lines suggested by Cass Sunstein, the more steps that are required to implement treaties, the more open the process will be and the greater the opportunity for deliberation, stable policy-making, and broader political acceptance.[68]

These benefits are not without trade-offs. Legislatures create space for more deliberation and include a broader base of political groups, but they are also slower and more fragmented, and they lack the expertise of those who sit in the executive branch. Legislators elected every two years might place short-term benefits over longer-term interests. Of greatest concern to the Framers, larger legislative bodies have more difficulty acting swiftly and secretly. In explaining the exclusion of the House from treatymaking, Alexander Hamilton wrote in *Federalist No. 75* that the numerous body lacked "accurate and comprehensive knowledge of foreign politics," "a steady and systematic adherence to the same views," "a nice and uniform

---

[63] Fernando R. Teson, *The Vexing Problem of Authority in Humanitarian Intervention: A Proposal*, 24 Wis. Int'l L.J. 761, 763–68 (2006).

[64] McGinnis & Somin, *supra* note 61, at 1210–17 (explaining that citizens' comparative ignorance of international law and the lack of transparency enable political elites to establish norms that run counter to the interests of ordinary citizens).

[65] For discussion on the problems involved in reviewing and adjusting the law, see Abram Chayes & Antonia Handler Chayes, The New Sovereignty: Compliance with International Regulatory Agreements 229–49 (1995).

[66] Daniel Farber & Philip Frickey, *The Jurisprudence of Public Choice*, 65 Tex. L. Rev. 873, 875–76 (1987).

[67] *See generally* Keith Krehbiel, Information and Legislative Organization (1991) (proposing a link between distributive and informational theories of legislative organization); Arthur Maass, Congress and the Common Good (1980) (discussing the relationship between political institutions, public opinion, political actors, and elections); William N. Eskridge, Jr., *Overriding Supreme Court Statutory Interpretation Decisions*, 101 Yale L.J. 331, 356–57 (1991) (discussing information theory and the creation of public policy).

[68] *Cf.* Cass Sunstein, *Interest Groups in American Public Law*, 38 Stan. L. Rev. 29, 33–35 (1985) (addressing the problem of factionalism in supplanting political discussion and debate).

sensibility to national character," and "decision, *secrecy*, and dispatch."[69] Hamilton believed that the management of foreign relations was executive in nature, and hence so too were treaties, but because the Supremacy Clause had given treaties the potential to operate as domestic laws, they had a legislative aspect that required the inclusion of the Senate. Requiring the joint participation of the President and Senate in treatymaking would produce greater "security" from abuse by their abilities to check each other. But including the House, Hamilton argued, would go too far toward paralysis, becoming a "source of so great inconvenience and expence."[70]

The President, on the other hand, can act swiftly and secretly, with vigor and energy.[71] But he cannot engage in the full-throated deliberation of Congress, nor call on the same broad base of political groups for support.[72] Some functions are more suited toward executive action, and some for legislative, depending on the type of function and on the relative priority of deliberation versus swiftness for the decision in question.[73] Looked at in this way, non-self-execution matches each branch to those aspects of the treaty process to which it is best suited. The executive branch retains control of the negotiation of international agreements, where speed, secrecy, and a broad national view are the most important. If the agreement requires domestic implementation, secrecy and speed are no longer important, but balancing competing societal values and building broad political support for policy become paramount. Legislative competence outweighs the executive once the forum moves to the domestic realm.

In fact, the odd man out is the Senate, which has not come to play the role that some Framers may have hoped for.[74] It was thought that the Senate would confer some of the benefits of an advisory council. Its smaller size would allow for secrecy, while its higher age requirement and appointment by the state legislatures would

---

[69] FEDERALIST No. 75, *supra* note 48, at 507 (Alexander Hamilton) (emphasis in original).

[70] *Id. See also* Yoo, *supra* note 13, at 2038–39 (explaining that some Framers wanted to require the House's approval before a treaty had legislative effect, but they ultimately decided to exclude the House from participating formally in treatymaking because of its perceived structural limitations).

[71] FEDERALIST No. 70, *supra* note 39, at 472 (Alexander Hamilton); HAROLD H. KOH, THE NATIONAL SECURITY CONSTITUTION: SHARING POWER AFTER THE IRAN-CONTRA AFFAIR 119 (1990).

[72] *See generally* KREHBIEL, *supra* note 67; MAASS, *supra* note 67; Eskridge, *supra* note 67.

[73] Scholars such as Neil Komesar, Cass Sunstein, and Adrian Vermeule have undertaken a similar approach to questions ranging from statutory interpretation to regulatory decision-making. See, for example, NEIL K. KOMESAR, IMPERFECT ALTERNATIVES: CHOOSING INSTITUTIONS IN LAW, ECONOMICS, AND PUBLIC POLICY (1994); Cass Sunstein & Adrian Vermeule, *Interpretation and Institutions*, 101 MICH. L. REV. 885, 917–19 (2003).

[74] *See* ELKINS & MCKITRICK, *supra* note 40, at 55–58 (describing President Washington's failed attempt to consult with the first Senate on treaties). Apparently, when President Washington appeared in the Senate, the noise and confusion led to the treaty matter being deferred to another day. President Washington left in a huff, and according to one story declared that "he would be damned if he ever went there again." *Id.* at 55.

produce "the most enlightened and respectable citizens," in the words of John Jay, "who have become the most distinguished by their abilities and virtue."[75] These structural advantages have disappeared over time. The Senate today has about 50 percent more members than the first House of Representatives, undermining the idea that the Senate as a body could act swiftly and secretly. Nor can the Senate make claim to greater stability, which the Framers believed would steady American foreign policy. Senators have longer terms, but their races are more highly contested, compared with incumbency retention rates in the House (which regularly hover around 90 percent).[76] Due to the Seventeenth Amendment, senators now are elected, rather than chosen by state legislatures, drawing them closer to popular wishes and further from the vision of a less accountable council of wise men. The Senate never actively participated in diplomatic negotiations, as some (such as Jay) had anticipated. Instead, it gives its advice and consent to treaties after the executive branch has already negotiated and signed them.[77]

Moreover, the House can now play a role equal to that of the Senate in foreign policy. It has its own committees on international relations, national security, and intelligence to oversee foreign relations. The House's structural equality to the Senate is especially relevant in regard to multilateral treaties which mimic domestic legislation in their regulation of private activity within national borders. Treaties that regulate chemicals, set tariff schedules, or define civil liberties do not demand that the United States act with secrecy or speed of action. Congress regularly passes legislation in these areas without any need for special procedures. Of course, there are treaties that are sensitive, where consideration by large bodies might be harmful to the national interest. These agreements, however, tend to be political or military alliances, which usually need little, if any, domestic legislation for their implementation and therefore do not run into the presumption of non-self-execution. House cooperation, in fact, is necessary, not to enforce the treaty domestically but to guarantee that the United States will live up to its political and military commitments. Only Congress, for example, can provide the long-term funds needed for the permanent deployment of military forces called for by security alliances. But such treaties do not require any implementing legislation, as called for by the non-self-execution presumption, because they do not regulate any domestic conduct or private parties.

Non-self-execution also enhances democratic decisionmaking by reserving foreign policy decisions for the political branches. It is true that non-self-execution raises the transaction costs of making international agreements with domestic effect. An international obligation, for example, would have to receive presidential support

---

[75] FEDERALIST No. 64 at 433 (Jacob E. Cooke ed. 1961) (John Jay).

[76] See NORMAN ORNSTEIN ET AL., VITAL STATISTICS ON CONGRESS, 57, 63–64, 77, 81 (2008).

[77] John Yoo, *Treaties and Public Lawmaking: A Textual and Structural Defense of Non-Self-Execution,* 99 COLUM. L. REV. 2218, 2242 (1999); LUZIUS WILDHABER, TREATY-MAKING POWER AND CONSTITUTION: AN INTERNATIONAL AND COMPARATIVE STUDY 59–61 (1971); Riesenfeld & Abbott, *supra* note 14, at 578–82.

and two-thirds of the Senate, and then undergo the enactment of implementing legislation by both Houses and presentment to the President. A purely domestic regulation of the same subject, without the international obligation, would only require bicameralism and presentment, not the two-thirds majority of the Senate. As McGinnis has observed, this extra step in implementing a treaty increases the transaction costs for entering into international agreements, which demands a higher level of political consensus and the production of more information.[78] While this may pose obstacles for treaties that regulate the same matters as domestic regulation, it may also bring a positive trade-off when treaties make claim to authority under *Missouri v. Holland* that is unavailable to normal statutes.

Another important effect of non-self-execution is the reduction of judicial control over foreign policy. If treaties do not take automatic effect as domestic law, then courts must await further guidance from Congress and the President before their implementation. Policy concerning treaties and, through them, international relations will be set primarily by the decisions of the branches most directly accountable to the people through regular elections, rather than by an appointed federal judiciary that is designed to be highly insulated from popular wishes.[79]

This has important functional advantages. While courts are the primary institutions in the U.S. system that interpret and apply laws, some of their key features undercut their ability in foreign affairs. Courts have limited access to information and are unable to take into account the broader context for making foreign policy. These limitations are not a general failing. They are part of the inherent design of the federal court system, which is intended to be independent from politics, to allow parties to dictate the course of litigation, and to consider information in formal and narrow ways. These characteristics support the ability of the federal courts to be neutral in disputes between citizens and their government, but they also make judges less-than-competent actors in achieving national goals in international relations.[80]

Take the gathering of information. Courts receive information almost entirely from litigating parties, which acquire it through the expensive process of discovery. Information provided to the court must survive evidentiary rules for relevance, credibility, and reliability. By contrast, the executive branch collects a wide variety of information through its own institutional experts and a wide network of contacts, unfiltered by courtroom rules of evidence.[81] Courts cannot update their decisions to reflect new information, but must continue to enforce statutory or treaty mandates even if the national interest would be better served by a change in policy.[82] They find

---

[78] McGinnis, *supra* note 5.

[79] *Cf.* Akhil Reed Amar, *Of Sovereignty and Federalism*, 96 YALE L.J. 1425, 1429–66 (1987) (arguing that true sovereignty lies with the people of the United States and that therefore all government must be limited).

[80] Julian Ku & John Yoo, *Beyond Formalism in Foreign Affairs: A Functional Approach to the Alien Tort Statute*, 2004 SUP. CT. REV. 153, 182.

[81] *Id.* at 183.

[82] *See, e.g.*, Thomas R. Lee, *Stare Decisis in Economic Perspective: An Economic Analysis of the Supreme Court's Doctrine of Precedent*, 78 N.C. L. REV. 643 (2000).

it difficult to use that information to reach quick decisions, and the structure of the federal court system is not ideally designed to produce feedback that can lead to the swift correction of mistakes.[83]

The political branches, by contrast, have superior institutional competencies. Unlike generalist judges, the executive branch possesses expertise in complex areas such as foreign affairs. The defense, diplomatic, and intelligence agencies are large bureaucracies solely focused on developing and implementing foreign policy, and they maintain a broad network to gather and process information.[84] Congress also has a specialized staff that can engage in both formal and informal methods for fact-finding through hearings or political contacts. Neither branch is required to consider problems through the narrow lens of a lawsuit, which may present anomalous parties and facts; instead, each branch can set policy with a broader perspective. Congress can enact nationwide rules more quickly than the courts, while the executive branch can respond with the greatest speed to changes in complex factual settings.

Which institutions ought to have the lead role should depend on their functional suitability and the normative goals for that subject area. In the area of civil liberties, for example, our legal system depends more heavily on courts because we have decided to provide the individual with protections against the actions of the majority.[85] The institution most insulated from political influence reduces the government's advantages vis-à-vis the individual; devoting more resources to formal information gathering and deliberation at the expense of speed becomes a virtue, rather than a fault. In functional terms, we worry more about the costs of errors than the costs incurred in making the decision itself.

Foreign policy, on the other hand, entails a different trade-off. The harms of reaching a decision too slowly may outweigh the costs of an erroneous policy. If the United States must react quickly to an overseas threat or sudden change in circumstances, the delay of a decision itself may be costly. The increased expense in using the judicial system to set policy may itself yield no reduction in errors, especially if the courts cannot access better information. Changes in foreign conditions require the United States to shift policies with speed, or to set policy with the broader national interest in view.

Treaty implementation forms a core element of foreign policy. The United States may wish to sign treaties, but implement only some of them domestically. It may want to adopt provisions in a certain way in order to improve its bargaining position. It may want to retain the flexibility to apply treaty obligations in different ways depending on other outstanding issues between itself and another state.

---

[83] See Martin Shapiro, *Toward a Theory of Stare Decisis*, 1 J. LEGAL STUD. 125, 125–34 (1972).

[84] *See* Ku & Yoo, *supra* note 80, at 194–95 (explaining that the State Department and foreign affairs agencies operate on a far greater budget than the federal judiciary and employ experts who understand the culture and politics of particular regions and who have access to classified data essential to understanding foreign policy).

[85] *See* JESSE H. CHOPER, JUDICIAL REVIEW AND THE NATIONAL POLITICAL PROCESS: A FUNCTIONAL RECONSIDERATION OF THE ROLE OF THE SUPREME COURT 67–70 (1980).

The United States may even want to preserve the ability to suspend the treaty, if the circumstances require it. Domestic politics may demand that no change in internal laws occur in order to win approval of an agreement in the Senate. Carrying out a treaty domestically, in other words, is intimately tied up with the question of whether the United States will fulfill international obligations and rules, or whether those obligations and rules even exist. Courts are poor institutional actors to make the type of delicate trade-offs and policy decisions involved. The political branches are better suited to international relations not just in terms of quality of information and speed of action, but also in balancing legal considerations against political, security, and economic values that are outside the judiciary's ken.

An important objection to requiring House implementation of treaty obligations is that it creates an unjustified gap in federal law. Treaties would be essentially read out of the Supremacy Clause's guarantee of law-of-the-land status because they could not be enforced by the courts. Carlos Vazquez, for example, argues that the Supremacy Clause demonstrates the intent to "adopt the very same mechanism for enforcing treaties, federal statutes, and the Constitution itself."[86] This logic falters, however, because it assumes that all species of federal law are automatically enforceable. Basic parts of the Constitution, such as the establishment of the federal courts and their jurisdiction, are not automatically enforceable, but wait upon congressional action to take life.[87] Statutory law also cannot be enforced directly in the courts unless Congress deliberately creates a right of action for private individuals.[88]

Asking the courts to fly a holding pattern until the political branches have decided whether and how to implement international agreements raises concerns held by the judiciary itself over its proper role in foreign affairs. The federal courts have expressed their relative lack of competence on international relations in the political question doctrine, which prohibits the judiciary from deciding certain questions of constitutional law that are textually committed to another branch or are impervious to judicially manageable standards.[89] Courts, for example, refused to hear cases challenging the President's use of military force without a declaration of war during

[86] Carlos Manuel Vazquez, *Treaty-Based Rights and Remedies of Individuals*, 92 Colum. L. Rev. 1082, 1108 (1992).

[87] Fallon et al., *supra* note 24, at 28. There is a strong debate, however, about whether certain classes of federal jurisdiction were considered mandatory and had to be vested by Congress in the federal courts. *See, e.g.*, Akhil R. Amar, *Neo-Federalist View of Article III: Separating the Two Tiers of Federal Jurisdiction*, 65 B.U. L. Rev. 205, 260–62; Amar, *supra* note 23; Robert N. Clinton, *A Mandatory View of Federal Court Jurisdiction: Early Implementation of and Departures from the Constitutional Plan*, 86 Colum. L. Rev. 1515, 1561–70 (1986).

[88] Fallon et al., *supra* note 24, at 840–41.

[89] *See generally* John Hart Ely, War and Responsibility: Constitutional Lessons of Vietnam and Its Aftermath 55–56 (1993); Thomas M. Franck, Political Questions/Judicial Answers: Does the Rule of Law Apply to Foreign Affairs? 3–9 (1992); Michael J. Glennon, Constitutional Diplomacy, xix—xxi (1990); Koh, *supra* note 71; Michael Tigar, *Judicial Power, the "Political Question Doctrine," and Foreign Relations*, 17 UCLA L. Rev. 1135, 1135–36 (1970).

the Vietnam conflict, interventions during the Reagan, Bush, and Clinton administrations, and the Iraq campaign.[90] As the Supreme Court recognized in *Baker v. Carr*, the progenitors of the modern political question doctrine included several cases in the foreign affairs area.[91] Justice Brennan observed, "[N]ot only does resolution of [foreign affairs] issues frequently turn on standards that defy judicial application, or involve the exercise of a discretion demonstrably committed to the executive or legislature; but many such questions uniquely demand single-voiced statement of the Government's views."[92] Similar concerns led a four-Justice plurality to dismiss *Goldwater v. Carter*, which challenged the President's unilateral termination of a mutual defense treaty with Taiwan.[93] Both cases echo Justice Sutherland's concerns in *United States v. Curtiss-Wright* that "in this vast external realm, with its important, complicated, delicate and manifold problems," the federal courts should defer to the political branches in their management of foreign relations.[94]

We should raise here two caveats. We are not arguing that the federal courts cannot decide any cases involving foreign relations. Obviously, they have decided and do decide such cases, and as the Court's growing intervention in the cases arising out of the detention of suspected terrorists at Guantánamo Bay shows, they may be deciding more such issues in the future than they have in the past.[95] Chapters 5 and 7 will explain the types of foreign affairs cases best decided by the courts and those best left to the political branches. Here, we raise these cases only to show that the courts themselves are aware of their deficiencies, from a comparative institutional perspective, in deciding issues that involve foreign affairs. Non-self-execution better accords with the structural differences between the political branches and the courts and with the Constitution's allocation of authority in foreign affairs. Waiting for congressional implementation of international law allows the courts to avoid the

---

[90] *See, e.g.,* DaCosta v. Laird, 405 U.S. 979, 979 (1972); Massachusetts v. Laird, 400 U.S. 886 (1970) (finding challenge to Vietnam War a nonjusticiable political question); Mor v. McNamara, 389 U.S. 934, 934 (1967); Dellums v. Bush, 752 F. Supp. 1141, 1146 (D.D.C. 1990) (holding that "the judicial Branch should not decide issues affecting the allocation of power between the President and Congress until the political branches reach a constitutional impasse"); Ange v. Bush, 752 F. Supp. 509, 512–15 (D.D.C. 1990); Lowry v. Reagan, 676 F. Supp. 333, 340 (D.D.C. 1987) (holding that the "judicial branch . . . is neither equipped or empowered to intrude into the realm of foreign affairs"). Sanchez-Espinoza v. Reagan, 770 F.2d 202, 210 (D.C. Cir. 1985) (dismissing a war powers claim as not ripe for judicial review); Crockett v. Reagan, 720 F.2d 1355, 1356 (D.C. Cir. 1983) (holding that the war powers issue presented a nonjusticiable political question); Holtzman v. Schlesinger, 484 F.2d 1307, 1310 (2d Cir. 1973).

[91] 369 U.S. 186 (1962).

[92] *Id.* at 211.

[93] 444 U.S. 996, 1002 (1979) (plurality opinion of Rehnquist, J.).

[94] 299 U.S. 304, 319 (1936). Scholars have not been kind to Justice Sutherland's analysis. For critical discussion of Curtiss-Wright, see David M. Levitan, *The Foreign Relations Power: An Analysis of Mr. Justice Sutherland's Theory,* 55 Yale L.J. 467 (1946); Charles A. Lofgren, *United States v. Curtiss-Wright Export Corporation: An Historical Reassessment,* 83 Yale L.J. 1 (1973); Henkin, *supra* note 9, at 19–20.

[95] *See, e.g.,* Boumediene v. Bush, 553 U.S. 723 (2008).

difficult policy questions inherent in determining how best to execute the nation's international obligations.

It should also be clear that non-self-execution does not prevent the United States from meeting its treaty obligations. The government can implement any treaty it chooses domestically so long as the law is created in the same way it would have been made had there been no international obligation. Thus, non-self-execution becomes a device that matches decision-making to institutional competence, rather than an obstacle to national compliance with treaties and international law. Non-self-execution advances constitutional values by enhancing the transparency and accountability of the process used to incorporate international law into the domestic legal system, and by keeping the federal government within the scope of its enumerated powers. Requiring Congress's participation to give treaties domestic legal effect will keep treaties from vesting the federal government with more power, vis-à-vis the states, than it would otherwise have done under the Constitution. Non-self-execution will prevent treaties from distorting the separation of powers, whose maintenance has been described by the Supreme Court as critical for the preservation of individual liberty.

5 Presidents and Customary International Law

Tensions between globalization and the domestic legal and political orders peak in the area of customary international law (CIL). At first glance, it is not obvious why unwritten international rules should threaten the disruption of the domestic constitutional system. We have seen that treaties create difficulties because, under the Supremacy Clause, they receive the status of federal law. Unwritten international law, by contrast, goes unmentioned in the Supremacy Clause or Article III's enumeration of the cases and controversies that fall within the jurisdiction of the federal courts. The Constitution only mentions CIL in Article I, Section 8, which gives Congress the power to "define and punish Piracies and Felonies committed on the high Seas, and Offenses against the Law of Nations."[1] As the "Law of Nations" was the rough eighteenth-century equivalent to today's CIL, the Constitution suggests that CIL does not operate within the United States unless Congress implements it. The Constitution treats CIL as a rare bird, seen only when Congress chooses.

Yet globalization has made CIL much more common than the Framers of the eighteenth century anticipated. Historically, most international rules were not codified in treaties, but instead were established through the long, consistent practice of nation-states. Even as early as the Washington administration, the meaning of CIL became a heated political issue. Confronted with the European wars, President

---

[1] U.S. Const. art. I, § 8.

Washington and his cabinet looked to CIL to decide whether the United States could suspend or terminate its alliance with France.[2] Today, CIL continues to play a similar role in high politics, as when the Clinton administration relied on rules of state succession to claim that the Anti-Ballistic Missile Treaty remained in force even after the collapse of the Soviet Union, and when the Bush administration relied on the laws of war to detain al-Qaeda terrorists for trial in military courts.[3]

As globalization has increased the impact of foreign activity on the United States, the presence of international rules has inevitably expanded. This has occurred in both the private and public spheres. In the private sphere, CIL provides rules governing trade, investment, business transactions, and even canons for interpreting treaties. For example, a claim by a new democratic regime that it should not have to pay the "odious debts" run up by its dictatorial predecessor would depend on CIL. In cases filed in U.S. courts under the Alien Tort Statute, plaintiffs from other nations rely on CIL to claim that multinational corporations have violated international norms when operating in their countries. In the public sphere, the United States claims support from CIL to protect its ships on the high seas and to use force to protect American citizens and interests abroad. Much as the common law operates in the domestic legal system, CIL provides the default rules for most areas of international affairs, while treaties extend primarily to discrete and specialized subjects.[4]

Globalization makes interpreting and applying CIL a necessity for the domestic legal system. It is not just important for the management of American economic relations with the world economy. It is also a permanent feature of American foreign relations. Compliance with CIL can advance U.S. goals when international

---

[2] Washington sent a list of thirteen questions to Hamilton, Jefferson, Knox, and Randolph concerning the interpretation of the 1778 treaties with France. Letter from President George Washington to Alexander Hamilton, Thomas Jefferson, Henry Knox, and Edmund Randolph (Apr. 18, 1793), in 14 THE PAPERS OF ALEXANDER HAMILTON 326–27 (Harold Syrett ed., 1965). Jefferson responded that international law did not permit suspension of the treaties, while Hamilton and Knox argued that the new circumstances threatening national security justified termination. Opinion on the Treaties with France (Apr. 28, 1973), in 25 THE PAPERS OF THOMAS JEFFERSON 608–18 (Julian P. Boyd ed., 1974); Letter from Hamilton & Knox to Washington (May 2, 1793), in 14 PAPERS OF ALEXANDER HAMILTON, at 367–96.

[3] Memorandum of Understanding Relating to the Treaty between the United States of America and the Union of Soviet Socialist Republics on the Limitation of Anti-Ballistic Missile Systems of May 26, 1972, Sept. 26, 1997. Republican Senators claimed that the fall of the Soviet Union terminated the ABM Treaty, but Clinton maintained that "there is no question that the ABM Treaty has continued in force and will continue in force, even if the MOU is not ratified." Letter from President William J. Clinton to Benjamin A. Gilman (May 21, 1998). For discussion of the rules of war and the use of military courts, see JOHN YOO, WAR BY OTHER MEANS: AN INSIDER'S ACCOUNT OF THE WAR ON TERROR 220–30 (2006); JOHN ALAN APPLEMAN, MILITARY TRIBUNALS AND INTERNATIONAL CRIMES (1971); WILLIAM WINTHROP, MILITARY LAW AND PRECEDENTS (2d ed. 1920).

[4] Restatement (Third) of the Foreign Relations Law of the United States, Introductory Note, §§ 111 cmt. d (1987) ("To this day, however, many rules about status, property, and international delicts are still customary law, not yet codified"). For a critical view of CIL's status as federal common law, see Curtis A. Bradley & Jack L. Goldsmith, *Customary International Law as Federal Common Law: A Critique of the Modern Position*, 110 HARV. L. REV. 815 (1997).

rules play to national advantage, such as the availability of neutrality during the French Revolution. Obeying CIL can also help signal the nation's commitment to keep its international obligations, creating a level of credibility that will ease future international cooperation. But this does not mean that the United States will achieve its national interest by obeying all rules of CIL at all times. At times, the stakes involved in a national security crisis may well outweigh any long-term benefits of automatic compliance with international law. While the rules of neutrality seemed to serve the United States well in the Anglo-French wars in the 1790s and 1800s, for example, they unduly constrained the nation from supporting the allies against Nazi Germany in the early years of World War II. Because of the national interests at issue in foreign relations, international law invokes another set of considerations that do not arise with compliance questions in domestic law.

Our legal system has had an uneasy relationship with CIL. With bilateral or multilateral treaties, the President and two-thirds of the Senate must consent before the United States becomes legally bound. But with CIL, the United States does not participate in a democratic lawmaking process. CIL arises through the practice of states, rather than a legislative assembly where the United States is formally represented. The majority of the states that have followed the practice may or may not be democratic themselves. Scholars believe that this practice can constitute a form of majority approval, but some scholars even believe that a rule of CIL can bind states that have not consented, so long as the practice is "universal" enough, or a state has not persistently and publicly objected to it.[5]

Some leading foreign relations scholars share the view that CIL even amounts to self-executing federal law that must be given direct effect by the courts, preempting state law and binding the President and Congress.[6] Surprisingly, little critical assessment of this contention exists, aside from that by Curtis Bradley and Jack Goldsmith, Philip Trimble, and Arthur Weisburd.[7]

Strong criticism of this expansive view of CIL is long overdue. Automatically-enforced CIL would pose an even greater challenge to popular sovereignty than

---

[5] See, e.g., Restatement (Third), *supra* note 4, at §§ 102 cmt. b (1987) ("Inaction may constitute state practice, as when a state acquiesces in acts of another state that affect its legal rights. . . A practice can be general even if it is not universally followed; there is no precise formula to indicate how widespread a practice must be, but it should reflect wide acceptance among the states particularly involved in the relevant activity"); Karol Wolfke, Custom in Present International Law 160–69 (2d ed. 1993); I. C. MacGibbon, *The Scope of Acquiescence in International Law*, 31 Brit. Y.B. Int'l L. 143 (1954). For critical perspectives of this conception of CIL, see Anthony D'Amato, The Concept of Custom in International Law 68–70 (1971). J. Patrick Kelly, *The Twilight of Customary International Law*, 40 Va. J. Int'l L. 449, 469–75 (2000).

[6] See, e.g., Harold Koh, *Is International Law Really State Law?*, 111 Harv. L. Rev. 1824 (1998); Lea Brilmayer, *Federalism, State Authority, and the Preemptive Power of International Law*, 1994 S. Ct. Rev. 295 (1994); Louis Henkin, *International Law as Law in the United States*, 82 Mich. L. Rev. 1555 (1984).

[7] See Philip R. Trimble, *A Revisionist View of Customary International Law*, 33 UCLA L. Rev. 665, 671 (1986); and Arthur M. Weisburd, *The Executive Branch and International Law*, 41 Vand. L. Rev. 1205 (1988).

other forms of international law and cooperation. Accepting CIL as self-executing federal law, for example, would have the revolutionary effect of circumscribing the President's authority as chief executive and Commander-in-Chief. There are some statements during the early Republic that suggest some Framers believed, after the Constitution's adoption, that federal law included CIL, but the significance of this history has been overinterpreted. Practice, when more completely read, seems to stand for the opposite proposition: that the Constitution does not automatically make CIL domestic law, nor are Presidents prohibited from taking actions under their constitutional authorities that run counter to CIL.[8]

Self-executing CIL would also remove significant policy-making discretion from the political branches in the area where their functional advantages are at their height—the management of foreign affairs. As international affairs impact the economy and society with ever greater influence, self-executing CIL would transfer authority over decisions that were once wholly the province of democratic decision-making processes to a branch of government (the courts) over which the people have relatively little control. For this reason, we argue that far from being "bound" by judicial interpretations of CIL, the President should have the authority to independently interpret CIL, and then allow it to assume the status of federal law only after congressional action. This would shore up the democratic basis for international law and harmonize it with the constitutional lawmaking process.

We are not arguing that presidents should ignore CIL: compliance, or at least *perceived* compliance, with international law is likely to be an asset in American foreign policy.[9] Nor are we addressing whether and how customary international rules legally bind the United States as a matter of international law. Our inquiry is limited to the status of customary international rules as domestic law and their relevance to the separation of powers. We will discuss customary international law's effects on federalism in the next chapter. Our Constitution does not recognize customary international rules as federal law unless the political branches actively incorporate them. Whether Presidents should follow CIL in the exercise of their constitutional authorities remains a policy question that is context specific, and the same is true for Congress and the courts.

---

[8] A few Founders stated that the Law of Nations was the law of the land during the neutrality prosecutions in the 1790s. See, e.g., Henfield's Case, 11 F. Cas. 1099, 1100–01 (C.C.D. Pa. 1793) (No. 6390) (Grand Jury charge of Jay, C.J.); *id.* at 1117 (Grand Jury charge of Wilson, J.). Alexander Hamilton, writing as Pacificus, stated that the Law of Nations was U.S. law, and Attorney General Edmund Randolph made a similar statement in a legal opinion. "Pacificus" Number 1 (June 1973), reprinted in 15 PAPERS OF ALEXANDER HAMILTON, *supra* note 2, at 40; 1 Op. Att'y Gen. 26, 27 (1792) (Attorney General Randolph). But see Robert Delahunty & John Yoo, Executive Power vs. International Law, 30 HARV. J. L. & PUB. POL'Y 73, 76–88 (2006) (arguing that customary international law should not be interpreted to bind the President).

[9] This point is made forcefully and repeatedly in DAVID KENNEDY, OF LAW AND WAR (2006). Equally, however, legal constraints can operate as liabilities in waging war, creating vulnerabilities and asymmetric opportunities for adversaries not so constrained. See ROGER W. BARNETT, ASYMMETRICAL WARFARE: TODAY'S CHALLENGE TO U.S. MILITARY POWER (2003).

I. THE FORMAL BASIS FOR THE PRESIDENT'S POWER OVER INTERNATIONAL LAW

If it is true that most states follow most international law most of the time, the same probably goes for presidents, too. Whether presidents follow international law out of a belief that they, and the United States, must comply with it, or whether they follow international law because much of it simply describes general patterns of state conduct, remains vigorously debated.[10] Presidents, however, have stretched or even violated CIL at significant moments in American history where important national security and foreign policy goals were at stake. Rather than executive overreaching, presidential ability to interpret CIL advances important democratic values and has been blessed by the courts. By recognizing the Executive's authority to interpret international law, our constitutional system can ensure that international rules take no effect until an elected and accountable branch of the government has decided to implement them. Without the President or Congress involved, international law would rule solely through the courts, the branch of government least accountable to the people, without undergoing the normal constitutional process for making binding federal law.

Yet this is not the position taken by many scholars of American foreign relations and international law. Recently, international law has served as a political rallying point against the antiterrorism policies of the Bush administration regarding the use of force, detention, interrogation, and military trial. Academic critics of the Bush administration made a broad argument: violations of CIL violate not only international law, but also the Constitution.[11] Repeating claims made against the Reagan administration, this argument asserts that the Constitution includes international law in the Laws of the Land under Article VI of the Supremacy Clause.[12] According to this argument, Article II's requirement that the President enforce the law includes the enforcement of international law. "There can be little doubt," Professor Louis Henkin has argued, "that the President has the duty, as well as the authority, to take

---

[10] Compare Louis Henkin, How Nations Behave (1979); with Jack Goldsmith & Eric Posner, The Limits of International Law (2005).

[11] See, e.g., David Golove, *Military Tribunals, International Law, and the Constitution: A Franckian-Madisonian Approach*, 35 N.Y.U. J. Int'l L. & Pol. 363, 364 (2003); Derek Jinks & David Sloss, *Is the President Bound by the Geneva Conventions?*, 90 Cornell L. Rev. 97 (2004); Jordan J. Paust, *Customary International Law and Human Rights Treaties Are Law of the United States*, 20 Mich. J. Int'l L. 301 (1999); Jordan J. Paust, *Executive Plans and Authorizations to Violate International Law Concerning Treatment and Interrogation of Detainees*, 43 Colum. J. Transnat'l L. 811, 855–56 (2005); Jordan J. Paust, *Judicial Power to Determine the Status and Rights of Persons Detained without Trial*, 44 Harv. Int'l L.J. 503, 518–19 (2003).

[12] Michael J. Glennon, *Raising the Paquete Habana: Is Violation of Customary International Law by the Executive Unconstitutional?*, 80 Nw. U. L. Rev. 321, 363 (1985); Henkin, *International Law as Law*, supra note 6, at 1566. See also Jonathan I. Charney, *The Power of the Executive Branch of the United States Government to Violate Customary International Law*, 80 Am. J. Int'l L. 913 (1986); Jules Lobel, *The Limits of Constitutional Power: Conflicts between Foreign Policy and International Law*, 71 Va. L. Rev. 1071, 1179 (1985).

care that international law, as part of the law of the United States, is faithfully executed."[13]

There are three possible versions of the argument against recognizing the President's authority to violate CIL.[14] By one account, international law is binding on the President unless he is exercising a statutory authority: he has no independent constitutional right to violate international law. A second view is that international law is binding on the President unless he is exercising his constitutional authority: a delegation of power from Congress is insufficient for that end. A third claim is that the President cannot violate certain forms of international law *regardless* of his domestic authority.[15] One corollary of holding that international law constitutes federal law under the Supremacy Clause is that federal courts should be able to enjoin the President from violating it in properly brought cases. All of these approaches, in our view, make the mistake of viewing CIL as federal law without any act of congressional or presidential adoption. But since CIL does not automatically have the status of law under our domestic constitutional system, Presidents have the greater power to violate CIL as well as the lesser power to interpret it at odds with the views of other nations.

The academic criticism of presidential violations of international law does not describe judicial opinion instead, it is normative in design. The leading Supreme Court case on the point, *The Paquete Habana*, states that "[i]nternational law is part of our law" but that "the customs and usages of civilized nations" will be given effect only if "there is no treaty, and no controlling executive or legislative act or judicial decision" to the contrary.[16] While supporters of CIL's restraint on presidential power take comfort from the first part of *The Paquete Habana*'s holding, the Court also clearly held that the President could override customary international law.[17] It did not distinguish between presidential acts that conflict with international law beforehand or afterward. As far as we are aware, no federal court of appeals has ever held that CIL limits presidential decisions,[18] and the only district court that comes

[13] Henkin, *International Law as Law, supra* note 6, at 1567.

[14] See John O. McGinnis & Ilya Somin, *Should International Law Be Part of Our Law?*, 59 Stan L. Rev. 1175 (2007).

[15] Lobel, *Limits of Constitutional Power, supra* note 12, at 1075.

[16] The Paquete Habana, 175 U.S. 677, 700 (1900).

[17] See *id.* See also Restatement of Law: Foreign Relations Law of the United States section 131 cmt. c: "the President, acting within his constitutional authority, may have the power under the Constitution to act in ways that constitute violations of international law by the United States"; see also Mike Paulsen, *The Constitutional Power to Interpret International Law*, 118 Yale L.J. 1762 (2009).

[18] See, e.g., Barrera-Echavarria v. Rison, 44 F.3d 1441, 1451 (9th Cir. 1995); Gisbert v. U.S. Att'y Gen., 988 F.2d 1437, 1448 (5th Cir. 1993); Garcia-Mir v. Meese, 788 F.2d 1446, 1454–55 (11th Cir. 1986). In fact, a recent decision of the U.S. Court of Appeals for the District of Columbia held that customary international law does not constrain the President's exercise of his Commander-in-Chief powers and powers delegated to him by Congress after the September 11 terrorist attacks. Al-Bihani v. Obama, 590 F.3d 866 (D.C. Cir. 2010), pet. for rehrg en banc denied, Al-Bihani v. Obama, No. 09-5051 (Aug. 31, 2010).

close to reaching such a conclusion was affirmed, though the court of appeals did not address the issue.[19] In the terrorism cases over the past ten years, the Supreme Court never held that CIL as interpreted by the courts binds the President. Rather, the Court has expanded the rights of alien detainees under the Constitution's habeas corpus and due process clauses or the acts of the political branches, such as the Geneva Conventions, the Uniform Code of Military Justice, and the Military Commissions Act.[20]

Much attention has focused on the applicability of CIL in domestic law through the Alien Tort Statute (ATS). So far, courts have found that sovereign immunity precludes ATS suits against the U.S. government and, presumably, the President.[21] Indeed, in *Sosa v. Alvarez-Machain*, the Supreme Court in 2005 dismissed the claim of a Mexican drug cartel doctor who claimed that his kidnapping by American agents had violated CIL.[22] The Justices held that a norm against arbitrary detention had not achieved the broad acceptance and specific definition necessary to win inclusion among the limited causes of action permissible under the ATS.[23] Since the CIL rule had not been incorporated by Congress, it could not supply a cause of action and had no domestic legal force of its own.

Arguments that CIL constitutes domestic law depend on the Supremacy Clause. Only if Article VI recognizes international law as constituting federal law would it fall within the President's Article II obligation to "take Care that the Laws be faithfully executed."[24] The Supremacy Clause itself only mentions one species of international law: treaties. "This Constitution, and the Laws of the United States which shall be made in Pursuance thereof; and all Treaties made, or which shall be made, under the Authority of the United States," Article VI declares, "shall be the supreme Law of the Land."[25] Article VI recognizes that treaties are federal law and therefore must be enforced by the President, subject to any powers he has to suspend or terminate them.

There are compelling textual reasons to conclude that the Supremacy Clause recognizes only treaties, and not unwritten forms of international law, as federal law. Article VI lists the Constitution first as receiving supremacy effect. In second place are not just laws, but "Laws of the United States which shall be made in Pursuance thereof." This phrasing suggests that it is the "Laws of the United States"

---

[19] Rodriguez Fernandez v. Wilkinson, 505 F. Supp. 787, 800 (D. Kan. 1980), aff'd, 654 F.2d 1382, 1388 (10th Cir. 1981).

[20] See Hamdi v. Rumsfeld, 542 U.S. 507 (2004); Hamdan v. Rumsfeld, 548 U.S. 557 (2006); Boumediene v. Bush, 553 U.S. 723 (2008).

[21] Sanchez-Espinoza v. Reagan, 770 F.2d 202, 207 (D.C. Cir. 1985) ("The Alien Tort Statute itself is not a waiver of sovereign immunity"); El-Shifa Pharm. Indus. Co. v. United States, 402 F. Supp. 2d 267, 272–73 (D. D.C. 2005) (holding [1] the ATS does not waive sovereign immunity and [2] the Administrative Procedure Act does not waive the sovereign immunity of the President, which is not an agency within the Act).

[22] 542 U.S. 692 (2004).

[23] *Id.* at 738.

[24] U.S. Const. art. II, § 3.

[25] *Id.* art. VI, cl. 2.

and not other sources of law that are supreme. The only place where the Constitution discusses the making of a "Law of the United States" is in Article I, Section 7's bicameralism and presentment clauses.[26] As Bradford Clark has argued, the Framers deliberately linked the Supremacy Clause with Article I, Section 7 in order to ensure that the Senate would be involved in the making of all species of federal law.[27] CIL never undergoes the Article I, Section 7 process and hence cannot assume that status.

The Supremacy Clause's use of the phrase "which shall be made" further disputes international law's status as federal law. This language indicates that the "Laws of the United States" were to be made in the future, that is, after the ratification of the Constitution. "Laws of the United States" did not already exist at the time of the writing or adoption of the Constitution, so they could not have included international law. The Law of Nations, as the Framers called it, existed prior to and independent of the Constitution. Another way of seeing this point is to compare the Supremacy Clause's description of statutes with its description of treaties. Article VI gives supremacy to treaties "made, or which shall be made." Supremacy extends both to treaties that the President and the Senate will agree to in the future and to treaties that existed before the Constitution. This latter category included most prominently the 1783 Treaty of Paris, which recognized the United States' independence from Britain.[28]

In Article VI, the Framers were quite specific about which laws and treaties would receive supremacy effect. It seems clear that they did not intend to incorporate a body of law that existed before the adoption of the Constitution, except for a handful of treaties. The Supremacy Clause explicitly distinguishes between different forms of international law, and gives only one of them supremacy effect. Article VI elevates treaties to the level of supreme federal law. It does not mention the other form of international law at the time, the "Law of Nations." This shows that the Framers knew how to distinguish between different types of international law (treaties and the Law of Nations) and that they were aware that they could give supremacy to a body of international law that existed before the Constitution. We know that the Framers were well aware of the Law of Nations because in Article I, Section 8, they gave Congress the power to define and punish its violation.[29] It would run counter to standard methods of interpretation to read the Supremacy Clause's "Laws of the United States" to include CIL when the Constitution separately mentions the Law of Nations.[30] Giving full effect to the Supremacy Clause's explicit

---

[26] See *id.* art. I, § 7, cl. 2–3.

[27] See, e.g., Bradford R. Clark, *Separation of Powers as a Safeguard of Federalism*, 79 Tex. L. Rev. 1321 (2001).

[28] Definitive Treaty of Peace between Great Britain and the United States, Sept. 3, 1783, U.S.-Gr. Brit., 48 Consol. T.S. 487.

[29] See U.S. Const. art. I, § 8, cl. 10.

[30] See, e.g., Keene Corp. v. United States, 508 U.S. 200, 208 (1993) ("where Congress includes particular language in one section of a statute but omits it in another . . . , it is generally presumed that Congress acts intentionally and purposefully in the disparate inclusion or exclusion")

mention of treaties recommends against importing the Law of Nations, which went unmentioned, into federal law.

The Supremacy Clause's use of the phrase "made in Pursuance thereof" requires that any laws of the United States entitled to supremacy must undergo the procedures set out in the Constitution. As one of us has argued elsewhere, this language even suggests that the laws made by Congress must comport with the Constitution, not just as a procedural but also as a substantive matter.[31] At a minimum, those who argue over the legitimacy of judicial review agree that "made in Pursuance thereof" requires that all laws of the United States undergo the procedural requirements of bicameralism and presentment. International law is not made pursuant to the Constitution, but by the practice and agreement of states. It does not undergo the same bicameralism and presentment that apply to the laws of the United States.[32]

Since *Marbury v. Madison*, courts have recognized the supremacy of the Constitution over all other types of the law in the U.S. system. In *Marbury*, Congress could not change the constitutional limits on the jurisdiction of the federal courts. Here, a valid exercise of constitutional authority cannot be restricted either by a statute or by international law, because neither source of law can override the Constitution. One might argue, however, that the President has a duty to enforce laws that go beyond positive federal law. Both Ernest Young and Michael Ramsey, for example, suggest that CIL enjoys the status of pre-*Erie* general federal common law that could provide a rule of decision in an appropriate case but would not preempt state law or give rise to federal question jurisdiction.[33] One implication of this, which Professor Ramsey seems to follow, is that international law might be included within the "Laws" in Article II's Faithful Execution Clause, even though it would not be within the Supremacy Clause's enumeration of federal law.[34]

This argument usually depends on the statements of Framers during the early Republic. There do not appear to be any comments during the ratification period itself, however, that support the claim. If this view were correct, the President could enforce CIL within the domestic United States in the absence of a statute. President Washington, for example, would have been on firm constitutional ground in ordering the prosecution of American citizens who violated the Proclamation of Neutrality

(quoting Russelo v. United States, 464 U.S. 16, 23 [1983]); Central Bank of Denver v. First Interstate Bank, 511 U.S. 165, 176–77 (1994) (applying the maxim of "Congress knows how to say" to show that the omission of certain terms was intentional).

[31] Saikrishna B. Prakash & John C. Yoo, *The Origins of Judicial Review*, 70 U. Chi. L. Rev. 887, 903–09 (2003).

[32] Cf. INS v. Chadha, 462 U.S. 919, 946–51 (1983) (discussing the Constitution's bicameralism requirement and presentment clauses).

[33] Michael D. Ramsey, *International Law as Non-preemptive Federal Law*, 42 Va. J. Int'l L. 555, 556–57 (2002); Ernest A. Young, *Sorting Out the Debate over Customary International Law*, 42 Va. J. Int'l L. 365, 392–94 (2002).

[34] See Ramsey, *supra* note 33, at 576–84.

in the French Revolutionary Wars,[35] even though Congress had yet to enact any criminal sanctions for its violation.[36] It is true that, while sitting as lower court judges, some Supreme Court Justices, such as Chief Justice John Jay, gave jury charges declaring international law to be enforceable federal law.[37] Although Washington and his cabinet believed that the President could unilaterally enforce CIL, juries acquitted defendants charged under the Proclamation. In response, President Washington asked Congress to enact a criminal law, which it did in 1794.[38] In 1812, the Supreme Court resolved any confusion in *United States v. Hudson & Goodwin*, which held that no federal common law of crimes exists.[39] At the very least, these events demonstrate that no consensus held sway among the Framing generation in favor of the idea that the President could enforce nonstatutory, non-treaty-based international law. If anything, the resolution of the Neutrality Proclamation prosecutions suggests the exact opposite.

Other parts of the Constitution also seem to challenge the view that international law has the status of federal law. Article I, Section 8 enumerates a variety of congressional powers, such as the authority of Congress "to define and punish Piracies and Felonies committed on the high Seas, and Offences against the Law of Nations."[40] This provision empowers Congress to incorporate customary international law into federal law, which would be unnecessary if the Law of Nations were already domestic law. If the Laws of Nations were already federal law, there would be no need for the Constitution to grant Congress an explicit power to criminalize their violation, because Congress would already have that discretion under the Necessary and Proper Clause (just as Congress can criminalize activity within reach of the Interstate Commerce Clause).

Requiring that Presidents obey CIL in the exercise of their Commander-in-Chief or chief executive authority would distort the constitutional structure by raising the authority of international law above that of ordinary federal statutes. Ordinary statutes cannot infringe on the President's valid constitutional power; for example, a statute could not forbid the President from exercising his removal authority over an executive branch official. This restriction arises from the same reasoning that forbids Congress from interfering with the Constitution's conferral of the judicial power on the federal courts.[41] The Constitution is the highest form of federal law, and its distribution of authority among the branches cannot be overridden by

---

[35] George Washington, Proclamation of Neutrality (1793), reprinted in 32 The Writings of George Washington from the Original Manuscript Sources 1745–1799, at 430–31 (John C. Fitzpatrick ed., 1939).

[36] Congress did not pass a criminal law enforcing neutrality until 1794. Neutrality Act, ch. 50, 1 Stat. 381 (1794).

[37] See Henfield's Case, *supra* note 8, at 1100–05.

[38] See Neutrality Act, ch. 50, 1 Stat. 381 (1794).

[39] United States v. Hudson & Goodwin, 11 U.S. 32 (1812). See also United States v. Coolidge, 14 U.S. 415 (1816).

[40] U.S. Const. art. I, § 8, cl. 10.

[41] Cf. Steve G. Calabresi & Kevin H. Rhodes, *The Structural Constitution: Unitary Executive, Plural Judiciary*, 105 Harv. L. Rev. 1153 (1992).

statute, executive order, or judicial decision. If CIL can limit, as a matter of domestic law, what would otherwise be a valid exercise of the Commander-in-Chief or chief executive power, it would have greater force within our system than an act of Congress or a judicial decision. CIL would even have a higher status if it were permitted to limit executive authority as a general matter, rather than just acting as an obstacle to an individual presidential act.

Giving CIL a limiting effect on presidential power would also create a strange deformation in the Constitution's allocation of the foreign affairs power. Under current practice, the Constitution gives the bulk of the foreign affairs power to the President. The Supreme Court has called the President the "sole organ"[42] of the nation in its external relations. Although this conception has sometimes been questioned, there is wide agreement that the President exercises broad powers to set foreign policy, protect the national security, and make international agreements. Critics of presidential power would preclude the President in these activities from violating international law. At the same time, however, it is relatively settled that Congress can supplant international law by statute—for some reason, advocates for CIL are willing to abide by this aspect of *The Paquete Habana*.[43] This legal interpretation would give Congress the authority to supplant international law while denying that authority to the President, even though the President is thought to exercise the bulk of the nation's foreign affairs power.

There is no indication that the Framers would have intended such a result. If anything, popular sovereignty rejects it. Under this theory, the government exercises power only because it serves as the agent of the people's will. As James Madison wrote in *Federalist No. 46*, "The federal and State governments are in fact but different agents and trustees of the people, instituted with different powers, and designated for different purposes."[44] Madison reminded critics of the proposed Constitution "that the ultimate authority, wherever the derivative may be found, resides in the people alone."[45] The government can exercise only that power which the people have delegated to it, which is codified in the Constitution. Any law that conflicts with the written Constitution is illegal, because it goes beyond the delegation of power from the people to the government. As Alexander Hamilton wrote in *Federalist No. 78*, "every act of a delegated authority, contrary to the tenor

---

[42] See United States v. Curtiss-Wright Export Corp., 299 U.S. 304, 319 (1936) ("As Marshall said in his great argument of March 7, 1800, in the House of Representatives, 'The President is the sole organ of the nation in its external relations, and its sole representative with foreign nations'") (quoting 10 ANNALS OF CONG., 598, 613 (1800)); Hamdi v. Rumsfeld, 542 U.S. 507, 581 (2004) (Thomas, J., dissenting) (quoting 10 ANNALS OF CONG., 613 (1800)).

[43] Glennon, *Raising the Paquete Habana, supra* note 12, at 325. For discussion of CIL and the executive branch, see Essays, *Agora: May the President Violate Customary International Law?* 80 AM. J. INT'L L. 913 (1986); Essays, *Agora: May the President Violate Customary International Law?* (Cont'd), 81 AM. J. INT'L L. 371 (1987); *The Authority of the United States Executive to Interpret, Articulate or Violate the Norms of International Law*, 80 AM. SOC'Y INT'L L. PROC. 297 (1986).

[44] THE FEDERALIST NO. 46, at 239 (James Madison) (Max Beloff ed., 1987).

[45] *Id.*

of the commission under which it is exercised, is void."[46] If this understanding did not prevail, a written constitution would prove inconsequential because the agents could simply exercise the powers as they saw fit, regardless of the will of the people.[47] Without the basic proposition that the agents could not act beyond the power granted in the Constitution, the government, rather than the people, would be sovereign. Or, as Hamilton wrote, it "would be to affirm, that the deputy is greater than his principal . . . that men acting by virtue of powers, may do not only what their powers do not authorize, but what they forbid."[48] To preserve the basic nature of a written constitution of limited, enumerated powers, the Constitution must be "superior, paramount law" to any actions of the government it creates.[49] Therefore, any law or government action that conflicts with the Constitution must be a nullity.

This theory of popular sovereignty has important implications for CIL. The Framers were concerned that their agents—the President, Congress, or the federal courts—would make law inconsistent with the people's fundamental grant of authority in the Constitution. Hence, they decided to rely on a written Constitution to police their agents. They held this concern even though their agents would be chosen through regular election or appointment by constitutional methods and thus would be accountable to the people. In a structural sense, the written Constitution serves as an ultimate safeguard should the regular political process fail to control government officials from acting against the people's wishes. The principal-agent problem that worried the Framers would have been compounded if there were a possibility that CIL, which is created outside the American political system, was automatically part of the Law of the Land.

Scholars have identified other structural problems with treating CIL as federal law.[50] Giving CIL this status undermines the treaty power and the doctrine of non-self-execution. Even if the United States refused to sign a multilateral treaty, or signed one with the understanding that it was non-self-executing, if enough nations joined it, it would conceivably assume the status of CIL and thus become federal law without the assent of the President or Senate. As Bradley and Goldsmith have prominently argued, raising CIL to the level of federal law would run counter to *Erie R.R. Co. v. Tompkins*[51] by reintroducing a general common law enforceable by the federal courts. Under *Swift v. Tyson*, CIL had formed part of the general common law applied by federal courts in diversity cases, but was not considered to be law of

---

[46] THE FEDERALIST No. 78, at 398 (Alexander Hamilton) (Max Beloff ed., 1987).

[47] As stated by the Supreme Court, "[t]he distinction, between a government with limited and unlimited powers, is abolished, if those limits do not confine the persons on whom they are imposed, and if acts prohibited and acts allowed, are of equal obligation." Marbury v. Madison, 5 U.S. (1 Cranch) 137, 176–77 (1803).

[48] THE FEDERALIST No. 78, *supra* note 46, at 398 (Alexander Hamilton).

[49] Marbury, 5 U.S. (1 Cranch) at 177.

[50] See Weisburd, *The Executive Branch and International Law*, *supra* note 7, at 1256–67.

[51] 304 U.S. 64 (1938).

the United States for federal question jurisdiction.[52] *Erie* replaced *Swift* in favor of specialized common law in limited areas that would amount to true federal law.[53]

Formally considering international law to be federal law could run afoul of the separation of powers by interfering with the President's duty to conduct foreign relations as the "sole organ" of the United States. A President may wish to violate international law in order to create a new rule of CIL, as President Reagan did when he unilaterally extended American maritime boundaries.[54] A President, acting on behalf of the United States, may disagree with the majority of other nations that a new rule of CIL should come into being. Considering CIL to be federal law would preclude the President from engaging in these courses of action, even though under our Constitution, as interpreted by the Supreme Court, he plays the leading diplomatic role on behalf of the United States.

Recognizing these problems, defenders of the view that CIL may limit the President respond with a definitional argument. They argue that the Commander-in-Chief power, by definition, is limited by CIL.[55] This argument is usually based on materials

[52] See Swift v. Tyson, 41 U.S. (Pet. 16) 1 (1842), overruled by Erie R.R. Co. v. Tompkins, 304 U.S. 64 (1938).

[53] For discussion of the nature of federal common law, see Henry J. Friendly, *In Praise of Erie—And of the New Federal Common Law*, 39 N.Y.U. L. Rev. 383, 405–07 (1964); Bradford A. Clark, *Federal Common Law: A Structural Reinterpretation*, 144 U. Pa. L. Rev. 1245 (1996); Thomas W. Merrill, *The Common Law Powers of Federal Courts*, 52 U. Chi. L. Rev. 1 (1985); Martha Field, *Sources of Law: The Scope of Federal Common Law*, 99 Harv. L. Rev. 881 (1986).

[54] See Douglas W. Kmiec, *Office of Legal Counsel, Legal Issues Raised by the Proposed Presidential Proclamation to Extend the Territorial Sea*, 1 Terr. Sea J. 1, 9–10 (1990) (OLC Opinion), cited in In re Air Crash off Long Island, 209 F.3d 200, 205 n.9 (2d Cir. 2000).

[55] See Golove, *Franckian-Madisonian Approach, supra* note 11, at 364; Jules Lobel, *International Law Constraints*, in The U.S. Constitution and the Power to Go to War 108–12 (Gary M. Stern & Morton H. Halperin eds., 1994). See also Ingrid Brunk Wuerth, *International Law and Constitutional Interpretation: The Commander-in-Chief Clause Reconsidered*, 106 Mich. L. Rev. 61, 73–82 (2007) (arguing that presidential power is at its lowest ebb when the President acts contrary to international law). Likewise, it has been argued that Congress's war powers, no less than the President's, are implicitly limited by customary international law (or at least those elements of it that have supposedly acquired "peremptory" status). See Lobel, *Limits of Constitutional Power, supra* note 12, at 1075. But the Supreme Court expressly refused to accept that claim in Miller v. United States, 78 U.S. (11 Wall.) 268 (1870). The plaintiffs contended that

> [a]lthough there are no express constitutional restrictions upon the power of Congress to declare and prosecute war, or to make rules respecting captures on land and water, there are restrictions implied in the nature of the powers themselves. The power to prosecute war is only a power to prosecute it according to the law of nations, and a power to make rules respecting captures is a power to make such rules only as are within the laws of nations.

Id. at 285–86. The Court continued:

> It is argued that though there are no express constitutional restrictions upon the power of Congress to declare and prosecute war, or to make rules respecting captures on land and water, there are restrictions implied in the nature of the powers themselves. Hence it is said the power to prosecute war is only a power to prosecute it according to the law of nations, and a power to make rules respecting captures is a power to make such rules only

from the early Republic that are said to show that the Framers believed that the President as Commander-in-Chief can only exercise those powers permitted to the United States as a belligerent under the laws of war, or the laws of armed conflict as they are known today.[56] These arguments, or at least their claim to support from the original understanding of the Constitution, instead depend on quotations from Alexander Hamilton and James Madison's 1793 Pacificus-Helvidius debates over the Neutrality Proclamation.[57] In *Pacificus No. 1*, Alexander Hamilton argued that "[t]he [Chief] Executive is charged with the execution of all laws, the laws of Nations as well as the Municipal law, which recognises and adopts those laws."[58] In *Helvidius No. 1*, Madison responded that when war is declared, normal peacetime laws are suspended and replaced by, "as *a rule for the executive*, a *new code* adapted to the relation between the society and its foreign enemy."[59] In a following Helvidius paper, Madison seemed to agree that the President "is bound to the faithful execution of these as of all other laws internal and external."[60] Hamilton and Madison's apparent agreement is taken as a sign that the Framers understood the Constitution as limiting the President's Commander-in-Chief power to the customary rules of war.

There is good reason to doubt this inference. As an initial matter, the Pacificus-Helvidius debates took place during the second Washington administration, not 1787–88. If they confirmed evidence from the drafting or ratification debates, they would be more decisive, but standing alone they do not show that the Framers held this understanding. The very fact that Hamilton and Madison were in such sharp disagreement over whether the President had the constitutional authority to declare

---

as are within the laws of nations. Whether this is so or not we do not care to inquire, for it is not necessary to the present case. It is sufficient that the right to confiscate the property of all public enemies is a conceded right.

Id. at 305. Later Supreme Court decisions left little doubt that it lay within the war powers of the government to violate customary international law, and that any remedy for such a violation would be political rather than legal in nature. In Young v. United States, 97 U.S. 39 (1877), the Court stated:

As war is necessarily a trial of strength between the belligerents, the ultimate object of each, in every movement, must be to lessen the strength of his adversary, or add to his own. As a rule, whatever is necessary to accomplish this end is lawful; and, as between the belligerents, each determines for himself what is necessary. If, in so doing, he offends against the accepted laws of nations, he must answer in his political capacity to other nations for the wrong he does.

Id. at 60.

[56] Golove, *Franckian-Madisonian Approach, supra* note 11, at 365.

[57] See JOHN YOO, THE POWERS OF WAR AND PEACE 198–204 (2005) (discussing the Neutrality Proclamation and Pacificus-Helvidius debates).

[58] "Pacificus" Number 1 (June 1793), reprinted in 15 THE PAPERS OF ALEXANDER HAMILTON, *supra* note 2, at 40.

[59] "Helvidius" Number 1 (Aug. 24, 1793), reprinted in 15 THE PAPERS OF JAMES MADISON 69 (Thomas A. Mason, Robert A. Rutland, & Jeanne K. Sisson eds., 1985).

[60] "Helvidius" Number 2 (Aug. 31, 1793), reprinted in 15 THE PAPERS OF JAMES MADISON, *id.* at 86.

neutrality demonstrates that the thinking of 1793 does not reflect an agreement on what the Framers believed. Reading Hamilton in this way, in particular, does not do his arguments full justice. Hamilton was defending President Washington's declaration of neutrality, which, in essence, derived from his constitutional authority to interpret the 1778 Franco-American Treaty of Alliance and to establish the nation's foreign policy. Hamilton argued that the President's right to enforce international law expanded, not limited, his constitutional power. Neither Hamilton nor Madison addressed the converse question because it was not at issue in the Neutrality Proclamation, and their quotes relied on by the critics of presidential power are tangential to their actual arguments at the time.

II. THE PRESIDENT'S FUNCTIONAL ADVANTAGE IN THE INTERPRETATION OF INTERNATIONAL LAW

If CIL does not rise to the level of binding federal law under the Constitution absent congressional codification, its interpretation becomes a policy choice. There may be very good reasons to follow CIL in any given case. Compliance with a rule of CIL may supply a focal point that allows nations to coordinate their independent actions. It might provide a way for nations to cooperate or to signal their credibility and reliability. Nonetheless, the benefit of interpreting and following international law must be balanced against other foreign policy considerations. More compelling interests in our international relations may dictate against following a particular interpretation of CIL. The power to interpret international law should fall within the normal allocation of authority for other foreign policy questions. Because our constitutional system gives the bulk of foreign policy decisions to the Executive, it would make sense that the question of interpreting international law stays within that institutional design. This is not to say that federal courts cannot play a role in the development and enforcement of CIL. Instead, we are making the second-order argument that as a matter of institutional competence, the federal judiciary suffers significant disadvantages in such a role compared to the executive branch. We necessarily base our institutional assessment on certain generalizations and assumptions about how these institutions work, because it would be difficult to conduct a sufficiently rigorous empirical test of these functional claims.

It is important to distinguish between both micro- and macro-level characteristics of the judiciary. Several characteristics of the federal courts at the micro level—the operation of individual judges in lawsuits—limit the information that flows to courts and the options available to them. At a macro level, certain system-wide features of the Article III judiciary may poorly equip it to carry out national policy on a global scale. Defining features of the federal courts make them superior to other branches in performing certain functions, but also make them comparatively less well suited to playing a leading foreign relations role. Federal courts are designed to be independent from politics, to allow parties to drive litigation, and to receive information in highly formal ways. These characteristics may make courts more neutral in their decision-making and more just in their attitude toward parties.

But they also may render them less effective tools in achieving national goals in international relations. Comparison of courts with other institutions may make these points more salient.

An initial difference between courts and other institutions is access. Compared with other institutions, courts have high barriers to access.[61] Congress has somewhat moderately difficult barriers—it is generally thought that interest groups must provide campaign contributions or political support in order to obtain access to congressional leaders.[62] The executive branch has lower barriers than Congress; it is probably easier for individuals and groups to provide information to and make requests of agencies, although perhaps with no greater chances of success. By contrast, courts have numerous doctrines that limit access. Under standing doctrine, for example, plaintiffs, to have their day in court, must have suffered an actual injury in fact that is traceable to conduct on the part of a defendant who can remedy the harm. The timing of the case must be just right, neither too early and therefore unripe nor too late and therefore moot. It cannot raise political questions whose determination is constitutionally vested in another branch. The plaintiff must actually be able to claim a potential benefit from a cause of action created under federal law. Litigation itself demands significant resources, at least in comparison with the means of accessing the executive or legislative branches.[63]

There are also significant differences in the way courts receive and process information. Courts gather knowledge through a painstaking and expensive process of discovery, conducted by the contending parties. That information must satisfy the federal rules of evidence—it must survive tests for relevance, credibility, and reliability—and the parties must present it to the court in accordance with formal courtroom procedures. By contrast, the executive branch collects information through agency experts, a national and global network of officials and agents, and links with outside groups and foreign governments. Congress can acquire information from the executive branch or outside groups via relatively inexpensive hearings. Also, a court generally cannot update its information except in the context of a new case. Thus, if a court has made a decision based on information available to it at a certain time, it generally will not continue to gather information thereafter—even if it would lead it to change its decision—until another case raises the same issue.[64]

Article III creates significant limitations on the ability of federal courts to integrate its actions with national foreign policy. Once the President and Congress

---

[61] Neil K. Komesar, Imperfect Alternatives: Choosing Institutions in Law, Economics, and Public Policy 125 (1994).

[62] See Robert D. Cooter, The Strategic Constitution 51–74 (2000) (discussing interest group theory of politics). Other studies, however, show that members of Congress are responsive to public pressure as reflected through the media and constituents.

[63] See, e.g., Lujan v. Defenders of Wildlife, 504 U.S. 555 (1992) (standing); DeFunis v. Odegaard, 416 U.S. 312 (1974) (mootness); United Public Workers v. Mitchell, 330 U.S. 75 (1947) (ripeness); Nixon v. United States, 506 U.S. 224 (1993) (political question doctrine).

[64] See, for example, Thomas R. Lee, Stare Decisis in Economic Perspective: An Economic Analysis of the Supreme Court's Doctrine of Precedent, 78 N.C. L. Rev. 643 (2000).

have enacted a statute or the President and the Senate have approved a treaty, the judiciary's constitutional responsibility is to execute those goals in the context of Article III cases or controversies. Federal judges cannot alter or refuse to execute those policies, even if the original circumstances that gave rise to the statute or treaty have changed.[65] If a federal court, for example, finds that a defendant has violated the Helms-Burton Act by "trafficking" in property confiscated by the Cuban government, it must render judgment for an American plaintiff who once owned that property.[66] Article III requires a federal court to reach that decision even if the effects of the judgment in that particular case would actually harm the national interest or conflict with other countries' view of CIL.

A last micro difficulty arises from the substantive challenge presented by CIL. CIL is a very different subject than that usually encountered by federal courts. Many observers admit that the very concept of CIL—law that "results from a general and consistent practice of states followed by them from a sense of legal obligation" rather than through positive enactment—is fraught with difficulty.[67] It is unclear whether CIL should prevail because of actual state consent to a rule, passive state acquiescence, or state practice that is assumed to reflect international consensus. It is unclear how widespread state practice must be, how long it must continue, and how consistent it must be to qualify as CIL.[68] It is not even clear what counts as state practice, whether it should be limited to actions or declarations, and whose practice—that of the great powers, the leading nations of each region in the world, or every nation in the world—matters. It is not clear when state practice can be said to arise out of a sense of legal obligation rather than through coincidence or expedient coordination. The positive sources of law are so uncertain that the International Court of Justice describes the views of scholars and publicists as a "subsidiary means" of identifying CIL, which is not only a controversial proposition concerning the legitimacy of international law but might even make the law more confusing.[69]

Even if the very nature of CIL were not so uncertain and ambiguous, it is likely that the federal courts would experience either a high error rate or high decision costs in determining its content. CIL involves sources that are not often encountered by federal judges or American lawyers. The very source of CIL—state practice—is not easily discoverable. State practice may not be reflected in publicly available documents but more likely lie in the obscure archives of the State

---

[65] For a contrary view, see GUIDO CALABRESI, A COMMON LAW FOR THE AGE OF STATUTES (1985).

[66] See John Yoo, *Federal Courts as Weapons of Foreign Policy: The Case of the Helms-Burton Act*, 20 HASTINGS INT'L & COMP. L. REV. 747 (1997).

[67] Restatement (Third), *supra* note 4, at § 102(2); Compare D'AMATO, CONCEPT OF CUSTOM, *supra* note 5, at 4; with IAN BROWNLIE, PRINCIPLES OF PUBLIC INTERNATIONAL LAW 5–6 (4th ed. 1990).

[68] See Prosper Weil, *Toward Relative Normativity in International Law?*, 77 AM. J. INT'L L. 413, 433 (1983). These well-known problems with CIL are also discussed in D'AMATO, CONCEPT OF CUSTOM, *supra* note 5, at 6–10.

[69] See Kelly, *The Twilight of Customary International Law*, *supra* note 5, at 500–01 (describing lack of agreement on sources of state practice for purposes of determining CIL); Jack Goldsmith & Eric Posner, *A Theory of Customary International Law*, 66 U. CHI. L. REV. 1113, 1176–77 (1999); Bradley & Goldsmith, *Critique of the Modern Position*, *supra* note 4, at 872–76.

Department and foreign ministries or rest in the incorporeal preserve of unwritten custom. American-trained judges—almost all of them generalists—would have to survey the actions of governments over the course of dozens, if not hundreds, of years and make fine-grained judgments not just about what states have done, but also about why they have done it. Take the most prominent example of a federal court attempting to divine CIL: the *Paquete Habana* case. Justice Gray surveyed centuries of policies, declarations, and naval actions to determine the legal status of coastal fishing vessels. It appears that he may have gotten the record of state practice wrong—states did not consistently refrain from seizing small fishing vessels during wartime. Even if Justice Gray had accurately described practice, he failed to show that the protection of coastal fishing vessels had arisen out of a sense of legal obligation, rather than out of an interest by states in coordinating their activities or because of a fear of retaliation.[70]

A useful analogy can be made here to the arguments about the use of legislative history. Whether courts should consult legislative history has become one of the focal points for broader debates about the nature of legislation, the competencies of the judiciary, and the purpose of interpretation. To summarize briefly, many who believe that courts should seek out Congress's "intent" or broader "purpose" find reliance on legislative history, along with other policy considerations, generally acceptable. A minority argues that legislative history ought not to be used, either because there is no such thing as a collective intent or because consulting legislative history evades the formal separation of powers. Professor Adrian Vermeule makes a similar argument to the one made here: even if courts should seek legislative intent, their "limited interpretive competence" suggests that they "might do better, even on intentionalist grounds, by eschewing legislative history than by consulting it." Judges may have limited abilities to understand and use legislative history properly, leading to high decision costs in conducting extensive reviews of legislative history without any corresponding reduction (and perhaps even an increase) in error costs.[71]

If this is true with legislative history, these costs will only be compounded with CIL. The sources of legislative history at least rest within the general bounds of American public law and so will be familiar to most judges. While expensive to gather and analyze in relation to other forms of American legal research,[72] legislative

[70] Goldsmith & Posner, *Theory of Customary International Law, supra* note 69, at 1148 n. 101.

[71] See, for example, William N. Eskridge, Jr., *Textualism, the Unknown Ideal?*, 96 Mich. L. Rev. 1509 (1998) (reviewing Antonin Scalia, A Matter of Interpretation: Federal Courts and the Law [1997]); Daniel A. Farber & Philip P. Frickey, *Legislative Intent and Public Choice*, 74 Va. L. Rev. 423 (1988); William N. Eskridge, Jr., & Philip P. Frickey, *Statutory Interpretation as Practical Reasoning*, 42 Stan. L. Rev. 321 (1990); John F. Manning, *Textualism as a Nondelegation Doctrine*, 97 Colum. L. Rev. 673 (1997); Frank H. Easterbrook, *Text, History, and Structure in Statutory Interpretation*, 17 Harv. J. L. & Pub. Pol'y 61, 68 (1994); Adrian Vermeule, *Legislative History and the Limits of Judicial Competence: The Untold Story of Holy Trinity Church*, 50 Stan. L. Rev. 1833 (1998).

[72] See, for example, Kenneth W. Starr, *Observations about the Use of Legislative History*, 1987 Duke L. J. 371, 377; Eskridge, *Textualism, supra* note 71, at 1541; Vermeule, *Untold Story of Holy Trinity Church, supra* note 71, at 1868–69.

history may well be cheap to use in comparison to sources of CIL, which comes in different languages, involves not just texts but also practices, and is recorded in sources that are often not publicly available. Even the use of more conventional public sources, such as multilateral treaties and the resolutions of the UN General Assembly, has serious interpretive problems. It is highly questionable, for example, that nations that refuse to sign treaties should be held to the same norms because they have "ripened" into custom, or that CIL should be read to go beyond the standards set by a widely joined treaty. Organs of the United Nations, particularly of the General Assembly, have no formal authority to declare CIL, if by definition CIL represents the practice of states, not the opinions of international organizations. The most pertinent evidence of state practice will be the most expensive to come by, and there is no empirical evidence yet showing that federal courts will perform better by employing it.[73]

The organization of the federal judiciary as an institution perhaps has even more significant effects on the comparative ability of the courts to achieve foreign policy goals. First, the federal judiciary is a generalist institution composed of generalist judges. Members of the judiciary are not usually chosen because of any expertise in any particular subject, unlike, say, the way in which scientists may be hired for work at the Department of Energy, the Environmental Protection Agency, or the Food and Drug Administration. This rings even more true in the case of foreign affairs. Judges are not chosen because of any background in specific regions or areas, nor are they selected because they have experience in national security issues. As an institution, the judiciary is unlikely to have great facility with international legal, political, or economic theories or materials, and its members are more likely to be chosen because of their prominence as litigators or public officials. It is difficult to recall more than a handful of judges who had significant foreign affairs experience before their appointment to the federal bench.

Second, of the three branches of government, the judiciary is the most decentralized. The front line of the judiciary is composed of 94 district courts, which are staffed by more than 667 judges.[74] Until appellate courts have ruled on a legal issue, the judges in these district courts can hold 667 different interpretations of the law. There are 13 federal courts of appeals, with 179 judges.[75] The Supreme Court currently hears between 70 and 85 cases per year, while about 60,000 cases a year are filed in the federal appellate courts and about 350,000 cases are filed a year in the

---

[73] The legitimacy of this "new" CIL is debated by Weil, *Toward Relative Normativity, supra* note 68, and Alain Pellet, *The Normative Dilemma: Will and Consent in International Lawmaking,* 12 Australian Y.B. Int'l L. 22 (1992), and is summarized in Antonio Cassese & Joseph H. H. Weiler eds., Change and Stability in International Lawmaking (De Gruyter 1988).

[74] Federal Courts, Understanding the Federal Courts, District Courts, at http://www.uscourts.gov/FederalCourts/UnderstandingtheFederalCourts/DistrictCourts.aspx; Judges & Judgeships, Federal Judges, at http://www.uscourts.gov/JudgesAndJudgeships/FederalJudgeships.aspx.

[75] Federal Courts, Understanding the Federal Courts, Courts of Appeals, at http://www.uscourts.gov/FederalCourts/UnderstandingtheFederalCourts/CourtsofAppeals.aspx; Judges & Judgeships, Federal Judges, at http://www.uscourts.gov/JudgesAndJudgeships/FederalJudgeships.aspx.

district courts.[76] Given the demands on the Supreme Court's caseload, it is doubtful that the Court could devote a significant portion of its docket to correcting errone-ous interpretation of international law, mistaken interference with foreign policy, or misapplications of the ATS. Unless this happens, the geographic organization of the federal courts may well produce disharmony on questions of foreign policy and a diversity of possible applications of international law.

In some areas outside CIL, this level of decentralization might not pose such a problem. Geographically organized courts may better tailor national policies to local conditions, allow for diversity and experimentation in federal policies, and provide a more effective voice for local communities in federal decision-making. As we argue in chapter 6, state governments might play this role, subject to presi-dential or congressional supervision. But these are not usually positive values in foreign affairs. The Constitution sought to centralize authority over foreign affairs to provide the nation with a single voice in its international relations, so as to pre-vent other nations from taking advantage of the disarray that had characterized the Articles of Confederation.[77] Indeed, in cases such as *Crosby v. National Foreign Trade Council* and *American Insurance Association v. Garamendi*, the Supreme Court recently has preempted state efforts to influence foreign nations precisely because of the need for a uniform foreign policy set by Congress or the President.[78] This rationale, although offered to justify national preeminence over the 50 states, applies with force to a federal judiciary of 94 district courts and 13 appellate courts. Judicial implementation of foreign policy promises disharmony where uniformity is supremely important.

Third, institutional structure suggests that judicial activity in foreign policy may be slow, in terms of both implementation and self-correction. Lawsuits can often take years to complete. Even when cases are expedited, they require many months to proceed from the time of filing to final judgment and appeal. To use *Sosa v. Alvarez-Machain* as an example, eleven years passed between the filing of the ATS claim in federal district court and the Supreme Court's decision. While they did not warrant extensive discovery or trial proceedings, recent Supreme Court cases on Massachusetts's efforts to sanction Burma and on California's efforts to provide remedies for Holocaust victims still took several years to adjudicate.[79]

Delay also affects not just initial decisions, but also monitoring and feedback, impeding the swift and effective execution of foreign policy. Delay infects the judi-ciary's institutional systems for communicating between its different units and for

---

[76] Judicial Caseload Indicators 2010, at http://www.uscourts.gov/Viewer.aspx?doc=/uscourts/Statistics/FederalJudicialCaseloadStatistics/2010/front/IndicatorsMar10.pdf.

[77] See generally, Frederick Marks, Independence on Trial: Foreign Affairs and the Making of the Constitution (1973).

[78] American Ins. Ass'n v. Garamendi, 539 U.S. 396, 413 (2003); Crosby v. Nat'l Foreign Trade Council, 530 U.S. 363, 372–73 (2000).

[79] The lawsuit in *Garamendi* began in 1999 and was not finally decided by the Supreme Court until 2003. 539 U.S. at 512. *Crosby* began in 1998 and was not decided by the Supreme Court until 2000. 530 U.S. at 371.

correcting errors. While the federal courts have an appellate court system for detecting and correcting errors, that system can take months, if not years, to bring finality to an issue. Even if a district or circuit judge acts in defiance of established circuit or Supreme Court precedent, litigation is needed to correct the error. Standards of review concerning fact-finding may even render some decisions immune from appellate review despite contrary or conflicting results reached by different trial courts in similar cases. Transmission of information identifying and correcting errors may become garbled within the system, which helps to explain the repeated cycles of appeal and remand that can occur in the context of a single case. Judicial errors or deviations may take years to reverse or may even go entirely uncorrected.[80] While these problems also afflict the resolution of purely domestic disputes, they may bring more harm to the national interest in this context because of the need to act swiftly and decisively in foreign affairs.

The judiciary's institutional characteristics render it superior to other institutions for certain kinds of decisions. It can address issues more fairly, with less interference from politics, and it can implement federal policy over a wide number of cases throughout the country. It can help solve political commitment problems between interest groups or between branches of government due to its high level of insulation from outside control.[81] Its virtues, however, also diminish its usefulness as an institutional actor in foreign affairs. Its evenhandedness and passivity impede it from efficiently gathering and processing information and coordinating its policies with other national actors. Its procedural fairness and geographic decentralization prevent it from acting swiftly in a unified fashion, and it lacks effective tools for the rapid assimilation of feedback and the correction of errors.

Even if American foreign policy goals include the development and enforcement of international law, the courts are by no means the most effective institutional mechanism. CIL suits would require courts to acquire information about events that usually have occurred abroad and that involve parties outside their jurisdiction. They demand that courts interpret and apply norms whose sources can be difficult to discover and discern. These cases often involve sensitive judgments that may impact broader, ongoing relations with other nations. This is not to say that courts could not perform this function if need be; courts have interpreted open-ended clauses of the Constitution and have attempted to manage institutions ranging from schools to prisons.[82] Rather, the central question is, from a comparative institutional perspective, whether there is reason to think that courts would be *equal or superior* to other branches of government in achieving national policy on international law or human rights.

---

[80] Martin Shapiro, *Toward a Theory of Stare Decisis*, 1 J. Leg. Stud. 125, 125–34 (1972).

[81] William M. Landes & Richard A. Posner, *The Independent Judiciary in an Interest-Group Perspective*, 18 J.L. & Econ. 875 (1975); Cooter, The Strategic Constitution, *supra* note 62, at 195–98.

[82] See John Yoo, *Who Measures the Chancellor's Foot?: The Inherent Remedial Power of the Federal Courts*, 84 Cal. L. Rev. 1121 (1996).

As Professors Sunstein, Vermeule, and Komesar have argued with regard to allo-cating decisions among courts, agencies, and markets, simply deciding on a social goal is not enough. We must also make comparative judgments on the ability of different institutions to achieve those goals. Such comparative institutional judg-ments have been applied in both constitutional and statutory interpretation.[83] Even if the judiciary would perform poorly at enforcing national policy in the interna-tional law area, it still may be the best institutional mechanism available. A compre-hensive analysis of the interpretation and enforcement of international law requires a judgment of the relative ability of the judiciary and the institution most likely to replace it: the Executive.

Evaluation of the comparative advantages and disadvantages of the judiciary versus the Executive in implementing foreign affairs goals parallels arguments surrounding the review of agency interpretations of law. In *Chevron U.S.A. Inc. v. Natural Resources Defense Council, Inc.*, the Court established a well-known two-part test for reviewing executive branch interpretation of ambiguous statutes. First, courts are to ask whether Congress has clearly addressed the interpretive question at hand. If not, then judges are to defer to the agency interpretation if it is based on a reasonable or permissible reading of the statute.[84]

We are not so much interested in whether *Chevron* establishes the correct rule as we are in the comparative institutional considerations that motivated the Court's holding. *Chevron* identified two reasons of judicial policy that support our analysis. First, judicial deference to reasonable agency interpretations assumes that agencies usually possess greater expertise in administering regulatory statutes than the judiciary. Second, deference recognizes that the executive branch can claim greater political accountability than the judiciary, implying that interpretation ought to pursue present policy goals and that the electorate ultimately could change unwanted interpretations.[85]

The Supreme Court recently has demarcated the limits of deference to agency interpretation at rule-making and formal adjudication, but not other forms of

---

[83] Cass Sunstein & Adrian Vermeule, *Interpretation and Institutions*, 101 Mich. L. Rev. 885, 917–19 (2003); Komesar, Imperfect Alternatives, *supra* note 61. Constitutional scholars such as John Hart Ely and Jesse Choper, for instance, have applied such comparative institutional analysis to defend their theory of constitutional interpretations. Choper's defense of political safeguards for federalism relied heavily on his assessment of the comparative institutional advantages of judicial versus political branch enforcement of federalism. Jesse Choper, Judicial Review and the National Political Process: A Functional Reconsideration of the Role of the Supreme Court (1981).

[84] 467 U.S. 837, 842–43 (1984). Curtis Bradley has also sought to draw upon Chevron in the foreign affairs context. His inquiry concerned whether Chevron principles support judicial deference to executive branch interpretation of different forms of international law. Curtis A. Bradley, *Chevron Deference and Foreign Affairs*, 86 Va. L. Rev. 649 (2000). Our approach is different: we seek to learn from Chevron's observations on the relationship between agencies and courts to reach judgments about the institutional abilities of each branch.

[85] On this point, see Laurence H. Silberman, *Chevron—The Intersection of Law and Policy*, 58 Geo. Wash. L. Rev. 821 (1990).

agency action, such as policy guidance and informal adjudication.[86] Agency expertise and accountability, however, continue to remain central justifications for judicial deference, and it is useful to understand them through an institutional lens. *Chevron* locates interpretation in the institution that has the superior level of technical competence. Unlike federal judges, agency personnel are experts at their subject, are trained and devoted to policy-making in a discrete specialty, and have access to technical experience and information accumulated by a wide bureaucracy.

To be sure, agency decision-making does not depend solely on technical decisions; rather, it requires officials to reach decisions involving a mixture of factual determinations and value judgments.[87] And agencies are not just run by civil servants but are managed by a thin crust of political appointees chosen by the President. Moreover, executive branch officials are more politically accountable than federal judges, and mistakes of agency interpretation are more likely to be corrected. Congress also has any number of formal and informal tools for pressuring agencies to reverse unwanted actions. Congress can hold hearings, refuse to confirm nominees to the agency, and reduce agency budgets for enforcement. Congress can use interest groups and the media to generate public opposition to executive policy.[88]

By contrast, the federal judiciary is designed to be outside the reach of normal politics. Federal judges have life tenure and a permanent salary, and for the most part have reached the end of their official careers, so they are not as beholden to political groups for their advancement. Because of its internal system of precedent, the federal courts generally do not reverse a decision simply because of political opposition or pressure. In order to change a judicial decision, Congress generally can resort only to the single formal process set out in Article I, Section 7 for the enactment of legislation. Because of the hurdles of bicameralism and presentment, this makes it far more difficult for Congress to correct mistakes in policy by the federal courts.[89]

In terms of comparative institutional advantage, it may be useful to express these values in terms of error and decision costs.[90] We can make the reasonable

---

[86] United States v. Mead Corp., 533 U.S. 218 (2001). Compare Matthew C. Stephenson & Adrian Vermeule, *Chevron Has Only One Step*, 95 VA. L. REV. 597 (2009), with Kenneth A. Bamberger & Peter L. Strauss, *Chevron's Two Steps*, 95 VA. L. REV. 611 (2009).

[87] There is a wide literature, for example, on whether cost-benefit analysis should be used by agencies and whether they are capable of following it properly. See, for example, Matthew D. Adler & Eric A. Posner, *Rethinking Cost-Benefit Analysis*, 109 YALE L. J. 165 (1999); Lisa Heinzerling, *Regulatory Costs of Mythic Proportions*, 107 YALE L. J. 1981 (1998).

[88] Edward Markey, *Congress to Administrative Agencies: Creator, Overseer, and Partner*, 1990 DUKE L.J. 967, 971; Barry Weingast & Mark Moran, *Bureaucratic Discretion or Congressional Control? Regulatory Policymaking at the Federal Trade Commission*, 91 J. POL. ECON. 765, 769–70 (1983); JOEL D. ABERBACH, KEEPING A WATCHFUL EYE: THE POLITICS OF CONGRESSIONAL OVERSIGHT 130–44 (1990); Peter Strauss, *The Place of Agencies in the Government: Separation of Powers and the Fourth Branch*, 84 COLUM. L. REV. 573 (1984).

[89] See, for example, COOTER, STRATEGIC CONSTITUTION, *supra* note 62.

[90] See Adrian Vermeule, *Interpretive Choice*, 75 N.Y.U. L. REV. 74, 88 (2000) ("The first advantage, getting more cases right, means that the doctrine minimizes *error costs*; the second advantage,

assumption that deference to agencies is likely to lead to lower error costs in decision-making. Their technical competence in specialized areas is less likely to produce incorrect decisions because agencies may be more familiar with the meaning of Congress's instructions in the context of a heavily regulated and factually complex field.[91] Their expertise and knowledge also make it more likely that they will set the appropriate technical standards within the parameters set by Congress. At the same time, however, agencies may well incur higher decision costs than courts. They reach their judgments after gathering broader amounts of information than judges, unconstrained from the form or context of litigation. Their decisions follow the amorphous standard of acting reasonably under the totality of the circumstances, rather than clear ex ante rules. Error correction by the political branches, however, seems superior to that of courts. Holding oversight hearings and threatening budget cuts present a far less difficult method to change incorrect agency interpretations than does the enactment of specific overriding legislation.[92]

A third justification for judicial deference did not appear in *Chevron* but implicates core questions of institutional design. A President provides a single policy vision that sets a uniform regulatory policy throughout the nation. Federal courts, by contrast, are organized into thirteen different circuit courts of appeals organized by geography. Because of the Supreme Court's limited docket, the decisions of the circuit courts represent the final word of the Article III judiciary in 99 percent of all cases. *Chevron*, in essence, promotes national uniformity in administrative law by ensuring that statutes will not be interpreted differently in different regions.[93] If federal courts could review agency interpretations de novo or under a less deferential regime, it is likely that administrative rules would be applied differently in different circuits.

These institutional considerations bear significantly on the choice between courts and the executive branch in foreign affairs. First, consider the factor of institutional structure. Putting aside the issue of the origins of the President's foreign affairs power, the executive branch seems much better structured for the conduct of

---

requiring less time and effort, means that the doctrine minimizes judicial *decision costs*").

[91] Sunstein & Vermeule, *Interpretation and Institutions, supra* note 83, at 927–30 (explaining that "by virtue of their specialized competence and relative accountability, agencies are in a better position to [resolve statutory ambiguities] than courts"); *see* International Bhd. of Elec. Workers v. NLRB, 814 F.2d 697,717 (D.C. Cir. 1987) (Buckley, J., concurring) (suggesting that "judges . . . have neither the time to review the entire history of a particular bill nor the experience to filter out the political overtones"); Reed Dickerson, *Statutory Interpretation: Dipping into Legislative History,* 11 Hofstra L. Rev. 1125, 1142 (1983) (arguing that "[m]ost courts simply have no realistic grasp of how legislation is put together"); Kenneth A. Shepsle, *Congress Is a "They," Not an "It": Legislative Intent as Oxymoron,* 12 Int'l Rev. L. & Econ. 239, 254 n.27 (1992) ("[C]ourts as currently constituted possess neither the resources nor the intellectual inclination to do the kind of systematic legislative history that is sensitive to supply-side institutional intricacies").

[92] *See, e.g.,* Cooter, Strategic Constitution, *supra* note 62, at 225–29 (explaining that a system that slows down legislation through constitutional separation of powers and party fragmentation increases the discretionary power of the courts).

[93] Peter Strauss, *One Hundred Fifty Cases per Year: Some Implications of the Supreme Court's Limited Resources for Judicial Review of Agency Action,* 87 Colum. L. Rev. 1093 (1987).

foreign relations than the courts. As Alexander Hamilton argued in *Federalist No. 70*, the Executive is structured for speed and decisiveness in its actions and is better able to maintain secrecy in its information gathering and deliberations. "Decision, activity, secrecy, dispatch will generally characterize the proceedings of one man, in a much more eminent degree, than the proceedings of any greater number; and in proportion as the number is increased, these qualities will be diminished."[94] In the years leading up to World War II, the Supreme Court made a similar observation. The *Curtiss-Wright* Court famously observed: "In this vast external realm, with its important, complicated, delicate and manifold problems, the President alone has the power to speak or listen as a representative of the nation." Quoting from a Senate report, the Court further explained that "[t]he nature of transactions with foreign nations . . . requires caution and unity of design, and their success frequently depends on secrecy and dispatch."[95] As Harold Koh describes it, "His decision-making processes can take on degrees of speed, secrecy, flexibility, and efficiency that no other governmental institution can match."[96] If anything, national security and foreign policy demands since World War II have led to even more concentration of authority in the executive branch. The history of American foreign relations has been the story of the expansion of the presidency, thanks to its structural abilities to wield power quickly, effectively, and in a unitary manner—a fact bemoaned by critics of the "imperial presidency."[97]

Institutional design leads to advantages in specialized competence. The United States operates large bureaucracies designed to develop and implement foreign policy. For fiscal year 2010, for example, the Obama administration's budget request for the State Department and other foreign affairs agencies totaled $53.9 billion. As of September 2009, the Executive Departments employed 2,773,878 officials and civil servants, and all independent federal agencies, including those involved in foreign affairs, employed an additional 866,972 workers.[98] These figures do not include the budget and personnel figures for the Defense Intelligence Agency, the Central Intelligence Agency, the National Security Agency, and the White House staff, all of which have significant roles in developing foreign policy. These agencies employ experts in specific subjects, such as arms control or human rights, or certain nations and regions, such as the State Department's Asia or Africa desks. Many of the staff who work on these issues have developed their areas of expertise by spending their careers immersing themselves in local cultures, learning languages, or gaining experience in

---

[94] FEDERALIST NO. 70 (Hamilton), in Merrill Jensen, John P. Kaminski, & Gaspare J. Saladino, eds., 16 THE DOCUMENTARY HISTORY OF THE RATIFICATION OF THE CONSTITUTION 397 (1986).

[95] 299 U.S. 304, 319 (1936).

[96] HAROLD KOH, NATIONAL SECURITY CONSTITUTION 119 (1990).

[97] *Id.* at 118–23; compare ARTHUR M. SCHLESINGER, JR., THE IMPERIAL PRESIDENCY (1973) with JOHN YOO, CRISIS AND COMMAND: A HISTORY OF EXECUTIVE POWER FROM GEORGE WASHINGTON TO GEORGE W. BUSH (2010).

[98] Table 1: International Affairs Request, at http://www.state.gov/documents/organization/124295. pdf; Table 2: Comparison of Total Civilian Employment of the Federal Government by Branch, Agency, and Area as of August 2009 and September 2009, at http://www.opm.gov/feddata/ html/2009/September/table2.asp.

the international politics of a region. The federal judiciary, by contrast, operates on a budget of roughly $6.9 billion with 33,754 employees, who must devote their efforts to the adjudication of disputes involving federal law.[99]

Executive branch agencies have access to broader forms of information about foreign affairs than those available to a court, such as that produced by clandestine agents or electronic eavesdropping, which cannot be publicly disclosed. Classified information cannot be produced in an open court, though it can provide invaluable data on the plans and intentions of other governments and the possible effects of American foreign policy. In terms of receiving and processing that information, the executive branch is not restricted by the structures that limit the information that a court may consider.

By contrast, the very nature of courts as decision-making institutions may impede their ability to perform a role in foreign affairs. Institutional reform cases, where courts have supervised the management of school, prisons, and other government agencies, have shown that courts are relatively poor at gathering information, especially when a case extends beyond the facts behind a single transaction or accident to broader political, economic, and social events and trends. Courts experience difficulty in weighing policy alternatives and in calculating costs and benefits. Courts have been shown to be unable to gather and absorb the sort of comprehensive, objective data required to make considered decisions when more than just historical fact and causation are involved.[100]

In addition to gathering and processing information, the executive branch has broader tools at its disposal to achieve foreign policy goals. In the field of foreign affairs, the discretion and authorities available to the President generally go beyond those enjoyed by agencies in domestic affairs. The President is the sole organ of the nation in its diplomatic relations, Commander-in-Chief of the military, and director of the clandestine services. These inherent authorities could be used in a variety of ways to achieve foreign policy goals. In the diplomatic realm, they range from negotiating and drafting international agreements to pressuring other nations to follow international norms to seeking to isolate rogue states. Intelligence agencies could take covert action to destabilize nations that threaten American national security. As Commander-in-Chief, the President could issue orders to the military to restore order in states where central authority has collapsed, as in Somalia or Haiti, or ultimately to use force to end abuse by states, as in Kosovo. Despite the controversy over its legitimacy, the Iraq war showed a President using a variety of tools to end Saddam Hussein's record of severe human rights abuses and his flagrant disregard for UN Security Council resolutions.

The executive branch can also make significant progress toward foreign policy goals without having to rely on inherent constitutional authority. Under the

---

[99] Garrett Hatch, *Financial Services and General Government Appropriations: FY2012 Budget Request Fact Sheet*, Congressional Research Service Report, R41655, June 16, 2011, at 2, at http://www.fas.org/sgp/crs/misc/R41655.pdf.
[100] Peter Schuck, Suing Government: Citizen Remedies for Official Wrongs, 394–404 (1983); Donald L. Horowitz, The Courts and Social Policy 156–61 (1977).

International Economic Emergency Powers Act (IEEPA), the President can impose sanctions against entities ranging from individuals to nations. If these nations pose a threat to U.S. national security and foreign policy, the President may declare a national emergency that then triggers the authority to freeze foreign assets in the United States or to restrict all commercial contacts with a foreign nation. Under the Export Administration Act, the President can place restrictions on exports to a nation that poses a threat to American national security or foreign policy.[101] The President can deploy these powers as a scalpel or as a hammer. They can be used in a fine-grained manner when aimed at a particular individual, such as apprehending Slobodan Milosevic. Or they can be used more broadly to try to coerce a nation to change its treatment of its own citizens, as with South Africa in the 1980s or with the former Yugoslavia and Iraq in the 1990s.

In comparison, courts have few effective tools to enforce compliance with their decisions, and those tools use monetary sanctions or the punishment of individuals to leverage broader policy or institutional changes. Again drawing from the institutional structure context, courts possess imperfect tools for communicating their decrees, and they must rely on other institutions and personnel to disseminate and implement their orders.[102] Courts have few resources to compel compliance on the part of defendants or to create positive incentives to encourage adherence to judicial orders. Aside from a contempt order, judges generally rely on the moral persuasiveness and the institutional legitimacy of their decisions to encourage compliance. These problems are only compounded with regard to foreign affairs. Parties will often be outside the United States and outside the reach of a federal district court or federal marshals.

Third, executive policy in foreign affairs is subject to greater political accountability. One advantage of the courts, in certain situations, is their relative insulation from political control. Delegation to courts may help to preserve a legislative majority's victories by making them more difficult to reverse in the future or by providing a means to overcome a commitment problem where parties to an agreement do not trust each other to live up to their obligations. In order to achieve the benefits of locking in policies or making credible commitments, however, Congress must accept a loss of flexibility in policy implementation, a reduction in institutional expertise, and a decrease in ability to reflect changing legislative wishes. Many of these arguments have been brought to bear on the study of delegation of authority to agencies; the primary insight is that bureaucracies can be "inefficient by design"

---

[101] International Economic Emergency Powers Act, 50 U.S.C. § 1701 et seq.; Export Administration Act, 50 U.S.C. App. § 2401 et seq.

[102] See, e.g., Paul J. Mishkin, *Federal Courts as State Reformers*, 35 Wash. & Lee L. Rev. 949 (1978); Raoul Berger, Government by Judiciary: The Transformation of the Fourteenth Amendment (1977); Horowitz, The Courts and Social Policy, *supra* note 100, at 249–98; Schuck, Suing Government, *supra* note 100, at 150–81; Lon L. Fuller, *The Forms and Limits of Adjudication*, 92 Harv. L. Rev. 353, 393–405 (1978); Robert F. Nagel, *Separation of Powers and the Scope of Federal Equitable Remedies*, 30 Stan. L. Rev. 661 (1978) (arguing that separation of powers limits the ability of the judiciary to undertake executive or legislative functions when ordering relief against federal officials).

because of the desire of groups in the legislature to insulate agencies that share their views from being overturned or influenced by later coalitions with different views.[103]

As a matter of comparative institutional analysis, it would seem that delegation to the courts would experience the aforementioned costs and benefits more intensely than delegation to executive branch agencies. Delegation of international law decisions to courts would lock in policies such that only overriding legislation could change national goals. Compared to the executive branch, courts are relatively impervious to oversight hearings, budget controls, and other informal political controls. They are also less subject to the formal political control of elections. Except for the use of the appointment power to name federal judges to the bench, only a statute would allow the President and Congress to force a change of direction in policy. While this gives courts greater political insulation, it also deprives the nation of the flexibility to adjust policy in light of changes in preferences, new circumstances, or new information and expertise.

Interpretation by the executive branch, rather than the courts, in the area of CIL also may make more sense because of the President's enhanced constitutional role in foreign affairs. As the sole representative of the nation in its international relations, the President develops foreign policy, communicates with other nations, and reaches international agreements. By custom, presidents also make a variety of informal commitments with other nations. As Commander-in-Chief, the President can use force to achieve foreign policy, but he can also use less violent forms of persuasion or coercion. International law, of course, has constituted an important element in American foreign policy. Presidents have appealed to human rights laws to undermine antagonistic regimes, as President Reagan did with the Soviet Union, or have pursued them as a goal in themselves, as did President Carter.

Effectiveness would arguably be enhanced if the same institution exercised control over international law as well as broader foreign policy. Otherwise, the United States might send conflicting signals to other nations about its policies. To take an extreme case, suppose the United States sought to wage a war to promote humanitarian goals, such as to end a genocidal conflict. Such a war would arguably violate the prohibition on the use of force contained in the UN Charter.[104] Indeed, the International Court of Justice has held that this rule is not just a positive rule of the Charter, but a rule of CIL.[105] Suppose an alien harmed by American military action in the war brought a suit against the U.S. government and its officials alleging the war violated CIL. A judicial decision to promote CIL could conflict with the decision of the executive branch to use force in the same case, to the point of

---

[103] See, for example, Rui J.P. de Figueiredo, Jr., *Electoral Competition, Political Uncertainty, and Policy Insulation*, 96 Am. Poli. Sci. Rev. 321 (2002).

[104] For a discussion of the international legal rules governing the use of force, see John Yoo, *Using Force*, 71 U. Chi. L. Rev. 729 (2004).

[105] Case Concerning Military and Paramilitary Activities in and against Nicaragua (Nicaragua v. United States), 1986 I.C.J. 14, 146.

frustrating the substantive improvement of human rights conditions in the area of conflict.

In light of these considerations, it seems that the executive branch is superior to the courts. The executive branch has better means for developing information on foreign affairs, has more tools to bring to bear against violators of international law, and can display more flexibility in responding to changing international conditions, all the while remaining more accountable politically. Congress, however, might still delegate authority in these areas to the courts rather than agencies, depending on the propensity of the executive branch to violate CIL itself. If the executive branch were to prove more likely to violate CIL than the courts, then Congress might choose to vest the authority for its enforcement in the latter.

Two considerations make it unlikely that this is the case. First, domestic law does not operate to prevent the United States from violating CIL because it does not override sovereign immunity. Second, the courts' own doctrines permit the President to violate CIL. *The Paquete Habana* itself recognizes that courts may only apply CIL in the absence of a "controlling executive *or* legislative act." This language recognizes that a President's order, legitimately taken pursuant to his constitutional authority, can override CIL.[106] In order to change CIL, the President may need to violate CIL because one of the ways to alter a CIL rule is to engage in state practice that establishes a different norm.[107] Presidents also may need to violate CIL in order to vindicate other foreign policy goals, such as using force to protect human rights (as in Kosovo) or to prevent the proliferation of weapons of mass destruction (as in Iraq).

III. EXAMPLES OF PRESIDENTIAL CONTROL OVER INTERNATIONAL LAW

History shows the advantages of presidential interpretation of international law, primarily through the Executive's ability to gear CIL toward American foreign policy goals. If CIL were assumed to bind the executive branch or were fixed in meaning by the courts, the Executive would be prevented from reading CIL flexibly to pursue policies that advanced the national interest. Cooperation between the President and Congress is required if CIL is to assume the form of binding domestic law rather than simply acting as a form of foreign policy, providing a built-in check on the President's powers.

President Washington's Proclamation of Neutrality in 1793 demonstrates these principles at work. After beheading King Louis XVI, revolutionary France declared

---

[106] The Paquete Habana, 175 U.S. at 700 (emphasis added).

[107] See, for example, Authority of the Federal Bureau of Investigation to Override Customary or Other International Law in the Course of Extraterritorial Law Enforcement Activities, 13 Op. Office Legal Counsel 163, 170–71 (1989) (discussing whether Congress and the Executive can override CIL).

war on Great Britain and Holland on February 1, 1793.[108] France's new ambassador to the United States, Edmund Genet, landed in early April, about the same time that news reached the United States of the upheaval on the Continent. The news threw the American government into a quandary concerning its obligations under the 1778 treaties with France. Article 11 of the Treaty of Alliance called upon the United States to guarantee French possessions in America, which meant that France could now demand American defense of the French West Indies from British attack.[109] Article 17 of the companion Treaty of Amity and Commerce gave French warships and privateers the right to bring prizes (vessels seized from an enemy) into American ports, while denying the same right to her enemies.[110] Article 22 prohibited the United States from allowing the enemies of France to equip or launch privateers or sell prizes in American ports.

Washington's cabinet was deeply split over whether to observe the treaties. On learning of the French declaration of war, Treasury Secretary Hamilton—"with characteristic boldness," in Jefferson's words—began to press for a suspension of the French treaties.[111] Hamilton feared that providing military assistance to the French, or even allowing France to use the United States as a base for naval warfare, would provoke British retaliation against the United States. While he acknowledged that international law did not generally allow a country to void treaties because of a change in government, he reasoned that the uncertain status of the French government and the dangerous wartime situation allowed the United States to suspend the 1778 agreements.[112] While Secretary of State Jefferson agreed that American military participation in the European war was out of the question, he favored observance of the 1778 agreements because international law in his view did not allow suspension of a treaty because of a change in government. Jefferson's interpretation of CIL happily fell in line with his sympathy toward the French Revolution and suspicion of political ties with Britain.

On April 18, Washington sent a list of thirteen questions concerning the position to take on the war to Hamilton, Jefferson, Secretary of War Henry Knox, and Attorney General Edmund Randolph, and ordered a cabinet meeting for their

---

[108] For the relevant historical details, I have relied on STANLEY M. ELKINS & ERIC L. MCKITRICK, THE AGE OF FEDERALISM 303–73 (1993); FORREST MCDONALD, THE PRESIDENCY OF GEORGE WASHINGTON 113–37 (1974); Editorial Note, Jefferson's Opinion on the Treaties with France, reprinted in 25 THE PAPERS OF THOMAS JEFFERSON, supra note 2, at 597–602; Letter from Alexander Hamilton to John Jay (Apr. 9, 1793), in 14 PAPERS OF ALEXANDER HAMILTON, supra note 2, at 297–98 n.4. These events are also discussed in David P. Currie, The Constitution in Congress: The Third Congress, 1793–1795, 63 U. CHI. L. REV. 1, 4–16 (1996).

[109] Treaty of Alliance, Feb. 6, 1778, U.S.-Fr., Treaty Series 82, art. XI, 7 Bevans 777.

[110] Treaty of Amity and Commerce, Feb. 6, 1778, U.S.-Fr., 8 Stat. 12., art. XVII.

[111] Notes on Washington's Questions on Neutrality and the Alliance with France (May 6, 1793), reprinted in 25 PAPERS OF THOMAS JEFFERSON, supra note 2, at 665–66.

[112] See Letter from Alexander Hamilton to John Jay (Apr. 9, 1793), in 14 PAPERS OF ALEXANDER HAMILTON, supra note 2, at 297–98.

discussion the next day.[113] He asked, for example: "Are the United States obliged by good faith to consider the Treaties heretofore made with France as applying to the present situation of the parties?" Washington also requested that the cabinet consider whether Article 11 of the Treaty of Alliance applied to an offensive war by France, whether the United States could observe the treaties and remain neutral, and under what conditions the United States could suspend or terminate the 1778 agreements. Everyone answered Washington's first question in the affirmative, stating that a proclamation of neutrality should be issued, but in order to assuage Jefferson's concerns, the word "neutrality" was not used. Washington issued the proclamation, drafted by Randolph, on April 22.[114] Acknowledging a state of war between France and the other European powers, he declared that the United States "should with sincerity and good faith adopt and pursue a conduct friendly and impartial toward the belligerent [sic] Powers." President Washington further saw fit to "declare the disposition of the United States to observe the conduct aforesaid towards those Powers respectfully" and "to exhort and warn the citizens of the United States carefully to avoid all acts and proceedings whatsoever, which may in any manner tend to contravene such disposition." The Proclamation also stated that the federal government would prosecute those who "violate the law of nations, with respect to the Powers at war." Everyone in the cabinet realized that the United States was in no position to be anything but neutral, and there was immediate agreement to issue the Proclamation.[115]

Two other questions met with unanimous answers. The cabinet agreed on Washington's second question, stating that the President should receive Genet, an implicit acceptance of the legitimacy of the new French government. The cabinet decided unanimously, and apparently with little discussion, in the negative on Washington's last question: "Is it necessary or advisable to ask together the two Houses of Congress with a view to the present posture of European affairs? If it is, what should be the particular objects of such a call?" Adjourning the meeting without reaching the other ten questions, Washington asked his advisers to submit written responses on the suspension or termination of the 1778 treaties.

In his response of April 28, Jefferson argued that nothing in international law allowed for the suspension or annulling of a treaty simply because of a change in government.[116] He also argued that France was unlikely to ask the United States to fulfill its obligation to defend the West Indies and that it would be better to wait for a request before deciding whether to terminate the treaty. Hamilton, joined by Knox, argued on May 2 that the uncertain outcome of the civil war in France

---

[113] Letter from President George Washington to Alexander Hamilton, Thomas Jefferson, Henry Knox, and Edmund Randolph (Apr. 18, 1793), in 14 PAPERS OF ALEXANDER HAMILTON, *supra* note 2, at 326–27.

[114] George Washington, Proclamation, reprinted in 1 COMPILATION OF THE MESSAGES AND PAPERS OF THE PRESIDENTS: 1789–1897, at 156 (James D. Richardson ed., 1900).

[115] ELKINS & McKITRICK, AGE OF FEDERALISM, *supra* note 108, at 338.

[116] Opinion on the Treaties with France (Apr. 28, 1793), in 25 PAPERS OF THOMAS JEFFERSON, *supra* note 2, at 608–18.

justified the United States in temporarily suspending the operation of the treaty.[117] They also argued that the treaty applied only to defensive wars, not one in which France had declared war first, and that international law would justify termination of the treaties due to the dangerous circumstances. Randolph's opinion, entered on May 6, agreed with Jefferson. Telling Jefferson the next day that he "never had a doubt about the validity of the treaty," Washington decided against suspension.[118]

These events show that President Washington and his cabinet unanimously assumed that the interpretation of CIL, as well as of the 1778 treaties, rested within presidential authority. Washington's April 22 Proclamation declared that the United States would remain neutral in the European conflict under CIL. Washington did not act pursuant to any congressional authorization; indeed, the cabinet unanimously agreed that the President should not call Congress into session to discuss the meaning of the treaties. More than a year later, Congress finally stepped in, providing legislation for federal prosecution of those who violated American neutrality.[119] This legislative act accepted Washington's interpretation of CIL and the 1778 treaties and implemented it at the domestic level.

Washington's Proclamation, dependent in part on his ability to interpret CIL, was unquestionably the right choice for the nation. Going to war with Great Britain to protect France's Caribbean possessions and to aid the revolutionary government would have been a strategic disaster, as the War of 1812 would prove. The United States had virtually no navy and a tiny army devoted primarily to border conflicts with the Indian tribes on the northwestern frontier. Great Britain was a European power that could pose a real threat to the United States—it had the world's finest navy and shared a long border along Canada. Remaining neutral gave the United States time to organize itself under its new Constitution and allowed it to profit handsomely by trading with all sides in the European wars. While it sparked the creation of an opposition political party, Jefferson's Democrat-Republicans, Washington's neutrality policy appeared to receive popular approval and led to an economic boom. These benefits would have gone unrealized without Washington's ability to interpret CIL in line with American interests.

The neutrality crisis also underscores the inability of the courts to act with the swiftness often necessary for foreign affairs. Before the Washington administration decided on its policy toward revolutionary France, it sought the Supreme Court's advice. On July 18, 1793, Secretary of State Thomas Jefferson submitted a series of questions to the Justices on the international rules of neutrality and the meaning of the 1778 treaties of alliance with France. On August 8, 1793, the Justices refused. They concluded that answering the questions would amount to an unconstitutional advisory opinion because the "judicial power" of the federal courts extended only to

---

[117] Letter from Alexander Hamilton & Henry Knox to President George Washington (May 2, 1793), in 14 PAPERS OF ALEXANDER HAMILTON, *supra* note 2, at 367–96.

[118] Notes on Washington's Questions on Neutrality and the Alliance with France, reprinted in 25 PAPERS OF THOMAS JEFFERSON, *supra* note 2, at 666.

[119] Neutrality Act, 1 Stat. 381 (June 5, 1794).

actual cases or controversies: "The Lines of Separation drawn by the Constitution between the three Departments of Government—their being in certain Respects checks upon each other—and our being Judges of a court in the last Resort—are Considerations which afford strong arguments against the Propriety of our extrajudicially deciding the questions alluded to." The Court could not provide any guidance on the meaning of CIL when it was most needed—at the time when the nation had to take a position on its relationship with France—because of the Constitution's limit on its power to cases or controversies. This only reinforces the need for executive branch interpretation of CIL.[120]

The Civil War provides a second example of presidential control of the interpretation of CIL. General William T. Sherman's Civil War 1864 campaigns in Georgia and the Carolinas rested on a new reading of the laws of war to permit a new kind of warfare. Doubtless Sherman's critics believed he was violating CIL, though that was less clear at the time.[121] Sherman's mode of warfare, which involved wreaking devastation on the civilian population and cities of the South, grew directly out of the strategic decisions of his Commander-in-Chief, President Abraham Lincoln.[122] As early as 1862, Lincoln had rejected General George McClellan's plea to carry on a conflict that "should not be at all a war upon population, but against armed forces

---

[120] See Letter from Chief Justice John Jay to President Washington (August 8, 1793), reprinted in PAUL M. BATOR ET AL., HART & WECHSLER'S THE FEDERAL COURTS AND THE FEDERAL SYSTEM 65–67 (3d ed. 1978).

[121] See Thomas G. Robisch, *General William T. Sherman: Would the Georgia Campaigns of the First Commander of the Modern Era Comply with Current Law of War Standards?*, 9 EMORY INT'L L. REV. 459 (1995); J. F. C. FULLER, THE CONDUCT OF WAR 1789–1961: A STUDY OF THE IMPACT OF THE FRENCH, INDUSTRIAL, AND RUSSIAN REVOLUTIONS ON WAR AND ITS CONDUCT 107–11 (1961) (condemning Sherman's methods); B. H. LIDDLE HART, SHERMAN: SOLDIER, REALIST, AMERICAN 426 (1929) (Sherman "deliberately aimed at the non-combatant foundation of the hostile war spirit" and viewed law and war "as two opposed states" such that "war began when law broke down").

[122] Lincoln and two of his most outstanding generals, Grant and Sherman, had begun fairly early in the war to contemplate a strategy of "total war" of the kind that Sherman was eventually to implement in Georgia and the Carolinas in 1864. See ULYSSES M. GRANT, PERSONAL MEMOIRS 198–99 (James M. McPherson ed. 1999) (After Shiloh, "I gave up all idea of saving the Union except by complete conquest"; this led him to the conclusion that it was necessary "to consume everything that could be used to support or supply armies," including "the property of the citizens whose territory was invaded"); James M. McPherson, *Lincoln and the Strategy of Unconditional Surrender*, in Gabor S. Borritt (ed.), LINCOLN: THE WAR PRESIDENT 45–47 (1992) (describing changes in Lincoln's and Grant's strategic thinking, beginning in 1862, about the need for "total" war); EDWARD HAGERMAN, THE AMERICAN CIVIL WAR AND THE ORIGINS OF MODERN WARFARE xii–xiv (1988) (discussing novel features of Sherman's method of waging war, and analyzing changed circumstances that appeared to dictate adoption of those methods); *id.* at 207–08 (describing development of Sherman's thinking, beginning in 1862, on the necessity of waging "total" war against civilian population and property). Moreover, as Eliot Cohen has shown in detail, Lincoln was a highly engaged and well-informed Commander-in-Chief who "exercised a constant oversight of the war effort from beginning to end." ELIOT A. COHEN, SUPREME COMMAND: SOLDIERS, STATESMEN, AND LEADERSHIP IN WARTIME 17 (2002).

and political organization."[123] Instead, Lincoln decided on a total war, directed against combatants and civilians alike.[124] By July 1863, the Union Army's conduct toward Confederate noncombatants and their property was so destructive that President Jefferson Davis wrote a personal letter to Lincoln calling his attention to these apparent violations of the laws of war and urging him to remedy them.[125] Lincoln never replied. In a letter of October 19, 1864, to his commander, Major General Henry Halleck, Sherman characterized the "not purely military or strategic" objectives of his Georgia and Carolinas campaign as an attempt to "illustrate the vulnerability of the South" by wreaking destruction on civilian property.[126] Lincoln, who was "ecstatic" over the news of Sherman's capture of Atlanta[127] and who had "unlimited confidence" in his general,[128] can therefore fairly be said to have authorized Sherman's practices in the Georgia and Carolinas campaigns.

[123] Letter of Major General George McClellan to President Abraham Lincoln (July 7, 1862), in HARRY S. STOUT, UPON THE ALTAR OF A NATION: A MORAL HISTORY OF THE CIVIL WAR 137 (2006). McClellan had urged Lincoln to conduct the war "upon the highest principles known to Christian civilization. It should not be a war looking to the subjugation of the people of any State in any event. It should not be at all a war upon population, but against armed forces and political organization. Neither confiscation of property, political executions of persons, territorial organizations of States, or forcible abolition of slavery should be contemplated for a moment. In prosecuting the war all private property and unarmed persons should be strictly protected, subject only to the necessity of military operation." *Id.*

[124] In response to McClellan's letter, Lincoln designated Major General John Pope as the commander of the new Army of Virginia. "After spending three weeks in Washington, D.C., with Lincoln and [Secretary of War] Stanton, Pope clearly understood the new course his commander wanted him to take." STOUT, UPON THE ALTAR OF A NATION, *supra* note 123, at 138. With Lincoln's approval, *id.* at 141, Pope issued a series of General Orders that brought the war home to Southern civilians. See Major General John Pope's General Orders No. 5, 7, 11, and 19, at http://www.civilwarhome.com/popesorders.htm. Within four months of receiving McClellan's letter, Lincoln relieved him from the command of the Army of the Potomac. Abraham Lincoln, Executive Order (Nov. 5, 1862), at http://www.presidency.ucsb.edu/ws/index.php?pid=69825#axzz1cmAyxq2Z.

[125] STOUT, UPON THE ALTAR OF A NATION, *supra* note 123, at 259.

[126] BROOKS D. SIMPSON & JEAN V. BERLIN (EDS.), SHERMAN'S CIVIL WAR: SELECTED CORRESPONDENCE OF WILLIAM T. SHERMAN 1860–1865 at 736 (1999). In that letter, Sherman went on to say: "They don't know what war means, but when the rich planters of the Oconee and Savannah see their fences and corn and hogs and sheep vanish before their eyes they will have something more than a mean opinion of the 'Yanks.' Even now our poor mules laugh at the fine cornfields, and our soldiers riot on chestnuts, sweet potatoes, pigs, chickens, &c." After Savannah fell to Sherman on December 21, 1864, he estimated that his army had caused $100 million in damage, four-fifths of which he characterized as "simple waste and destruction." PHILIP HOWES, THE CATALYTIC WARS: A STUDY IN THE DEVELOPMENT OF WARFARE 1860–1870 at 267 (1998).

[127] STOUT, UPON THE ALTAR OF A NATION, *supra* note 123, at 368. Sherman also made a "Christmas gift" of the city of Savannah to President Lincoln in 1864. See Matthew C. Waxman, *Siegecraft and Surrender: The Law and Strategy of Cities as Targets*, 39 VA. J. INT'L L. 353, 379 (1999). On that occasion, Lincoln wrote a personal letter to Sherman, telling him that his success "brings those who sat in darkness [i.e., the South's civilian population] to see a great light." Letter of President Abraham Lincoln to General William T. Sherman (Dec. 26, 1864), quoted in MEMOIRS OF GENERAL WILLIAM T. SHERMAN 641 (Charles Royster ed., 1990) (1885).

[128] SIMPSON & BERLIN, SHERMAN'S CIVIL WAR, *supra* note 126, at 782 (Letter of December 31, 1864).

To the extent that the law of war applied to Sherman's campaigns, it was chiefly in the form of the Lieber Code, which President Lincoln had himself issued.[129] The Lieber Code represented an unstable compromise between the demands of the form of warfare that was emerging from the rise of the modern nation-state and the more traditional military practices of eighteenth and early nineteenth-century Europe.[130] The code included several important provisions that maintained the traditional distinction between combatants and civilians—a distinction that the emerging model of total national mobilization threatened to undermine. Among these provisions was one that generally prohibited the unannounced bombardment of cities except when a surprise assault was being prepared.[131] It is this provision that Sherman arguably violated when he bombarded the city of Atlanta without warning, then ordered it to be evacuated and burned.[132] Sherman ordered the evacuation and destruction of the city even after the defending Confederate Army had left and he was free to enter it without resistance, and he deliberately destroyed privately owned Confederate civilian property. Both acts arguably also violated the law of war, at least as it was understood before the Civil War.[133] Yet given the unsettled state of the law of war at the time and as the war unfolded, Sherman's bombardment and subsequent treatment of Atlanta might arguably have been defended as a "military necessity" in the emerging circumstances of "total war."

A third example of presidential interpretation of CIL is supplied by President John F. Kennedy's actions during the Cuban Missile Crisis. Faced with the alarming disclosure that Soviet missiles were being introduced into Communist Cuba, President Kennedy grappled with the American response. Although the Cold War had already lasted for well over a decade, the United States was not in a state of war with either the Soviet Union or Cuba. Although the introduction of the Soviet missiles to a place within close range of the United States' major East Coast cities undoubtedly constituted a grave threat to the nation's security, the threat could not by itself have reasonably been considered an "armed attack" within the meaning of

---

[129] See Waxman, *Siegecraft and Surrender, supra* note 127, at 372–74.

[130] *Id.*

[131] "Commanders, whenever admissible, inform the enemy of their intention to bombard a place, so that the noncombatants, and especially the women and children, may be removed before the bombardment commences. But it is no infraction of the common law of war to omit thus to inform the enemy. Surprise may be a necessity." General Orders, No. 100, Instructions for Government of Armies of the United States in the Field, art. 19 (April 24, 1863) (Lieber Code).

[132] See Robisch, *Would the Georgia Campaigns, supra* note 121, at 477–78; Richard Shelly Hartigan, Lieber's Code and the Law of War 21 (1983); J. M. Spaight, War Rights on Land 171 (1911) (Sherman's unannounced bombing "cannot be reconciled with the principle laid down in" Article 19 of the Lieber Code). Sherman's orders also may have been inconsistent with the law of war as interpreted by General Henry Halleck, the author of an 1861 treatise on the subject. H. W. Halleck, International Law; or Rules Regulating the Intercourse of States in Peace and War ch. xix, § 24 at 466 (1861) ("The general rule by which we should regulate our conduct toward an enemy, is that of moderation, and on no occasion should we unnecessarily destroy his property").

[133] See Robert J. Delahunty & John Yoo, *Executive Power vs. International Law*, 30 Harv. J. L. & Pub. Pol'y 73 (2006).

Article 51 of the UN Charter. It was widely understood that an armed attack was necessary before the right to take lawful armed countermeasures in self-defense was triggered.[134] At best, a nation could act in anticipatory self-defense if an attack were imminent, and even this principle remains controversial (both in whether it exists and whether it is prone to abuse).[135] A unilateral American naval blockade of Cuba, even though defensive in nature, could well be regarded as an unlawful act of aggression in violation of Article 2(4) of the Charter.

The Kennedy administration was greatly concerned with international law when considering whether to institute a naval blockade. To minimize legal objections, it characterized the action as a "quarantine" rather than a "blockade," because the latter constituted an act of war under international law. It limited the action to interdicting the flow of offensive military equipment into Cuba, rather than erecting a general blockade.[136] When it could not obtain UN Security Council authorization for its action (which the Soviet veto obviously made impossible), the Kennedy administration sought authorization for the use of force from the Organization of American States.[137] While these maneuvers succeeded in their aim of altering international perceptions of the American action, they hardly silenced the objections to it on grounds of international law.[138]

Again, the arguable limitation in international law does nothing to cloud the President's constitutional authority to act as Kennedy did. That President Kennedy had the constitutional authority to order the "quarantine" of Cuba was incontestable, whatever the legality of that action under international law. And regardless of the constitutional authority, which as far as we know went unchallenged, it seems undeniable that JFK's interpretation of international law provided great benefit to the nation. JFK understood the right to use force in self-defense to include threats, such as a rapid change in the balance of power, which did not qualify as an "imminent" attack. Forcing the Soviets to remove the intermediate-range ballistic missiles from Cuba protected American national security and removed a potentially destabilizing factor from the Cold War's balance of terror. JFK's interpretation of international law also provided the tool—the "quarantine"—that applied pressure to the Soviets without escalating the crisis into an open military conflict. The administration was able to use international law to assist American foreign

---

[134] See, e.g., IAN BROWNLIE, INTERNATIONAL LAW AND THE USE OF FORCE BY STATES 258–61 (1963). In the event, the State Department advised, and the Kennedy Administration agreed, not to defend the naval intervention as an act of self-defense. See ABRAM CHAYES, THE CUBAN MISSILE CRISIS: INTERNATIONAL CRISES AND THE ROLE OF LAW 65 (1974); see also Eugene V. Rostow, *Until What? Enforcement Action or Collective Self-Defense?*, 85 AM. J. INT'L L. 506, 515 (1991).

[135] John Yoo, *Using Force*, *supra* note 104.

[136] See LAWRENCE FREEDMAN, KENNEDY'S WARS: BERLIN, CUBA, LAOS, AND VIETNAM 183, 187–88, 191 (2000).

[137] See *id.* at 203.

[138] See Quincy Wright, *The Cuban Quarantine*, 57 AM. J. INT'L L. 546, 553–65 (1963) (arguing quarantine was unlawful). But see Myres S. McDougal, *Editorial Comment, The Soviet-Cuban Quarantine and Self-Defense*, 57 AM. J. INT'L L. 597 (1963) (defending legality of quarantine as self-defense).

policy in ending the crisis with the peaceful removal of the Soviet missiles from Cuba.

IV. CONCLUSION

We do not underestimate the importance of CIL in a globalizing world. Indeed, we suggest that CIL will remain an important set of rules affecting decisions by national decision-makers. The United States has been an important contributor to the development of particular norms of CIL in the past, and it is likely to remain so in the future.

CIL's importance as a manifestation of globalization does not mean, however, that CIL is automatically enforceable as self-executing domestic law that binds the President, Congress, or the courts. Rather, as we have argued here, CIL should not be considered domestic law unless and until Congress chooses to incorporate a CIL norm via statute. Absent congressional action, we take the view that CIL is left to presidential interpretations to which the other branches should defer. As a policy choice, there is little doubt that the President is a more effective institutional decision-maker on how and whether to accept, reject, interpret, or apply CIL norms. As such, we believe the President, and not the courts, is the entity best positioned to mediate between the increasing demands of CIL and the U.S. constitutional system.

6 Globalization and the States

As its name suggests, the United States was founded as a union of previously sovereign and independent states. The Constitution would not have been adopted without guarantees that each state would receive equal representation in the Senate, and it is one of only three provisions of the Constitution that cannot be amended. Even today state governments dominate many areas of law and public policy in the United States. The main source of law in the early United States was the English common law, which largely entered the American legal system through the actions of state governments. Although federal law has expanded dramatically over the past century, it was, and in many ways still is, meant to operate interstitially—as specialized law that acts against the background of state common law. The federal government relies on the cooperation of the states, which possess the great bulk of judicial and executive officials in the country, to administer many social and regulatory programs. The Constitution's enumeration of the powers of the federal government over discrete subjects ensures that states will play the primary role in regulating the conduct of private citizens and entities.

Thus, the states have remained a vital and central component of the American governmental system in the twenty-first century. The impact of globalization cannot change this reality. As we explained in chapters 2 and 3, globalization's pressures have transformed subjects that are primarily and often exclusively regulated at the state level into matters of international relations and regulation. Because the U.S. constitutional system allocates power over foreign affairs to the federal government, some commentators have suggested that international or national governmental bodies will ultimately displace the states from areas of globalized public policy. Such a diminished role for the states might seem a logical consequence of globalization.

We disagree. The states can and should play a prominent role in the accommodation of globalization with the popular sovereignty of the Constitution. In this chapter, we describe a division of state and federal authority that preserves an independent (albeit limited) role for the states even in areas implicating foreign affairs and international law. Such a division of authority is consistent with the constitutional primacy of the federal government to preempt state policies in foreign affairs. As we will further explain, the political arms of the federal government—the executive and legislative branches—have shown little inclination to preempt state activities that implicate foreign affairs. Rather, they have brought the states into the foreign policy process by allocating to the states a measure of independent discretion in the implementation of international law obligations. Indeed, given the states' primary role in regulating most areas of American civil society and the vast administrative resources at their command, successful adaptation to globalization demands their active cooperation with the policies of the federal government.

I. GLOBALIZATION, THE NEW INTERNATIONAL LAW, AND THE STATES

The collision between state autonomy and globalization arises largely from the changes in contemporary international law. As we discussed in chapter 2, traditional international law governed relations between nation-states. Consistent with the conception of Westphalian sovereignty, domestic affairs and regulations were left to the "absolute and exclusive" control of nation-states and could not be a matter for international regulation without a nation-state's consent.

Traditional international law rarely collided with domestic matters regulated in the United States by the state governments. When such collisions did occur, they invariably involved matters directly implicating relations with another state, such as foreign sovereign immunity, diplomatic and consular relations, the treatment of aliens, and the laws of war. These rarely implicated state law, which has traditionally dominated areas of law such as criminal law, public morals, contracts, torts, property, trusts and estates, and family law. State laws in these areas were typically challenged under traditional international law only when a foreign government or foreign national was a party with an interest. State law that only affected American citizens rarely had to take traditional international law into account.

The acceleration of globalization and cross-border activity has led, as we described in chapter 2, to the explosive growth of international law. Most significantly, the "new" international law has increasingly concerned itself with a nation-state's treatment of its own citizens as well as relationships between citizens of different nation-states. Freedom of religion, to take just one of many examples, is guaranteed not just by the First Amendment of the U.S. Constitution, but also by the International Covenant on Civil and Political Rights. Certain rules with respect to adoption, child custody, and parental access are limited by the Hague Convention on the Civil Aspects of International Child Abduction or the Hague Convention on Intercountry Adoption. Government procurement, even by local governments, is not just a matter for the domestic appropriations process, but also a question for U.S. obligations under international trade agreements.[1] This shift in the subject matter for international regulation has naturally increased the likelihood of greater conflicts between state laws and international law.

The explosion of cross-border trade has resulted in an increasingly elaborate and complex system of trade agreements. Such agreements originally focused on the administration of tariffs and other customs duties, which are subjects of law controlled by the federal government. Modern trade agreements, however, have increasingly sought to reduce or eliminate nontariff barriers to the trade of goods and services, government subsidies of domestic industries, and government procurement practices. Nontariff barriers have been found to include many laws that impact the sale of foreign goods and services, including environmental laws, health and safety regulations, and even the regulation of public morals. Subsidies for local state exports, such as Florida's support for its citrus industry, are also subject to challenge under international trade agreements. Even state procurement practices for local infrastructure projects can be challenged under modern international trade agreements.

Globalization has also fostered a wide variety of cross-border activity between private individuals. Individuals today engage in a bewildering variety of international commercial transactions, from the simple sale and transportation of goods to trade in national currencies and securities to Internet gambling. New international treaties facilitate these transactions by establishing rules governing contracts for the international sale of goods, the choice of dispute resolution mechanisms, and the enforcement of foreign judgments, among others. Noneconomic private cross-border activity has further spurred the creation of new international treaties regulating matters such as the recognition of wills and the administration of estates, divorce and child custody, and adoptions. Treaties in both the economic and noneconomic realm could potentially displace or at least modify areas of law currently controlled by the states.

Most dramatically, globalization has led to the proliferation of international human rights law. Unlike agreements relating to foreign trade or cross-border private activity, international human rights treaties do not require any foreign connection. Instead, they regulate a nation-state's relations with its own citizens. Together, the leading international human rights treaties create a broad array of rights and obligations that directly intersect with many aspects of state law and policy. In addition to guaranteeing a broad array of individual rights that are similar to those protected by the U.S. Constitution, human rights treaties also guarantee economic, social, and cultural rights that overlap with a state government's provisions

---

[1] See Appendix to Subpart B of 2 CFR part 176—U.S. States, Other Sub-Federal Entities, and Other Entities Subject to U.S. Obligations under International Agreements (as of February 16, 2010), 75 Fed. Reg. 14324 (tabulating U.S. trade agreements and their applicability to U.S. states).

for the same. State control over domestic relations and family law are the subject, for example, of the Convention on the Rights of the Child and the Convention for the Elimination of Discrimination against Women. Many countries believe that international instruments prohibit American states from imposing the death penalty in a variety of contexts, even though the United States has taken reservations from international human rights agreements that ban the punishment.

The United States has not joined all of the treaty regimes discussed here. But many, if not most, are under consideration by the U.S. government. Some of the treaties that have been ratified by the vast majority of countries in the world, such as the Convention on the Rights of the Child, might become customary international law in the view of many academics and international lawyers. Whether all of these treaties are ultimately used to challenge state laws and policies is not the primary concern. Instead, what matters most is the direction of the new international law. That direction clearly points toward conflicts with traditional areas of state control.

II. A FORMAL DEFENSE OF STATE AUTONOMY IN FOREIGN AFFAIRS

As a doctrinal matter, many courts and commentators have a simple solution for conflicts between globalization and state autonomy. Invoking the federal government's dominance over foreign affairs, they have argued against any independent role for states in matters implicating foreign affairs. In this section, we offer a three-pronged formal doctrinal defense of state autonomy in foreign affairs. In the next section, we offer a functional defense of this outcome.

First, while the Supreme Court has found that the federal government preempted a number of state activities in recent years, the Court has refrained from endorsing a theory of federal exclusivity over foreign affairs. This means that the states are generally free to engage in foreign policy activities absent express preemption by Congress or the President. It also means that federal courts cannot override state foreign affairs activities without authority from the political branches. Second, the Supreme Court has continued to impose constitutional prohibitions on the commandeering of state governors and other state executive officials, thus limiting the ability of the federal government to force state governments to fulfill a particular foreign affairs goal. Third, the federal government itself has relied on states to carry out international obligations and to fulfill foreign policy goals. All of this suggests that the Constitution permits states to maintain an autonomous role in foreign affairs that includes the accommodation of many aspects of globalization

A. The Retreat from Federal Exclusivity

Federal exclusivity prevents state governments from encroaching on matters implicating foreign affairs, whether or not the federal government has actually approved a treaty, statute, executive agreement, or declaration on the particular foreign policy issue. This view holds broad support among commentators, and a number of the Court's decisions have also embraced this approach. For instance, on one occasion the Supreme Court declared that, for purposes of foreign affairs, the "state[s] . . . do[] not exist."[2] The most powerful judicial articulation of the theory of federal exclusivity in foreign affairs is found in the 1968 decision *Zschernig v. Miller*. In *Zschernig*, the Supreme Court invalidated an Oregon statute limiting the rights of foreigners to inherit real property if the inheriting foreign national's home country did not give U.S. citizens similar rights. The Court's decision depended on a theory of exclusivity because the Court did not find that the state statute had been expressly preempted by any treaty, statute, or presidential order. Rather, the Court held that state laws "must give way if they impair the effective exercise of the Nation's foreign policy."[3] *Zschernig* represented a substantial innovation in the Court's approach to foreign affairs preemption because it authorized federal courts to preempt inconsistent state law based on their own determination of the nation's foreign policy interests. This theory of federal exclusivity has very little support in the original understanding of the Constitution. In fact, as Michael Ramsey has argued, the historical record strongly suggests that the Founders anticipated that only Congress and the President would have the power to preempt state actions through treaty, statute, or executive agreements.[4] There is no evidence from this period supporting an independent federal judicial power to preempt state foreign policy activities.[5]

It is not surprising, therefore, that the Court has not reaffirmed the federal exclusivity approach in the forty-plus years since *Zschernig*. Subsequent decisions eschewed federal exclusivity in favor of actual preemption by statute or executive action.[6] The Court's most recent decision in this area, *American Insurance Association v. Garamendi*, represents an important departure from *Zschernig*. Although a lower court had invoked *Zschernig* to invalidate a California statute targeting foreign insurance companies for failing to pay World War II–related policies, the Supreme Court took a different approach. In his opinion for the Court, Justice Souter relied

---

[2] United States v. Belmont, 301 U.S. 324, 331 (1937). For academic commentary in support of this broad proposition, see Louis Henkin, Foreign Affairs and the U.S. Constitution 163–65 (1996) (describing view that states are excluded from foreign affairs even without action by federal political branches); Bradford R. Clark, *Federal Common Law: A Structural Reinterpretation*, 144 U. Pa. L. Rev. 1245, 1297 (1996) (concluding that "the Constitution appears to preclude the states from exercising direct authority over foreign relations"); Brannon P. Denning & Jack H. McCall, Jr., *The Constitutionality of State and Local "Sanctions" against Foreign Countries: Affairs of State, States' Affairs, or a Sorry State of Affairs?*, 26 Hastings Const. L.Q. 307 (1999) (arguing that state foreign policy activities are unconstitutional); David Schmahmann & James Finch, *The Unconstitutionality of State and Local Enactments in the United States Restricting Business Ties with Burma (Myanmar)*, 30 Vand. J. Transnat'l L. 175 (1997) (arguing that state and local sanctions on Burma may be unconstitutional). For a summary of the Supreme Court case law in this vein, see Michael D. Ramsey, *The Power of the States in Foreign Affairs: The Original Understanding of Foreign Policy Federalism*, 75 Notre Dame L. Rev. 341, 350–65 (1999).

[3] Zschernig v. Miller, 389 U.S. 429, 440 (1968).

[4] Ramsey, *supra* note 2, at 369–90.

[5] Jack L. Goldsmith, *Federal Courts, Foreign Affairs, and Federalism*, 83 Va. L. Rev. 1617 (1997).

[6] *See, e.g.,* Crosby v. Nat'l Foreign Trade Council, 530 U.S. 363 (2000).

on executive agreements between the United States and German governments as evidence that the federal government had preempted California's statute. Although these agreements did not explicitly preempt California's statutes, the Court found them to be evidence of an "unmistakabl[e]" policy to negotiate a resolution to the insurance coverage dispute.[7]

The Court suggested that its approach followed Justice Harlan's concurrence in *Zschernig*, which would require preemption of state law if "state legislation will produce something more than an incidental effect in conflict with express foreign policy of the National Government . . ." The Court must weigh the "strength of the state interest, judged by standards of traditional practice, when deciding how serious a conflict must be shown before declaring the state law preempted." Justice Harlan suggested that the strength of the state interest in a particular policy could reduce the likelihood of finding that state law in conflict with federal law.[8] In following the Harlan approach, the *Garamendi* approach implicitly rejected the sweeping version of federal exclusivity adopted by the *Zschernig* majority.

Garamendi itself has been criticized for giving the federal executive branch too much discretion in its power to preempt state law.[9] Even so, *Garamendi*'s approach still leaves room for a system of state autonomy in foreign affairs. Had the Court revived *Zschernig*'s approach, almost all of the state activities involving foreign affairs would be subject to immediate preemption by federal courts, even in the absence of presidential or congressional action. Under *Garamendi*, states are still free to take acts that impact foreign affairs substantially unless and until the President or Congress acts to preempt. And even when the President or Congress acts via a treaty, statute, executive agreement, or presidential declaration, the Court would, per *Garamendi*, weigh the strength of the state's interest against the federal claim of preemption.

The Court confirmed its commitment to this approach in *Medellín v. Texas*.[10] In *Medellín*, the Court refused to stay the Texas execution of a foreign national for capital murder, even though the execution would likely have violated U.S. treaty obligations and conflicted directly with the President's foreign policy goals. As we explained in chapter 4, the *Medellín* Court relied on the non-self-execution doctrine

---

[7] American Insurance Ass'n. v. Garamendi, 539 U.S. 396, 420–21 (2003). Most notably, the Court avoided invoking a broad Zschernig-style approach to preemption in Barclays Bank v. Franchise Tax Board of California, 512 U.S. 298 (1994), when it upheld a state tax that appeared to conflict with a broader federal international tax policy.

[8] Garamendi, 539 U.S. at 420. Although Justice Souter had no difficulty finding a necessary conflict in this case, he did suggest that there must be some point at which the strength of the state interest in vindicating the claims of Holocaust survivors might displace the federal standard. But because the federal government has the same interest, he held, the "humanity underlying the state statute could not give the State the benefit of any doubt in resolving the conflict with national policy." *Id.* at 426–27.

[9] See *id.* at 430 (Ginsburg, J., dissenting); Brannon P. Denning & Michael D. Ramsey, *American Insurance Association v. Garamendi and Executive Preemption in Foreign Affairs*, 46 Wm. & Mary L. Rev. 825, 898–925 (2004).

[10] Medellín v. Texas, 552 U.S. 491 (2008).

to reach its decision. But the Court's decision to permit Texas to act in conflict with express federal policy set by the President further confirms the end of the *Zschernig* conception of federal exclusivity over all matters affecting foreign affairs.

B. Commandeering

Under the nonexclusivity approach, the federal government's control over the states is limited to action by the political branches to preempt through treaty, statute, or executive act. But even this federal power is constrained because it is limited by the constitutional prohibitions against the commandeering of states. The Supreme Court has imposed limitations on the federal government's ability to "commandeer" state governments to carry out federal policies, having derived these "anti-commandeering" principles from the Tenth Amendment's recognition of the states' residual sovereignty.[11] The modern anti-commandeering doctrine began with *New York v. United States* (1992), which invalidated a federal regulatory scheme requiring states to dispose of low-level radioactive waste. The federal law was invalidated for impermissibly intruding on state sovereignty by commandeering the state governments to "enact and enforce a federal regulatory program."[12] Five years later, the Court extended this principle to state executive officials. In *Printz v. United States*, the Court held that the federal government could not require state law enforcement officers to carry out federal gun background checks. Justice Scalia's opinion for the Court held that the ban on commandeering applied to both state legislatures and executives (though not judiciaries). "Congress cannot circumvent that prohibition by conscripting the state's officers directly."[13]

Unlike the Court's other federalism decisions, *New York* and *Printz* do not impose limitations on the subject matter of federal regulations. Rather, the decisions limit how the federal government may pursue otherwise valid objectives. According to the Court, the prohibition on anti-commandeering reflects the Constitution's commitment to maintaining a dual system of sovereignty of federal and state governments. Justice O'Connor's opinion for the Court in *New York* stated this principle broadly:

States are not mere political subdivisions of the United States. State governments are neither regional offices nor administrative agencies of the Federal Government. The positions occupied by state officials appear nowhere on the Federal Government's most detailed organizational chart. The Constitution instead "leaves to the several States a residuary and inviolable sovereignty," reserved explicitly to the States by the Tenth Amendment.[14]

---

[11] See, e.g., Printz v. United States, 521 U.S. 898 (1997); New York v. United States, 505 U.S. 144 (1992).

[12] New York, 505 U.S. at 161.

[13] Printz, 521 U.S. at 927, 935.

[14] New York, 505 U.S. at 188 (citation omitted).

Neither the *New York* nor the *Printz* Court discussed whether the constitutional prohibition on commandeering also applies to the federal government's power to conduct foreign affairs. Nor has the Court addressed this question in subsequent anti-commandeering cases.[15] Scholars, however, have highlighted the potential significance of the anti-commandeering doctrine, particularly as it was applied in *Printz*, to the federal government's efforts to exercise its foreign affairs powers against the states through the treaty power.

Professor Vazquez, however, argues that the primary legal justification for the anti-commandeering principle does not apply to exercises of the federal treaty power. Citing Justice Holmes's holding in *Missouri v. Holland* that the treaty power is not limited by any "invisible radiation" of the Tenth Amendment, Vazquez concludes that the federal treaty power does not violate the Tenth Amendment because there are no limitations on the subjects that can be regulated by treaties.[16] This critique, however, fails to grapple with the important distinction between the power to make a treaty and the power to implement a treaty's obligations. The Constitution plainly allocates to the federal government the exclusive power to make treaties with foreign governments. This power to make treaties is not reserved to the states by the Tenth Amendment. However, it does not follow that the Constitution also allocates to the federal government the exclusive power to implement a treaty's obligations as a matter of domestic law.[17]

A common mechanism for implementing a treaty's obligations, as Chief Justice Marshall noted in *Foster v. Neilson*, is a new federal statute specifically designed to implement the treaty.[18] But this is not the only mechanism. Some treaties may be implemented by presidential action, others by state governments.[19] The variety of domestic legal mechanisms for implementing treaties suggests that the power to implement is not coterminous with the power to make a treaty. The fact that the President or Congress has some power to implement treaties, for instance, does not mean that either institution's implementing actions are free of constitutional

---

[15] In fact, no court has addressed the foreign affairs implications of *Printz* and *New York*. The First Circuit briefly considered the issue, but found that the litigant had waived the argument. See, e.g., Nat'l Foreign Trade Council v. Natsios, 181 F.3d 38, 61 n.17 (1st Cir. 1999).

[16] Vazquez therefore argued that the *Printz* limitation should be read very narrowly. Professor Flaherty added a review of historical materials that generally agreed with this analysis and called for reconsideration of *Printz* and *New York* even in the domestic context. See Martin S. Flaherty, *Are We to Be a Nation? Federal Power v. "States' Rights" in Foreign Affairs*, 70 U. Colo. L. Rev. 1277, 1296 (1999).

[17] The treaty power is only one of the foreign affairs powers that might be invoked against the states. A similar distinction might limit the federal government's power to invoke customary international law against the states. While Congress and the President hold the power to recognize rules of customary international law as binding on the U.S. government, their power to implement these rules against the states are still constrained by the Constitution's anti-commandeering prohibitions.

[18] Foster v. Neilson, 27 U.S. (2 Pet.) 253, 314 (1829).

[19] See Julian G. Ku, *The State of New York Does Exist: How the States Control Compliance with International Law*, 82 N.C. L. Rev. 457, 499–510 (2004) (describing state implementation of treaties involving private international law); Exec. Order No. 13, 107, 63 Fed. Reg. 68,991 (Dec. 10, 1998) (implementing U.S. obligations under various international human rights treaties).

constraints imposed by either federalism or separation of powers. As Nicholas Rosenkranz has forcefully argued, Congress may not be able to rely on its delegated authority under the Necessary and Proper Clause when implementing a treaty by legislation.[20] Rather, Congress may need to rely on its other delegated powers to enact legislation implementing a treaty.

Under this view, when the federal government implements a treaty, it is limited by the Tenth Amendment in the same manner as any other federal statute. To be sure, this view of the Necessary and Proper Clause's limited scope with respect to the treaty power remains disputed.[21] The most effective critique follows an argument first developed by Alexander Hamilton in his defense of the controversial Jay Treaty during the 1790s. In short, Hamilton argued that neither Congress nor the states could limit the implementation of a treaty. Hamilton's argument was contested at the time by other Founders, such as James Madison, who sought to allocate to Congress an independent power of implementing treaties distinct from the treaty-making power itself. Indeed, the issue of implementation remained contested from the outset.

Additionally, neither Hamilton nor Madison confronted a treaty that purports to commandeer states in a manner much more intrusive than treaties at the time would have required. In the consular relations context, for instance, the federal government agreed that the United States would notify consulates whenever a foreign national was arrested. State officials are primarily responsible for carrying out the obligation, since state and local law enforcement carry out the vast majority of arrests. Without having any input in the development of the policy, states are thus "put in the position of taking the blame for [a federal obligation's] burdensomeness and for its defects."[22] In short, these concerns for state autonomy likely helped animate the court's anti-commandeering precedents and their application to treaties.

Alternative methods can accomplish federal policy goals and alleviate state burdens without commandeering states. The federal government could implement its obligations by, for instance, creating a private right of action in federal courts for foreign nationals to challenge violations of their consular rights.[23] It could pass legislation that requires state and local officials to comply with treaty obligations in order to receive related federal funding.[24]

[20] See Nicholas Quinn Rosenkranz, *Executing the Treaty Power*, 118 HARV. L. REV. 1868, 1880–1912 (2005) (arguing that Congress's legislative power under Article I to implement treaties is limited to matters it otherwise would have domestic authority to regulate).

[21] See, e.g., Carlos M. Vazquez, *Missouri v. Holland's Second Holding*, 73 MO. L. REV. 939 (2008) (arguing that, for Founders, "[l]eaving the implementation of treaty commitments to the States would have been anathema").

[22] Printz, 521 U.S. at 930 (discussing the burden created by a federal law not pursuant to a treaty).

[23] For instance, the Court has stated that a treaty can serve as the basis for a private lawsuit invalidating a state law. Asakura v. City of Seattle, 265 U.S. 332 (1924).

[24] See South Dakota v. Dole, 483 U.S. 203, 210–11 (1987) (rejecting "independent constitutional bar" on use of spending power to compel state action). Compare Jesse Choper & John Yoo, *Who's So Afraid of the Eleventh Amendment?*, 105 COLUM. L. REV. 213 (2006) (arguing that Spending Clause can be used to achieve federal policies barred by limits on Commerce Clause).

Alternative methods to facilitate state cooperation do not render anti-commandeering limitations meaningless. Rather, by imposing a limitation on how the federal government limits the role of states in foreign affairs, we can preserve an independent role for states in a variety of important contexts. Either the federal government acts through its political branches to implement a foreign policy obligation, or it leaves that decision for the states. But it cannot commandeer the states to carry out its foreign policy obligations on its behalf.

C. Federal Political Branch Support for State Autonomy

Even with the prohibition against commandeering, the federal government has broad powers to eliminate state activities that interfere in foreign affairs. While it has refrained from commandeering states to comply with demands from foreign governments, it has the acknowledged power to preempt state activities through treaty, statute, executive agreement, or executive declaration.[25] Surprisingly, the federal government has rarely chosen to exercise this power, but instead has limited its own ability to preempt state activity through treaties. The result of this choice amounts to even more space for states to affect foreign policy.

The most pronounced examples of the federal government's self-imposed limitations are found in reservations, understandings, and declarations attached to the ratification of international agreements. RUDs are usually conditions imposed by the Senate before giving advice and consent to treaties. In the trade context, the limitations are contained in legislation approving and implementing trade agreements. Although RUDs take different forms, all usually have the same legal consequence: they prevent international agreements from preempting, commandeering, or otherwise restricting the ability of state officials to act in matters affecting foreign affairs.[26] For instance, foreign nations have gone to international tribunals to challenge a number of state laws and activities as violations of U.S. obligations under international trade agreements.[27] But states are largely free to ignore findings by international tribunals, which do not have direct domestic effect. In approving international agreements, Congress specifically prevented such agreements from

---

[25] The first three methods have long been recognized. See HENKIN, *supra* note 2, at 157–58 (explaining that "there is no reason why a treaty, an executive agreement, a judicial doctrine or any federal regulation" should not preempt state law). The fourth method was recognized by the Supreme Court in Am. Ins. Ass'n v. Garamendi, 539 U.S. 396, 401 (2003).

[26] See generally Curtis A. Bradley & Jack L. Goldsmith, *Treaties, Human Rights, and Conditional Consent*, 149 U. PA. L. REV. 399 (2000) (providing a general overview of the system of reservations, understandings, and declarations).

[27] See Appellate Body Report, United States—Measures Affecting the Cross-Border Supply of Gambling and Betting Services, WT/DS285/AB/R (Apr. 7, 2005) (reviewing the compatibility of certain state gambling regulations and trade treaty obligations); Final Award of the Tribunal, Methanex Corp. v. United States (Aug. 3, 2005) (considering and then rejecting argument that California gasoline regulation violated NAFTA obligations), available at http://www.state.gov/documents/organization/51052.pdf. Although the United States essentially prevailed in both cases, they do illustrate the exposure of state law to international trade obligations.

having any preemptive effect except in a lawsuit brought by the U.S. government itself.[28]

Even though the federal government has never availed itself of the option, it did preserve its ability to preempt inconsistent state law by lawsuit when it made trade agreements. But no such provision is found in the RUDs attached to U.S. ratification of leading international human rights treaties. For instance, in ratifying the ICCPR, the United States attached a "federalism" understanding stating that the federal government would implement the treaty obligations within its existing jurisdiction "and otherwise by the state and local governments; to the extent that state and local governments exercise jurisdiction over such matters . . ."[29] The understanding reflects the President's and Senate's belief that the treaty does not alter the existing division of authority between the federal and state governments.

The most recent treaties approved by the U.S. Senate strengthen this principle. Upon ratifying the recent Convention against Transnational Crime in 2005, the U.S. Senate attached a reservation declaring that the U.S. government is not bound by the treaty to the extent that it required the federal government to "address conduct which would fall within" a sphere of local activity governed exclusively by state law.[30] In essence, the reservation removes any implication that the treaty could authorize federal preemptive authority over state activities, even if those activities affected the subject matter of the treaty. Similar reservations were proposed to at least two other treaties under consideration by the Senate.[31]

Treaties, executive agreements, and implementing statutes are the key mechanism by which the federal government preempts inconsistent state law. By imposing federalism limitations on the domestic effect of international agreements, the federal government has deliberately deprived itself of a key tool to compel state compliance with its foreign policies. Because the federal government has effectively handcuffed itself, state governments remain the only institution authorized to fulfill U.S. treaty obligations in matters where states traditionally exercise jurisdiction.

---

[28] See 19 U.S.C. § 3312(b)(2), § 3512(2)(A) (2000).

[29] See U.S. Senate Resolution of Advice and Consent to Ratification of the International Covenant on Civil and Political Rights, 138 CONG. REC. S4783 (daily ed. Apr. 2, 1992).

[30] See, e.g., Resolution of Advice and Consent, United Nations Convention against Transnational Organized Crime, S. Treaty Doc. No. 108-16, at § 2(a)(1), available at http://thomas.loc.gov/cgibin/ntquery/D?trtys:1:./temp/ ~trtysELvPEE (Oct. 7, 2005).

[31] See, e.g., United Nations Convention against Corruption, S. Treaty Doc. No. 109-6 ("The Government of the United States of America the right to assume obligations under this in a manner consistent with its fundamental of federalism, pursuant to which both federal and state criminal laws must be considered in to the conduct addressed in the Convention. The Government of the United States of America therefore reserves to the obligations set forth in the Convention to the extent they (1) address conduct that would fall within this narrow category of highly localized activity or (2) involve preventive measures not covered by federal law governing state and local officials"); see also Letter of Submittal, Convention on Cybercrime, S. Treaty Doc. No. 108-11 [SC2: year?] (Nov. 23, 2001), available at 2001 WL 34368783 ("The United States of America, pursuant to Articles 41 and 42, reserves the right to assume obligations under Chapter II of the Convention in a manner consistent with its fundamental principles of federalism").

III. A FUNCTIONAL DEFENSE OF STATE AUTONOMY IN FOREIGN AFFAIRS

As we have argued, formal constitutional doctrine permits the existence of state autonomy in foreign affairs, and the federal political branches have allowed such autonomy to flourish. We freely concede, however, that our reading of the doctrine is disputed: federal exclusivity over foreign affairs remains attractive to many courts and commentators. Moreover, even if states enjoy autonomy in foreign affairs, this does not necessarily mean that the federal political branches will allow it to continue. For these reasons, we offer a functional analysis of a system of state autonomy. Given the particular pressures and challenges created by globalization, there are strong functional reasons to prefer a system where the federal government's political branches, rather than the federal courts, determine how and whether states will have autonomy over a matter implicating foreign affairs.

In a system of state autonomy in foreign affairs, state governments will take the lead in determining how and whether to implement certain U.S. obligations under international law that uniquely affect local and state interests. States will also participate in certain foreign policy activities that relate to their particular localized interests. In all of these activities, state decision-makers act either because the federal political branches have remained silent on the subject or because they have allocated this authority to the states. The federal decision-makers—Congress, the Senate, or the President—can control the states by refusing to delegate or by overriding state policies with a treaty, statute, or executive declaration.

In this system, the key institutions for deciding how to accommodate globalization's pressures are those that are most politically sensitive: Congress, the treaty-makers, the President, or the state governments. The institution with the smallest role is the federal courts, which can only intervene pursuant to a valid treaty, statute, or executive declaration. We have already analyzed the functional advantages of allocating decisions relating to foreign affairs to the political branches versus federal courts in the context of treaty interpretation and customary international law. As we argued in the previous two chapters, the executive and legislative branches possess substantial institutional advantages over federal courts in the speed and flexibility of their decision-making as well as in their superior ability to obtain information.

Many of these same advantages come into play in the context of a system of state autonomy in foreign affairs. But the functional argument for state autonomy in foreign affairs requires more than simply establishing the institutional advantage of relying on the federal political branches over the federal courts. It also requires establishing the institutional competence of state governments in certain activities that affect foreign affairs.

If the federal courts possessed a greater institutional competence in the assessment of foreign policy goals than the state governments did, then a functional analysis might still support a regime of court-supervised federal exclusivity.

But we have already considered the general institutional features of the federal courts that render them unfit to interfere in foreign policy. In many respects, a comparison of federal courts and state decision-makers is likely to be similar to the

Table 6.1 Summary of Federal Comparative Institutional Competence in Foreign Affairs

	Access to Information	Expertise in Processing Information	Speed	Transparency	Flexibility
Congress	High	High	Low	High	Medium
President	High	High	High	Medium	High
Courts	Low	Low	Medium	High	Low
States	Medium	Medium	High	Medium	High

comparison of federal courts to federal political decision-makers. At the state level, the primary decision-makers for engaging in activities affecting foreign affairs are the state legislatures and state executive branches. Both institutions have the same functional characteristics as the federal political branches. The major difference between federal political branches and state political branches is that state decision-makers have almost no access to clandestine information, nor do they possess comparable levels of institutional expertise in foreign policy activities. But in contrast with federal courts, state decision-makers possess many of the same institutional advantages in decision-making as the federal political branches. As table 6.1 suggests, while the states are unlikely to possess competence over foreign policy decisions superior to that of the federal congress or executive, it is still likely that they possess superior competence over federal courts. To give just one example, the decision by Massachusetts to limit state entities from purchasing services from companies doing business with Burma, a decision later overturned by the U.S. Supreme Court, was based on the state legislature's investigations and research into Burmese affairs.[32] The executive officers of Massachusetts received under the statute a certain amount of discretion in designating companies that did business with Burma. None of the federal courts' institutional characteristics we have identified could have allowed them to carry out the same investigations and research that Massachusetts did in assessing the policy goals of adopting the Massachusetts Burma Law. Thus, federal courts are unlikely to have greater competence in these matters than state governments do.

For areas of law and policy within their traditional control, states possess information and information-processing expertise that are superior to those of federal courts. States are likely to possess superior local knowledge about how an international law obligation or foreign affairs issue would modify or change local law and policy. States may well have greater local expertise in certain areas than even the federal political branches. For instance, when considering how best to deal with an international agreement for the recognition of wills, the states have superior local

---

[32] Crosby v. National Foreign Trade Council, 530 U.S. 363 (2000).

knowledge and expertise in assessing the effects of adopting the international agreement. States not only control almost all law related to wills; they also control the institutions charged with administering wills and resolving any disputes related to them. In contrast, neither the federal courts nor the federal government in general is responsible for wills. The same is true for many areas of the new international law affecting criminal procedure, domestic relations, and private commercial law. Yet there is no doubt that administering or recognizing wills from foreign countries has an impact on foreign affairs, especially if such activities involve the application or interpretation of international agreements or the rights of foreign nationals.

To be sure, the federal courts do possess one unquestionable advantage over state governments. Unlike the states, federal courts are part of a single bureaucracy answerable to a single decision-maker: the U.S. Supreme Court. Thus, federal courts can achieve a greater level of uniformity in their decision-making. In contrast, no individual state can impose a single policy on the other states. Left on their own, states can only achieve uniformity by mechanisms of joint cooperation. States, for instance, can enter into compacts with each other (subject to federal approval). They can also participate in voluntary systems of lawmaking. But unlike federal courts, the states cannot guarantee uniformity among their different decision-makers. In certain cases, state policy will suffer from collective action problems that will lead them to compete in a destructive, costly manner.

In our conception, the federal government should have the ultimate authority to unify disparate state policies that impact foreign affairs. The only question is which branch of the federal government is best positioned to decide how to unify these policies. Federal courts, as we have already argued, possess no functional advantages over the federal political branches. To vest federal courts with the same authority would require us to accept that a single unified national foreign policy is *always* superior to a system of state autonomy. This appeal to the overriding necessity of uniformity is often called the "one voice" argument. As many scholars have pointed out, the Supreme Court has stated on a number of occasions that it is necessary for the United States to speak with "one voice" on matters involving foreign policy. There is ample evidence that the Founding generation sought to prevent states from violating treaties and causing foreign policy consequences for the nation as a whole.[33]

The functional imperative for "one voice" in all circumstances, however, has been overstated. Not all foreign policy questions are created equal. To be blunt, some matters of foreign policy are more important than others. Adhering with "one voice" to certain international obligations simply may not be as important as

---

[33] See, e.g., Jack N. Rakove, *Making Foreign Policy—The View from 1787*, in Robert A. Goldwin & Robert A. Licht, eds., FOREIGN POLICY AND THE CONSTITUTION 1–3 (1990) (describing importance of creating uniform foreign policy among Constitution's Framers); THE FEDERALIST No. 3 (Jay) ("Because, under the national government, treaties and articles of treaties, as well as the laws of nations, will always be expounded in one sense and executed in the same manner,—whereas adjudications on the same points and questions in thirteen states . . . will not always accord or be consistent . . .").

maintaining a commitment to constitutional norms such as federalism or separation of powers. The recognition that the United States may sometimes prefer to violate international law over interfering with domestic law is embodied in doctrines such as the "last in time" rule[34] and reflected in the Supreme Court's refusal to exempt treaties from the Bill of Rights.[35]

It is true that in analogous doctrinal areas, such as the dormant commerce clause, federal courts are required to police state interference in interstate commerce even if Congress has not provided any guidance. The functional rationale for judicial interference is that Congress cannot effectively monitor every state action that affects interstate commerce. But asking federal courts to police state activities in foreign affairs has a different functional balance. The dormant commerce clause doctrine allows federal courts to focus on state economic regulations and assess their impact on overall interstate commerce. In a dormant foreign affairs doctrine, federal courts would have to assess the foreign policy impact of a wide range of state activities ranging from matters of social policy to private commercial law to public morality. The functional balance of state interests, expertise, and the overall effect on national foreign policy is substantially more complex and nuanced than the types of assessments made in the dormant Commerce Clause area.

For this reason, it is not irrational for Congress to prefer a method of implementation that, while probably not perfect, creates a balance between respecting state autonomy over a wide range of issues and fulfilling international law obligations. Depending on the relative importance of a particular international obligation, then, the federal government could (as it has done in most cases) choose to leave the incorporation and implementation of certain international obligations to the states and even tolerate nonuniformity. Such a system is hardly radical or absurd. In fact, it is essentially the same result as the system of treaty implementation adopted by Canada.[36]

IV. EXAMPLES OF STATE AUTONOMY IN FOREIGN AFFAIRS

In this section, we provide examples of how globalization is affecting the states and how the states have responded by operating with a certain level of autonomy in foreign affairs. In light of these examples, as well as the formal and functional foundations we offered in Parts II and III, we are confident that states will play a central role in the accommodation of the effects of globalization within the United States.

---

[34] See Whitney v. Robertson, 124 U.S. 190, 194 (1888).

[35] See Reid v. Covert, 354 U.S. 1, 18 (1957) (plurality).

[36] See, e.g., A.G. Can.V. A.G. Ont. et al. (Labour Conventions Case), [1937] 1 D.L.R. 673 ("federal government cannot pass implementing legislation in areas that fall within provincial jurisdiction"). See also Canada v. Ontario, [1937] A.C. 326, 354 (P.C.) (appeal taken from Can.) (national government of Canada cannot expand its powers vis-à-vis the Provinces by entering into treaties).

A. Making International Agreements

In response to globalization, for example, states have gone beyond implementing international obligations to negotiating and entering into international agreements in areas such as tax allocation, motor vehicle regulation, natural resources management, and even greenhouse gas emissions.[37] While almost all of these policies may be preempted by the federal government, the decision to do so is reserved to the executive or legislative branches of the federal government in an exercise of their political judgment. A meaningful role for states is not unprecedented. States have always exercised a certain amount of autonomy in foreign affairs, especially in ensuring compliance with international obligations that affect areas of traditional state regulation. The importance of this autonomous state role will only increase as the new international law expands further into matters of traditional state control.

The most common and unremarkable form of state international agreement is a bicultural exchange agreement with a foreign government. As a report released by the National Governors Association observed, states use bilateral cultural exchange agreements to bolster their economic relationships with certain foreign countries. To take just one example, at least twenty-five states have signed bilateral trade, cultural, and educational agreements with Israel.[38] Such agreements are generally made when a state governor makes a visit to a particular foreign country. For instance, Governor Gray Davis of California signed an agreement for cooperation in the development of biotechnology during his 1999 visit to Israel.[39] Although many of these agreements are phrased in nonbinding terms, they are important mechanisms for governors seeking to bolster their state's international economic profile for attracting trade, investment, and tourism.[40]

More significantly, governors of border states have sought deep levels of cooperation with Canadian provincial governments. A number of states, for instance, have

---

[37] See Raymond Spencer Rodgers, *The Capacity of States of the Union to Conclude International Agreements: The Background and Some Recent Developments*, 61 Am. J. Int'l L. 1021, 1024–28 (1967) (describing several agreements between states and Canada).

[38] See National Governors Association Center for Best Practices, How States Are Using Arts and Culture to Strengthen Their Global Trade Development 27 (2003) [hereinafter NGA Study], at http://www.nga.org/portal/site/nga/menuitem.9123e83a1f6786440ddcbeeb501010 a0/?vgnextoid=2763303cb0b32010VgnVCM1000001a01010aRCRD. The states include: Alabama, Arizona, California, Colorado, Connecticut, Florida, Georgia, Illinois, Indiana, Iowa, Kentucky, Maryland, Michigan, Minnesota, Missouri, Nebraska, New Jersey, New York, Pennsylvania, Ohio, Oklahoma, South Carolina, Tennessee, Texas, and Vermont.

[39] See, e.g., Memorandum of Understanding between the Israel Biotechnology Organization and the California Commission on Bioscience, Oct. 29, 1999, at http://www.jewishvirtuallibrary.org/ jsource/US-Israel/cabio.html (establishing a "formal relationship between the Israel Biotechnology Organization and the California Governor's Commission on Bioscience in order to foster technology, business development and educational opportunities, through business interaction in the public and private sectors").

[40] See NGA Study, *supra* note 38, at 1. A general review of these activities, including "sister-city" agreements, is discussed in Richard Bilder, *The Role of States and Cities in Foreign Relations*, 83 Am. J. Int'l L. 821 (1989).

entered into bilateral reciprocal agreements with the province of Quebec for the treatment of traffic sanctions and the inspection of commercial vehicles. Traffic agreements require each state or province to recognize traffic offenses committed by their residents in the other party's jurisdiction for purposes of driver's license suspensions. Reciprocal inspection agreements allow one party's inspection to satisfy inspection requirements in the other party's jurisdiction. States have also made similar reciprocal agreements in the area of child-support regulation.[41]

States have also negotiated broad multilateral agreements involving multiple states and foreign provinces. Perhaps the most successful example of a state multilateral agreement is the Great Lakes Charter, an agreement among seven U.S. states and two Canadian provinces to cooperate in the management of the waters of the Great Lakes.[42] The original charter, signed in 1985, committed the parties to develop mechanisms for cooperative management. A subsequent 2001 agreement committed the parties to prepare "[b]asin-wide binding agreement(s), such as an interstate compact and such other agreements, protocols or other arrangements between the States and Provinces." The states and provinces finalized this commitment in December 2005 when they agreed to a prohibition on diversions of water from the Great Lakes, subject to certain limitations. This latest agreement is also accompanied by a "compact" that includes all the parties to the 2001 agreements except for the Canadian provinces.[43] While the precise definition of a "compact" is uncertain, compacts may include agreements between different U.S. states as well as agreements between U.S. states and foreign states. Both kinds of compacts require federal congressional approval.[44]

---

[41] See, e.g., Regulation Respecting a Reciprocal Agreement between the Gouvernement du Québec and the Government of the State of Maine Concerning Drivers' Licenses and Traffic Offenses (Sept. 25, 1991), at http://www.canlii.org/qc/laws/regu/c-24.2r.0.1.2.2/20060213/whole. html; Regulation Respecting the Reciprocal Agreement between the State of New York and Québec Concerning Drivers' Licences and Traffic Offences (Feb. 4, 1988), at http://www.canlii.org/qc/laws/ regu/c-24.2r.0.1.2/20050809/whole.html; Regulation Respecting Reciprocal Commercial Vehicle Registration Agreements between the Gouvernement du Québec and Certain American States (Feb. 17, 1993), at http://www.canlii.org/qc/laws/regu/c-24.2r.0.1.5/20051019/whole.html) (listing agreements between Quebec and forty-one different states); Regulation Respecting an Agreement between the Gouvernement du Québec and the Government of the State of New York Respecting the Mechanical Inspection of Buses (1990), at http://www.canlii.org/qc/laws/regu/c-24.2r.0. 1.2.1/20051019/whole.html). See Dehart, *Comity, Conventions, and the Constitution: State and Federal Initiatives in International Support Enforcement*, 28 FAM. L.Q. 89 (1994).

[42] COUNCIL OF GREAT LAKES GOVERNORS, THE GREAT LAKES CHARTER: PRINCIPLES FOR THE MANAGEMENT OF GREAT LAKES WATER RESOURCES 1–2 (1985), available at http://www.glc.org/ wateruse/wrmdss/finalreport/pdf/GreatLakesCharter.pdf; *see also* Michael J. Donahue, *Strengthening the Binational Great Lakes Management Effort: The Great Lakes Commission's Provincial Membership Initiative*, 1998 TOL. J. GREAT LAKES' L. SCI. & POL'Y 27, 33.

[43] Council of Great Lakes Governors, Great Lakes—St. Lawrence River Basin Sustainable Water Resources Compact (2005), available at http://www.cglg.org/projects/water/docs/12-13-05/Great_ Lakes-St_Lawrence_River_Basin_water_resources_compact.pdf.

[44] U.S. CONST. art. I, § 10 ("No state shall, without the Consent of Congress . . . enter into any Agreement or compact with another State, or with a foreign Power . . ."); see Edward T. Swaine,

Compacts represent a form of state foreign policy. Agreements such as the Great Lakes Charter were negotiated by governors directly with other governors and with foreign provincial leaders. The federal executive played no official role in the negotiations.[45] It did not, for instance, sign any of the agreements. Congress may act only to approve or disapprove the compact negotiated by the governors.

In some cases, the U.S. government has entered into international agreements that depend on the consent of individual states before having effect. For instance, only thirty-seven states have agreed to participate in the Agreement on Government Procurement, and the scope of each state's obligations is determined by each state's government.[46] The U.S. government has also entered into other agreements that effectively permit states to opt out of compliance.[47]

The Great Lakes Charter illustrates how states can act as foreign policy actors in cooperation with the federal government. States played the role usually held by the federal government by negotiating a typical international agreement. Indeed, because the distinction between a compact requiring congressional approval and an agreement that can be made by the states alone is hardly self-evident, states may have the authority to make agreements with foreign governments that are never reviewed by the federal government. At least one state high court has recognized that some agreements with foreign governments do not rise to the level of a "compact" requiring federal approval,[48] and the U.S. Supreme Court has held that preliminary negotiations to a compact are not always prohibited.[49]

States have also negotiated and entered into international agreements that may actually differ from federal policy. A number of U.S. states, for instance, have joined

---

Does Federalism Constrain the Treaty Power?, 103 COLUM. L. REV. 403, 499–510 (2003) (arguing that the judicial definition of "foreign compact" remains flexible).

[45] The absence of the federal government is surprising, given that both the Supreme Court and the federal Executive take the view that states cannot negotiate with any foreign governments. See, e.g., Holmes v. Jennison, 39 U.S. (14 Pet.) 540, 574 (1840) (Taney, C. J.) (describing the Framers' intention that "there would be no occasion for negotiation or intercourse between the state authorities and a foreign government"); 5 GREEN HAYWOOD HACKWORTH, DIGEST OF INTERNATIONAL LAW 25 (1943) (quoting a State Department letter rejecting proposed Florida-Cuba compact negotiations).

[46] See Final Act Embodying the Results of the Uruguay Round of Multilateral Trade Negotiations, Annex 4, Plurilateral Trade Agreements, Agreement on Government Procurement. For a list of participating states, see WTO GPA Annex 2.

[47] See, e.g., Convention on Cybercrime, S. Treaty Doc. No. 108-11, November 23, 2001, article 41 ("1 A federal State may reserve the right to assume obligations under Chapter II of this Convention consistent with its fundamental principles governing the relationship between its central government and constituent States or other similar territorial entities provided that it is still able to co-operate under Chapter III"). Convention (NO. 182) for Elimination of the Worst Forms of Child Labor.

[48] See McHenry County v. Brady, 163 N.W. 540 (1917) (upholding an agreement between North Dakota and a Canadian town as not violating the Compact Clause).

[49] See Virginia v. Tennessee, 148 U.S. 503 (1893) (finding that Virginia-Tennessee boundary negotiations did not violate the Compact Clause).

with some Canadian provinces to set greenhouse gas reduction goals.[50] This agreement committed parties to reduce greenhouse gas emissions to 1990 levels by 2010, and to 10 percent below 1990 levels by 2020.[51] These goals were similar to (and even more ambitious than) the reduction goals set in the Kyoto Protocol to the U.N. Framework Convention for Climate Change.[52] During the Bush administration, the United States refused to ratify the Kyoto Protocol and rejected the Protocol's aggressive targets for the reduction of greenhouse gas emissions.[53]

The pressures of economic and social globalization have not only pushed states to improve their mechanisms for transnational cooperation, but have also increased states' opportunities to regulate business with transnational effects. State legislatures have enacted a number of statutes that directly impact foreign affairs. The most controversial state statutes required businesses that apply for state contracts to certify that they avoid business transactions with certain foreign countries.[54] Less aggressively, some statutes require businesses applying for state contracts to certify that their business in certain foreign countries complies with certain nondiscriminatory principles.[55] State governments have also required state executive officials to avoid investing state pension funds in certain foreign countries.[56] In a different vein, a number of states have enacted statutes imposing special disclosure requirements on foreign insurance companies as part of state regulation of the insurance industry.[57] While some of these state statutes have been challenged in the Supreme Court as an impermissible encroachment on federal foreign policy powers, the Court has refused to invalidate all such statutes categorically unless it determines that state laws have been preempted by an express federal or state activity.[58] While we

---

[50] New England Governors/ Eastern Canadian Premiers, Climate Change Action Plan 2001 (2001), available at http://www.scics.gc.ca/pdf/850084011_e.pdf. See Ken Colburn & Amy Royden, *New England States and Eastern Canadian Provinces Team Up to Tackle Climate Change*, ABA SEC. ENV'T, ENERGY & RES. CLIMATE CHANGE AND SUSTAINABLE DEVELOPMENT NEWSLETTER, June 2003, available at http://abanet.org/environ/committees/climatechange/newsletter/june03/newengland/home.html.

[51] *Id.* at 7.

[52] Kyoto Protocol to the United Nations Convention on Climate Change art. 3(1), available at http://unfec.int/resource/docs/convkp/kpeng/html (requiring member states to reduce emissions to 5 percent below 1990 levels by 2008–12).

[53] See Letter from the President to Senators Chuck Hagel, Jesse Helms, Larry Craig, and Pat Roberts (Mar. 13, 2001) (explaining opposition from himself and from the Senate to joining the Kyoto Protocol), available at http://www.whitehouse.gov/news/releases/2001/03/20010314.html.

[54] See, e.g., An Act Regulating State Contracts with Companies Doing Business with or in Burma (Myanmar), 1996 Mass. Acts 239 (codified at MASS. GEN. LAWS ANN. CH. 7 §§ 7:22G–7:22M (West 2002)).

[55] See, e.g., Mass. Gen. Laws Ann. ch. 7, § 22C (West 2002) (requiring businesses operating in Northern Ireland to certify nondiscriminatory practices).

[56] See, e.g., Conn. Gen. Stat. Ann. § 3-13h (West 2000) (restricting use of state investment funds in Northern Ireland).

[57] See, e.g., Cal. Ins. Code §§ 13800–13807 (West 2005). Cal. Civ. Proc. Code § 354.5 (West Cum. Supp. 2003).

[58] See, e.g., Am. Ins. Ass'n v. Garamendi, 539 U.S. 396, 401 (2003) (invalidating a California statute on the basis that it impermissibly interfered with the federal government's conduct of foreign

agree with some scholars that more federal supervision of such state activities is desirable, we think that the growing state autonomy in foreign affairs is, on balance, a welcome trend.[59] It suggests that the U.S. system has already found ways to accommodate the effects of globalization on the state governments by allowing limited state participation in foreign affairs.

B. Implementing International Law Obligations

States also exercise autonomy in foreign affairs by playing a role in the implementation of national obligations under international law. Only the United States can undertake an obligation under international law, but how it carries out its obligations is a matter of its own law. The U.S. constitutional system relies heavily on the independent action of the states to carry out many obligations under treaties and customary international law.

States often play a central role in whether and how some international law obligations are carried out in areas of their traditional control. Three models for state control over the implementation of international agreements have emerged. First, states may, as in the case of an international agreement on wills, implement a non-self-executing treaty by enacting uniform legislation expressly designed to implement the treaty. Second, states may adopt legislation implementing treaties that have not yet been ratified by the Senate (and for which ratification is not assured). In these circumstances, the states actually undertake international obligations even though the United States as a whole has not. Finally, in some cases states have implemented treaties through legislation in tandem with federal implementing legislation or a self-executing treaty. All of these mechanisms rely on independent determinations by state legislatures and executives before giving these agreements domestic effect.

In 1973, the United States hosted negotiations for the Convention on the Form of an International Will under the auspices of UNIDROIT in Washington, D.C. The purpose of the Washington Convention "is to provide testators with a way of making wills that will be valid as to form in all countries joining the Convention."[60] The Convention relied on two key mechanisms for ensuring recognition of wills across borders. First, all states would adopt a uniform law that recognizes an "international will" that is created in the form agreed upon by the Convention.[61] Second, the

---

relations, because it required insurance companies doing business in California to disclose all information relating to policies sold in Europe by the company or anyone "related" to it between 1920 and 1945); Crosby v. Nat'l Foreign Trade Council, 530 U.S. 363, 372–73 (2000) (finding that federal law preempted a Massachusetts statute barring state entities from buying goods or services from companies that did business with the nation of Burma).

[59] For a sharp critique of the constitutionality of such state international agreements, see Duncan Hollis, *Unpacking the Compact Clause*, 88 Texas L. Rev. 741 (2010).

[60] Unif. Probate Code art. II, pt. 10 prefatory note (2001).

[61] Washington Convention, art. I

uniform law would define and specify "authorized persons" to verify and validate an international will.[62]

The Washington Convention was submitted in 1986 to the Senate, which gave its advice and consent in 1991.[63] What is unusual about the Washington Convention, however, is that it specifically contemplated and required state-by-state implementation. The states had to implement the treaty via adoption of a revised Model Probate Code or an International Wills Act. The President was to withhold final ratification until the Convention was implemented through state legislation.

From the outset, the subject matter of the Washington Convention raised concerns about federal encroachment on areas of state control. Indeed, one commentator accused the Convention's drafters of seeking "not merely the resolution of international probate problems, but knowing[ly] undert[aking] the subversion of the traditional role of the American states in enforcing their own rules for testing the validity of testamentary instruments."[64]

Although the Washington Convention specifically allowed nation-states to assign implementation to particular subunits, the United States did not make such a declaration.[65] On the other hand, despite one influential commentator's recommendation,[66] the U.S. government also refused to implement the treaty by federalizing probate law with respect to international wills.

It would be undesirable, however, to rely exclusively on federal legislation to bring both aspects of the Convention—the execution of international wills as well as their recognition—into force. Our testators and their attorneys are not accustomed to consulting federal statutes for guidance on the formalities for making wills; they should continue to be able to place primary reliance on state law rather than federal law for this purpose. Therefore, it was recommended to Congress that the making of international wills within the United States be governed by state legislation, with each state free to decide whether it wishes to make it possible for testators to execute wills in its jurisdiction in this new form.[67]

Not only did the federal government agree with this recommendation; it essentially chose to use the uniform laws system to implement its treaty obligations under the Washington Convention.[68] Thus, the National Conference of Commissioners for Uniform State Laws was enlisted to adopt model legislation implementing

---

[62] Washington Convention, art. III.

[63] President's Message to Congress Transmitting the Convention Providing a Uniform Law on the Form of an International Will, 1986 Pub. Papers 905-06 (July 2, 1986), available at 1973 U.S.T. LEXIS 321; Convention Providing a Uniform Law on the Form of an International Will, 102d Cong., 137 CONG. REC. S12131 (daily ed. Aug. 2, 1991) (Sup. Docs. No. X/A.102/1:137/121).

[64] See Jerome J. Curtis, The Convention on International Wills, 23 AM. J. COMP. L. 119, 121 (1975).

[65] See Submittal Letter, 1973 UST LEXIS at *12–*13.

[66] See Kurt Nadelmann, The Formal Validity of Wills and the Washington Convention 1973 Providing the Form of an International Will, 23 AM. J. COMP. L. 365, 375 (1974) (arguing for federal statutory implementation).

[67] Id.

[68] See Richard D. Kearney, The International Wills Convention, 18 INT'L L. 613, 628 (1984).

the treaty.[69] Although the federal government was supposed to pass implementing legislation to require uniform recognition of international wills by "authorized persons," the amendments to the Uniform Probate Code guaranteed the same result.[70] In theory, the promoters of the Washington Convention expected federal legislation to impose on all states the requirement of recognizing wills executed in accordance with the Convention.[71] However, no such federal legislation was actually introduced, thus resulting in what one commentator called a "bizarre patchwork of states which do and do not have state implementing legislation."[72]

Not only did this "bizarre patchwork" exist, but it existed even prior to the Senate's granting of advice and consent in 1991. Indeed, nine states enacted amendments to the Model Probate Code specifically designed to implement the Washington Convention before 1991.[73] Even today, although no federal legislation has been passed, sixteen states have essentially decided to enter into the Washington Convention themselves through their enactment of laws implementing that convention.[74] Testators in those states can execute wills under the Convention, and

---

[69] See National Conference of Commissioners for the Uniform State Laws, Prefatory Notes and Comments, Uniform International Wills Act (1977).

[70] See, e.g., International Wills Act, art. I ("A will shall be valid as regards form, irrespective particularly of the place where it is made, of the location of the assets and of the nationality, domicile or residence of the testator, if it is made in the form of an international will complying with the provisions set out in Articles 2 to 5 hereinafter").

[71] See Kearney, *supra* note 68, at 628.

[72] TIM COVELL, LEGISLATION SHOULD PROMPT STATES TO ENACT INTERNATIONAL WILLS LAWS, TRUSTS AND ESTATES 42 (1994).

[73] See, e.g, Uniform Probate Code, Art. II, Part 10. Actions by States. California: While California has not adopted the Uniform Probate Code, it adopted the Uniform International Wills Act (Part 10 of Article 2 of the Code) originally in West's Ann.Cal.Probate Code, § § 60 to 60.8 by L.1979, c. 632, effective Jan. 1, 1980. L.1983, c. 842, effective Jan. 1, 1985, repealed West's Ann.Cal.Probate Code § 60 to 60.8, which constituted the Uniform International Wills Act, and reenacted the same as West's Ann.Cal.Probate Code § § 6380 to 6389. L.1990, c. 79, repealed West's Ann.Cal.Prob. Code, § § 6380 to 6389, which constituted the Uniform International Wills Act and reenacted said act as new § § 6380 to 6390. Colorado: As part of its adoption of the Uniform Probate Code, Colorado has adopted the Uniform International Wills Act (see West's C.R.S.A. § § 15-11-1001 to 15-11-1011). Connecticut: While Connecticut has not adopted the Uniform Probate Code, it has adopted the Uniform International Wills Act (Part 10 of Article 2 of the Code) in C.G.S.A. § § 50a-1 to 50a-9, by P.A. 87-369, effective July 1, 1987. Illinois: While Illinois has not adopted the Uniform Probate Code, it has adopted the Uniform International Wills Act (Part 10 of Article 2 of the Code) in S.H.A. 755 ILCS 10/1 to 10/10. by L.1990, P.A. 86-1291. Minnesota: As part of its adoption of the Uniform Probate Code, Minnesota has adopted the Uniform International Wills Act (see M.S.A. § § 524.2-1001 to 524.2-1010). Montana: As part of its adoption of the Uniform Probate Code, Montana has adopted the Uniform International Wills Act (see MCA 72-2-901 to 72-2-910). New Mexico: As part of its adoption of the Uniform Probate Code, New Mexico has adopted the Uniform International Wills Act (see NMSA 1978 § § 45-2-1001 to 45-2-1010). North Dakota: As part of its adoption of the Uniform Probate Code, North Dakota has adopted the Uniform International Wills Act (see NDCC § § 30.1-08.2-01 to 30.1-08.2-09). Oregon: While Oregon has not adopted the Uniform Probate Code, it has adopted the Uniform International Wills Act (Part 10 of Article 2 of the Code) in O.R.S. 112.232, by L.1981, c. 481.

[74] See Act of May 1, 1990, ch. 79, 1990 Cal. Legis. Serv. 79 (West) (codified as amended at Cal. Prob. Code §§6380-6390 (1991)); Act effective Apr. 17, 1989, 1989 Colo. Legis. Serv. 180 (West) (codified as amended at Colo. Rev. Stat. §§15-11-1001 to -1011 (2002)); Act of June 19, 1987, 1987 Conn.

foreign international wills will be recognized in those states. Testators in the other thirty-four states, however, cannot invoke the Convention despite the Senate's advice and consent.

The Washington Convention thus illustrates how states can play a central role in the fulfillment of international obligations. Facing the choice between federalizing an area of traditional state regulation or permitting states to control compliance themselves, the federal government has chosen the latter—despite Congress's broad authority to regulate via its treaty power, as recognized in *Missouri v. Holland*. As a practical matter, therefore, compliance with the International Wills Convention now rests with the willingness of individual state legislatures to adopt implementing legislation.

This model of state-by-state implementation through the Uniform Laws system has also been adopted with respect to other signed but not ratified conventions, including the Hague Convention on the Conflicts of Laws Relating to the Form of Testamentary Dispositions[75] and the Hague Convention on the Law Applicable to Trusts on Their Recognition.[76] State-by-state implementation of treaties is not limited to matters involving private law. In the context of international human rights treaties, the several states are understood to play an important part. For instance, the Senate ratification of the ICCPR was accompanied by this declaration:

The United States understands that this Covenant shall be implemented by the Federal Government to the extent that it exercises legislative and judicial jurisdiction over the matters covered therein, and otherwise by the state and local governments; to the extent that state and local governments exercise jurisdiction over such matters, the Federal Government shall take measures appropriate to the Federal system to the end that the competent authorities of the state or local governments may take appropriate measures for the fulfillment of the Covenant.[77]

Legis. Serv. 369 (West) (codified as amended at Conn. Gen. Stat. Ann. §§50a-1 to -9 (West 1994)); Act effective Jan. 1, 1991, 1990 Legis. Serv. P.A. 86-1291 (West) (codified as amended at 755 Ill. Comp. Stat. Ann. 10/0.01-10/10 (West 1992)); Act effective Mar. 24, 1978, ch. 525, 1978 Minn. Laws 153 (codified as amended at 19 Minn. Stat. Ann. §§524.2-1001 to -1010 (West 2002)); Act of Feb. 27, 1991, ch. 62, 1991 Mont. Laws 170 (codified as amended at Mont. Code Ann. §§72-2-901 to -910 (2001)); Act effective July 1, 1993, ch. 66, 1992 N.M. Laws 748 (codified as amended at N.M. Stat. Ann. §§45-2-1001 to -1010 (Michie 1995)); Act of Mar. 15, 1979, ch. 376, 1979 N.D. Laws 915 (codified as amended at N.D. Cent. Code §§30.1-08.2-01 to -09 (1996)); Act of July 28, 1981, ch. 481, 1981 Or. Laws 519 (codified as amended at Or. Rev. Stat. §112.232 (1997)). Act effective Jan. 1, 1997, ch. 75, 1996 Alaska Sess. Laws 308, 308 (codified as amended at Alaska Stat. §§13.12.912 to 13.12. 921 (Michie 2002)); Act effective June 25, 1997, ch. 81, 71 Del. Laws 177, 177 (1997) (codified as amended at Del. Code Ann. tit. 12 §§251-59 (2001)); Act effective Apr. 1, 2000, No. 386, 1998 Mich. Pub. Acts 1738, 1738 (codified as amended at Mich. Comp. Laws Ann. §§700-2951 to 700-2959 (West 2002)); Act approved Mar. 20, 1995, 1995 Va. Acts ch. 443, 637, 637 (codified as amended at Va. Code Ann. §§64.1-96.2 to 64.1-96.11 (Michie 2002)).

[75] Model Probate Code Art. 2, 2-1002; Eugene Scoles, *The Hague Convention on Succession*, 42 Am. J. Comp. L. 85 (1994).

[76] Unif Trust Code s. 107 cmt. (2000).

[77] U.S. Senate Resolution of Advice and Consent to Ratification of the International Covenant on Civil and Political Rights, 138 Cong. Rec. S4783 (daily ed. Apr. 2, 1992).

Similar understandings were attached to the ratification of two other international human rights treaties[78] to which the United States is a party, and such understandings have been proposed for two other treaties still being considered.[79] To be sure, the legal purpose of the "understandings" is hardly self-evident. Because they are not "reservations," they do not appear to limit the United States' obligations under international law. They do not specifically limit the treaty obligations to asking for state implementation in the same way as the so-called federal-state clauses in treaties do. On the other hand, the understandings are clearly conditions on which ratification takes place, and the federal government has, at various times, suggested that it intends the understandings to limit America's obligations under international law.

For instance, when submitting the Convention against Torture and Other Cruel, Inhuman or Degrading Treatment or Punishment (the Torture Convention), the State Department attached what it called a "federalism understanding" that would limit the scope of U.S. obligations to implement the Torture Convention.[80] It further explained that the United States would implement obligations to provide for training of persons involved in the treatment of detainees "with respect to law enforcement forces acting under its authority or control."[81] However, with respect to state and local law enforcement forces, "the Federal Government would take appropriate measures to the end that the competent authorities of the states may take appropriate measures for the fulfillment of the Convention Articles."[82]

One possible reading of this far from pellucid language is that the federal government's implementation, with respect to state and local law enforcement, would be to the same "end" or extent as whatever "appropriate measures" the states take to fulfill the Torture Convention. This implies that the federal government was asserting its right to take the same "appropriate measures" that the states could or would take. Such a reading is unlikely, however, given the stated purpose of attaching this statement. The language originated in President Carter's original submission of four treaties to the Senate. In that submission, the State Department described the understanding as a "reservation designed to deal with . . . provisions . . . which impose obligations whose fulfillment is dependent on the legal power of the state and local governments as well as the federal government."[83]

---

[78] U.S. Senate Resolution of Advice and Consent to Ratification of Convention Against Torture and Other Cruel, Inhuman or Degrading Treatment or Punishment, 136 Cong. Rec. S17904-01 (Oct. 27, 1990); U.S. Senate Resolution of Advice and Consent to the Ratification of the International Convention on the Elimination of All Forms of Racial Discrimination, 145 Cong. Rec. E139-04 (June 24, 1994) (hereinafter Racial Discrimination Ratification).

[79] Senate Report Recommending Ratification of the Convention on the Elimination of All Forms of Discrimination Against Women, S. Exec. Rep. No. 107-9 (2002); Message from the President of the United States Transmitting Four Treaties Pertaining to Human Rights, S. Exec. Doc. No. 95-2 (1978) (hereinafter Carter Message) (recommending ratification of four treaties with federalism understandings, including International Covenant on Economic, Social and Cultural Rights).

[80] Report of the Senate Committee on Foreign Relations, S. Exec. Rep. No. 101-30, 13, 36 (1990).

[81] Id. at 23.

[82] Id.

[83] Carter Message, *supra* note 79, at viii.

The better reading is that U.S. implementation at the state and local level would be up to the states. This second reading is strengthened by an amendment to the language by Senator Helms (working with the State Department), which modified the first clause to read that the "Federal Government shall take measures appropriate to the Federal system . . ." This amendment (and perhaps the well-known views of its sponsor as well)[84] strengthens the reading that the federal government's "appropriate measures" are limited by the "Federal system" to whatever "appropriate measures" are taken by the states. The modified "federalism understanding" language was also adopted with respect to ratifications of the ICCPR and the Racial Discrimination Convention.[85] Although such understandings do not necessarily limit the federal government's power to subsequently adopt legislation to implement these agreements, they reflect a strong federal commitment to leave the implementation of international treaty obligations to the state governments.

By conditioning its consent on the federalism understandings, the Senate has limited U.S. obligations under those treaties to whatever powers the federal government already possesses without the treaties. Congress is thus limited to its traditional Article I powers when implementing those treaties. The federalism understandings suggest that the states are responsible for treaty obligations that are beyond the scope of Congress's Article I powers.

Unlike state implementation of private international law treaties via the adoption of uniform laws, no state appears to have expressly passed legislation for the purpose of implementing U.S. international human rights treaty obligations. The closest example arose in the context of the U.S. Supreme Court's decision to uphold the University of Michigan Law School's affirmative action program.[86] As Justice Ginsberg observed in her concurrence, the majority's suggestion of a twenty-five-year limit on affirmative action programs accords with the understanding of both the Racial Discrimination Convention and CEDAW.[87] Although her concurrence did not further explain the relevance of these treaties, amici curiae suggested that Michigan's programs could be understood as attempts to fulfill U.S. obligations under these treaties. Although this theory could have offered a separate basis for meeting the compelling state interest prong of the Court's review of the program's constitutionality, it failed to win the concurrence of a majority of the Court.

[84] Senator Jesse Helms of North Carolina served as chairman of the Senate Foreign Relations Committee from 1994 to 2001 before retiring from the Senate. His skepticism of international institutions and defense of what he called "American sovereignty" made him the bête noire of many internationalists and international law advocates. Prior to becoming the chairman of the Committee on Foreign Relations, Senator Helms was an outspoken member of that same committee at one point attaching a separate statement to the committee report recommending ratification of the Genocide Convention filled with criticisms of international institutions and their encroachment on American sovereignty. See generally Separate Statement of Senator Jesse Helms, *Report on the Convention on the Prevention and Punishment of the Crime of Genocide*, S. Exec. Rep. No. 98-50 (1984).

[85] See, e.g., ICCPR Ratification, *supra* note 77; Racial Discrimination Ratification, *supra* note 78.

[86] Grutter v. Bollinger, 539 U.S. 306, 344 (2003) (Ginsberg, J. concurring).

[87] *Id.*

V. CONCLUSION

Although globalization has brought many areas of traditional state control within the ambit of the new international law, states continue to remain independent actors in the accommodation of the new international law within the U.S. legal system. States have historically played a central role in the implementation of treaty obligations that impact subjects of their traditional control, and we see no reason for this role to diminish or change in the future. Globalization has only increased the opportunities for the states to engage in their own transnational activities. Most prominently, the frequency of transborder interactions has spurred state participation in certain types of international agreements as well as state efforts to impose transnational sanctions. The easy movement of people, goods, and services means that more international activity will fall within the territorial jurisdiction of the states. Globalization actually increases, rather than decreases, the importance of states as players in domestic and international lawmaking.

The possibility of conflicts in the system of dual sovereignties contemplated by the Constitution has intensified with the rise of globalization. For instance, states have traditionally held independent authority to regulate matters such as gambling, local health and safety, and criminal punishment. The forces of globalization have exposed all of these areas to the prospect of international regulation. Indeed, if the federal exclusivity approach is adopted, many independent state policies and laws would eventually give way to federal control.

But it does not follow that internationalization *always* requires nationalization. Rather, states have continued to exercise autonomy in many areas of law and policy even though those areas impact overall national foreign policy. States play a central role in the implementation of international law obligations that affect areas of their traditional control, and they even engage in limited outward foreign affairs activities.

As a formal matter, we believe such a system of state autonomy is permissible as long as the federal government's political branches can override or unify inconsistent policies pursuant to a treaty, statute, or executive declaration. This formal understanding comports fully with a functional comparison of the institutional competence of the federal legislature, executive, and judiciary. Indeed, a functional analysis also suggests that states possess substantial functional advantages in the integration of international norms and policies with areas of local policy and law.

In the long run, the existence of a state autonomy operates as a pragmatic constitutional accommodation of the internationalizing demands of globalization and the continuing conception of the United States as a federal system. The federal government continues to retain its authority to enter into more international commitments, even over matters that were previously controlled by the state governments. But the federal government leaves implementation of those obligations, along with the power to respond to greater international scrutiny of state policies, to the state governments.

7 Globalization and Constitutional Controversy

In this chapter, we put our proposals to the test. In the last decade, globalization and the concomitant demands for international cooperation have placed increasing pressure on the American constitutional system. Like tectonic plates moving against each other, the contact between these two forces has erupted in several constitutional controversies. And like many constitutional or political controversies today, they have found their way into the American federal courts.

These cases show that our concerns about the effect of globalization on American politics and the Constitution are not just an abstract hypothetical. They are real. Judicial struggles with these cases directly illuminate the impact of globalization on our governmental system and the manner in which some seek directly to incorporate international legal norms into the domestic order without approval by democratic means. In *Sosa v. Alvarez Machain*, the Supreme Court took up the case of an accused drug cartel doctor who claimed that his overseas arrest and return to the United States violated international standards for judicially approved detention.[1] In *Medellín v. Texas*, a Mexican national convicted of capital murder in the United States challenged his sentence because he was not informed of his right, called for by treaty, to contact consular officials of his nation.[2] In *Hamdan v. Rumsfeld*, Taliban

---

[1] 542 U.S. 692 (2004).
[2] 552 U.S. 491 (2008).

and al Qaeda detainees argued that their continuing detention and proposed trial by military commission violated the Geneva Conventions.[3]

In these cases, the Supreme Court confronted exactly the type of challenge posed by globalization that we have described in earlier chapters. Usually aided by NGOs, academics, activists, and even foreign states, private party appellants sought the incorporation of various international norms into United States law. These norms took varied forms: CIL, UN decrees, non-self-executing treaties, and international court decisions. What these norms had in common was that they had not received the direct approval of the political branches for their incorporation into American law. In essence, private parties sought to sidestep the regular public lawmaking process and the Constitution's normal allocation of power over international relations by leveraging international norms through the courts. If the Supreme Court had adopted these aggressive claims, the nation's freedom of action in the international sphere would have been limited, and domestic policy would have been set or reset, without the considered judgment of the President and Congress.

As we have argued throughout this book, the courts are poor institutions for making policy choices on international relations. But globalization is forcing them to confront these questions anyway. The emerging tangle of international law and institutions that have risen in response to globalization cannot suffer obstacles to their reach, and American courts pose the path of least resistance. This can result in policies on important issues such as relations with important neighboring countries like Mexico, or the pursuit of drug cartels, or even the waging of war, being subject to a fragmented, uncoordinated, and slow judicial process that does not take overall national costs and benefits into account.

This is not to say that every decision by every judge in every case would harm American interests. It may well be that a judicial decision would reach the right result for overall national policy. Our claim is only that the courts, as an institution, are functionally ill-suited to setting foreign policy and that the political branches will reach superior decisions over time. Our solutions—non-self-executing treaties, presidential interpretation of international law, and a state role in implementation—thus serve a dual purpose. They funnel decision-making on areas of American law most affected by globalization to the political branches, and they restrain the courts from intervening. A review of *Sosa*, *Medellín*, and *Hamdan* will show the virtues of our approach and the costs of a court-centric vision of American law and globalization.

I. SOSA V. ALVAREZ-MACHAIN

Although customary international law has historically played a relatively small role in the U.S. legal system, in recent decades it has become a potentially important point of entry for international norms into the domestic legal system. Leading academics

---

[3] 548 U.S. 557 (2006).

and nongovernmental organizations have argued that federal courts may interpret and enforce CIL as federal common law without any specific congressional authorization. Advocates of this "modern position" have supported sophisticated litigation strategies that use CIL to shape or even override domestic legal norms through the vehicle of the Alien Tort Statute.

The *Sosa* Court's decision recognized many of these tensions with the U.S. constitutional system, but it also refused to stop the lower courts from recognizing causes of action under CIL.[4] In this section, we critique the Court's failure to follow the logic of its own analysis, though we are sympathetic to its effort to limit the role of the judiciary in incorporating international human rights norms directly into American law without the intervention of the President or Congress. We then offer our own approach to resolving the structural problems recognized by the *Sosa* Court, an approach that permits the accommodation of CIL within the U.S. constitutional framework by allocating decision-making to the state courts, subject to supervision by the President.

A. The Alien Tort Statute and the Supreme Court

Sosa marked Dr. Alvarez-Machain's second trip to the Supreme Court, and he could not have fared less well than he did in his first.[5] In 1985, members of a Mexican drug cartel kidnapped, interrogated, tortured, and then murdered Enrique Camarena-Salazar, an agent of the Drug Enforcement Agency. From 1984 to 1985, Agent Camarena-Salazar had proven extremely successful in frustrating the operations of the cartel, with one raid alone seizing billions of dollars' worth of marijuana. Dr. Alvarez-Machain allegedly prolonged Agent Camarena-Salazar's life to extend the torture and interrogation. Five years later, a U.S. grand jury indicted Dr. Alvarez-Machain, and a warrant was issued for his arrest. After failed efforts to persuade the Mexican government to hand Dr. Alvarez-Machain over, the DEA hired Mexican bounty hunters—including the ultimate defendant in the case, Jose Francisco Sosa—who abducted him and then transferred him to the United States for arrest.[6]

Alvarez-Machain's first trip to the Supreme Court challenged his abduction as a violation of the U.S.-Mexico extradition treaty. Writing for a 6–3 majority,

---

[4] For discussions of Sosa, see Curtis A. Bradley, Jack L. Goldsmith, & David H. Moore, *Sosa, Customary International Law, and the Continuing Relevance of Erie*, 120 Harv. L. Rev. 869 (2007); William S. Dodge, *Bridging Erie: Customary International Law in the U.S. Legal System after Sosa v. Alvarez-Machain*, 12 Tulsa J. Comp. & Int'l L. 87 (2004); William A. Fletcher, *International Human Rights in American Courts*, 93 Va. L. Rev. 653 (2007); Eugene Kontorovich, *Implementing Sosa v. Alvarez-Machain: What Piracy Teaches about the Limits of the Alien Tort Statute*, 80 Notre Dame L. Rev. 111 (2004); Ralph G. Steinhardt, *Laying One Bankrupt Critique to Rest: Sosa v. Alvarez-Machain and the Future of International Human Rights Litigation in the U.S. Courts*, 57 Vand. L. Rev. 2241 (2004); *Customary International Law as Federal Law after Sosa v. Alvarez-Machain*, 101 Am. Soc'y Int'l L. Proc. 261 (2007).

[5] United States v. Alvarez-Machain, 504 U.S. 655 (1992).

[6] United States v. Alvarez-Machain, 504 U.S. 655 (1992). Additional facts can be found in United States v. Zuno-Arce, 44 F.3d 1420 (9th Cir. 1995).

Chief Justice Rehnquist held that the agreement did not explicitly forbid abductions that occurred outside the extradition process. Instead, the Court applied the *Ker-Frisbie* doctrine, which holds that a federal court may exercise jurisdiction over a criminal defendant brought before it through a forcible abduction and that due process is satisfied so long as the defendant receives a fair trial on the substantive charges themselves.[7] The Court reversed the Ninth Circuit's holding that the treaty applied to Alvarez-Machain's abduction and permitted his prosecution to proceed.

Upon remand, the district court tried Alvarez-Machain and ultimately granted a motion for acquittal. Alvarez-Machain then brought a suit under the Alien Tort Statute (ATS) against Sosa for arbitrary arrest, which he claimed violated the Law of Nations (another term for CIL).[8] The district court granted summary judgment in favor of Alvarez-Machain and awarded him $25,000. Upon Sosa's appeal, Alvarez-Machain found a sympathetic hearing before a panel of the Ninth Circuit and a subsequent en banc court, which agreed that Alvarez-Machain's arbitrary arrest constituted a violation of CIL that supported a cause of action under the ATS.[9]

Reversing, the Supreme Court found that the ATS did not provide a cause of action for Alvarez-Machain's claim of arbitrary arrest. In winning the battle, however, opponents of the ATS may well have lost the war. First, the Court rejected the argument that the ATS merely granted jurisdiction to the federal courts and that any private causes of action would have to await future congressional action. This was a surprising outcome, because Justice Souter at times declared that the ATS was indeed jurisdictional in nature and did not *sua sponte* create any new causes of action. "All Members of the Court agree that §1350 is only jurisdictional," he remarks at one point.[10] Yet while the ATS appears to be jurisdictional according to Justice Souter, it must have gone beyond granting jurisdiction because of the Framers' concerns about the national government's inability to enforce international law within the United States.[11] As several historical studies have shown, one of the problems that had beset the Articles of Confederation was that the Continental Congress was responsible for foreign policy, such as making treaties, but possessed no domestic legislative or funding powers to actually implement them.[12] In particular, the Court referred to a 1781 appeal by the Continental Congress that the states provide punishments for violating international law, and a well-known incident in which a French diplomat was attacked in 1784 and no federal

---

[7] Alvarez-Machain, 504 U.S. at 661–63. The doctrine takes its name from Ker v. Illinois, 119 U.S. 436 (1886), and Frisbie v. Collins, 342 U.S. 519, rehearing denied, 343 U.S. 937 (1952).

[8] He also brought a tort claim under the Federal Tort Claims Act against the United States, which the Court dismissed and we do not discuss here. Sosa, 542 U.S. at 698–710.

[9] Alvarez-Machain v. United States, 266 F.3d 1045, 1051 (9th Cir. 2001), aff'd, 331 F.3d 604, 641 (9th Cir. 2003) (en banc).

[10] Sosa, 542 U.S. at 729.

[11] *Id.* at 716–18.

[12] For one such review of the history of this period, see John Yoo, *Globalism and the Constitution: Treaties, Legislative Power, and the Original Understanding*, 99 Colum. L. Rev. 1955 (1999).

remedy was available.[13] This history led Justice Souter to conclude that "there is

every reason to suppose that the First Congress did not pass the ATS as a jurisdictional convenience to be placed on the shelf for use by a future Congress or state legislature that might, some day, authorize the creation of causes of action or itself decide to make some element of the law of nations actionable for the benefit of foreigners." The Court, however, could not provide any direct historical evidence to support this point, as conventional legislative history from this period is almost nonexistent.[14] Rather, Justice Souter relied on what he called "[t]he anxieties of the pre-constitutional period" in rejecting the idea "that the statute was not meant to have a practical effect."[15]

Second, the Court reached back to historical sources to give substantive content to its odd jurisdictional-but-not-jurisdictional interpretation of the ATS. For a plaintiff to enter federal court, Congress must enact a law that grants jurisdiction over the subject matter of the case, and the subject must fall within the Constitution's list of topics over which the federal courts have competence. The two primary sources of jurisdiction are over cases involving federal questions (where the meaning of a federal law, treaty, or constitutional provision is involved) and diverse parties (where the plaintiff and defendant come from different states or countries). Reviewing the Framing-period evidence, Justice Souter claimed that the Law of Nations, as it existed in the late eighteenth century, regulated private individual conduct by guaranteeing safe conducts, prohibiting attacks on ambassadors, and outlawing piracy.[16] Therefore Congress could only have intended the ATS to provide jurisdiction for this limited set of violations. But how can this be reconciled with the Court's observation that the ATS does more than simply create jurisdiction? According to Justice Souter, the ATS not only recognized a limited set of torts under the international law of 1789, but also anticipated that the common law could add others of similar seriousness in the future. Justice Souter summarized:

[A]lthough the ATS is a jurisdictional statute creating no new causes of action, the reasonable inference from the historical materials is that the statute was intended to have practical effect the moment it became law. The jurisdictional grant is best read as

---

[13] Sosa, 542 U.S. at 715–717.

[14] For different views on the original meaning of the ATS, see Anne-Marie Burley, *The Alien Tort Statute and the Judiciary Act of 1789: A Badge of Honor*, 83 AM. J. INT'L L. 461 (1989); Curtis A. Bradley, *The Alien Tort Statute and Article III*, 42 VA. J. INT'L L. 587 (2002); William R. Casto, *The Federal Courts' Protective Jurisdiction over Torts Committed in Violation of the Law of Nations*, 18 CONN. L. REV. 467 (1986); William S. Dodge, *The Historical Origins of the Alien Tort Statute: A Response to the "Originalists,"* 19 HASTINGS INT'L & COMP. L. REV. 221 (1996); Thomas H. Lee, *The Safe-Conduct Theory of the Alien Tort Statute*, 106 COLUM. L. REV. 830 (2006); John M. Rogers, *The Alien Tort Statute and How Individuals "Violate" International Law*, 21 VAND. J. TRANSAT'L L. 47 (1988); Joseph Modeste Sweeney, *A Tort Only in Violation of the Law of Nations*, 18 HASTINGS INT'L & COMP. L. REV. 445 (1995); Arthur Weisburd, *The Executive Branch and International Law*, 41 VAND. L. REV. 1205 (1988).

[15] Sosa, 542 U.S. at 719.

[16] *Id.* at 714 (citing 4 W. BLACKSTONE, COMMENTARIES ON THE LAWS OF ENGLAND 68 (1769)).

having been enacted on the understanding that the common law would provide a cause of action for the modest number of international law violations with a potential for personal liability at the time.[17]

Despite opening the door (to borrow the Court's metaphor) to a reading of the ATS as enforcing substantive norms itself, the Court appeared determined to limit the possible causes of action. As Justice Souter wrote,

[T]here are good reasons for a restrained conception of the discretion a federal court should exercise in considering a new cause of action of this kind. Accordingly, we think courts should require any claim based on the present-day law of nations to rest on a norm of international character accepted by the civilized world and defined with a specificity comparable to the features of the 18th-century paradigms we have recognized.[18]

What are those "good reasons"? It seems that they are the same ones that have been offered by the ATS's critics. First, the Court acknowledged that the nature of the common law has changed between 1789 and today—it is no longer transcendental law "discovered" by the state and federal courts; rather, it is made. Second, the foundational *Erie Railroad Co. v. Tompkins*[19] in 1938 changed the role of federal courts by denying the existence of a general federal common law and permitting only interstitial federal common lawmaking; *Erie* left open only a few narrow areas for judge-made law. As the Court explained, "[T]he general practice has been to look for legislative guidance before exercising innovative authority over substantive law. It would be remarkable to take a more aggressive role in exercising a jurisdiction that remained largely in shadow for much of the prior two centuries."[20] Third, the Court in recent years has made clear that it will not infer a private cause of action for a domestic statute unless it expressly creates one.[21]

These reasons are not unique to foreign affairs, but apply to all statutes generally and reflect the federal courts' seeming reluctance in the wake of *Erie* to engage in lawmaking. They would certainly be familiar arguments to the scholars who have explored the scope and processes of federal common law over the last decades, several of whom have come to doubt the modern case for the place of CIL as federal law.[22] The Court, however, added two more reasons, specific to the foreign affairs context. First, because of changes in international law, ATS suits now can call on federal courts to declare that foreign governments have violated the rights of their

---

[17] *Id.* at 724.

[18] *Id.* at 725.

[19] Erie R. Co. v. Tompkins, 304 U.S. 64 (1938).

[20] Sosa, 542 U.S. at 726.

[21] *Id.* at 727. (citing Correctional Services Corp. v. Malesko, 534 U.S. 61, 68 (2001); Alexander v. Sandoval, 532 U.S. 275, 286–87 (2001)).

[22] See, for example, Ernest A. Young, *Sorting Out the Debate over Customary International Law*, 42 Va. J. Int'l L. 365 (2002); Daniel J. Meltzer, *Customary International Law, Foreign Affairs, and Federal Common Law*, 42 Va. J. Int'l L. 513 (2002).

own citizens. This, according to Justice Souter, risks "impinging on the discretion of the Legislative and Executive Branches in managing foreign affairs."[23] Second, to the extent that the political branches have addressed the issue, they have generally refused to make human rights treaties self-executing or to create new statutory causes of action to enforce international law.[24]

Despite these considerations, however, the Court refused to "close the door" on the notion that the ATS gives rise to some causes of action, or that new substantive standards could emerge as international law evolved. Justice Scalia, joined by Chief Justice Rehnquist and Justice Thomas, argued in concurrence that the ATS was *only* jurisdictional and could not even permit claims based on the three substantive norms (safe passage, ambassadors, piracy) recognized in the late eighteenth century. In response, Justice Souter declared that federal common lawmaking could continue, albeit cautiously and reluctantly. "[W]e are persuaded that federal courts should not recognize private claims under federal common law for violations of any international law norm with less definite content and acceptance among civilized nations than the historical paradigms familiar when §1350 was enacted."[25] In applying this test, the Court found that Alvarez-Machain's claim of arbitrary detention did not rise to the level of universal recognition, binding obligation, and specificity that characterize only the highest norms of CIL and hence are cognizable under the ATS. In part, the Court clearly was troubled by the practical implications of recognizing such a cause of action, which would require the federal courts to review "any arrest, anywhere in the world, unauthorized by the law of the jurisdiction in which it took place."[26] The Court considered Alvarez-Machain's purported norm to be aspirational in nature, lacking both a specific definition and the universal acceptance by civilized nations sufficient to qualify as a binding rule of customary law.

Although Alvarez-Machain lost his case, supporters of an independent judicial role in the incorporation of international law could gain a great deal of succor from the decision. Justice Souter's opinion essentially left intact much of the existing ATS case law, as developed primarily by the Second and Ninth Circuit Courts of Appeals. Alvarez-Machain's fault was not that he sought a remedy through the ATS, but that he failed to show that a right against arbitrary detention had truly become a rule of CIL.

The Court's analysis in *Sosa*, and the debate between the majority and minority opinion, took place on fairly rigid formalist grounds. There was no doubt that if Congress, under its Article I, Section 8 power to define offenses under the Law of Nations, had decided to incorporate international law through a statute, it could have. The only question was whether the ATS ought to be interpreted as authorizing

---

[23] Sosa, 542 U.S. at 727.

[24] With one notable exception, the Torture Victim Protection Act of 1991, Pub. L. No. 102-256, 106 Stat. 73 (codified at 28 U.S.C. § 1350 (2006)), enacted to implement in part the Convention against Torture of 1984, ratified by the United States in 1991.

[25] Sosa, 542 U.S. at 732.

[26] *Id.* at 736.

federal courts to do so. To reach an answer, the Court began with an analysis of the ATS's text and original understanding, moved on to the structural arguments involving the role of the courts in federal common lawmaking and in foreign affairs, and analyzed the attitude of the current Congress. Justice Scalia's concurrence chided the majority for not following the logic of those considerations to their natural conclusion. Because Congress had not authorized the courts to engage in any common lawmaking in this area, the Court should not read the ATS to allow the creation of any causes of action to enforce CIL norms.

Nonetheless, the Court could not bring itself to shut the door completely on any federal judicial role in the enforcement of CIL. The Court's reasons, however, were anything but convincing. The historical materials on which it placed so much importance fail to show that the members of the First Congress understood the ATS to create substantive causes of action.

Justice Souter relied on three pieces of historical evidence. First, he considered it significant that Oliver Ellsworth had drafted the ATS because he had been a member of the Continental Congress in 1781 when it requested that states enact laws punishing attacks on ambassadors and violations of safe passage and because he'd been a member of the Connecticut legislature when it complied with that request. Second, the First Congress had enacted criminal statutes prohibiting violation of safe conducts, piracy, and attacks on ambassadors,[27] which Justice Souter believed showed that Congress would not have enacted a civil statute that waited upon further action to become effective.[28] Third, international law authorities of the time, most notably Vattel, declared that states should not only criminally punish those who attack ambassadors, but provide for compensation as well.[29]

To put it charitably, this historical evidence is weak. Standing alone, Ellsworth's membership in the Continental Congress and the Connecticut legislature tell us virtually nothing about the intentions of the First Congress in enacting the ATS. The Court provides no statements from Ellsworth or any of his contemporaries about the ATS, nor shows any consistent train of thought on Ellsworth's part regarding enforcement of CIL. This stands in sharp contrast, for example, to the clear public positions that leading Framers, such as James Madison and Alexander Hamilton, took on the question of the enforcement of another species of international law, treaties, both before and after the ratification.[30] Justice Souter's second piece of evidence undermines his own conclusion. If Congress was capable of enacting specific criminal statutes addressing an issue, why would it instead enact a statute that almost everyone concedes is ambiguous and unclear to address this very same conduct? Justice Souter makes a third odd historical inference from Vattel's comments. While Vattel does believe that states should compensate victims of attacks that violate

---

[27] An Act for the Punishment of Certain Crimes against the United States, § 8, 1 Stat. 113–114; *Id.* § 28, at 118.

[28] Sosa, 542 U.S. at 719.

[29] *Id.* at 723–24. (citing E. de Vattel, *Law of Nations* 463–64 (J. Chitty et al. transl. and ed. 1883)).

[30] Yoo, *Globalism, supra* note 12, at 2010–21, 2078–82.

international law, his comment cannot be read to specify whether such compensation should come about as a matter of civil suits. It is more likely that, in Vattel's time, compensation would be made by the transfer of funds from the treasury of one nation to another.

In response to Justice Scalia's concurrence, the Court sought further support in two precedents, *Banco Nacionale de Cuba v. Sabbatino*[31] and *The Paquete Habana*.[32] In the former, Justice Souter observed, the Court had commented that "it is, of course, true that United States courts apply international law as a part of our own in appropriate circumstances,"[33] while in the latter the Court declared: "International law is part of our law, and must be ascertained and administered by the courts of justice of appropriate jurisdiction, as often as questions of right depending upon it are duly presented for their determination."[34] From these cases, Justice Souter drew the conclusion that for 200 years "the domestic law of the United States recognizes the law of nations," and issued the rejoinder that "[i]t would take some explaining to say now that federal courts must avert their gaze entirely from any international norm intended to protect individuals."[35]

Neither of these cases, however, has anything to do with the ATS. Close examination of their contexts and holdings show that, if anything, they undermine the idea that the federal courts have power to enforce CIL as federal law. *Sabbatino*, for example, applied the act of state doctrine in an action arising out of the nationalization of foreign assets by the Cuban government. An American middleman purchased sugar that had been owned by a Cuban firm, CAV, whose assets the Cuban government had expropriated; after it took possession of the goods, the American company paid the proceeds to CAV rather than the Cuban government.[36] Invoking diversity jurisdiction, Banco Nacional sued under state law in federal district court for the money, and claimed that the legality of the expropriation could not be reviewed because of the act of state doctrine. In applying that doctrine, the Court rejected the notion that its use was compelled by international law, but instead found that it derived from the separation of powers in foreign affairs. As Justice Harlan wrote for the Court, the act of state doctrine "arises out of the basic relationships between branches of government in a system of separation of powers. It concerns the competency of dissimilar institutions to make and implement particular kinds of decisions in the area of international relations."[37] While the Court observed

---

[31] Banco Nacionale de Cuba v. Sabbatino, 376 U.S. 398 (1964).

[32] The Paquete Habana, 175 U.S. 677 (1900).

[33] Sabbatino, 376 U.S. at 423.

[34] The Paquete Habana, 175 U.S. at 700. The Court also cited The Nereide, 13 U.S. (9 Cranch) 388, 423 (1815) (Marshall, C. J.) ("[T]he Court is bound by the law of nations which is a part of the law of the land"); and Texas Industries, Inc. v. Radcliff Materials, Inc., 451 U.S. 630, 641 (1981) (recognizing that "international disputes implicating . . . our relations with foreign nations" are one of the "narrow areas" in which "federal common law" continues to exist).

[35] Sosa, 542 U.S. at 730.

[36] Sabbatino, 376 U.S. at 401.

[37] Id. at 423.

that *Erie Railroad* did not apply to the act of state doctrine, it emphasized that the rule was necessary to promote judicial restraint, or "a basic choice regarding the competence and function of the Judiciary and the National Executive in ordering our relationships with other members of the international community."[38] Thus, to the extent that *Sabbatino* enshrined the act of state doctrine as federal common law, federal courts still had no mandate to incorporate international law norms as federal law. Rather, the Constitution's separation of powers required courts to refrain from interfering with the Executive's control over foreign relations. Not only does *Sabbatino* not mention the ATS; its separation-of-powers concerns actually militate against Justice Souter's reading and toward judicial abstention from unilateral recognition of causes of action based in international law.

The *Paquete Habana* voyages even further from the ATS. During the Spanish-American War, American warships captured two coastal fishing vessels off the coast of Cuba.[39] After a federal district court condemned the ships as prizes, the crew of the vessels appealed to the Supreme Court on the ground that that the commander of the American naval vessel had captured the ships in violation of CIL. They claimed, and the Court agreed after a lengthy historical analysis of state practice from the 1400s, that CIL prohibited the seizure of such civilian vessels during wartime. However, several factors distinguish *The Paquete Habana* from *Sosa*, such as to make them almost completely different cases. First, the rule of the case is not simply the oft-quoted "International law is part of our law." Rather, the Court continues, courts should consult "the customs and usages of civilized nations" when "there is no treaty, and no controlling executive or legislative act or juridical decision."[40] Thus, an executive order standing alone could override the application of CIL, even though generally an executive order could not overrule judicial interpretation of a federal statute. Second, the case arose in prize jurisdiction, where, like admiralty jurisdiction, the courts had developed and applied federal common law rules, rather than pursuant to the ATS or any specific federal statute. There was no "tort" as the phrase was used in the ATS; rather, the cause of action arose under the laws of war. Third, in *The Paquete Habana* itself, the President had ordered the military to carry out its blockade in Cuba in accordance with the international laws of war—providing the Court with just the "controlling executive" action required.[41] In addition to the fact that the ATS was not even at issue, *The Paquete Habana* contains a significant difference from *Sosa* (or even the first *Alvarez-Machain* case) in that there was no conflict between executive policy and international law, and thus no occasion for the judiciary to examine whether CIL independently applied.

---

[38] *Id.* at 425.

[39] The Paquete Habana, 175 U.S. 677.

[40] *Id.* at 700.

[41] *Id.* at 712; see also Curt Bradley & Jack Goldsmith, *The Current Illegitimacy of International Human Rights Litigation*, 66 Fordham L. Rev. 319 (1997); Michael J. Glennon, *May the President Violate Customary International Law?: Can the President Do No Wrong?*, 80 Am. J. Int'l L. 923, 923 n. 6 (1986).

Despite this, cases such as *The Paquete Habana* and *Sabbatino* are usually cited for the more tenuous proposition that federal courts have the power to incorporate CIL as federal law directly, without the intervention of a statute.[42] The reasoning must run, we suppose, that if federal courts can directly incorporate international law as federal law, much in the way that the judiciary on its own authority derives rules to govern interstate disputes and federal instrumentalities, then doing so pursuant to a statute (here the ATS) is a far smaller step. This certainly seems to have been the reasoning of the lower courts, most prominently the Second Circuit, which relied on these cases when it gave birth to modern ATS litigation in *Filartiga*.[43] Of course, as we have explained above, the Court has never truly approved the direct incorporation of CIL as federal law, but rather has upheld international legal norms to advance judicial restraint in foreign affairs or to enforce presidential directives in war. Moreover, as we explain below, the Court has repeatedly refused to review state court decisions applying CIL on the ground that the Court lacked appellate jurisdiction to review a state court interpretation of CIL.[44]

Lastly, the Court relied on a series of questionable assumptions about congressional awareness of judicial activity in the international law arena. According to the Court, Congress's silence on the ATS must signify some level of implicit agreement with the lower courts' expanded application of the ATS over the last two decades. Put aside for the moment that, even accepting the Court's argument at face value, legislative silence today could only inform us about the current Congress's preferences, not the intentions of the First Congress that enacted the ATS in 1789. Also put aside the fact that the Supreme Court does not employ a strong form of stare decisis in statutory interpretation cases, but instead overrules precedents in this area with some regularity.[45] Justice Souter assumes that ATS cases are sufficiently important to outweigh other important items on Congress's limited agenda (a doubtful proposition these days), that silence reflects the wishes of a majority (rather than, perhaps, the opposition of a filibustering minority or a President and one-third of the Senate), and that Congress regularly overrides judicial interpretations with which it disagrees. The accuracy of these assumptions depends on facts for which no conclusive empirical data exist,[46] and there are certainly plausible arguments that run in the other direction.

---

[42] See, for example, Ryan Goodman & Derek Jinks, *Filartiga's Firm Footing: International Human Rights and Federal Law*, 66 FORDHAM L. REV. 463, 481 (1997).

[43] Filartiga v. Pena- Irala, 630 F.2d 876, 887 (2d Cir. 1980).

[44] See, for example, Ker v. Illinois, 119 U.S. 436 (1886).

[45] See, for example, Hubbard v. United States, 514 U.S. 695, 715 (1995); William N. Eskridge, Jr., *The Case of the Amorous Defendant: Criticizing Absolute Stare Decisis for Statutory Cases*, 88 MICH. L. REV. 2450, 2462 (1990).

[46] In the leading empirical study on this question, William Eskridge concluded that Congress does monitor judicial decisions involving statutory interpretation and will override "textualist" decisions more often than those that rely on legislative history or congressional purpose. William N. Eskridge, Jr., *Overriding Supreme Court Statutory Interpretation Decisions*, 101 YALE L.J. 331 (1991). Adrian Vermeule, however, has raised significant doubts about whether Eskridge's data actually supports that conclusion. See Adrian Vermeule, *Interpretive Choice*, 75 N.Y.U. L. REV. 74, 104–06 (2000).

Sosa purported to settle the ATS question using standard formalist tools of text, history, structure, and precedent. None of these arguments proved convincing. Indeed, as Justice Scalia's concurrence pointed out, the formalist arguments, if anything, should have led the Court to the opposite holding. The ruling perhaps should have come as no surprise, because it mirrors the stalemate that has prevailed in the academic literature. After an initial burst of writing in the wake of Curtis Bradley and Jack Goldsmith's 1997 attack on ATS litigation, academics have made little progress in reaching a consensus. In fact, this stalemate may have contributed to the odd nature of the Court's decision in *Sosa*, which seems to acknowledge both sides of the debate, but does not really choose between them. While the Court seems to admit the compelling nature of the formalist arguments against federal common lawmaking in general and incorporation of CIL in particular, it would not adopt their conclusion. At the same time, the Court could not develop any convincing reasons of its own, based in the text, structure, or history of the ATS, to keep the door open to judicial development of substantive causes of action under the ATS.

B. Customary International Law, the States, and Presidential Review

The Court might have decided to maintain an independent judicial role in the incorporation of CIL for reasons unrelated to its unconvincing formalist rationales. Indeed, many defenders of the *Sosa* decision have hailed the importance of this judicial role to ensure broad U.S. compliance with and development of norms of CIL.[47] From our perspective, however, the *Sosa* Court's confidence in preserving this role for federal courts is misplaced.

As we argued in chapter 4, federal courts are unlikely to have the best institutional characteristics for accommodating the various types of international law within the U.S. constitutional system. The defining institutional characteristics of federal courts—independence from politics, litigation-driven schedules for decision-making, and highly formalized limits on information gathering—strongly suggest that federal courts would have difficulty incorporating CIL norms within a broader context of international and national policy goals. At the very least, our functional analysis of federal courts suggests that they would be less effective and competent in this task than either the executive or the legislative branch. Indeed, the *Sosa* Court recognized this functional advantage by its emphasis on the importance of limiting the discretion of federal courts in the ATS context and by suggesting that deference to executive suggestions would be appropriate in certain cases.[48]

---

[47] See, for example, Beth Stephens, *Sosa v. Alvarez-Machain: The Door Is Still Ajar for Human Rights Litigation in U.S. Courts*, 70 Brook. L. Rev. 533, 535 (2004–2005) ("the decision is a clear victory for those human rights advocates who view the statute as a means to hold the most egregious perpetrators accountable for the most egregious violations of international law").

[48] *Sosa*, 542 U.S. at 733. ("Another possible limitation that we need not apply here is a policy of case-specific deference to the political branches").

We would take the *Sosa* Court's institutional intuitions to their logical conclusion and reject an independent role for federal courts in the incorporation of CIL through the ATS. But we recognize that there has been a long tradition of judicial participation in the application of CIL in the U.S. system. As a doctrinal matter, we accept *The Paquete Habana*'s declaration that "international law is part of our law" and must exist in some part of the domestic legal system cognizable by courts. But we believe there is a way to reconcile this doctrinal tradition with the U.S. constitutional structure's commitment to maintaining popular sovereignty. Like the rest of the pre-*Erie* general common law, we believe CIL should be treated as part of the common law of the states.

Interestingly, the perceived implausibility of this proposal has been one of the chief arguments for maintaining the federal status of CIL. As Koh has argued, treating CIL as state law could result in fifty different state interpretations of CIL and would be inconsistent with the traditional "one voice" conception of U.S. foreign relations law.[49]

This is a serious objection to the reading of the ATS that we propose here. As we argued in chapter 6, however, states already have the formal and functional ability to participate in matters affecting foreign affairs, including international law. Such participation can be further reconciled with our constitutional system by recognizing the power of the President to supervise and preempt divergent state interpretations of CIL by statements of national policy. Thus, removing CIL from the federal courts does not leave it to the whims of fifty different state court systems. Rather, it places CIL in the state and federal courts under the direct supervision of the federal executive. This reflects both our criticism of the centrality of federal courts in the control of CIL and our belief in the importance of maintaining a role for states in the accommodation of globalization.

As the *Sosa* Court pointed out, the Supreme Court has long "affirmed that the domestic law of the United States recognizes the law of nations."[50] But the *Sosa* majority failed to acknowledge that, prior to *Filartiga*, this affirmation of CIL had been the task of state courts operating independently and without the supervision of the federal courts.

Prior to the seminal *Erie* case, most scholars agreed that CIL formed part of the general common law.[51] In contrast to the post-*Erie* system, federal courts were not bound by state court interpretations of general common law, and state courts were not bound by federal court interpretations of general common law.

---

[49] See Harold H. Koh, *Is International Law Really State Law?*, 111 Harv. L. Rev. 1824, 1841 (1998).

[50] *Sosa*, 542 U.S. at 729.

[51] See, for example, Restatement (Third) of Foreign Relations Law of the United States, pt. I, ch. 2 introductory note, 41 (1986); Young, *Sorting Out the Debate over Customary International Law*, supra note 22, at 374; Gerald Neuman, *Sense and Nonsense about Customary International Law: A Response to Professors Bradley and Goldsmith*, 66 Fordham L. Rev. 371, 373 (1997); Beth Stephens, *The Law of Our Land: Customary International Law as Federal Law after Erie*, 66 Fordham L. Rev. 393, 400–01 n. 34 (1997). See also *Sosa*, 124 S. Ct. at 2770.

Thus, when cases involving the application of CIL fell within the jurisdiction of state courts, those courts applied CIL independently and without the possibility of appeal to the federal courts or the Supreme Court. Similarly, federal courts applied CIL without being bound by state court interpretations. Each system applied CIL independently.[52]

The Supreme Court consistently confirmed this understanding of the pre-*Erie* status of CIL, holding that CIL "is one of those questions of general jurisprudence" or general common law.[53] On a number of occasions, the Court also confirmed that it held no appellate jurisdiction over state court interpretations and applications of CIL. In 1875, the Court refused to accept appellate jurisdiction over a state court decision applying the "general laws of war, as recognized by the law of nations" because such a case did not involve the "Constitution, laws, treaties, or executive proclamations of the United States" under the federal question jurisdiction statute as it existed then.[54]

Less than a decade later, the Court similarly refused to review a state court decision affirming the conviction of a criminal defendant who had been abducted overseas in violation of CIL because "the decision of that question is as much within the province of the state court as a question of common law, or of the law of nations."[55] Although some commentators have simply rejected these and other decisions reaching the same result as erroneous,[56] the fact remains that no Supreme Court decision in the pre-*Erie* regime ever held that state court interpretations of CIL could be reviewed by federal courts.[57] The historical record, as Professors A. J. Bellia and Bradford Clark have confirmed in a recent study, shows that state courts have always developed and interpreted certain aspects of the traditional Law of Nations, such as private international law, without federal court supervision.[58]

While the pre-*Erie* regime of CIL as general common law persisted for a substantial period of time, in some cases the system resulted in inconsistent interpretations or applications of CIL. Such inconsistencies have fueled critics of Judge Learned

---

[52] For the leading account of the operation of the general common law system, and its difference from the modern, positivistic understanding of federal and state common law, see William A. Fletcher, *The General Common Law and Section 34 of the Judiciary Act of 1789: The Example of Marine Insurance*, 97 Harv. L. Rev. 1513 (1984).

[53] Huntington v. Atrill, 146 U.S. 657, 683 (1892).

[54] See New York Life Insurance v. Hendren, 92 U.S. 286 (1875).

[55] Ker v. Illinois, 119 U.S. 436, 444 (1883).

[56] See Neuman, *Sense and Nonsense about Customary International Law*, supra note 51, at 374 n. 14; Restatement (Third), supra note 51, at § 111, n. 4.

[57] Indeed, one of the interesting aspects of the scholarly debate is that while there is virtually no judicial precedent prior to Filartiga supporting federal court control over the interpretation and application of CIL, leading scholars managed to achieve wide acceptance for this view. See, for example, Restatement (Third), supra note 51, at § 111. This consensus was achieved despite the fact that the only federal court to directly consider the question of CIL after Erie prior to Filartiga, Judge Learned Hand in the Second Circuit, essentially followed Erie and past practice and treated CIL as part of New York's common law. See Bergman v. De Sieyes, 170 F.2d 360 (2d Cir. 1948).

[58] See, e.g., Anthony J. Bellia, Jr., & Bradford R. Clark, *The Federal Common Law of Nations*, 109 Colum. L. Rev. 1, 81 (2009).

Hand's view that CIL has become part of the common law of the several states after *Erie*. After all, adopting Judge Hand's conclusion would result in fifty different interpretations of CIL doctrines, with chaotic implications for the ability of the United States to maintain a unified voice on foreign affairs.[59]

However, there is no reason to believe that granting federal courts broad authority over CIL development, as the Court did in *Sosa*, will result in a superior system. Federal courts suffer from many disabilities that make them less than ideal arbiters of CIL, especially in matters implicating sensitive issues of foreign relations. Rather, both the historical record and functional considerations support giving the executive branch, rather than the federal courts, the power to supervise CIL development as a matter of domestic law. The Supreme Court's decision in *American Insurance Association v. Garamendi*[60] confirms and strengthens this belief.

In *Garamendi*, the Supreme Court considered the constitutionality of the Holocaust Victim Insurance Relief Act (HVIRA), a California statute requiring insurance companies to disclose information about World War II–era insurance policies held by Holocaust victims.[61] An association of insurance companies, including foreign insurance companies who bore the brunt of the disclosure requirements, challenged HVIRA, claiming the state law impermissibly intruded into the federal government's exclusive authority over foreign affairs. The governments of the United States and Germany filed briefs in support of the insurance companies. By a 5–4 majority, the Court agreed that the state law was preempted.[62]

What makes *Garamendi* important for our purposes is not that the Court decided to preempt a state law, but the basis for the preemption. A trial court had invalidated HVIRA on the grounds that it interfered with the federal government's exclusive control over foreign affairs.[63] The trial court had relied on the Supreme Court's decision in *Zschernig v. Miller*[64] that authorized federal courts to preempt state laws that intruded into foreign affairs, even without a direct conflict with a federal statute, treaty, or executive agreement.[65] The *Garamendi* Court did not reject *Zschernig*. On the other hand, it also did not extend *Zschernig*'s endorsement of an independent federal court power to supervise foreign relations. Instead, the Court found the California law preempted because the law created a clear conflict with a "consistent Presidential foreign policy."[66] Importantly, the Court did not rely on a treaty, statute, or executive agreement to find preemption. Rather, it gleaned this "consistent Presidential foreign policy" by reviewing statements made by U.S. officials responsible for negotiating settlement agreements with foreign governments

[59] Koh, *Is International Law Really State Law?*, *supra* note 49, at 1841.

[60] American Ins. Ass'n v. Garamendi, 539 U.S. 396 (2003).

[61] See Cal. Ins. Code §§ 13800–13807.

[62] Garamendi, 539 U.S. 396.

[63] See, for example, Gerling Global Reinsurance Corp. of Am. v. Quackenbush, 2000 U.S. Dist. LEXIS 8815 (June 9, 2000).

[64] Zschernig v. Miller, 389 U.S. 429 (1968).

[65] Gerling Global, 2000 U.S. Dist. Lexis at 19.

[66] Garamendi, 539 U.S. at 421.

and insurers.[67] Because these statements by executive branch officials indicated a national policy to encourage voluntary repayment of insurance policies rather than mandatory disclosures, "state law must give way where, as here, there is evidence of clear conflict between the policies adopted" by the "federal executive authority" and the states.[68]

Thus, the *Garamendi* Court neatly sidestepped the main criticism of *Zschernig*, in that it empowered federal courts independently to preempt state laws in the complete absence of any input from the wishes of the President or Congress. By relying on executive "statements" of national policy, the *Garamendi* Court avoided the problem of unchecked federal courts by empowering the executive branch to settle future disputes over state interference with foreign affairs by issuing statements of national policy.

Although the decision did not involve state court interpretations of the CIL, *Garamendi* shows that the power of the federal courts independently to oversee state activities in foreign affairs is deeply intertwined with federal court power to control the development of CIL. As suggested above, supporters of the ATS have argued that control over CIL must remain under the authority of the federal courts because only federal courts can unify disparate and inconsistent interpretations of CIL.[69] In this view, CIL is simply one part of the larger foreign relations law controlled and developed by federal courts. Just as states cannot intrude on matters involving foreign relations by enacting laws like HVIRA, states also cannot be allowed to intrude on foreign relations by developing and interpreting CIL independently.

For this reason, *Garamendi* only serves to strengthen the Executive's already well-established role in the supervision of CIL. *Garamendi*'s preference for using statements by subcabinet officials to determine whether a state law conflicts with national policy reaffirms the ability of such officials to control the development of CIL in lower courts as well. *Garamendi* reminds us that federal courts are not the only institutions capable of providing a coherent national approach to CIL.

Under this understanding of *Garamendi*, and consistent with past practice, the President controls CIL in three different ways. First, the President has the authority to declare, on behalf of the United States, adherence, rejection, or interpretation of CIL on the international plane. Most CIL requires state consent, and most scholars agree that the President holds the primary authority to issue or withhold such consent for the United States. One of the more uncontroversial examples of this practice is President Truman's 1945 proclamation declaring that the United States would control the underwater continental shelf abutting the coasts of the United States as part of U.S. territory.[70] A more controversial example of this practice is President

---

[67] *Id.*

[68] *Id.*

[69] See, for example, Koh, *Is International Law Really State Law?, supra* note 49, at 1841.

[70] Policy of the United States with Respect to the Natural Resources of the Subsoil and Sea Bed of the Continental Shelf, Proclamation no. 2667, 10 Fed. Reg. 12,303 (Oct. 2, 1945).

Bush's 2001 determination that al Qaeda and Taliban detainees captured in Afghanistan are not subject to the full protections of the customary laws of war.[71]

Second, the President may declare a national policy to adhere to, reject, or interpret a principle of CIL that preempts the entire field of CIL from state common law development. For example, in the aforementioned laws of war example, any presidential determination on the limited rights of unlawful combatants under the laws of war would likely completely preempt any independent state adjudication of CIL of those rights, including lawsuits by individuals seeking to challenge the President's interpretation. Otherwise, state courts might claim authority to make rules of international law as part of their general subject matter jurisdiction, which allows them to hear both federal and state law questions. Thus, if an unlawful combatant (say, from Guantánamo Bay) sues for violations of the law of war, the whole field would be controlled by presidential determinations of the applicability of the CIL of war.[72]

Third, the President may declare a national policy to adhere to, reject, or interpret a principle of CIL that comes into conflict with a specific interpretation of CIL under a state's common law. If a state adopts a rule, for instance, that head-of-state immunity protects a particular current head of state, the President can override that particular interpretation while still leaving the state the authority to interpret other, related forms of CIL such as whether head-of-state immunity applies to former heads of state.[73]

Of course, the President's authority to issue such declarations or interpretations is not exclusive. Rather, it is subject to congressional override for matters falling within the shared powers of Congress and the President. In the absence of congressional intervention, however, the President's interpretation of CIL would be the final word.[74]

While *Garamendi* provides formal doctrinal support for our proposal for state court control over CIL (supervised by the federal executive), critics are likely to offer a number of objections. We consider each in turn.

Perhaps the most counterintuitive component of our proposal is the idea that CIL will form part of the common law of the states rather than federal law. As proponents of the modern position have argued, CIL seems to fall logically within the purview of the federal government because foreign affairs is clearly a

---

[71] See, for example, John Yoo & James Ho, *The Status of Terrorists*, 44 Va. J. Intl L. 207 (2003).

[72] This would not prevent such an individual from bringing a suit on other grounds, however, including violations of constitutional or other domestic law rights.

[73] Compare Republic of Austria v. Altmann, 541 U.S. 677, 699–700 (2004).

[74] We limit our argument to the President's ability to interpret CIL in the absence of congressional action and do not address the related, but distinct question of the President's authority to interpret treaties. For a detailed discussion of this issue, see John C. Yoo, *Treaty Interpretation and the False Sirens of Delegation*, 90 Cal. L. Rev. 1305 (2002), and Michael P. Van Alstine, *The Judicial Power and Treaty Delegation*, 90 Cal. L. Rev. 1263 (2002).

national rather than a state matter. Moreover, as we have pointed out, CIL needs to be unified.

The first response is that under our proposal CIL would form part of the common law of the states, but the President would be responsible for unifying the treatment of CIL for the United States as a whole. As we explained in chapter 5, the executive branch has many more resources at its disposal for assessing and interpreting CIL. Unlike federal courts, which rely on private litigants to remove cases to their jurisdiction and properly brief the issues before them, the executive branch can intervene wherever and whenever it chooses to by the simple expediency of issuing a document similar to the Tate Letter.[75] Indeed, in a brief filed in the recent Supreme Court decision *Samantar v. Yousuf,* the executive branch argued that it retained this power to determine the applicability of foreign sovereign immunity to foreign government officials.[76] Although the Court did not explicitly accept this view, it remanded the case to the district court, which promptly followed the executive branch's suggestion.[77]

Moreover, even if one accepted the idea that state governments have no role in the administration and interpretation of CIL (an idea that one of us has disputed at length elsewhere),[78] our proposal will almost certainly result in most CIL litigation returning to federal courts. The difference will be that such litigation must satisfy federal diversity jurisdiction requirements and will be governed by the common law of the state where the federal court resides. Thus, even if state courts and institutions were deemed somehow inferior, as a functional matter, to federal courts, our proposal does not preclude plaintiffs from going to federal courts anyway (assuming they can satisfy diversity requirements).

Indeed, treating CIL as state common law actually protects the independence of federal courts. Under the current system, if the Executive seeks to stop a court from adhering to a principle of CIL, a court empowered by the *Sosa* decision to interpret CIL cannot automatically defer to the President's views without threatening its judicial independence. Under current doctrine with respect to the interpretation of treaties, for instance, courts give "great weight" but not conclusive authority to executive interpretations of treaties. Judicial independence requires at least some independent judgment, and if "[t]he Government equates deference to submission," then it "would conflate 'great weight' with surrendered judicial independence."[79]

---

[75] Just how the Executive intervenes remains somewhat unsettled after Garamendi, although the majority seemed to rely on its belief that the policy requiring preemption was "expressed unmistakably" in statements of executive branch officers responsible for negotiating the executive agreements in question. Garamendi, 539 U.S. at 442. In any event, Garamendi makes it clear such preemption may occur without a formal executive agreement, statute, or treaty.

[76] Samantar v. Yousuf, 130 S. Ct. 2278 (2010). See Brief for the United States as Amicus Curiae Supporting Affirmance at 5, Samantar, 130 S. Ct. 2278 (No. 08-1555)

[77] See Yousuf v. Samantar, 1:04cv1360 (LMB/JFA) (Feb. 15, 2011).

[78] Julian G. Ku, *The State of New York Does Exist: How the States Control Compliance with International Law,* 82 N.C. L. Rev. 457 (2004).

[79] Tachiona v. Mugabe 186 F. Supp. 2d 383, 393 (S.D.N.Y. 2002).

Presumably, similar concerns would arise in the context of executive views on CIL if such views were absolutely binding on federal courts. In other words, federal courts would hardly remain an independent branch of government if they were required to leave "[r]esolution of so fundamental a constitutional issue . . . [to] the shifting winds at the State Department."[80] On the other hand, the Court has never explicitly rejected its prior precedent requiring substantial deference to executive determinations on the requirements of sovereign immunity, even after the passage of the Foreign Sovereign Immunities Act.[81]

Needless to say, this continuing tension between judicial independence and executive competence could be largely avoided if state courts or federal courts sitting in diversity are merely applying CIL as a doctrine of state common law. Absolute deference by the state courts to executive statements of CIL would not threaten the separation of powers, since federal courts still act as an independent judicial system for federal matters delegated to federal courts by treaty or statute. Moreover, the Supreme Court's precedents consistently permit greater presidential leeway over state law as opposed to the other branches of the federal government. As *Garamendi* illustrates, the Court has determined that the President, who holds the "vast share of responsibility for foreign affairs," already holds the unilateral ability to preempt state law based on his determination of a "consistent . . . foreign policy."[82] And as we have explained above, this doctrinal result has sound functional benefits given the President's numerous institutional advantages over federal courts in the determination of national policy toward CIL and international human rights law. Just as importantly, this result also helps to preserve the role of federal courts as fair institutions relatively independent of political manipulation.

The second main objection to our proposal is that it would confer too much power on the President with respect to the interpretation and application of CIL. It is true that our proposal gives the President the discretion to interpret, apply, and even violate CIL. But we do not find this objection problematic.

First, it is well settled that the United States, as a sovereign, has the authority to violate CIL. U.S. courts, for instance, have long recognized that Congress has the power to violate treaties and CIL for purposes of domestic law. Hence, courts will enforce statutes passed later in time than treaties, and courts will also enforce statutes that violate CIL (although they will try to interpret both to avoid conflict).[83]

---

[80] Zschernig v. Miller, 389 U.S. 429, 443 (1968) (Stewart J., concurring).

[81] The Court suggested that the State Department's authority to control application of foreign sovereign immunity determinations exists alongside the FSIA's statutory requirements. Republic of Austria v. Altmann, 541 U.S. 677, 702 (2004) ("[S]hould the State Department choose to express its opinion on the implications of exercising jurisdiction over particular petitioners in connection with their alleged conduct, that opinion might well be entitled to deference as the considered judgment of the Executive on a particular question of foreign policy").

[82] Garamendi, 539 U.S. at 414 (quoting Youngstown Sheet & Tube Co v. Sawyer, 343 U.S. 579, 610–611 (1952)), 421.

[83] Whitney v. Robertson, 124 U.S. 190 (1888); Murray v. The Schooner Charming Betsy, 6 U.S. 64 (1804). For a discussion of the issues raised by conflicts between treaties and federal statutes, see

Similarly, the Supreme Court has recognized that even though international law is "part of our law," it is subject to preemption by a "controlling executive act."[84]

Second, the executive branch is the institution in the best position to determine whether and how the United States as a whole should adhere to a rule of CIL. As we have explained, much of CIL is determined by state practice, and under the U.S. system, the President is the chief interlocutor with foreign nations and international institutions. If the United States has the power to violate CIL, which it undoubtedly has, then the presidency is the logical institution to determine when and how to do so.

Third, under our view, Congress has the authority to override most presidential interpretations of CIL as well as presidential decisions to violate CIL. After all, Congress has the power to "define and punish offences against the Law of Nations."[85] Moreover, it has been delegated a number of specific powers to regulate foreign commerce and the military.[86] While there are some matters allocated by the Constitution to the President exclusively, many CIL questions do not fall within that category and can be regulated by Congress if it chooses. Additionally, as we explained above, Congress exercises substantially more influence over the executive branch than it does over the courts because it does not have to rely solely on its legislative power to override a decision. It can hold oversight hearings, change budget allocations, and block the appointment of executive officers, to name just a few of the nonlegislative mechanisms that would enable it to oversee executive interpretations of CIL. If Congress chooses not to act, either formally or informally, we believe the President, rather than the federal courts, should retain the authority to determine U.S. policy toward CIL.

Sosa uneasily endorses independent judicial participation in the interpretation and enforcement of CIL, a role supported by the majority of international legal scholars and advocates. Though *Sosa* recognized the force of both formalist critiques of the basis for such judicial powers under the ATS and functional critiques of the dangers of conflicts with other branches of the government, the Court was ultimately persuaded that the ATS litigation was necessarily a job for the federal courts. It refused to accept that "federal courts must avert their gaze from CIL" and that it was required by the formalist critique to remove "independent judicial recognition" of CIL.[87]

We believe there is a better way of dealing with the traditional status of CIL as "part of our law." Rather than eliminate CIL from U.S. domestic law entirely, we believe CIL can be accommodated as a form of state common law supervised by the President. In this way, CIL, and the global norms that develop under CIL, can

Julian G. Ku, *Treaties as Laws: A Defense of the Last-in-Time Rule for Treaties and Federal Statutes,* 80 Ind. L.J. 319 (2005).

[84] The Paquete Habana, 175 U.S. 677, 700 (1900).

[85] U.S. Const. art I, § 8.

[86] *Id.*

[87] Sosa, 542 U.S. at 729–730.

be absorbed into the U.S. system. At the same time, however, the institution with the greatest institutional competence for this task—the President—can manage this process while maintaining a certain level of autonomy for the states. In this way, the basic constitutional commitments to separation of powers and federalism—commitments that lie at the heart of the popular sovereignty theory of the Constitution—can be maintained.

II. MEDELLÍN V. TEXAS

Medellín v. Texas offers another case study of the complexity of challenges posed by globalization to the U.S. constitutional system. The root cause is the easy mobility of individuals across national borders. As foreign nationals enter the United States, some will commit crimes and become subject to the criminal justice system; as travel increases, the number of alien criminals will correspondingly increase. International regulatory agreement, in the form of a multilateral treaty, attempts to accord certain procedural rights to aliens arrested for crimes in another country, but American states may not follow—or even be aware—of those norms.

In this 2007 case, a Texas state court convicted a Mexican national of capital murder. From those basic facts arose a complicated case involving state, federal, and international law. The Supreme Court had to adjudicate issues involving a potential delegation of federal power to an international court, the independence of states in a matter implicating both foreign affairs and areas of traditional state control, and the role of the President in the enforcement of international law.[88] *Medellín* arose from the confluence of the new pressures unleashed by globalization. Such pressures included an assertive and independent international organization, an international treaty that NGOs and human rights advocates claimed regulated U.S. administration of the death penalty, and the willingness of foreign governments to use these legal mechanisms to challenge U.S. government policies.

Medellín also demonstrates the virtues of our proposed strategy of legal accommodation. Despite the various momentous issues before the Court, Chief Justice Roberts's opinion focused almost exclusively on the doctrine of non-self-execution. The Court's determination that the relevant treaties did not constitute enforceable domestic law allowed it to navigate between U.S. obligations to cooperate with an international court, on the one hand, and the right of the states to manage criminal procedure, on the other.

The Court's resolution of these challenges relied on a robust rejection of a central judicial role in the management of foreign affairs problems that intersect with domestic policy. *Medellín* requires a treaty text to contain a clear statement of an intent to delegate powers to an international tribunal. It further demands that Congress implement any domestic effect of the decisions of international tribunals by statute. This approach has the functional benefit of limiting and controlling (but

---

[88] 552 U.S. 491 (2008).

not prohibiting) the delegation of judicial power to international tribunals while allocating decision-making on how to manage the consequences of such delegations to the legislative and executive branches.

A. Dueling Courts and the Vienna Convention

Medellín was the final chapter in a tug-of-war between the U.S. Supreme Court, the executive branch, and the International Court of Justice that stretched back more than a decade. The dispute centered on the meaning and enforcement of the Vienna Convention on Consular Relations (VCCR), which was ratified by the United States in 1969.[89] The VCCR contains two provisions regulating communication and contact between consulates and nationals of foreign states. First, paragraph 1 of Article 36 created a right to consular notification for an arrested foreign national.[90] Second, paragraph 2 of Article 36 obliged states to ensure that its domestic laws conformed to these requirements, though also "in conformity with the laws and regulations" of the state. These provisions became the central focus of litigation against the United States in the International Court of Justice (ICJ).

Additionally, while disputes over consular relations had traditionally been handled via bilateral diplomacy, the VCCR offered states-parties a mechanism to resolve their disputes.[91] Pursuant to the Optional Protocol to the VCCR, "disputes arising out of the interpretation or application of the Convention shall lie within the compulsory jurisdiction of the International Court of Justice . . ."[92] This provision gave the ICJ jurisdiction to resolve disputes between states under the VCCR. The United States ratified the Optional Protocol at the same time that it ratified the VCCR.[93]

The VCCR lay dormant in U.S. domestic litigation for the first three decades after its ratification.[94] The federal government took measures to implement the treaty with respect to its immigration regulations,[95] but there was no additional legislation at either the federal or the state level. In the mid-1990s, spurred by domestic and international NGOs opposed to America's policies on capital punishment, a number

---

[89] Vienna Convention on Consular Relations and Optional Protocol on Disputes, Apr. 24, 1963, 21 U.S.T. 77, 596 U.N.T.S. 261.

[90] VCCR and Optional Protocol, art. 36(1)(b), *supra* 21 U.S.T. at 78.

[91] *Id.*

[92] *Id.*

[93] *Id.*

[94] The first case to consider article 36 of the VCCR occurred in 1979 in the context of immigration service regulations. United States v. Calderon-Medina, 591 F.2d 529 (9th Cir. 1979).

[95] Proceedings to Determine Deportability of Aliens in the United States: Apprehension, Custody and Detention, 8 C.F.R. s. 22.2(g) (1993); Inspection and Expedited Removal of Aliens; Detention and Removal of Aliens; Conduct of Removal Proceedings; Asylum Procedures, 62 Fed. Reg. 10312, 10360 (1997). Another example of the change in federal law appeared in Department of Justice arrest procedures, which state that an officer arresting a foreign national must inform him of his right to notify his consulate. *See* Notification of Consular Officers upon the Arrest of Foreign Nationals, 28 C.F.R. s. 50.5(a)(1) (1993).

of countries began to challenge the failure of state and local officials in the United States to confer consular notification rights under the VCCR to foreign nationals. These challenges took place both in domestic U.S. courts and in three separate cases brought by foreign nations against the United States in the ICJ.

The ICJ VCCR litigation illustrates how NGOs, foreign countries, and international institutions can combine to challenge the U.S. government's administration of domestic laws. Domestic and international opposition to capital punishment first took the form of domestic litigation, followed by international litigation. The VCCR, especially its Optional Protocol granting jurisdiction to the ICJ, became an important vehicle for pursuing an anti-capital punishment agenda.[96]

The ICJ's first two judgments involving violations of the VCCR did not directly raise questions of judicial enforceability in U.S. courts. In *Breard v. Greene*, decided in 1998, the Supreme Court took up the case of a Paraguayan national who was convicted of capital murder in Virginia but did not receive the required warning on arrest that he had the right to contact his consulate.[97] The Justices held that the petitioner had defaulted his right to raise the treaty claim in federal habeas because he had failed to raise it in state court first. Congress had enacted this procedural requirement, the Court observed, in 1996, later in time than U.S. adoption of the VCCR, so it conditioned any rights held by Breard. "Breard's ability to obtain relief based on violations of the Vienna Convention is subject to this subsequently-enacted rule, just as any claim arising under the United States Constitution would be."[98] In a second case involving two Germans convicted in Arizona, the Supreme Court refused to stop their executions (for a variety of procedural, constitutional, and treaty-based reasons), even though the ICJ found that their VCCR rights had been violated and ordered the United States to take measures to stay the proceedings.[99]

The Court did consider, and reject, the notion that the VCCR delegated authority to make decisions or interpret the VCCR to the ICJ. In *Sanchez-Llamas v. Oregon*, the Court took up the cases of Mexican and Honduran nationals convicted of state crimes without the benefit of their rights to consular notification.[100] The defendants and their amici contended that the United States was obligated to comply with the Vienna Convention as interpreted by the ICJ, which had held (post-*Breard*) that domestic procedural default rules should not bar a remedy for a VCCR violation. The Court rejected the argument: "although the ICJ's interpretation deserves 'respectful consideration,' we conclude that it does not compel us to reconsider our understanding of the Convention in *Breard*."[101] Relying on *Marbury v. Madison*, the Court held that nothing in the creation or the powers of the ICJ could supersede

---

[96] For an account of how the Medellín litigation serves this function, see Margaret E. McGuinness, *Medellín, Norm Portals, and the Horizontal Integration of International Human Rights*, 82 NOTRE DAME L. REV. 755 (2006).

[97] Breard v. Greene, 523 U.S. 371 (1998).

[98] *Id.* at 376.

[99] Federal Republic of Germany v. U.S., 526 U.S. 111 (1999).

[100] 548 U.S. 331 (2006).

[101] *Id.* at 353.

the Supreme Court's constitutional role as the final interpreter of federal law for the federal judiciary. "If treaties are to be given effect as federal law under our legal system, determining their meaning as a matter of federal law 'is emphatically the province and duty of the judicial department,' headed by the 'one supreme Court' established by the Constitution."[102]

In the final decision in the ICJ trilogy, *Mexico v. United States (Avena)*,[103] the ICJ held that the VCCR required a host state to "provide, by means of its own choosing, review and reconsideration of the convictions and sentences of the [affected] Mexican nationals" to determine whether the violations "caused actual prejudice."[104] But this meant more than simply providing executive clemency review and implied that procedural default rules should not bar such review.[105]

The *Avena* decision thus presented the first opportunity for U.S. courts to consider the domestic enforceability of an ICJ order whose binding force under international law was uncontested. The Supreme Court case was brought by Jose Medellín, a Mexican national who had been sentenced to death by the state of Texas.[106] At the time of the ICJ's final judgment in *Avena*, Medellín had already exhausted his state appeals and lost his first petition for habeas corpus relief in federal district court.[107] On appeal, the Fifth Circuit denied Medellín a certificate of appealability, finding that ICJ holdings were not directly enforceable in court.

Although the Supreme Court granted Medellín's petition for a writ of certiorari, its review was interrupted by a remarkable brief filed by the U.S. Solicitor General on behalf of the United States. Siding with Texas that the Supreme Court lacked the authority to enforce ICJ judgments, the Solicitor General also argued that the President held the exclusive authority to do so. In an executive order, President Bush ordered state courts to "give effect" to the ICJ's VCCR decisions "in accordance with general principles of comity."[108] The President's unusual intervention upended the Court's consideration of the case. In a close decision, the Court withdrew its review of the case, while at the same time denying Medellín's motion for a stay of the case pending his return to Texas courts to implement the President's order.[109]

---

[102] *Id.* at 353–54 (citations omitted).

[103] Case Concerning Avena and Other Mexican Nationals (Mex. v. U.S.), 2004 ICJ 12 (Judgment of Mar. 31, 2004) (available at 2004 WL 2450913).

[104] *Id.* at para. 121.

[105] *Id.* at para. 138, 143.

[106] Medellín v. Dretke, 371 F.3d 270, 273–74 (5th Cir. 2004) (describing background and posture of the case).

[107] *Id.* at 274.

[108] *Id.* at 38–40 ("I have determined, pursuant to the authority vested in me as President by the Constitution and the laws of the United States of America, that the United States will discharge its international obligations under the decision of the International Court of Justice in the Case Concerning Avena and Other Mexican Nationals (Mexico v. United States of America) (Avena), 2004 ICJ 128 (Mar. 31), by having state courts give effect to the decision in accordance with general principles of comity in cases filed by the 51 Mexican nationals addressed in that decision").

[109] Medellín v. Dretke, 544 U.S. 660, 661–662 (2005) (discussing motion for stay).

Despite the President's memorandum, the Texas courts continued to reject Medellín's motion for relief based on violation of his VCCR rights. Lower courts refused to give domestic effect to the ICJ's judgment in *Avena* and interpreted the President's memorandum as nonbinding. The case then returned to the Supreme Court, squarely presenting two questions: (1) whether the ICJ's *Avena* judgment was directly binding on Texas courts and, (2) if not, whether the President's memorandum nonetheless required courts to give effect to the ICJ's order.

Chief Justice Roberts's opinion for the Court began by focusing not on the VCCR obligations, but on the treaty obligations underlying the ICJ's claim of authority. The Court's analysis centered on the Optional Protocol to the VCCR[110] and Article 94 of the UN Charter.[111] The Optional Protocol provides that "[d]isputes arising out of the interpretation or application of the Convention shall lie within the compulsory jurisdiction of the International Court of Justice . . ."[112] Article 94, in turn, obligates each member of the United Nations to "undertake[] to comply with the decision of the International Court of Justice in any case to which it is a party."[113]

Medellín argued that the Optional Protocol's grant of "compulsory jurisdiction" to the ICJ over disputes arising under the VCCR, combined with the U.S. obligation under Article 92 to "undertake[] to comply" with ICJ decisions, required U.S. courts to give effect to ICJ judgments.[114] Analogizing this legal framework to treaties requiring the enforcement of foreign court or arbitral judgments, Medellín argued that the Supreme Court was merely being asked to enforce a foreign judgment, which U.S. courts do all the time. Alternatively, Medellín argued that the President's memorandum provided a separate authority for enforcing the *Avena* judgment.

Chief Justice Roberts rejected this reading of the two treaties. While not disputing that the *Avena* judgment constitutes an "international law obligation" on the United States, he emphasized that the Court has "long recognized the distinction between treaties that automatically have effect as domestic law, and those that . . . do not by themselves function as binding federal law."[115] In other words, the primary issue is whether the treaties underlying the ICJ judgment were self-executing.

To determine whether a treaty is self-executing, the Court looked for the intent of the treatymakers in the language of the treaty. Looking at the first treaty source, the Optional Protocol, the Court held that it is most naturally read as a "bare grant of jurisdiction."[116] The Optional Protocol lacked any language, common to international arbitration agreements, requiring parties to be bound by the ICJ's judgments.

---

[110] Vienna Convention on Consular Relations and Optional Protocol on Disputes, Apr. 24, 1963, 21 U.S.T. 77, 596 U.N.T.S. 261, 292.

[111] U.N. CHARTER art. 92.

[112] Optional Protocol, art. I.

[113] U.N. CHARTER art. 94, para. 1.

[114] Brief for Petitioner, Medellín v. Texas, 552 U.S. 491 (2008) (No. 06-984), 2007 WL 1886212.

[115] Medellín v. Texas, 552 U.S. 491, 504 (2008).

[116] *Id.* at 507.

The Protocol "says nothing about the effect of an ICJ decision and does not itself commit signatories to comply with an ICJ judgment."[117] Nor does it mention an enforcement mechanism.

Turning to Article 94 of the UN Charter, the Court found that the obligation to "undertake[] to comply" with an ICJ decision is merely a commitment for future action by UN member countries to comply. The Court contrasted the phrase "undertake[] to comply" with mandatory language such as "shall" or "must." This reading, the Court held, is further supported by Article 94(2)'s provision for a referral to the UN Security Council in the event of noncompliance with an ICJ judgment. The existence of Article 94(2), the Court held, suggests that ICJ judgments were meant to be international rather than domestic legal obligations. The United States ratified the UN Charter with the understanding that the enforcement of ICJ judgments is a political matter to be dealt with in the Security Council or in negotiations with foreign states.

Giving ICJ judgments automatic effect as federal law would undermine the Constitution's allocation of power in foreign affairs. Reading Article 94 to require direct judicial enforcement, the Court said, would undermine the UN Charter's emphasis on enforcement. The U.S. political branches would be unable to choose an option of noncompliance. Accepting Medellín's reading, the Court warned, would transfer "sensitive foreign policy decisions" to state and federal courts, which could not refuse enforcement.[118] The Court's reading was confirmed both by postratification practice under the Optional Protocol and Article 94 and by the views of the executive branch, which is entitled to "great weight" on questions of treaty interpretation.

Having found that the relevant treaties are non-self-executing, the Court went on to reject Medellín's argument that the President's memorandum constituted a separate and independent basis for enforcing the ICJ judgment. In issuing his memorandum, the President relied on his duty to take care that the laws are faithfully executed, which the United States argued included the VCCR as well as federal laws and other treaties. Noting that the President has broad powers to enforce international obligations, the Court nonetheless held that the President cannot "unilaterally convert[] a non-self-executing treaty into a self-executing one."[119] Only Congress can make domestic law, and therefore only Congress can implement a non-self-executing treaty in a way that would create binding domestic law.

The Court rejected the United States' claim that the UN Charter should be read as an implicit authorization to implement treaty obligations. A "non-self-executing treaty is by definition, one that was ratified with the understanding that it is not to have domestic effect of its own force."[120] No implicit authorization can therefore be read into such a treaty. Indeed, the only proper inference is that a non-self-executing treaty implicitly *prohibits* presidential implementation. The Court denied

---

[117] *Id.* at 507–508.
[118] *Id.* at 511.
[119] *Id.* at 525.
[120] *Id.* at 527.

Medellín's petition and affirmed the lower Texas court decisions. Medellín was executed by Texas about nine months later.

The character of Medellín's claim was more than a mere action to enforce the judgment of a foreign court. Medellín argued that the Supreme Court was bound by the ICJ's judgment despite the fact that the Court had previously interpreted the same treaty provision differently.[121] In other words, the Court was essentially being asked to disregard its own past interpretations of the same legal provision due to the authority granted to the ICJ by the Optional Protocol and the UN Charter. Medellín sought enforcement of this treaty over well-established precedents giving state governments near-exclusive power to set procedural rules for state court habeas proceedings.

A dizzying array of nongovernmental organizations, international legal academics, governments, and international organizations filed briefs in support of Medellín's argument on this point. All of these petitions emphasized the importance of complying with international tribunal judgments.[122] A number of prominent international law experts argued that "all courts in the United States are obliged to exercise their judicial powers within their respective jurisdictions consistently with the *Avena* judgment."[123] In this view, the Court should act to fulfill the U.S. foreign policy goal of compliance with international law by implementing the ICJ's judgment, whether or not the executive branch had instructed the Court to do so.

This aspect of Medellín's claim thus transforms itself from a mere foreign judgment enforcement action into a much stronger claim of judicial power. Unlike the enforcement of a foreign judgment, *Medellín* here argued that federal statutes required enforcement without exception—whether or not there were public policy ramifications to enforcement, and whether or not federalism would constrain congressional power over the states. In a typical foreign judgment enforcement proceeding, U.S. courts have the discretion to invoke public policy or constitutional norms to reject the enforcement of foreign judgments.[124] Instead, like a higher court, the judgment of the ICJ bound the Supreme Court and all lower federal and state courts regardless of domestic public policies, or even constitutional allocations of authority to the state governments.

The most accurate understanding of Medellín's argument is as a "delegation" of the judicial power granted to the federal courts under Article III of the Constitution that, by virtue of the treaty power, is not constrained by Tenth Amendment

---

[121] Brief for Petitioner, *supra* note 114, at 19.

[122] See, e.g. Brief Amicus Curiae of Ambassador L. Bruce Laingen and Lieutenant Colonel John J. Swift et al., in Support of Petitioner at 9–15, Medellín v. Texas, 554 U.S. 759, 2007 WL 18862; Brief of Former United States Diplomats as Amici Curiae in Support of Petitioner at 13–22, Medellín v. Texas, 554 U.S. 759, 2007 WL 1886206; Brief of Foreign Sovereigns as Amici Curiae in Support of Petitioner Jose Ernesto Medellín, *supra* note at 15–18; Brief of the American Bar Ass'n as Amicus Curiae in Support of Petitioner at 22–25, Medellín v. Texas, 554 U.S. 759, 2007 WL 1886209; Brief of International Court of Justice Experts as Amici Curiae in Support of Petitioner at 14–28, Medellín v. Texas, 554 U.S. 759, 2007 WL 906700.

[123] Brief of International Court of Justice Experts as Amici Curiae in Support of Petitioner at 2, Medellín v. Texas, 554 U.S. 759, 2007 WL 906700.

[124] Uniform Foreign Money Judgments Recognitions Act, § 3, 13 Pt. II U.L.A. 39 (2002); Somportex Ltd. v. Phila. Chewing Gum Corp., 453 F.2d 435, 440 (3d Cir. 1971).

principles protecting the autonomy of state governments. The ICJ's authority to order U.S. courts to follow its judgments is akin to the authority of the Supreme Court to order state courts to enforce federal law regardless of local state policies and conflicting state law.[125]

Although the Court's opinion did not explicitly call this argument a "delegation" argument, it did note the remarkable and extraordinary consequences of agreeing with Medellín's position:

> An ICJ judgment, the argument goes, is not only binding domestic law but is also unassailable. As a result, neither Texas nor this Court may look behind a judgment and quarrel with its reasoning or result. (We already know, from *Sanchez-Llamas*, that this Court disagrees with both the reasoning and result in *Avena*.) Medellín's interpretation would allow ICJ judgments to override otherwise binding state law; there is nothing in his logic that would exempt contrary federal law from the same fate. And there is nothing to prevent the ICJ from ordering state courts to annul criminal convictions and sentences, for any reason deemed sufficient by the ICJ. Indeed, that is precisely the relief Mexico requested.[126]

The Court did not complete this analysis, however, by analyzing the constitutional concerns created by Medellín's argument. What, precisely, would be the problem with preventing Texas or the Supreme Court from "quarrel[ing] with [the] reasoning and result [of the ICJ's judgment]"?[127] Or allowing the ICJ to "order[] state courts to annul criminal convictions and sentences"?[128] The Court does not say. Yet the most obvious understanding of its expressions of concern is that such a grant of power to an international tribunal's judgments would undermine both the federal judiciary's power to give definitive interpretations of federal law (treaties) and state courts' abilities to do the same for state law on matters that lie within the state's competence. With respect to the diminution of federal judicial power, it could be understood as a violation of Article III's exclusive grant of the federal judicial power to federal courts.

Still, the Court does not go so far as to suggest that Medellín's argument creates constitutional problems. On the other hand, it emphasizes that the unusual consequences of this argument require heightened attention to the intent of the ratifying parties. "Given that ICJ judgments may interfere with state procedural rules, one would expect the ratifying parties to the relevant treaties to have *clearly stated* their intent to give those judgments domestic effect, if they had so intended."[129] Justice John Paul Stevens, in his concurring opinion, concluded that there was no such clear statement in the text of either the Optional Protocol's grant of "compulsory

---

[125] See Martin v. Hunter's Lessee, 14 U.S. 304 (1816).

[126] Medellín v. Texas, 552 U.S. 491, 517–518 (2008) (citations omitted).

[127] *Id.*

[128] *Id.* at 518.

[129] *Id.* at 517 (emphasis added).

jurisdiction" or Article 92's language requiring the United States to "undertake[] to comply" with ICJ judgments.[130]

It is this analysis that is both the doctrinal weakness and functional strength of the majority opinion. If, as the opinion suggests, the case is simply a plain-vanilla treaty interpretation case, then there is a strong case for applying the self-execution doctrine. The *Restatement (Third) of Foreign Relations Law of the United States* declares that "[c]ourts in the United States are bound to give effect to . . . international agreements of the United States" unless the agreement is non-self-executing.[131] In this view, non-self-execution occurs only if an agreement "manifests an intention that it shall not become effective as domestic law without the enactment of implementing legislation."[132] In other words, unless there is an express manifestation of an intent toward non-self-execution, the *Restatement*'s default rule is that all treaties are self-executing. Indeed, Justice Breyer's dissent fairly criticized the majority for adopting a "new" clear statement rule for self-execution.[133]

There is a well-founded basis, however, for nonetheless applying a presumption in favor of non-self-execution in this context. It is a well-accepted canon of statutory interpretation that a court should, whenever possible, adopt an interpretation that avoids a finding of unconstitutionality. As a number of scholars have observed, this prudential approach has become the primary mechanism by which constitutional doctrines like nondelegation are applied.[134] In other words, rather than apply the nondelegation doctrine to find a statute unconstitutional, courts are more likely to seek an interpretation that avoids an excessive delegation. Indeed, a number of influential scholars have argued that, in the statutory context, the emphasis on avoiding a finding of unconstitutionality has led courts to require a clear statement before interpreting a statute to delegate. The application of this prudential doctrine acts as a constitutional constraint, although not as a constitutional bar, to excessive delegations.

The clear statement requirement for statutes can be adapted to the treaty context through the doctrine of non-self-execution. By requiring a clear statement before interpreting a treaty to result in an international delegation, courts can place constitutional constraints on treatymakers while avoiding the complications of an actual finding of unconstitutionality. Importantly, it also channels decisions on international affairs to the more politically accountable branches. If the President and the Senate so wish, they can make a treaty self-executing in the course of making the agreement, or Congress and the President can enact subsequent domestic law to implement the terms. While there may or may not be constitutional limitations

---

[130] *Id.* at 534–35 (Stevens, J., concurring).

[131] Restatement (Third) of Foreign Relations Law of the United States § 111(3) (1987).

[132] *Id.* § 111(4)(a).

[133] Medellín, 552 U.S. at 538–40 (Breyer, J., dissenting).

[134] See William N. Eskridge, Jr., & Philip P. Frickey, *Quasi-Constitutional Law: Clear Statement Rules as Constitutional Lawmaking*, 45 VAND. L. REV. 593, 597 (1992); Cass R. Sunstein, *Nondelegation Canons*, 67 U. CHI. L. REV. 315, 330–37 (2000) (discussing how courts use nondelegation canons to impose constraints on administrative power).

as to how far the treatymakers or Congress can go in delegating authority to institutions wholly outside the U.S. constitutional system, non-self-execution requires that the democratically elected make the basic decision whether to test those limits.

As we argued in chapter 4, non-self-execution shifts these decisions to the political branches, which accrues at least two important functional benefits. First, it forces political accountability for decisions and consequences of an international tribunal by shifting the decision of how and whether to comply with a tribunal's judgment to the political branches.[135] This does not mean that the United States will always defy that tribunal's judgments. Indeed, the President's intervention in the *Medellín* case is a classic example of how the executive branch can take responsibility for compliance with an international tribunal judgment. Even if the U.S. Supreme Court does not intervene, the President will often have a strong political desire to implement an international tribunal judgment.

Forcing the political branches to clarify their intentions about judicial enforcement prevents them from avoiding responsibility for the consequences of an international tribunal's judgment. In many, if not most, instances, the political branches will act to limit the independent judicial role in the enforcement of international obligations, as they have done in the proposed conditions for ratification of the Law of the Sea Treaty. If they do not take steps to limit such a rule, the fact that the enforcement provision is a clear statement prevents future claims that an activist domestic or international court is wrongly interpreting such a provision.

Second, the non-self-execution doctrine shifts the decision on compliance with an international tribunal judgment to the institutions of the government with the greatest expertise in foreign affairs: the executive and legislative branches. International tribunal judgments do not always represent simple determinations of legal obligations. They often take place amid a complex bilateral or multilateral relationship. For instance, at the time that Mexico was suing the United States in the ICJ in *Avena*, the United States was attempting to win Mexico's vote to support the UN Security Council Resolution to invade Iraq.[136] Less dramatically, U.S. compliance with decisions of trade tribunals often occurs within a complex multilevel trade relationship. Attempts by the United States to comply with WTO requirements by altering U.S. tax laws, for instance, were finely tuned political efforts to modify the laws in ways least disadvantageous to U.S. corporations.

---

[135] As Nicholas Rosenkranz has observed, the use of a clear statement rule as an interpretive rule operates in a similar manner to default rules in the private law context. *See* Nicholas Quinn Rosenkranz, *Federal Rules of Statutory Interpretation*, 115 HARV. L. REV. 2085, 2122–23 (2002). Legal scholars like Ian Ayres and Robert Gertner have noted that certain doctrines of contract law act as default rules forcing the parties to reveal information to each other in order to reach the fairest and most efficient outcome. See, e.g., Ian Ayres & Robert Gertner, *Filling Gaps in Incomplete Contracts: An Economic Theory of Default Rules*, 99 YALE L.J. 87, 91 (1989).

[136] See Andres Oppenheimer, *Bush Putting Mexican President on Hold*, MIAMI HERALD, Mar. 27, 2003, at 18A (describing Mexico's eleventh-hour decision to oppose a UN Resolution authorizing the use of force in Iraq).

To complicate matters further, only some countries grant international tribunal judgments self-executing effect in their domestic courts. For instance, most, if not all, countries that are parties to the ICJ do *not* grant the ICJ's judgments self-executing effect in their domestic courts.[137] Without a clear statement rule, the several states, U.S. government officials, and possibly the U.S. government itself could be subject to lawsuits in their own courts by private parties and foreign governments seeking to enforce an international tribunal judgment. Thus, a foreign government could ask a U.S. court to enforce an international tribunal judgment even if the U.S. government has rejected that judgment as a matter of domestic law. A court would have to determine whether and how to enforce judgments absent reciprocity.

All of this suggests that the judiciary is the institution least competent in determining how or whether to comply with an international tribunal's judgment. A court is, by design, not privy to the broader information about the U.S. relationship with other countries or particular international tribunals. Nor does it have any expertise in assessing that relationship and the proper way to deal with other countries or international institutions. In some instances, courts will be asked to play that role, despite their functional shortcomings. But a clear statement requirement ensures that the political branches have made the proper deliberations about what kind of international adjudicatory regime is best suited for judicial enforcement.

Medellín provides an excellent example of the benefits of this non-self-execution approach to treaties. Medellín raised questions of both separation of powers and federalism. Automatic enforcement of ICJ decisions as federal law opened a potential delegation of judicial power to an international institution that was not part of the U.S. constitutional system. At the same time, the scope of the ICJ's substantive decision potentially infringed on traditional matters of state regulation by attempting to regulate the states' operation of their criminal justice systems. The Court's decision avoided these troubling and weighty constitutional questions by its wise and appropriate application of the non-self-execution doctrine.

Interpreting the UN Charter provisions and the Optional Protocol as non-self-executing does not create a constitutional bar to future U.S. cooperation with the ICJ or with international dispute resolution systems in general. Instead, it shifts the decision-making locus to Congress and requires full congressional cooperation over how and whether to incorporate international decision-makers into the U.S. legal system. It not only gives the House of Representatives an opportunity, but also forces the House (along with the Senate and the President) to consider the consequences of an international delegation on domestic law and policy. In other international dispute resolution schemes, the House and Senate have done just that and clearly stated a desire to delegate such authority to an international tribunal.

---

[137] See Brief for Professors of International Law, Federal Jurisdiction and the Foreign Relations Law of the United States as Amici Curiae in Support of Respondent, Medellín III, at 23–24.

In other situations, most notably the WTO system, Congress has decided to retain control over compliance with WTO judgments.[138]

In some cases, Congress may choose not to act, as it did in the *Medellín* case. In that circumstance, the decision becomes a question for the state governments. Justice Stevens recognized the importance of the state government's discretion, and his concurring opinion urged Texas independently to grant Medellín the relief sought by the ICJ. While holding that neither the Court nor the President had power to require Texas to act, Justice Stevens accepted that such decisions implicating foreign policy may also be left to the states.

There are further benefits to a presumption of non-self-execution in the context of international delegations. By guaranteeing full consideration by Congress (or forcing a clear statement by the Senate), this prudential approach should reduce uncertainty about entering into long-term cooperative arrangements with international organizations. If ambiguous treaty language would be enough to transfer broad authority to international organizations, the Senate might be less inclined to enter into such a treaty in the first place. Non-self-execution creates a safe harbor for treaties, ensuring that, absent a clear statement, no international delegation will take place.

Moreover, non-self-execution should improve foreign policy decision-making. Scholars have observed elsewhere that clear statement rules can have information and deliberation forcing effects. By requiring more decision points in the legislative process, non-self-execution can require more deliberation to occur. Deliberation will encourage the production of information, cause viewpoints on the extreme ends of legislator preferences to confront more moderate views, and result in the giving of public justifications and reasons for decisions.[139] Deliberation also has its potential costs, including delay in decision, but the context of setting domestic rules of general application on questions such as criminal procedure may not incur high costs in this area.

Medellín will not be the last time that U.S. courts will face a difficult and complex problem arising out of new international law obligations, active NGOs, and international institutions. For this reason, it is encouraging that *Medellín* offers future courts a sensible, workable approach to these problems. Grounded in history and precedent, the non-self-execution doctrine permits a court to allocate most of the decision-making to the political branches of the federal government or the state governments. Such allocations respect the Constitution's design by inviting those political branches to take control over how best to respond to the challenges of globalization.

---

[138] See Uruguay Round Trade Agreements Act, 19 U.S.C. § 3512(b)(2)(A) (2005) (barring anyone other than the United States from challenging U.S. or state action or inaction based on its consistency with the Uruguay Round Agreements); Uruguay Round Agreements Act: Statement of Administrative Action, H.R. Rep. No. 103-316, at 675–77, 1043–44 (1994), reprinted in 1994 U.S.C.C.A.N. 4040, 4054–56, 4327.

[139] See, e.g., ADRIAN VERMEULE, MECHANISMS OF DEMOCRACY: INSTITUTIONAL DESIGN WRIT SMALL 222–23 (2008).

Handed down on the last day of the 2005 term, the Supreme Court's decision in *Hamdan v. Rumsfeld* was perhaps its most significant on the war on terrorism.[140] The Court held that the Bush administration's military commissions, created by executive order, could not be used to try enemy detainees without congressional authorization. While some might read *Hamdan* as an example of the Court relying on international law to constrain presidential wartime action, we believe that it actually advances in many ways the popular-sovereignty-protecting themes outlined in earlier chapters.

This is not to say that *Hamdan* was a victory for the presidential role in interpreting international law. Quite the opposite. Still, *Hamdan* did not fundamentally alter the separation of powers, as did *Youngstown Sheet & Tube v. Sawyer*[141] or *United States v. Nixon*.[142] Rather, *Hamdan* rested solely on the interpretation of three kinds of nonconstitutional law: federal statutes relating to military justice, treaties relating to the treatment of military detainees, and the customary international laws of war. *Hamdan*'s startling departure was to reject the Executive's reasonable interpretations of the relevant laws on war. *Hamdan* provides the occasion for examining the solid pedigree for deference to executive interpretation of international law and explaining its functional basis. The executive branch has strong institutional advantages over the courts in the interpretation of laws relating to the conduct of war; judicial intervention only raises the transaction costs for policy-making without any serious benefits and potentially at large costs.

Equally significant, however, is the way the Court reached its outcome. Although it rejected presidential interpretation of international law, it made no move to claim that international law was directly binding on the executive branch through the domestic courts. Rather, it concluded that sources of international rules, such as the Geneva Conventions and the customary laws of war, limited executive policy only because Congress had specifically incorporated them by domestic statute. We have serious doubts about whether the Court correctly interpreted the relevant laws, as

---

[140] Hamdan v. Rumsfeld, 548 U.S. 557 (2006). For discussion of the issues in Hamdan, see Captain Brian C. Baldrate, *The Supreme Court's Role in Defining the Jurisdiction of Military Tribunals: A Study, Critique, & Proposal for Hamdan v. Rumsfeld*, 186 Mil. L. Rev. 1 (2005); Curtis A. Bradley, *Military Commissions Act, Habeas Corpus, and the Geneva Conventions*, 101 Am. J. Int'l L. 322 (2007); Curtis A. Bradley & Jack L. Goldsmith, *Congressional Authorization and the War on Terrorism*, 118 Harv. L. Rev. 2047 (2005); Samuel Estreicher & Diarmuid O'Scannlain, *Hamdan's Limits and the Military Commissions Act*, 23 Const. Comment 403 (2006); Richard H. Fallon, Jr., & Daniel J. Meltzer, *Habeas Corpus Jurisdiction, Substantive Rights, and the War on Terror*, 120 Harv. L. Rev. 2029 (2007); Louis Fisher, *Detention and Military Trial of Suspected Terrorists: Stretching Presidential Power*, 2 J. Nat'l Sec. L. & Pol'y 1 (2006); George P. Fletcher, *Hamdan Confronts the Military Commissions Act of 2006*, 45 Colum. J. Transnat'l L. 427 (2007); Neal Katyal, *Equality in the War on Terror*, 59 Stan. L. Rev. 1365 (2007); Mark Tushnet, *The Political Constitution of Emergency Powers: Some Lessons from Hamdan*, 91 Minn. L. Rev. 1451 (2007).

[141] Youngstown Sheet & Tube v. Sawyer, 343 U.S. 579 (1952).

[142] United States v. Nixon, 418 U.S. 683 (1974).

did Congress, which swiftly reversed *Hamdan* in the Military Commission Act of 2006. Nonetheless, the important point is that the Court did not attempt to apply international law directly, but instead based its decision on the enactments of the elected branches. While *Hamdan* took issue with the allocation of powers over interpreting international law advanced in this book, it maintained the basic line that preserves American sovereignty.

A. The 9/11 Attacks and Military Commissions

On September 11, 2001, al Qaeda operatives hijacked four commercial airliners and used them as guided missiles against the World Trade Center and the Pentagon. Resisting passengers brought down a fourth plane apparently headed toward either the Capitol or the White House. The attacks caused about 3,000 deaths, disrupted air traffic and communications, and caused billions of dollars in losses. In part, the United States responded by sending forces to Afghanistan, where the ruling Taliban militia had harbored al Qaeda for several years.

One aspect of the war on terrorism focuses on the detention and trial of captured al Qaeda members. Military commissions are a form of tribunal used to try captured members of the enemy for violations of the laws of war. American generals have used them from the Revolutionary War through World War II.[143] These tribunals are not created by the Uniform Code of Military Justice (UCMJ), enacted by Congress in 1950, which governs courts-martial, but instead have been established by Presidents and military commanders in the field. On November 13, 2001, President Bush declared that al Qaeda's massive attacks had "created a state of armed conflict," and he established military commissions to try captured members of al Qaeda. The military commissions apply to any individual who there is "reason to believe" is or was "a member of al Qaeda" or has engaged in or conspired to commit terrorist attacks against the United States.[144]

Military commissions had traditionally operated according to the customary international law of war. They did not have a specific code of procedure, nor did they punish a statutory listing of offenses. Procedures were flexible to accommodate the demands of warfare, and punishable crimes were those recognized by a common law of war that was not reduced to a single text. Under President George W. Bush's military order, the Defense Department exercised delegated authority to issue two lengthy codes, one defining the elements of the crimes triable by commission, the other setting out the procedures. The Defense Department's regulations, for example, set the standard for conviction at proof beyond a reasonable doubt and require

---

[143] For a critical review of the history, see Louis Fisher, Military Tribunals & Presidential Power: American Revolution to the War on Terrorism (2005).

[144] Military Order of Nov. 13, 2001, Detention, Treatment, and Trial of Certain Non-Citizens in the War Against Terrorism §§ 1(a), 2(a)(1)(i–ii), 66 Fed. Reg. 57,833, 57,833 (Nov. 16, 2001). The order also applies to those who knowingly harbor al Qaeda members who plan to commit terrorist attacks against the United States. *Id.* at § 2(a)(1)(iii).

the prosecution to turn over any exculpatory evidence to the defense counsel. They also recognize the right against self-incrimination and the right of cross-examination and require a unanimous vote of the commission members for the death penalty.[145] Similarly, the Bush Defense Department's articulation of the crimes subject to trial by military commission went well beyond past practice. FDR's definition of the jurisdiction of military commissions, for instance, reached "sabotage, espionage, hostile or warlike acts, or violations of the law of war."[146]

Salem Ahmed Hamdan was captured by U.S. allies in November 2001 during the fighting in Afghanistan. American forces took custody of Hamdan and transferred him in 2002 to the detention facility at the U.S. Naval Station at Guantánamo Bay, Cuba. President Bush designated him for a trial by military commission the following year. In 2004, military prosecutors charged Hamdan with conspiracy to attack civilians, commit murder, and terrorism. According to the government, from 1996 to 2001, Hamdan had served as the bodyguard and personal driver for al Qaeda leader Osama bin Laden, had transported weapons for bin Laden, and had received weapons training at al Qaeda camps. A Combatant Status Review Tribunal, convened under a July 2004 military order, found Hamdan's continued detention to be justified.

In 2004, Hamdan filed a petition for writs of habeas corpus and mandamus. He based his challenge on both domestic and international law grounds. He argued that the military commission violated the Constitution's separation of powers because it had not received congressional authorization. It was undisputed that Congress had not passed any specific statute regarding military commissions after the September 11 attacks. The government, however, responded that the broad Authorization to Use Military Force (AUMF), passed by Congress on September 18, 2001, had amounted to authorization and that the UCMJ had left the historical jurisdiction of

---

[145] See U.S. Dep't of Defense, Military Commission Order No. 1, Procedures for Trials by Military Commissions of Certain Non-United States Citizens in the War against Terrorism para. 5 ("Procedures Accorded the Accused) and para. 6 ("Conduct of the Trial") (Mar. 21, 2002), available at http://www.defenselink.mil/news/Mar2002/d20020321ord.pdf; Crimes and Elements for Trials by Military Commissions, 32 C.F.R. § 11.3.

[146] Take, for example, the Bush Defense Department's effort to define spying:

(6) Spying—(i) Elements. (A) The accused collected or attempted to collect certain information;
(B) The accused intended to convey such information to the enemy;
(C) The accused, in collecting or attempting to collect the information, was lurking or acting clandestinely, while acting under false pretenses; and
(D) The conduct took place in the context of and was associated with armed conflict.
(ii) Comments. (A) Members of a military organization not wearing a disguise and others who carry out their missions openly are not spies, if, though they may have resorted to concealment, they have not acted under false pretenses.
(B) Related to the requirement that conduct be wrongful or without justification or excuse in this case is the fact that, consistent with the law of war, a lawful combatant who, after rejoining the armed force to which that combatant belongs, is subsequently captured, can not be punished for previous acts of espionage. His successful rejoining of his armed force constitutes a defense. 32 C.F.R. § 11.6.

commissions untouched. But even if Congress had recognized historical practice, Hamdan responded, it did not meet the umpire's requirement that commissions be used only when other forms of trial were unpractical.[147]

Hamdan also claimed that the military commissions violated the Geneva Conventions under international law. He argued that the Third Geneva Convention prohibited the trial of a prisoner of war by courts that did not also exercise jurisdiction over the country's own troops. In the event that the court found him not to be a prisoner of war, which was the conclusion reached by the President and Judge Randolph in the federal appeals court in Washington, D.C., Hamdan claimed that the tribunals still violated Common Article 3 of the Conventions. Common Article 3, so called because it is a provision common to all four of the 1949 Conventions, requires that detaining nations impose sentences on detainees that are pronounced "by a regularly constituted court affording all the judicial guarantees which are recognized as indispensable by civilized peoples." Hamdan argued that the Geneva Conventions were self-executing treaties directly enforceable in domestic courts, a contention rejected by the D.C. Circuit.[148]

B. Military Commissions and the Supreme Court

The Supreme Court reversed, but did not rely on the idea that international law by its own force limited the use of military commissions. As an initial matter, it found that the military commissions had run counter to UCMJ policies that demanded uniformity in military trial procedures—which had nothing to do with international law. Our main interest here, though, is on the second basis for the Court's decision. The Court found that the military commissions violated the customary international laws of war, but only because it found that Congress had incorporated the applicable customary laws of war into the UCMJ. While the Court agreed with Hamdan that Common Article 3 limited the use of military commissions, it did not hold that the Geneva Conventions were self-executing. We critique the Court's analysis of the meaning of the umpire's provisions: the important point is that it was Congress's enactments, and not international law operating of its own force, that provided the rules of decision.

The Court found that Article 21 of the UCMJ limits military commission jurisdiction to cases in compliance with the law of war. Titled "jurisdiction of courts-martial not exclusive," Article 21 declares that "[t]he provisions of this code conferring jurisdiction upon courts-martial shall not be construed as depriving military commissions, provost courts, or other military tribunals of concurrent jurisdiction in respect of offenders or offenses that by statute or by the law of war may be tried by such military commissions, provost courts, or other military tribunals."[149]

---

[147] Hamdan v. Rumsfeld, 415 F.3d 33 (D.C. Cir. 2005).

[148] *Id.* at 40.

[149] 10 U.S.C. § 821.

Article 21's plain language is concerned with preserving the concurrent jurisdiction of military commissions and other military tribunals. Nonetheless, the Court construed Article 21 to regulate the operation, not just the jurisdiction, of military commission trials according to the laws of war.[150] This is an odd reading. Article 21's text refers to the law of war to mark out the jurisdiction of military commissions. There is no indication that Article 21 was intended to regulate the procedures and operations of military commissions once jurisdiction was established. The Court, however, read Article 21 to require that military commissions follow the laws of war in both their procedures and the elements of the substantive crimes charged. The Court held that the phrase "law of war" incorporated the 1949 Geneva Conventions, particularly focusing on the Third Geneva Convention regulating the treatment of prisoners of war.[151]

The Court's heavy and nearly exclusive reliance on the Geneva Conventions suggests that it failed to understand that much of the law of war remains customary. There is no international agreement, for example, defining the elements of criminal violations of the laws of war. Rather, that common law is composed of treaties (such as the 1907 Hague Regulations, the Geneva Conventions, and the Statute of Rome establishing the International Criminal Court), state practice (such as domestic criminal legislation defining and punishing war crimes), and judicial decisions (such as the opinions of the Nuremberg Tribunal or the International Criminal Tribunal for the Former Yugoslavia). Indeed, the Geneva Conventions explicitly describe themselves as "complementary" to some of the 1907 Hague Regulations, which in turn explicitly incorporate customary law.[152] In construing the phrase "law of war," the Court should have surveyed all of these materials as well as American practice itself, because the United States has perhaps been involved in the most armed conflicts since World War II. Although Justice Stevens did consider these broader sources of law in his opinion for four Justices of the Court on the law of war's treatment of conspiracy, his opinion relied almost exclusively on the Geneva Conventions to give content to the law of war.

As an initial matter, the Court had to confront the argument that the Geneva Conventions are not judicially enforceable. Indeed, the Court's own prior decision in *Johnson v. Eisentrager* held that the Geneva Conventions could not be enforced in domestic courts.[153] German soldiers, convicted by military commission for continuing to fight in China after the end of World War II, claimed that their trial violated the Geneva Conventions. The *Eisentrager* Court found that the 1929 Geneva

---

[150] Hamdan, 548 U.S. at 627.

[151] The Court focused on the Third Geneva Convention. Geneva Convention Relative to the Protection of Civilian Persons in Time of War, Aug. 12, 1949, [1955] 6 U.S.T. 3316, T.I.A.S. No. 3364.

[152] See Geneva Convention Relative to the Protection of Civilian Persons in Time of War, Aug. 12, 1949, [1955] 6 U.S.T. 3316, T.I.A.S. No. 3364, art. 135 (describing Third Geneva Convention as "complementary" to regulations in Hague Convention respecting the Laws and Customs of War on Land); Hague Convention respecting the Laws and Customs of War on Land, Oct. 18, 1907.

[153] Johnson v. Eisentrager, 339 U.S. 763 (1950).

Conventions, which were largely identical to the 1949 Conventions, placed the "responsibility for observance and enforcement of these rights . . . upon political and military authorities" only.[154]

Nonetheless, *Hamdan* found that *Eisentrager* was not controlling because "compliance with the law of war is the condition upon which the authority set forth in Article 21 is granted."[155] The Court must have assumed either that Article 21 of the UCMJ had effectively overruled *Eisentrager*, or that the 1949 Geneva Conventions called for domestic judicial enforcement in a way that the 1929 Conventions did not. The enforceability of the Geneva Conventions could not have resulted from any change in Article 21 itself. When *Eisentrager* was decided, the statutory predecessor to Article 21 contained exactly the same language regarding "the law of war."[156] Thus, when the *Eisentrager* Court held that the Geneva Conventions were not judicially enforceable, military commissions were *already bound* by statute to comply with the laws of war. *Eisentrager* did not find that the laws of war, incorporated through Article 21, required anything more than an inquiry into whether the military commission properly exercised jurisdiction over the defendants.[157]

Put differently, Justice Stevens could be arguing that passage of the UCMJ had shifted the legal ground radically. He suggests that *Eisentrager* no longer controlled because Congress enacted the UCMJ after that 1950 case and therefore provided a new domestic law ground for enforcement of rights under the laws of war. Indeed, Justice Stevens could even claim that he was giving proper deference to the political branches in wartime, because Congress had enacted and the President had signed the UCMJ. The problem with his argument, however, is that the UCMJ was not a new enactment on the laws of war that had filled a vacuum. Rather, the UCMJ merely continued verbatim the existing provisions requiring military commissions to follow the laws of war under the Articles of War. Congress had enacted the Articles of War as long ago as 1806 (they had first been promulgated by the Continental Congress in 1775), and they had undergone significant revision in 1920. The UCMJ, therefore, could not have done the heavy lifting claimed by Justice Stevens, because Congress gave no indication that it intended to change the *Eisentrager* rule—in fact, it did everything it should have to make clear that it wanted the status quo to be maintained.

Even if the Court believed that the new Article 21 was intended to override *Eisentrager*, it would still err because events could not have happened that way. Congress enacted the UCMJ, and Section 821's unchanged recognition of military commissions, on May 5, 1950.[158] It would have been impossible for Congress to have understood that the UCMJ would overrule *Eisentrager* and render the Geneva Conventions judicially enforceable in domestic courts because *Eisentrager* was not

---

[154] *Id.* at 789 n. 14.

[155] Hamdan, 548 U.S. at 627.

[156] See 10 U.S.C. § 1485 (1949 (Article 15 is the predecessor provision)).

[157] Eisentrager, 339 U.S. at 786–87.

[158] Uniform Code of Military Justice (UCMJ), Pub. L. No. 81-506, 64 Stat. 107 (May 5, 1950).

decided until June 5, 1950.[159] In other words, Congress could not have understood the UCMJ to reject *Eisentrager's* rule on the nonenforceability of the Geneva Conventions because *Eisentrager* did not announce its rule until after Congress had enacted the new UCMJ.

If Section 821 did not change, then the Geneva Conventions must have changed. The majority, however, did not claim that the 1949 Geneva Conventions reversed the rule of the 1929 Conventions—enforcement was still to come from political or military channels. There was no textual difference indicating that those who negotiated, signed, or ratified the treaties on behalf of the United States believed the 1949 agreements to be self-executing. No federal court had ever held that the 1949 treaties were self-executing,[160] and the executive branch, which generally interprets international law on behalf of the United States, had never interpreted the 1949 Conventions to be self-executing either. Without some signal from the political branches, federal courts usually have not interpreted international agreements to bestow judicially enforceable individual rights.[161]

Having found that Article 21 incorporated the Geneva Conventions, the Court held that Common Article 3 applied to the U.S. conflict with al Qaeda, even though al Qaeda is not a signatory to the treaties. The Court concluded that the war with al Qaeda in Afghanistan (where Hamdan was captured) qualifies as a "conflict not of an international character occurring in the territory of one of the High Contracting Parties." Because Afghanistan is a High Contracting Party to the Geneva Conventions, the Court held that Hamdan was entitled to the protection of Common Article 3, which prohibits the humiliating and degrading treatment of detainees and requires the use of "regularly constituted court[s], affording all the judicial guarantees which are recognized as indispensable by civilized peoples."[162] The Geneva Conventions themselves do not define any of these obviously ambiguous terms.

The government, however, had argued that the war with al Qaeda did not fall into the category of a "conflict not of an international character." On February 7, 2002, President Bush had determined that al Qaeda detainees were not legally entitled to prisoner-of-war status because al Qaeda had neither signed the Geneva Conventions

---

[159] Eisentrager, 339 U.S. 763 (1950).

[160] One federal court did apply the Geneva Conventions on the assumption that they were judicially enforceable, although the issue of self-execution was not raised and the defendant himself was found to have no remedies under the Conventions. See United States v. Noriega, 746 F. Supp. 1506, 1525–29 (S.D. Fla. 1990).

[161] For discussion of the non-self-execution issue, see John C. Yoo, *Treaties and Public Lawmaking: A Textual and Structural Defense of Non-Self-Execution*, 99 Colum. L. Rev. 2218 (1999); John C. Yoo, *Globalism and the Constitution: Treaties, Non-Self-Execution, and the Original Understanding*, 99 Colum. L. Rev. 1955 (1999). For a different view, see Martin S. Flaherty, *History Right?: Historical Scholarship, Original Understanding, and Treaties as "Supreme Law of the Land,"* 99 Colum. L. Rev. 2095 (1999); Carlos Vazquez, *Laughing at Treaties*, 99 Colum. L. Rev. 2154 (1999).

[162] Geneva Convention Relative to the Protection of Civilian Persons in Time of War, art. 3, Aug. 12, 1949, [1955] 6 U.S.T. 3316, T.I.A.S. No. 3364.

nor voluntarily accepted its obligations.[163] Further, al Qaeda combatants did not fall within Common Article 3, which the administration read as applying only to internal civil wars. The government argued that the war with al Qaeda stretched far beyond Afghanistan and was a quintessentially international, rather than localized, conflict.[164]

The Court rejected this interpretation. Citing Jeremy Bentham for support, it argued that "the phrase 'not of an international character' bears its literal meaning" as referring only to matters between nations.[165] The Court treated Common Article 3 as a general catch-all provision to include all armed conflicts not involving clashes between nations. Although it acknowledged that the commentaries written at the time of the Geneva Conventions' drafting suggested otherwise, the *Hamdan* majority relied on changes to Common Article 3's text during the drafting process and developments in the laws of war postratification for its interpretation.

The Court's reasoning here was weak. While Bentham was one of the first writers to conceive of "international" law, rather than the Law of Nations, the Court presented no reason to think that those who drafted or ratified the 1949 Conventions held his understanding. Such a reading would not comport with modern understandings of "international," which in practice extends beyond matters "between nations" to include matters of global or transnational scope. "International" human rights law would be an oxymoron under the *Hamdan* majority's definition, as would the regulation of global commons, such as the space and the seas, under "international" environmental law. Nor did the Court identify any materials from a primary touchstone for the interpretation of treaties—for example, the understandings of the treaty text held by the President and Senate at the time of the latter's advice and consent—that supported its reading of Common Article 3.[166] The Geneva Conventions' drafters would have had the Spanish or Chinese civil wars in mind in expanding protections to conflicts "not of an international character," and in fact they rejected proposals to include new, unconventional conflicts, such as those surrounding decolonialization, or age-old supranational struggles, such as those over religion. Thinking on the law of war at that time simply had not developed to the point where it could consider the status of conflicts fought by nonstate actors such as al Qaeda against nation-states. World War II cases involving resistance fighters, or even those involving armed militias such as contemporary attacks on the new state of Israel, would have fallen under the Geneva Conventions category for wars between nation-states and their forces (whether regular or irregular).

---

[163] Memorandum for the Vice President, Secretary of State, Secretary of Defense, Attorney General, Chief of Staff to the President, Director of Central Intelligence, Assistant to the President for National Security Affairs, Chairman of the Joint Chiefs of Staff, Re: Humane Treatment of al Qaeda and Taliban Detainees (Feb. 7, 2002).

[164] For a discussion of the administration's reasoning, see John Yoo & James Ho, *The Status of Terrorists*, 44 Va. J. Int'l L. 207 (2003).

[165] Hamdan, 548 U.S. at 630.

[166] For discussion of the method of interpreting treaties, see John Yoo, The Powers of War and Peace: The Constitution and Foreign Affairs after 9/11 215–249 (2005).

The Geneva Conventions give no other indication that such conflicts were instead the grounds for extending Common Article 3 to cover a new, third type of conflict between nations and organizations unconnected to a state. Finally, the Court ignored subsequent executive branch decisions that rejected amendments to the Geneva Conventions, known as the 1977 Additional Protocols, which would have extended certain Geneva Convention protections to nonstate actors such as terrorist groups.[167] The fact that the drafters of the Geneva Conventions would have felt a need to add protocols in order to encompass nonstate actors like terrorist groups strongly suggests that the original Geneva Conventions did not apply to such groups.

The Court faced one final interpretive obstacle to finding Hamdan's military commission invalid. Reading Common Article 3's phrase "regularly constituted courts" to require the use of courts-martial, the majority held that military commissions can qualify as "regularly constituted courts" only if they comply with Article 21's practicability and uniformity requirements. But as Justice Alito pointed out in his separate dissent, the phrase "regularly constituted court" may be more naturally construed to require that the "court be appointed or established in accordance with the appointing country's domestic law."[168] Given the majority's own admission that military commissions had long been established or appointed by the President pursuant to executive orders and recognized by federal statute, the military commissions seem to satisfy Common Article 3's "regularly constituted court" requirement. Any problem with the procedures *applied* by the military commission does not speak to the manner in which the court was *constituted*. At the very least, the Court's interpretation of "regularly constituted" departed from that phrase's natural meaning.

Four members of the Court offered an even more forceful objection to Hamdan's military commission. According to these four Justices, the government's charge against Hamdan for conspiring to commit the September 11 attacks did not violate the law of war.[169] Justice Kennedy's refusal to join these portions of this opinion deprived this view of a majority. But the Stevens opinion still is worth discussing because it illustrates how at least four members of the Court have asserted broad authority to interpret CIL in conflict with the interpretations advanced by the President.

Hamdan was charged with participating in a conspiracy extending back from 1996 to attack the United States on September 11, 2001. As the plurality noted, none of the overt acts charged occurred in a theater of war or after September 11.[170] According to the plurality, violations of the law of war require activity in a war zone after the conflict has actually begun. Justice Stevens also argued for a high standard of

---

[167] See Message to the Senate Transmitting a Protocol to the 1949 Geneva Conventions (Jan. 29, 1987), reprinted in 133 CONG. REC. S1428 (daily ed. Jan. 29, 1987) (rejecting Protocol); Protocol Additional to the Geneva Conventions of 12 Aug. 1949 and Relating to the Protection of Victims of Non-International Armed Conflicts, June 8, 1977, S. Treaty Doc. No. 100-02, 1125 U.N.T.S. 609.

[168] Hamdan, 548 U.S. at 726 (Alito, J., dissenting).

[169] See *id.* at 600–602.

[170] *Id.* at 611–612.

acceptance for recognizing violations of the law of war. "When . . . neither the elements of the offense nor the range of permissible punishments is defined by statute or treaty, the precedent must be plain and unambiguous."[171] Although conspiracy had sometimes been tried in law-of-war courts in the United States, it had never been the sole basis for a military court's jurisdiction.

This standard for recognizing a violation of the law of war departs substantially from the Court's prior precedents. In *In re Yamashita*, for instance, the Court upheld a conviction (and execution) of a Japanese commander for war crimes despite substantial doubts over whether he had been properly charged with a violation of the law of war.[172] The new Stevens standard resembles the Court's more recent decision in *Sosa v. Alvarez-Machain*, requiring broad and universal acceptance before a federal court could recognize a violation of customary international law.[173]

If Justice Stevens were applying the difficult *Sosa* standard in the analysis of conspiracy, it is strange that he failed to apply that high standard to his other major interpretation of CIL. In another part of his plurality opinion that Justice Kennedy refused to join, Justice Stevens held that the right of an accused to be privy to all of the evidence against him is an "indisputabl[e] part of customary international law."[174] But rather than conducting the kind of searching, skeptical inquiry into the status of this right under customary international law demanded by *Sosa*, Justice Stevens merely cited Article 75 of the Protocol I to the Geneva Conventions and a number of U.S. cases endorsing the importance of this right.[175] None of the U.S. cases claim to be expounding a rule of customary international law. Instead, most seem to be explicating the U.S. constitutional right that Justice Stevens did not claim applied. Article 75 of Protocol I to the Geneva Conventions does provide evidence for a rule of CIL, but nothing in that provision actually requires an accused to be privy to all evidence against him.[176] Admittedly, Justice Stevens was interpreting the UCMJ, rather than determining whether international custom had coalesced into a firm rule that bound the United States. But because he claimed that the UCMJ in fact only implemented CIL, his reading required him to apply the same method to the question as called for by *Sosa*. Or, at least, Justice Stevens would have had to qualify the right in *Hamdan* by acknowledging that it did not meet the universality of consensus required for a rule of CIL that could give rise to an ATS claim—which would have been difficult, because both cases involved a claim that the United States

---

[171] *Id.* at 602.

[172] In re Yamashita, 327 U.S. 1 (1946).

[173] See Sosa v. Alvarez-Machain, 542 U.S. 692 (2004). Whether that standard is really so difficult to meet is debatable. See Julian Ku & John C. Yoo, *Beyond Formalism in Foreign Affairs: A Functional Approach to the Alien Tort Statute*, 2004 Sup. Ct. Rev. 153, 169–70.

[174] Hamdan, 548 U.S. at 564 (opinion of Stevens, J.).

[175] See *id.*

[176] The U.S. government appears to have recognized Article 75 as an "articulation of safeguards to which all persons in the hands of an enemy are entitled." See William H. Taft IV, *The Law of Armed Conflict after 9/11: Some Salient Features*, 28 Yale J. Int'l L. 319, 322 (2003). Article 75 does require an accused to have the right to examine witnesses, but it does not suggest that any and all evidence used against him must be disclosed. See Protocol I to the Geneva Conventions of 1949, art. 75(4).

had detained an individual in violation of international law, and in fact, in *Hamdan*, had done so during an armed conflict, where the balance in favor of the state is greater.

Justice Stevens's foray into the interpretation of CIL lacked a consistent interpretive methodology. His opinion therefore failed to offer a persuasive basis for rejecting conspiracy as a violation of the law of war but accepting the "right to be present" as a rule of CIL (or vice versa). His analysis also demonstrates the majority's lack of capacity in a highly technical area long given to the political branches. Justice Stevens missed the fundamental point that much of the law of war is customary, not written. Prosecutions of Nazi leaders at the Nuremberg war crimes trial for the crime of aggression did not enforce any written international criminal code. Justice Stevens's failure to understand that the crime of conspiracy might be part of the customary law of war undermines the precedent of Nuremberg and one of the main engines of development for the law of war.

Despite all of its flaws, it is important to recognize that the Court's decision did not promote the conflict between international rules and domestic sovereignty that is our concern. While it rejected the interpretation of the executive branch, *Hamdan* did not turn directly to CIL or treaties for authority. Instead, the Justices grounded their ruling on military commissions in their reading of the UCMJ. According to the Court, the basis for its holding was not that the Geneva Conventions were self-executing, but rather that the UCMJ had adopted the Conventions as a standard for measuring the legality of the commissions. In the Court's view, it was the choice of Congress to incorporate the laws of war, rather than the force of the international laws themselves, that provided the legal rule of decision. For the reasons we detail here, we believe that the Court's reading of Congress's intent with respect to the use of the phrase "law of war" in Article 21 is incorrect. But at least the Court's approach kept the exercise of sovereign authority *within* the U.S. government, even though the *Hamdan* case itself represented a conflict between the branches of the government. This preserved the ability of Congress to reverse the Court's result, which it did in the Military Commission Act of 2006.

C. The War on Terrorism and the Judicial Role

It should be clear that *Hamdan*'s readings of the substantive law are not the only plausible interpretations. Against each of Justice Stevens's interpretations of the UCMJ, the Geneva Conventions, and CIL, the government offered a reasonable (and often a more compelling) alternative interpretation. The existence of reasonable alternatives should have tipped the balance in favor of the government in the manner explored earlier in this book. Well-settled doctrines require courts to defer to executive interpretations of certain laws relating to foreign affairs. Yet *Hamdan* barely acknowledges the existence or relevance of these doctrines, much less justifies its departure from them.

In the breach, *Hamdan* provides a good example of the functional reasons for judicial deference to the other branches in interpreting and applying international law. While courts are the primary institutions in the U.S. system for interpreting and applying laws, some of their key institutional characteristics undercut their ability in the foreign affairs law context. In particular, courts have access to limited information in foreign affairs cases and are unable to take into account the broader context underlying the application of laws in such areas.

These limitations are not a failing. They are part of the inherent design of the federal court system, which is intended to be independent from politics, to allow parties to drive litigation in particular cases, and to receive information in highly formal and limited ways. While these characteristics are helpful for the purposes of neutral decision-making, they also may render courts less effective tools in resolving ambiguities in laws designed to achieve national goals in international relations. Such inflexibility surely advances the goals of a domestic legal system in uniformity, predictability, and stability in the interpretation and application of federal law. For these reasons, deference doctrines do not require judicial abdication to the executive branch. Rather, they typically allow the courts to make the initial judgment about the proper meaning of a statute or treaty. Where such statutes or treaties are ambiguous or broadly phrased, however, resort to a rigid, slow, inflexible, and decentralized decision-making process based on limited information is hard to justify.

This is not to say that courts cannot interpret ambiguous statutes when necessary. Rather, the central question is, from a functional perspective, whether there is reason to think that courts would be *equal or superior* to the other branches of government in resolving ambiguities in laws designed to achieve national foreign policies. The *Hamdan* Court's refusal to follow the deference doctrines only illustrates the institutional weaknesses of courts in foreign affairs.

In each of its interpretive moves, the Court resolved the ambiguity in a statute, treaty, or CIL against the government and in favor of the enemy combatant detainee. For instance, the Court's refusal to defer to the executive branch's interpretation of Common Article 3 required it to assess whether the war with al Qaeda was an armed conflict not "of an international character." The Court admitted that the provision appeared to apply to civil wars and other purely domestic conflicts, but ultimately relied on commentaries suggesting that the article should be interpreted as broadly as possible.[177] But the nature of the war with al Qaeda demands more than a myopic assessment of the meaning of the phrase "international character." It requires an analysis of the nature of the military conflict with al Qaeda and the likely effect of U.S. compliance with Common Article 3. It seems obvious that the Court has little competence or access to information that would allow it to make such a judgment.

Hamdan's enforcement of Common Article 3 also intrudes upon the political and diplomatic methods that had traditionally been used to implement the Geneva Conventions. The Geneva Conventions rely on the International Committee of the Red Cross to perform various services in monitoring and mediation.

---

[177] Hamdan, 548 U.S. at 628–630.

The Conventions specifically contemplate that the state parties will "bring into force" their terms through "special agreements." The Conventions rely only on political and diplomatic means, not judicial; indeed, some of the terms in Common Article 3 are so vague that they contemplate future executive and legislative interpretation. Geneva nowhere explicitly calls for direct enforcement by domestic judiciaries of its terms; such an approach would have been, at the time, utterly revolutionary.

Finally, the plurality's discussion of conspiracy and the "right to be privy to all evidence" was an inherently difficult and complex enterprise. Despite the Court's efforts to present the "right to be privy to all evidence" as indisputable, its failure to cite any serious evidence of state practice in the context of a military trial suggests that CIL had yet to coalesce. The executive branch, which is largely responsible for directing U.S. state practice on the law of war, is likely to have more expertise, information, and ability to assess the effect of rejecting or accepting conspiracy as a war crime or the right to be privy to evidence.

Hamdan ignored the Court's traditional deference to the delegation of authority, or power-sharing, in foreign affairs and national security. There are several reasons why courts have generally accepted interbranch cooperation in war and foreign affairs. From a formal perspective, the President has greater independent constitutional powers when foreign affairs and war are concerned than during peacetime. The September 11 attacks triggered the President's Commander-in-Chief power, which would provide him with broader authority to make policy decisions, at both the strategic and tactical level, than in peacetime. Even if one believes that only Congress can authorize wars, Congress authorized the war on terrorism when it enacted the AUMF in 2001.

Intrusive judicial review over warmaking does not advance the goals of the separation of powers. In the domestic context, the Court has identified the preservation of individual liberty as an important goal of the separation of powers. As the Court observed in *Bowsher v. Synar*, the Framers believed that the separation of powers would prevent any single branch of the government from expanding its power and threatening the freedoms of its citizens.[178] "Even a cursory examination of the Constitution reveals the influence of Montesquieu's thesis that checks and balances were the foundation of a structure of government that would protect liberty."[179] This echoed James Madison's explanation in the *Federalist* for the interlocking nature of the separation of powers and federalism. Due to the division of power between the branches of the federal government, and then between the federal government and the states, "a double security arises to the rights of the people. The different governments will control each other; at the same time that each will be controuled [*sic*] by itself."[180]

---

[178] Bowsher v. Synar, 478 U.S. 714, 721–22 (1986).

[179] *Id.* at 722.

[180] THE FEDERALIST No. 51, at 351 (James Madison) (Jacob E. Cooke ed., 1961).

In wartime, the government may be forced to reduce the individual liberties of aliens suspected of enemy activity in order to fight the war more effectively. A wartime government may even pursue policies that, in retrospect, appear to overreact to the threat. But our constitutional system places the interest in effectively waging war first. As Alexander Hamilton wrote in *Federalist No. 23*, because "the circumstances which may affect the public safety are [not] reducible within certain determinate limits, . . . it must be admitted, as a necessary consequence that there can be no limitation of that authority which is to provide for the defense and protection of the community in any matter essential to its efficacy."[181] James Madison agreed that the federal government had to possess all of the powers necessary to defend the country. "Security against foreign danger is one of the primitive objects of civil society. . . . The powers requisite for attaining it must be confided to the federal councils."[182] The limits of this power could not be defined precisely. Hamilton wrote that the federal government should possess "an indefinite power of providing for emergencies as they might arise."[183] The Framers did not appear to believe that a strict understanding of the separation of powers should prevail during wartime over interbranch cooperation that advanced the goal of defeating the enemy.

One could argue (as Justice Breyer's concurrence did) that *Hamdan* preserved the prerogatives of Congress, rather than the Court, by demanding a specific authorization for military commissions. But as positive political theorists have argued, Congress's collective action problems and the rational self-interest of its members make it difficult for the legislature to act where uncertainty is high, information and expertise are expensive, and costly political repercussions probable.[184] Political scientists such as William Howell have found that the greatest degree of delegation will occur in the area of foreign affairs and national security and that this is also an area where we would expect unilateral presidential action accompanied by congressional acquiescence. Legislators are less likely to develop their own policies and more likely to delegate authority to the executive branch when the matter involves high risks over which they have little control—which perhaps better describes war than any other area. Because of these political imperatives, the executive and legislative branches have settled on a stable system that provides broad delegation to the President in foreign affairs and national security. *Hamdan* identifies no benefits for U.S. war policies in overthrowing this arrangement, fails to grapple with the higher transaction costs and greater uncertainty it has created, and does not claim that the political process had malfunctioned in some way that caused the President and Congress to act in wartime matters contrary to the wishes of the electorate.

---

[181] The Federalist No. 23, at 122 (Alexander Hamilton) (Jacob E. Cooke ed., 1961).

[182] The Federalist No. 41, at 224 (James Madison) (Jacob E. Cooke ed., 1961).

[183] The Federalist No. 34, at 175 (Alexander Hamilton) (Jacob E. Cooke ed., 1961).

[184] See, e.g., William G. Howell, Power without Persuasion: The Politics of Direct Presidential Action (2003); David Epstein & Sharyn O'Halloran, Delegating Powers: A Transaction Cost Politics Approach to Policy Making under Separate Powers 73–77 (1999).

Enforcing a strict rule-based approach to delegation does not adequately address the situation presented by war, yet *Hamdan* essentially chooses a rule over a standard in delegating power.[185] Rules reduce decision costs because they are clear and easy to apply, create greater predictability, and require less information to implement. Rules, however, do not allow a careful application of law to all relevant facts, and so they are inevitably overinclusive or underinclusive.[186] Standards, which allow for consideration of more factors and facts, increase decision costs and reduce error costs. Consideration of a greater variety of factors reduces the underinclusiveness or overinclusiveness of the law, but it requires more information and produces less predictability and more uncertainty.

Rules and standards also bear differences in the discretion available to the decision-maker at the time of implementation. Delegators may choose a rule if they believe future decision-makers will make mistakes or will lack good information.[187] A rule gives more authority to those who write the law by narrowing the discretion of future decision-makers. A standard is superior when the decision-makers enjoy greater competence and have better information. Standards vest more authority in those who apply the law to a given case, rather than those who wrote the law.

Under this approach, narrow delegations governed by strict rules make the most sense when Congress enjoys a superior vantage point for making decisions. A rule will save decision-making costs, because the executive branch will not have to expend significant resources in implementation. But a rule requires Congress to predict with high certainty the universe of future cases, and draft rules anticipating them. Broad delegations via standards, on the other hand, will make more sense if Congress cannot anticipate future cases. A President with broadly delegated power will be able to fit policy to the circumstances at hand, though at higher decision-making costs.

Unless Congress is confident that it can predict the enemy's strategies and tactics, a rule-based delegation makes little sense in the context of war. War is perhaps the most extreme example of an issue where the executive branch will have superior information and can make decisions swiftly, while Congress will suffer from collective action problems. The costs of errors in war are extremely high. Given that mistaken policies can damage the national security and result in lost lives, it seems clear that war requires delegations that provide broad discretion.

Hamdan, by contrast, applies the opposite principle. It imposes a requirement that Congress act through rules when it attempts to delegate its war powers to the President. The Court's clear statement rule, however, does not appear to promote any specific policy that is more important or valuable than flexibility in wartime.

---

[185] See, for example, Adrian Vermeule, *Interpretive Choice*, 75 N.Y.U. L. Rev. 74, 91 n. 68 (2000) (collecting sources); Cass R. Sunstein, *Problems with Rules*, 83 Cal. L. Rev. 953 (1995); Louis Kaplow, *Rules versus Standards: An Economic Analysis*, 42 Duke L. J. 557 (1992); Richard A. Epstein, Simple Rules for a Complex World 30–36 (1995).

[186] See Vermeule, *supra* note 185, at 91.

[187] See generally *id.* at 92–93.

As William Eskridge and Philip Frickey have observed, clear statement rules embody policy choices by the Court, such as the rule of lenity's protection for criminal defendants. If anything, they have argued, in past cases the Court had applied clear statement rules to protect the Executive's prerogatives in managing foreign affairs.[188] *Hamdan* fails to explain what policy value is advanced by reversing this rule, and why that value outweighs the benefits of flexibility in war decisions.

Hamdan illustrates both the benefits of a more accommodating approach and the pitfalls of ignoring it. Although *Hamdan* rejected an important foreign policy initiative of the President in wartime, it did so in a way that relied on Congress's authority and judgment rather than its own. Congress reversed the effects of the *Hamdan* decision quickly, without having to amend or abrogate international treaty or customary international law obligations.

On the other hand, *Hamdan*'s interpretations of the relevant international laws, both treaty and customary, departed from the deference typically afforded to the President's interpretation of international law and foreign affairs statutes. This deference, as we argued in chapter 5, has a deep structural logic as well as a strong functional basis. The Court's failure to give, or even explain its failure to give, this deference has troubling implications for the ability of the political branches to act effectively and efficiently in wartime.

IV. CONCLUSION: BOUMEDIENE

Hamdan did not end the story. In response to the Court's invalidation of military commissions, President Bush immediately sought authorization from Congress. In the Military Commissions Act (MCA) of 2006, Congress again stripped the federal courts of jurisdiction over habeas corpus petitions brought by alien enemies held outside the territorial United States. It rejected Justice Stevens's claim in *Hamdan* that Congress, in the Detainee Treatment Act (DTA) of 2005, had removed habeas jurisdiction over Guantánamo Bay only over future (but not pending) cases.[189] In *Boumediene v. Bush*, a 5–4 majority of the Court held the restriction on habeas to be a violation of the Constitution's Suspension Clause, which states: "Privilege of the Writ of Habeas Corpus shall not be suspended, unless when in Cases of Rebellion or Invasion the public Safety may require it." Because Congress had not declared it was suspending the writ under these circumstances, the Court concluded that jurisdiction continued to reach to enemy combatants held at Guantánamo Bay.[190]

While we disagree with the Court's expansion of habeas corpus in wartime, this question is wholly of domestic law and outside the ambit of this book. To be sure, some commentators hailed *Boumediene* as a victory for international law over American counterterrorism policies. They greeted with praise the Court's refusal to

---

[188] William N. Eskridge, Jr., & Philip P. Frickey, *Quasi-Constitutional Law: Clear Statement Rules as Constitutional Lawmaking*, 45 Vand. L. Rev. 593, 615–19 (1992).

[189] Military Commissions Act of 2006, § 7(a), Pub. L. No. 109-366, 120 Stat. 2600, 2635 (2006).

[190] Boumediene v. Bush, 553 U.S. 723, 128 S. Ct. 2229 (2008).

bend to the joint decision of the President and Congress to return the courts to their traditional position of wartime deference. What remains important, but was unaddressed by the *Boumediene* Court, is the political branches' initiative to implement the nation's international law obligations in the wake of *Hamdan*. A careful understanding of the story shows that the constitutional system more closely follows our account of the implementation of international law in the domestic legal system.

Recall, for example, *Hamdan*'s use of the UCMJ to reverse the *Eisentrager* Court's finding that the Geneva Conventions were non-self-executing. On this point, in our view, *Hamdan* disregarded decades of precedent and the better reading of the constitutional structure. Then Congress simply overruled *Hamdan*. Section 3 of the MCA declares: "no alien unlawful enemy combatant subject to trial by military commission" may raise a claim in federal court using "the Geneva Conventions as a source of rights."[191] Not only does this show that Justice Stevens's reading of Congress's intent in the UCMJ (as with the DTA) was mistaken, but the MCA also restored the traditional understanding that the political branches, and not the courts, were to decide how to implement the nation's treaty obligations.

Congress gave similar treatment to *Hamdan*'s application of the Geneva Conventions. Once he had found the Geneva Conventions to create domestic law, Justice Stevens argued that Common Article 3 required the use of courts-martial to try enemy prisoners for war crimes. Again, the President and Congress simply overturned *Hamdan*. Section 3 of the MCA declared a military commission to be "a regularly constituted court, affording all the necessary 'judicial guarantees which are recognized as indispensable by civilized peoples' for purposes of common Article 3 of the Geneva Conventions."[192] While the political branches made some concessions to the *Hamdan* Court on military commission procedures, they nonetheless continued to claim their preeminence over national security and international relations by reestablishing the commission system along the same lines as before. Congress and the President made clear that the United States would use military commissions in the current conflict, despite *Hamdan*. The MCA authorized military commissions "to try alien unlawful enemy combatants engaged in hostilities against the United States for violations of the law of war and other offenses triable by military commission." The political branches rejected the Court's suggestion that terrorists were either civilians or enemy prisoners of war deserving of court-martial. They defined an "unlawful enemy combatant" subject to military commission trial as "a person who has engaged in hostilities or who has purposefully and materially supported hostilities against the United States or its co-belligerents who is not a lawful enemy combatant (including a person who is part of the Taliban, al Qaeda, or associated forces)."[193]

The MCA shows the political branches playing the role we have urged, not just in reversing *Hamdan*, but also in implementing international law in the domestic

---

[191] MCA, § 3, 120 Stat. 2602.

[192] *Id.*

[193] *Id.* at 120 Stat. 2601.

legal system. Congress and the President did not meekly accept the Supreme Court's views on the laws of war. Instead, they reaffirmed the use of military commissions for terrorism cases and even went further in choosing among the different laws of war standards to apply (or not) in trials. Congress, for example, defined a list of crimes triable by military commission—including murder, attacking civilians and civilian objects, pillaging, denying quarter, taking hostages, rape, and torture. This enumeration of individual conduct that is punishable under the laws of war represents Congress's interpretation and implementation of international law. Likewise, the MCA's establishment of the procedures for military commissions—including the rules of evidence, burdens of proof and persuasion, the right to counsel, trial rules, the role of the judge and commission members, and appellate procedure—amounts to Congress's understanding of the minimal requirements demanded by the customary international laws of war for the operation of military tribunals. Congress further used the MCA to clarify the scope of the War Crimes Act, which had made a "grave breach" of Common Article 3 of the Geneva Conventions a federal offense.[194] Common Article 3 itself used terms, such as a prohibition on "outrages on personal dignity" and "humiliating and degrading treatment," which Congress believed to be too ambiguous. In the MCA, it interpreted those phrases by enumerating exactly which acts qualified as violations.

As of this writing, the Supreme Court has not yet examined any of the substantive provisions of the MCA. Its only decision remains *Boumediene.* The Court could respond by holding that some military commission provisions violate international law, but it is difficult to believe that it would follow this course. Such a decision would both ignore the last-in-time rule and expand the judicial role into a type of international policy-making that has traditionally remained in the political branches. Because of this tradition, it is more likely, in our view, that the Court will ground any reversal in constitutional, rather than international, law.

As we have argued in this book, functional reasons demand that the courts defer to the President and Congress in the interpretation and implementation of international law. Only the political branches can weigh the political costs and benefits of obeying, altering, or violating international norms against other policy values. Only they can represent the wishes of the majority in the process of transforming international law into domestic law. The Court recognized this fact in *Medellín,* and was sensitive to the need for careful limitations on courts in *Sosa* as well. Only in *Hamdan* did the Court appear to ignore the allocation of decision-making that we have advocated. Even then, however, the quick and decisive repudiation of *Hamdan* by the President and Congress demonstrates their willingness to intervene to pursue the appropriate international policy goals. The federal courts would best serve the constitutional structure by deferring to their judgment.

---

[194] MCA, § 6, 120 Stat. 2632.18 U.S.C. §2441.

8 Foreign Law and the Constitution

Our analysis has focused on ways that the Constitution's structures can control international efforts to regulate globalization within the U.S. legal system. In our view, the judiciary should defer to the decisions of the President and Congress expressed in their making of treaties and interpreting international law. For the most part, the courts have played this role.

There is one area, however, where the courts have ventured forth on their own: interpreting the Constitution in line with foreign and international opinion. In recent years, Supreme Court Justices have increasingly looked to foreign and international courts for advice in deciding controversial, high-profile issues. This represents another way for globalization to impact the U.S. system: international judicial cooperation that does not undergo the normal public lawmaking process of congressional enactment or presidential interpretation. For this reason, this practice threatens to undermine the Constitution's advancement of popular sovereignty as the basic authority for government within the United States.

Once an isolated practice limited to a few concurrences or dissents, the turn to foreign and international law has recently been adopted by majorities of the Supreme Court. In 2010, for example, *Graham v. Florida* held that the Constitution prohibits sentencing juveniles to life imprisonment without the possibility of parole. *Roper v. Simmons* in 2005 outlawed application of the death penalty to offenders who were under eighteen when their crimes were committed. In 2003, *Lawrence v. Texas* struck down a state law that criminalized homosexual sodomy. *Atkins v. Virginia* a year earlier held against the execution of mentally retarded capital defendants. All four cases looked to foreign and international precedents for help in interpreting the meaning of the prohibition on "cruel and unusual" punishment in the Constitution's Eighth Amendment and the protection of "due process" rights guaranteed by the Constitution's Fourteenth Amendment against the states.[1]

Foreign courts, of course, are usually interpreting their own constitutions or international law, not the U.S. Constitution. Nonetheless, some Supreme Court Justices believe that foreign and international opinions can remain relevant to their duty to interpret the Constitution. In *Roper*, for example, Justice Kennedy found for the majority that it is "proper that we acknowledge the overwhelming weight of international opinion against the juvenile death penalty. . . . The opinion of the world community, while not controlling our outcome, does provide respected and significant confirmation for our own conclusions."[2] The Court relied on a provision of the United Nations Convention on the Rights of the Child—a treaty the United States has not ratified—and on amicus briefs by the European Union and interested foreign observers. In *Lawrence*, Justice Kennedy's majority opinion again cited decisions of the European Court of Human Rights to conclude that prohibiting homosexual sodomy is at odds with the current norms of Western civilization.[3] In *Atkins*, the majority opinion by Justice Stevens relied on an amicus brief filed by the European Union to claim that executing the mentally retarded is "overwhelmingly disapproved."[4] References to foreign decisions have appeared not just in cases expanding individual rights, but also in dissents from opinions defining the balance of powers between the federal and state governments.[5]

It is possible that the Justices cite foreign decisions and international law merely as ornaments.[6] While providing aesthetic support, foreign and international law may contribute little of analytical value and may have no real effect on actual American decision-making. Even had the foreign decisions come out differently, the Supreme Court would have reached its preferred result anyway. Foreign and international law precedents may provide only tangential value to bolster decisions reached on more traditional grounds.

There are, however, two reasons to think that use of foreign decisions extends beyond mere ornamentation, one grounded in the expressed views of several Justices and the other in academic opinion.

First, several Justices have been explicit proponents of the use of foreign law. Justice Breyer has been the most prominent. In a speech, he enthusiastically claimed

---

[1] Graham v. Florida,130 S. Ct. 2011 (2010); Roper v. Simmons, 543 U.S. 551 (2005) (plurality opinion); Lawrence v. Texas, 539 U.S. 558 (2003); Atkins v. Virginia, 536 U.S. 304 (2002).

[2] Roper, 543 U.S. at 578.

[3] 539 U.S. at 573 (citing Dudgeon v. United Kingdom, 45 Eur. Ct. H.R. (1981) ¶ 52).

[4] 536 U.S. at 316 n.21.

[5] See Printz v. United States, 521 U.S. 898, 976 (1997) (Breyer, J., dissenting).

[6] Thus, Professor Alford suggests that the Court's use of international and foreign materials in constitutional cases may be mere "bricolage." See Roger P. Alford, *Misusing International Sources to Interpret the Constitution*, 98 Am. J. Int'l L. 57, 64–65 (2004).

that a "global legal enterprise . . . is now upon us."[7] Justice Breyer's remarks in that instance built on arguments he had previously made in judicial opinions.[8] Justices Stevens,[9] O'Connor,[10] and Ginsburg[11] have also advocated the use of foreign law in constitutional adjudication. Indeed, Justice Breyer has even argued that the "judgment of other nations" should help "guide this Court" in Eighth Amendment cases. Justice O'Connor has even gone further in claiming that "we should not be surprised to find congruence between domestic and international values" in the Eighth Amendment context.

Other Justices have expressed hostility to the use of foreign or international decisions in interpreting the U.S. Constitution. In *Atkins*, Chief Justice Rehnquist declared: "I fail to see . . . how the views of other countries regarding the punishment of their citizens provide any support for the Court's ultimate determination."[12] According to him, "if it is evidence of a *national* consensus for which we are looking, then the viewpoints of other countries simply are not relevant."[13] Justices Scalia and Thomas have similarly maintained that foreign precedents are irrelevant because

---

[7] Stephen Breyer, Associate Justice, Supreme Court of the United States, The Supreme Court and The New International Law, remarks to the American Society of International Law (April 4, 2003), available at http://www.supremecourt.gov/publicinfo/speeches/viewspeeches.aspx?Filename=sp_04-04-03.html.

[8] See, e.g., Nixon v. Shrink Mo. Gov't PAC, 528 U.S. 377, 403 (2000) (Breyer, J., concurring) (citing European and Canadian judicial decisions for their treatment of First Amendment issue); Foster v. Florida, 537 U.S. 990, 993 (2002) (Breyer, J., dissenting from denial of certiorari) ("'[A]ttention to the judgment of other nations'. . . can help guide this Court when it decides whether a particular punishment violates the Eighth Amendment" (quoting THE FEDERALIST No. 63 (James Madison))); Knight v. Florida, 528 U.S. 990, 995–97 (1999) (Breyer, J., dissenting from denial of certiorari) (finding the opinions of former British Commonwealth nations "particularly instructive" in constitutional death penalty adjudication).

[9] See Thompson v. Oklahoma, 487 U.S. 815, 830–31 (1988) (plurality opinion).

[10] See, e.g., Roper, 543 U.S. at 604–05 (O'Connor, J., dissenting) ("I disagree with Justice Scalia's contention . . . that foreign and international law have no place in our Eighth Amendment jurisprudence. Over the course of nearly half a century, the Court has consistently referred to foreign and international law as relevant to its assessment of evolving standards of decency. . . . [T]his Nation's evolving understanding of human dignity certainly is neither wholly isolated from, nor inherently at odds with, the values prevailing in other countries. On the contrary, we should not be surprised to find congruence between domestic and international values . . ."); Sandra Day O'Connor, *Keynote Address at the 96th Annual Meeting of the American Society of International Law* (March 13–16, 2002), in 96 AM. SOC. INT'L L. PROC. 348, 350 (2002) ("Although international law and the law of other nations are rarely binding upon our decisions in U.S. courts, conclusions reached by other countries and by the international community should at times constitute persuasive authority in American courts"); Sandra Day O'Connor, *Broadening Our Horizons: Why American Lawyers Must Learn about Foreign Law*, 45 FED. LAW. 20 (Sept. 1998).

[11] See, e.g., Grutter, 539 U.S. at 344 (Ginsburg, J., joined by Breyer, J., concurring) (relying on international treatment of affirmative action); Ruth Bader Ginsburg, *Looking Beyond Our Borders: The Value of a Comparative Perspective in Constitutional Adjudication*, 22 YALE L. & POL'Y R. 329 (2004); Ruth Bader Ginsburg & Deborah Jones Merritt, *Affirmative Action: An International Human Rights Dialogue*, 21 CARDOZO L. REV. 253, 282 (1999).

[12] Atkins, 536 U.S. at 324–25 (Rehnquist, C. J., dissenting).

[13] *Id.*

they interpret the constitutional documents of other nations.[14] Dissenting in *Roper*, Justice Scalia contended that "the basic premise of the Court's argument—that American law should conform to the laws of the rest of the world—ought to be rejected out of hand."[15] The Court's use of foreign law was inconsistent and unprincipled, as shown by the deviation between American and foreign case law on the exclusionary rule, church-state relations, and abortion. Justice Scalia concluded: "[t]he Court should either profess its willingness to reconsider all these matters in light of the views of foreigners, or else it should cease putting forth foreigners' views as part of the *reasoned basis* of its decisions. To invoke alien law when it agrees with one's own thinking, and ignore it otherwise, is not reasoned decisionmaking, but sophistry."[16]

Second, legal academics have urged the Supreme Court Justices to engage in a "dialogue" with their foreign counterparts. Four academic projects are particularly noteworthy: Professor Bruce Ackerman has advocated "world constitutionalism";[17] Professors Vicki Jackson and Mark Tushnet have become interested in the possibilities of comparative constitutional analysis;[18] Professor Harold Koh has argued that the Court has looked and should look beyond American law when interpreting a constitutional requirement (like unreasonable searches or due process) that "implicitly refers to a community standard";[19] and international law scholar Anne-Marie Slaughter has argued in favor of transnational communication between courts.[20] These academics appear to be attempting to construct an intellectual framework that could justify more extensive use of foreign judicial decisions in the future. This may presage further federal judicial reliance, at least in part, on foreign and international law.

It is important to identify precisely what is and what is not in controversy. In appropriate cases, foreign and international law has long been invoked in accordance with conflict of law principles or canons instructing courts to avoid

---

[14] See, e.g., Lawrence, 539 U.S. at 598 (Scalia, J., dissenting) ("The Court's discussion of these foreign views . . . is therefore meaningless dicta"); Foster v. Florida, 537 U.S. 990, 990 n.*. (Thomas, J., concurring in denial of certiorari).

[15] Roper, 543 U.S. at 624 (Scalia, J., dissenting).

[16] *Id.* at 627 (italics in original).

[17] Bruce Ackerman, *The Rise of World Constitutionalism*, 83 Va. L. Rev. 771 (1997). See also David S. Law, *Generic Constitutional Law*, 89 Minn. L. Rev. 652 (2005).

[18] Vicki C. Jackson, *Ambivalent Resistance and Comparative Constitutionalism: Opening Up the Conversation on "Proportionality," Rights and Federalism*, 1 U. Pa. J. Const. L. 583 (1999); Mark Tushnet, *The Possibilities of Comparative Constitutional Law*, 108 Yale L. J. 1225 (1999).

[19] Harold H. Koh, *International Law Part of Our Law*, 98 Am. J. Int'l L. 43, 46 (2004).

[20] Anne-Marie Slaughter, *A Typology of Transnational Communication*, 29 U. Rich. L. Rev. 99 (1994); Anne-Marie Slaughter, *Judicial Globalization*, 40 Va. J. Int'l L. 1103 (2000). In addition to the scholars cited, other scholars, even while critical of aspects of the Court's use of foreign and international law sources, believe that those sources may be relevant to some questions of constitutional interpretation. See, e.g., Michael Ramsey, *International Materials and Domestic Rights: Reflections on Atkins and Lawrence*, 98 Am. J. Int'l L. 69, 71 (2004) (arguing that "[i]nternational sources are obviously relevant to the scope of the Constitution's structural provisions defining the international powers of the U.S. government").

interpretations of statutes that violate international law. Such uses of foreign and international law are largely unremarkable because these methods do not affect the interpretation of the U.S. Constitution.

In the context of constitutional interpretation, some Justices believe that foreign and international legal practices and opinions can serve, at a minimum, to illuminate possible solutions to questions similar to those that U.S. courts must address (just as our federal courts may learn from our state courts, and vice versa). Foreign materials can provide relevant empirical information about the practical effects of particular social policies. Or, like law review articles, they can furnish original legal arguments. To the extent that foreign and international legal materials serve these purposes, they also seem unobjectionable. Some Justices may also think it is desirable for U.S. constitutional law to converge with the constitutional law of other (especially European) legal systems. These Justices might give decisional effect to those materials, thus allowing them to determine the outcome in constitutional cases. So used, foreign or international law would have legal force in deciding important questions, including the rights of criminal defendants, the constitutionality of parental notification requirements, the reasonableness of searches by law enforcement, the extent of governmental leeway in religion cases, and the validity of various forms of capital punishment under the Eighth Amendment.

It is this last approach to foreign and international law that falls afoul of the Constitution's structure and the principles of popular sovereignty. In our judgment, foreign and international laws are not legitimately used in an outcome-determinative way to decide questions of constitutional interpretation except in one narrow category of cases: where the text of the Constitution itself refers to international or foreign law. Article I, Section 8, for example, vests Congress with the powers to "define and punish . . . Offences against the Law of Nations"[21] or to "declare War."[22] Under those clauses, the Constitution gives Congress the authority to promulgate rules of international law. As we discuss below, the Supreme Court held in the early days of the Republic that public international law (or, more precisely, the Law of Nations) could be used to interpret the scope of Congress's power to "declare War."[23] That holding makes perfect sense, given that the power to "declare War" is seen by many scholars (including one of us) as an exceptional grant of authority to Congress to make legal rules in the *international* sphere.[24] Likewise, the scope of Congress's power to define and punish offenses against the "Law of Nations" can be legitimately established by reference to that body of law.[25]

---

[21] U.S. CONST. art. I, § 8, cl. 10.

[22] U.S. CONST. art. I, § 8, cl. 11.

[23] See Brown v. United States, 12 U.S. (8 Cranch) 110, 125 (1814).

[24] See 1 JAMES KENT, COMMENTARIES 56–58 (Da Capo Press 1971) (1826) (explaining the meaning of the Declaration of War Clause).

[25] The Constitution also refers to international law in certain grants of power to the federal courts, for example, when it authorizes those courts to try "all Cases of admiralty and maritime Jurisdiction." U.S. CONST. art. III, § 2, cl. 1. Maritime and admiralty law "has strong roots in international custom. In extending judicial power 'to all cases of admiralty and maritime jurisdiction,' the framers of the

Such unusual cases aside, foreign and international law should not be available as a basis for interpreting the Constitution.

This chapter makes three arguments against the Supreme Court's practice of relying on foreign and international decisions. First, we argue that nonornamental use of foreign decisions undermines the separation of powers and violates the constitutional rules against delegation of federal authority to bodies outside the control of the national government. Second, the use of foreign decisions undermines the limited theory of judicial review, as set out in *Marbury v. Madison*.[26] There, Chief Justice Marshall justified the federal courts' power to ignore enacted laws that were inconsistent with the Constitution on the ground that such statutes fell outside the delegation of authority by the people to the government, as expressed in the Constitution.[27] Relying on decisions that interpret a wholly different document runs counter to the notion that judicial review derives from the Court's duty to enforce the Constitution. Finally, we consider the relevance of the Constitution's Supremacy Clause and Law of Nations Clause to the Court's emerging use of foreign and international law.

As noted above, in four cases in the last few years, the Court used foreign and international precedents to analyze the application of the Eighth Amendment and the Due Process Clause. These controversies called on the Court to measure state action against social norms. To determine whether the life imprisonment or execution of juveniles, capital punishment of the mentally retarded, and the criminalization of homosexual sodomy violated social norms, the Court looked to Europe. It considered European precedents to represent world opinion on the question.[28]

The Court's use of foreign and international law in these cases has the potential to turn into a standard of deference. Though the arguments for deferring to foreign

Constitution apparently had English admiralty practice in mind, itself based on the civil law of continental Europe." James A. R. Nafziger, *The Evolving Role of Admiralty Courts in Litigation Related to Historic Wreck*, 44 Harv. Int'l L. J. 251, 266 (2003). See also William Blackstone, 4 Commentaries on the Laws of England *67 (1778) (Law of Nations is "universal law" that encompasses "mercantile questions, such as bills of exchange and the like," "all marine causes," "the law-merchant," and "disputes relating to prizes, to shipwrecks, to hostages, and ransom bills"); Edward Dumbauld, *John Marshall and the Law of Nations*, 104 U. Pa. L. Rev. 38, 39 (1955) (quoting the statement of Lord Mansfield that "the maritime law is not the law of a particular country, but the general law of nations").

[26] 5 U.S. (1 Cranch) 137 (1803).

[27] *Id.* at 176 ("That the people have an original right to establish, for their future government, such principles as, in their opinion, shall most conduce to their own happiness, is the basis, on which the whole American fabric has been erected").

[28] Roper, 543 U.S. at 577 ("The United Kingdom's experience bears particular relevance here. . . . As of now, the United Kingdom has abolished the death penalty in its entirety; but, decades before it took this step, it recognized the disproportionate nature of the juvenile death penalty; and it abolished that penalty as a separate matter"); Lawrence, 539 U.S. at 572 ("The sweeping references by Chief Justice Burger to the history of Western civilization and to Judeo-Christian moral and ethical standards did not take account of other authorities pointing in an opposite direction") (emphasis added); Atkins, 536 U.S. at 317 n. 21 ("[W]ithin the world community, the imposition of the death penalty for crimes committed by mentally retarded offenders is overwhelmingly disapproved").

precedents are not precise, an analogy can be made to the standards of deference that courts apply to administrative agencies. The strongest of these standards, *Chevron* deference, requires courts to defer to agency interpretations of an ambiguous statutory provision if Congress's intent does not clearly dictate otherwise and if the interpretation is a permissible or not unreasonable reading of the provision.[29] "Deference under Chevron to an agency's construction of a statute that it administers is premised on the theory that a statute's ambiguity constitutes an implicit delegation from Congress to the agency to fill in the statutory gaps."[30] Under a weaker standard of deference, *Skidmore* deference, the weight given to an agency interpretation rests on "the thoroughness evident in its consideration, the validity of its reasoning, its consistency with earlier and later pronouncements, and all those factors which give it power to persuade, if lacking power to control."[31] Both *Chevron* and *Skidmore* exist in administrative law, with the former applying to agency interpretations of ambiguous law, while the latter extends less deference to less formal forms of agency action that lack the force of law, such as enforcement guidelines or policy statements.[32]

A *Chevron* sort of deference to foreign decisions would be unconstitutional. It would subject American citizens to the judgments of foreign and international courts. As we argued in chapter 3, the Constitution makes no provision for the transfer of federal power to entities outside our system of government. To the contrary, the Appointments Clause limits the transfer of federal power.[33] Much writing on this clause has focused on the balance of power between the President and Senate in the appointment of federal judges.[34] However, the Clause also functions as a mechanism to conserve federal power. In recent decisions, the Supreme Court has recognized that the Appointments Clause restricts the exercise of federal power to those officials appointed through the processes set out in the Clause.[35]

---

[29] Chevron U.S.A., Inc. v. Natural Res. Def. Council, Inc., 467 U.S. 837, 842–45 (1984). For a classic exposition of Chevron, see Laurence H. Silberman, *Chevron—The Intersection of Law & Policy*, 58 GEO. WASH. L. REV. 821 (1990).

[30] FDA v. Brown & Williamson Tobacco Corp., 529 U.S. 120, 159 (2000). On this point, see John Manning, *The Nondelegation Doctrine as a Canon of Avoidance*, 2000 SUP. CT. REV. 223.

[31] Skidmore v. Swift & Co., 323 U.S. 134, 140 (1944); see also United States v. Mead Corp., 533 U.S. 218, 227, 234 (2001) (distinguishing Chevron deference from Skidmore deference).

[32] See Christensen v. Harris County, 529 U.S. 576 (2000). Useful overviews of these issues can be found in Cass Sunstein, *Chevron Step Zero*, 92 VA. L. REV. 187 (2006); Thomas W. Merrill & Kristin E. Hickman, *Chevron's Domain*, 89 GEO. L.J. 833 (2001).

[33] John C. Yoo, *The New Sovereignty and the Old Constitution: The Chemical Weapons Convention and the Appointments Clause*, 15 CONST. COMMENT. 87, 96 (1998) ("[T]he Constitution erects limits on the ability of the federal government to transfer or delegate power to entities that are not directly responsible to the American people"); see also John C. Yoo, *Treaty Interpretation and the False Sirens of Delegation*, 90 CAL. L. REV. 1305 (2002).

[34] See John C. Yoo, *Choosing Justices: A Political Appointments Process and the Wages of Judicial Supremacy*, 98 MICH. L. REV. 1436, 1437 n.4 (2000) (collecting sources).

[35] See, e.g., Edmond v. United States, 520 U.S. 651, 663 (1997); Ryder v. United States, 515 U.S. 177, 180–84 (1995); Weiss v. United States, 510 U.S. 163, 169–76 (1994); Freytag v. Comm'r, 501 U.S. 868, 884 (1991); Buckley v. Valeo, 424 U.S. 1, 135 (1976) (per curiam).

This restriction ensures that federal power is limited to officials who are accountable solely to elected representatives. International and foreign courts do not meet this standard.

The Court's discussions of the Appointments Clause in *Edmond v. United States* and *Printz v. United States*[36] affirm the notion that Congress may not transfer responsibility for the execution of federal law to officers outside the control of the executive branch. In *Edmond*, the Court observed that the Appointments Clause "is among the significant structural safeguards of the constitutional scheme."[37] In *Printz*, the Court held that Congress could not delegate the power to enforce the Brady Act to state officials because such delegation would leave federal law enforcement free of "meaningful Presidential control" and would undermine the effectiveness of a unitary Executive.[38] "That unity would be shattered, and the power of the President would be subject to reduction, if Congress could act as effectively without the President as with him, by simply requiring state officers to execute its laws."[39] *Printz* made clear that the Appointments Clause would be offended not only if Congress sought to transfer federal law enforcement to officers of its own selection, but also if it attempted to delegate that power to officials outside the executive branch of the federal government.[40]

The Appointments Clause also concerns itself with the general scope and execution of national power. The Clause's requirement that all individuals who exercise significant federal authority become officers of the United States, appointed pursuant to Article II, Section 2, ensures that the federal government cannot blur the lines of accountability between the people and their officials. As Chief Justice Rehnquist wrote for the Court in *Ryder v. United States*, "The Clause is a bulwark against one branch aggrandizing its power at the expense of another branch, but it is more: it 'preserves another aspect of the Constitution's structural integrity by preventing the diffusion of the appointment power.'"[41] *Buckley v. Valeo*[42] first made clear the link between the Appointments Clause and the exercise of federal power. The *Buckley* Court rejected the proposition that Congress could appoint individuals to exercise federal power who were not officers of the United States, observing, "We think . . . [that the Appointments Clause's] fair import is that any appointee exercising significant authority pursuant to the laws of the United States is an 'Officer of the United States,' and must, therefore, be appointed in the manner prescribed by [the Clause.]"[43] Individuals appointed by Congress, therefore, did not qualify as officers of the United States and could only perform duties not involving the enforcement of federal law.

---

[36] Edmond, 520 U.S. at 659; Printz, 521 U.S. at 922–23.

[37] 520 U.S. at 659.

[38] 521 U.S. at 922.

[39] *Id.* at 923.

[40] *Id.*

[41] 515 U.S. at 182 (quoting Freytag, 501 U.S. at 878).

[42] 424 U.S. 1.

[43] *Id.* at 126.

Two other elements of the Constitution's text and structure confirm the Appointments Clause's careful husbanding of federal power. First, Article III vests the federal judicial power "in one supreme Court, and in such inferior Courts as the Congress may from time to time ordain and establish."[44] This provision suggests that the federal judicial power, which includes the authority to decide cases or controversies under federal law, cannot be exercised by any other branch of the federal government, with the narrow and debatable exception of the Senate's role in trying cases of impeachment.[45] The logical implication is that no part of the Article III authority to decide federal cases and controversies, from which springs the judicial power to interpret the Constitution, can be delegated or transferred outside the U.S. government.

Of course, Congress could have declined to create any lower federal courts. Furthermore, restrictions on the subject matter jurisdiction of federal courts cause many federal constitutional issues to arise first in state courts, whose judges are not members of the federal government.[46] Any damage to the separation of powers from state courts is not, however, insurmountable. State judicial decisions can be reviewed by the U.S. Supreme Court, and state courts are still part of the American political system. The potential violation of separation of powers is, therefore, greater when the courts defer to foreign laws or courts. Transferring judicial power outside the Article III courts and the federal government would ignore the vesting of federal judicial power in the Supreme Court and undermine the accountability of government. Members of the electorate could not hold accountable officials who stand completely outside the structure of American government.

The second element of the Constitution's text and structure that confirms the Appointments Clause's conservation of power is the nondelegation doctrine. The doctrine prohibits Congress from delegating rulemaking authority to another branch unless Congress has stated intelligible standards to guide administrative discretion.[47] This requirement ensures that the exercise of delegated power can be

---

[44] U.S. Const. art. III, § 1.

[45] See, e.g., Akhil Reed Amar, *A Neo-Federalist View of Article III: Separating the Two Tiers of Federal Jurisdiction*, 65 B.U. L. Rev. 205 (1985); Steven G. Calabresi & Kevin H. Rhodes, *The Structural Constitution: Unitary Executive, Plural Judiciary*, 105 Harv. L. Rev. 1153 (1992). Legislative attempts at jurisdiction stripping, however, may obscure this concept. Commentators who believe that Congress has the authority to strip the federal courts of jurisdiction include Paul M. Bator, *Congressional Power over the Jurisdiction of the Federal Courts*, 27 Vill. L. Rev. 1030, 1030–32 (1982); Gerald Gunther, *Congressional Power to Curtail Federal Court Jurisdiction: An Opinionated Guide to the Ongoing Debate*, 36 Stan. L. Rev. 895, 898 (1984); and Henry M. Hart, Jr., *The Power of Congress to Limit the Jurisdiction of Federal Courts: An Exercise in Dialectic*, 66 Harv. L. Rev. 1362, 1362–66 (1953).

[46] The well-pleaded complaint rule precludes almost all defendants in state courts from removing their cases to federal courts. Federal defenses to state law claims made by plaintiffs are therefore adjudicated almost exclusively by state judges. See Louisville & Nashville R.R. v. Mottley, 211 U.S. 149 (1908); 28 U.S.C. § 1331 (2001).

[47] See, e.g., Whitman v. Am. Trucking Ass'ns, 531 U.S. 457 (2001); cf. Clinton v. New York City, 524 U.S. 417 (1998).

monitored and controlled, and even reversed. Although the Supreme Court has not invalidated a statute on nondelegation grounds since the New Deal,[48] it remains an important structural principle that finds its expression in canons of construction.[49] The delegation of lawmaking power outside the federal government would prevent lower courts, Congress, and the public from monitoring whether the delegated authority was being exercised consistent with legislative standards.[50]

Giving deference to foreign judicial decisions would cause considerable tension with these constitutional structures. Under the Appointments Clause, anyone who possesses the power to interpret and execute federal law must be an officer of the United States. When the Court applies *Chevron* deference, it is deferring to officials who are appointed by the President or those responsible to him, consistent with the Appointments Clause. Those who make and interpret federal law, whether federal judges or agency officials, remain ultimately responsible to the American electorate. Foreign judges, by contrast, have received neither presidential nomination nor senatorial consent, and thus should not exercise significant federal power. To the extent that a foreign decision determines outcomes or triggers application of *Chevron* deference, it would raise serious problems with the constitutional requirement established by the Appointments Clause. If, of course, federal courts do not provide *Chevron* deference, but instead are only reviewing foreign or international decisions for their persuasive effect, or are mining them for good ideas, there would be no structural problem because these decisions would not be exerting any legal effect within the U.S. system.

Reliance on foreign decisions also undermines the policies animating the Appointments Clause and the nondelegation doctrine, namely, accountability and control. Delegation to federal agency officials seems tolerable because those officials are part of an executive branch responsible to the President, Congress, the courts, and the public. Though the courts may defer, an agency that goes beyond its statutory mandate is still subject to the checks of congressional oversight, budget cuts, statutory amendments, presidential removal, public criticism and, ultimately, elections.[51] The same mechanisms do not constrain foreign judges, who are neither responsible to the American political system nor required to adapt their exercise of interpretive authority to federal constitutional or statutory principles. Reliance on foreign and international decisions would evade the Constitution's conferral of the

[48] See A.L.A. Schlechter Poultry Corp. v. United States, 295 U.S. 495 (1935); Pan. Ref. Co. v. Ryan, 293 U.S. 388 (1935).

[49] Cass R. Sunstein, *Nondelegation Canons*, 67 U. Chi. L. Rev. 315 (2000); Manning, *supra* note 30.

[50] See Julian G. Ku, *International Delegation and the New World Court Order*, 81 Wash. L. Rev. 1 (2006). For recent discussion of the nondelegation doctrine, compare Eric A. Posner & Adrian Vermeule, *Interring the Nondelegation Doctrine*, 69 U. Chi. L. Rev. 1721 (2002) with Gary Lawson, *Delegation and Original Meaning*, 88 Va. L. Rev. 327 (2002).

[51] Congressional attempts to shield itself from popular accountability have been struck down. See Metro. Wash. Airports Auth. v. Citizens for the Abatement of Aircraft Noise, 501 U.S. 252 (1991) (striking down law that allowed a nine-member Board of Review made up of members of Congress to review the decisions of the airport authority).

power to implement and interpret federal law to officers of the United States who are accountable to the electorate.

Issues of delegation or deference aside, reliance on sources exogenous to the American political system in interpreting the Constitution undermines the textual and structural basis for judicial review. This criticism does not extend to all uses of foreign decisions by the federal courts. Such sources might be relevant to judicial interpretation of other types of federal law, such as treaties, statutes, and perhaps even federal common law. We argue, however, that when it comes to the Constitution, federal courts are limited to materials that derive from the American legal system.

The touchstone is the nature of judicial review under the Constitution. Some support it for functional reasons, such as the protection of individual rights or its moderating role among the political branches.[52] We offer a more modest explanation. Judicial review finds its origins in the nature of the Constitution as a manifestation of popular sovereignty, in the supremacy of constitutional law to statutory law, and the duty of every federal officer to obey that higher law when confronted with the inconsistent actions of other branches of government.[53]

The structural foundation for judicial review lies in the nature of the Constitution and its relationship with the officers of the federal government. According to the theory of popular sovereignty, the government is a creation of the people of the several states rather than of the federal state or a monarch. The government exercises power only because it serves as the agent of the people's will. As James Madison wrote in *Federalist No. 46*: "The federal and State Governments are in fact but different agents and trustees of the people, constituted with different powers and designed for different purposes."[54] Madison reminded critics of the proposed Constitution that "the ultimate authority, wherever the derivative may be found, resides in the people alone . . ."[55]

It follows from this that the government may exercise only the power that the people have delegated to it. A written constitution serves to specify and limit those powers. Any exercise of authority beyond the grant of power in the written constitution is therefore invalid because it goes beyond the delegation from the people and undermines popular sovereignty. As Alexander Hamilton explained in *Federalist No. 78*, "[E]very act of a delegated authority, contrary to the tenor of the commission under which it is exercised, is void."[56] A written constitution would prove inconsequential if its agents could simply exercise the powers that they saw fit, regardless of the will of the people. Chief Justice John Marshall declared in *Marbury v. Madison*: "The distinction between a government with limited and

---

[52] See, e.g., JESSE H. CHOPER, JUDICIAL REVIEW AND THE NATIONAL POLITICAL PROCESS: A FUNCTIONAL RECONSIDERATION OF THE ROLE OF THE SUPREME COURT (1980); TERRI JENNINGS PERETTI, IN DEFENSE OF A POLITICAL COURT (2001).

[53] See Saikrishna B. Prakash & John C. Yoo, *The Origins of Judicial Review*, 70 U. CHI. L. REV. 887 (2003).

[54] THE FEDERALIST No. 46, at 294 (James Madison) (Clinton Rossiter ed., 1961).

[55] *Id.*

[56] THE FEDERALIST No. 78, at 467 (Alexander Hamilton) (Clinton Rossiter ed., 1961).

unlimited powers is abolished, if those limits do not confine the persons on whom they are imposed, and if acts prohibited and acts allowed, are of equal obligation."[57] In order for the Constitution to successfully establish written limitations on the powers of the branches of government, it must establish a rule of decision that places it above the organs it creates.

The task of policing federal and state governmental actors has largely fallen to the federal courts.[58] In *Federalist No. 78*, Hamilton specifically emphasized the role of the federal courts as "an intermediate body between the people and the legislature in order, among other things, to keep the latter within the limits assigned to their authority."[59] Following Hamilton, Chief Justice Marshall in *Marbury* spelled out, through a series of *reductio ad absurdum* arguments, the necessity of such a judicial role. The view that the courts could not examine the constitutionality of a statute before them, or pronounce it void if they found it repugnant to the Constitution, "would subvert the very foundation of all written constitutions."[60] Marshall explained:

It would declare that an act which, according to the principles and theory of our govern-ment, is entirely void, is yet, in practice, completely obligatory. It would declare that if the legislature shall do what is expressly forbidden, such act, notwithstanding the express prohibition, is in reality effectual. It would be giving to the legislature a practi-cal and real omnipotence, with the same breath which professes to restrict their powers within narrow limits.[61]

Neither the *Federalist* nor *Marbury* makes the claim, however, that it is solely the function of the judiciary to decide whether the acts of the other branches of govern-ment are unconstitutional and hence ought not be obeyed.[62] Popular sovereignty suggests that each branch has an obligation to refuse to obey commands that violate the Constitution. As Thomas Jefferson wrote to William Jarvis:

You seem . . . to consider the judges as the ultimate arbiters of all constitutional questions; a very dangerous doctrine indeed, and one which would place us under the

---

[57] 5 U.S. (1 Cranch) 137, 176–77 (1803).

[58] This is in part because of the phenomenon of "agency costs," which can make it effectively impos-sible for a principal to monitor the performance of its agents and so ensure that they are not acting outside the scope of the authority delegated to them. In order to maintain control over its agents, a principal may therefore delegate to one of those agents a lead role in monitoring the actions of the others. To be sure, such a delegation may itself be abused, precisely because close monitoring of that agent may also be unduly costly for a principal. See, e.g., Michael C. Jensen & William H. Meckling, *Theory of the Firm: Managerial Behavior, Agency Costs and Ownership*, 3 J. FIN. ECON. 305, 308–310 (1976).

[59] The Federalist No. 78, *supra* note 56, at 467 (Alexander Hamilton).

[60] 5 U.S. (1 Cranch) at 178.

[61] *Id.*

[62] Indeed, Marshall later went to some length to specify a class of "political" cases in which the consti-tutionality of the actions of another branch is not open to judicial review. See, e.g., Foster v. Neilson, 27 U.S. (2 Pet.) 253, 307–09 (1829) (international boundaries a political question); United States v. Palmer, 16 U.S. (3 Wheat.) 610, 634–35 (1818) (recognition of international status a political question); Rose v. Himely, 8 U.S. (4 Cranch) 241, 272 (1808) (independence of French colony a political question).

despotism of an oligarchy. . . . The constitution has erected no such single tribunal. . . . It has more wisely made all the departments co-equal and co-sovereign within themselves.[63]

Andrew Jackson, in his Veto Message of July 10, 1832, stated:

It is as much the duty of the House of Representatives, of the Senate, and of the President to decide upon the constitutionality of any bill or resolution which may be presented to them for passage or approval as it is of the supreme judges when it may be brought before them for judicial decision. The opinion of the judges has no more authority over Congress than the opinion of Congress has over the judges, and on that point the President is independent of both.[64]

To infer that *Marbury* holds otherwise, Gerald Gunther observed, "confuses Marshall's assertion of judicial authority to interpret the Constitution with judicial exclusiveness."[65]

The Oaths Clause provides textual evidence that the power to interpret the Constitution is not exclusively judicial. It declares that "[t]he Senators and Representatives before mentioned, and the Members of the several State Legislatures, and all executive and judicial Officers, both of the United States and of the several States, shall be bound by Oath or Affirmation, to support this Constitution . . ."[66] The Clause makes clear that all officials of both the federal and state governments have a basic obligation not to violate the Constitution. *Marbury* suggested that oath-takers should disregard the actions of other institutions when they conflict with the Constitution.[67] To make that determination, oath-takers would have to interpret the Constitution themselves.

Under this interpretation, judicial review is neither unique nor special. It is merely the manner in which federal judges fulfill their obligation to follow the Constitution when deciding Article III cases or controversies—to obey the written limits on the people's delegation of power to their government. Members of the other branches must obey the same obligation to enforce the Constitution when performing their particular responsibilities—whether it is a congressman who votes against

---

[63] Thomas Jefferson, Letter to William C. Jarvis, Sept. 28, 1820, in 10 The Writings of Thomas Jefferson 160 (Paul L. Ford ed., 1899).

[64] Andrew Jackson, Veto Message to the Senate, July 10, 1832, in 2 Messages and Papers of the Presidents 576, 582 (James D. Richardson ed., 1896).

[65] Gerald Gunther, *The Subtle Vices of the "Passive Virtues"—A Comment on Principle and Expediency in Judicial Review*, 64 Colum. L. Rev. 1, 25 n.155 (1964).

[66] U.S. Const. art. VI, § 1, cl. 3.

[67] 5 U.S. (1 Cranch) at 180 (noting, with respect to the Oaths Clause and the judges it binds, "How immoral to impose it on them, if they were to be used as the instruments, and the knowing instruments, for violating what they swear to support!").

legislation that he believes to be unconstitutional or a President who vetoes legislation for the same reason.[68]

Judicial review arises from the principle that each branch of government is coordinate, independent, and responsible for interpreting and enforcing the Constitution when fulfilling its particular constitutional role. While the federal judiciary enjoys no constitutional authority to force the other branches to adopt its interpretations of the Constitution in the performance of their unique functions, neither can the other branches dictate constitutional meaning to the judiciary.[69]

There has been much debate between those who interpret the separation of powers formally and those who interpret it functionally. Both sides can agree on the several points that follow. The Constitution makes clear that the three branches are coordinate, in the sense that they are equal to each other. As James Madison wrote in *Federalist No. 49*: "The several departments being perfectly co-ordinate by the terms of their common commission, neither of them, it is evident, can pretend to an exclusive or superior right of settling the boundaries between their respective powers ..."[70] Each branch exercises authority granted directly by the people through the Constitution, and no branch is subordinate to the others.

In addition to being coordinate, the branches are separate. While some powers are shared, such as those regarding treaties and appointments, each branch executes certain core functions that belong to it alone. Only Congress can enact legislation within the field of authority given to the federal government by Article I, Section 8 and the Reconstruction Amendments; only the President may execute federal laws; and only the judiciary may decide Article III cases or controversies. In the course of performing its constitutional responsibility to decide cases or controversies, the judiciary must give primacy to the Constitution over other actions of the federal or state governments.[71] Federal judges interpret the Constitution in the course of resolving conflicts that arise between federal or state law and the Constitution.

Judicial review's roots in the constitutional text and structure explain why reliance on foreign decisions creates difficulties. Judicial review operates because the Court, in carrying out its Article III duties, must follow the higher law of the Constitution

---

[68] See Michael Stokes Paulsen, *The Most Dangerous Branch: Executive Power to Say What the Law Is*, 83 Geo. L.J. 217, 343 (1994) ("The President may exercise a power of legal review . . . over acts of Congress and refuse to give them effect insofar as his constitutional authority is concerned."); see also Frank H. Easterbrook, *Presidential Review*, 40 Case W. Res. L. Rev. 905, 906–09 (1990) (discussing the presidential practice of vetoing legislation on constitutional grounds); John O. McGinnis, *Executive Branch Interpretation of the Law*, 15 Cardozo L. Rev. 21 (1993) (addressing the relationship between the Supreme Court and the President).

[69] See, e.g., City of Boerne v. Flores, 521 U.S. 507 (1997); U.S. v. Klein, 80 U.S. (13 Wall.) 128 (1871).

[70] The Federalist No. 49, at 314 (James Madison) (Clinton Rossiter ed., 1961).

[71] Marbury, 5 U.S. (1 Cranch) at 178 ("So if a law be in opposition to the constitution; if both the law and the constitution apply to a particular case, so that the court must either decide that case conformably to the law, disregarding the constitution; or conformably to the constitution, disregarding the law; the court must determine which of these conflicting rules governs the case. This is of the very essence of judicial duty").

above any inconsistent federal or state statutes. When interpreting the scope and meaning of that delegation of power to the federal government, the federal courts should have no recourse to foreign decisions. Foreign courts, after all, interpret documents entirely differently from the U.S. Constitution. The European Court of Human Rights (ECHR), for example, enforces the European Convention on Human Rights of 1950, which was created by the member states of the Council of Europe.[72] The beliefs of the member states of the Council of Europe about the scope of various individual rights circa 1950 have little to do with the extent of the powers that the American people delegated to their government in 1788, 1791, or 1865–70. The European Convention and the ECHR's decisions do not even purport to relate to our Constitution's delegation or power. The European Convention is an international agreement in which the party states committed to abide by certain requirements.[73] By relying on foreign and international sources of law to interpret the Constitution, the Court undermines the very delegation of authority that gives it the power of judicial review.

We should also focus on "the People" as the originator of the Constitution and the delegator of all powers under it. The states that are parties to the European Convention, no matter how worthy or progressive in their approach to human rights, are not part of the American polity and were not in 1787 or 1791. If anything, we enjoy our current Constitution precisely because the Americans of the late eighteenth century rejected their relationship with Europe.[74] Our Union was largely designed to serve as an "effective barrier against the Europeanization of American politics."[75]

Even before the Framing, the Declaration of Independence had denounced King George III for "subject[ing] us to a jurisdiction foreign to our constitution, and unacknowledged by our laws," and for "taking away our Charters, abolishing our most valuable Laws, and altering fundamentally the Forms of our Government."[76] If the Framers considered English law oppressive, it is unlikely that they would have wanted the Constitution's interpreters to defer to the laws and practices of Bourbon France or Spain, Habsburg Austria, Hohenzollern Prussia, or the Papal States. Tens of millions of living Americans descended from people who fled to the United States after the Constitution's adoption precisely to escape Europe. Nor is there any indication that the American people at any point in their history have wanted their

[72] Convention for the Protection of Human Rights and Fundamental Freedoms, Nov. 4, 1950, 213 U.N.T.S. 221.
[73] The agreement's preamble opens: "The Governments signatory hereto, being Members of the Council of Europe . . ." *Id.* at 221 (emphasis added).
[74] See Larry D. Kramer, *The Supreme Court, 2000 Term—Foreword: We the Court*, 115 HARV. L. REV. 5, 73–74 (2001) ("The colonial experience of resisting King and Parliament served as the model from which the Founders constructed their theories, and the Revolution itself, beginning with the Stamp Act protests, provided their blueprint for opposing a government that exceeded its constitutional authority").
[75] PETER ONUF & NICHOLAS ONUF, FEDERAL UNION, MODERN WORLD: THE LAW OF NATIONS IN AN AGE OF REVOLUTIONS, 1776–1814 at 176 (1993).
[76] THE DECLARATION OF INDEPENDENCE para. 17, 25 (U.S. 1776).

delegation of authority to the national government to be construed consistently with the constitutions of foreign nations. Certainly the Framers would not have thought any European treaties in existence at that time should provide a model for constitutional rights; indeed, the framework of international human rights that we have today would have been foreign to them.[77]

A "living constitution" approach to constitutional interpretation—the conviction that the Constitution should be interpreted in light of contemporary attitudes and values—also does not justify reliance on foreign precedents. There is no indication that the American people today believe that their constitutional rights and delegation of powers should be interpreted in light of foreign judicial decisions. In fact, American attitudes toward international human rights indicate the opposite. The United States has entered into relatively few human rights treaties, and those agreements to which it has consented have been ratified only with significant reservations, understandings, and declarations (RUDs).[78] The RUDs usually contain provisions making clear that the United States considers its existing laws to meet the requirements of the treaty and that the treaty is non-self-executing.[79] Such a practice undermines the claim that international human rights agreements, even those to which the United States is a party, should be given domestic effect. Certainly, the argument for judicial deference to international agreements to which the United States is not a party is even weaker.

Nevertheless, the majority opinion in *Roper* discounted the reservation, proposed by the President and accepted by the Senate, to the International Covenant on Civil and Political Rights (ICCPR).[80] This reservation was addressed to article 6(5) of the ICCPR, which prohibits the juvenile death penalty and was intended to enable the United States and its component states to retain that form of punishment if they saw fit. The reservation stated: "The United States reserves the right, subject to its Constitutional constraints, to impose capital punishment on any person (other than

---

[77] How attentive an ear the Court should give to the intent of the Constitution's Framers is often disputed. There is little doubt, however, that the Court itself often claims to place at least some importance on the intended design of the Framers. See generally Jacobus ten Broek, *Use by the United States Supreme Court of Extrinsic Aids in Constitutional Construction*, 27 CAL. L. REV. 399, 399 (1939) ("[The Court] has insisted, with almost uninterrupted regularity, that the end and object of constitutional construction is the discovery of the intention of those persons who formulated the instrument . . .").

[78] Many scholars who complain of the United States' unwillingness to join fully the international community readily admit that the cause may be a reluctance to do so on the part of American elected officials. See, e.g., Harold Hongju Koh, *On American Exceptionalism*, 55 STAN. L. REV. 1479 (2003); Johan D. van der Vyver, *American Exceptionalism: Human Rights, International Criminal Justice, and National Self-Righteousness*, 50 EMORY L.J. 775 (2001).

[79] At least three modern treaties to which the United States is a party have been qualified with RUDs: the Convention against Torture and Other Cruel Inhuman or Degrading Treatment or Punishment, Dec. 10, 1984, 1465 U.N.T.S. 85; the International Covenant on Civil and Political Rights, Dec. 19, 1966, 999 U.N.T.S. 171 [hereinafter Political Rights Covenant]; and the International Convention on the Elimination of All Forms of Racial Discrimination, opened for signature Mar. 7, 1966, 660 U.N.T.S. 195.

[80] Political Rights Covenant, *supra* note 79, 999 U.N.T.S. at 171.

a pregnant woman) duly convicted under existing or future laws permitting the imposition of capital punishment, including such punishment for crimes committed by persons below eighteen years of age."[81] Despite agreement by the nation's treatymaking branches, the Court effectively stripped the RUD out of the treaty.[82] The Court cited article 6(5) of the ICCPR to support its conclusion that the juvenile death penalty is unconstitutional.[83] Moreover, the majority opinion gave considerable weight to the prohibition on the juvenile death penalty in article 37 of the Convention on the Rights of the Child, despite the United States' failure to ratify that treaty.[84] Little wonder that an exasperated Justice Scalia was led to ponder whether "the Court ha[d] added to its arsenal the power to join and ratify treaties on behalf of the United States . . ."[85]

In addition to nondelegation and judicial review, we assess the relevance of the Supremacy Clause and the Law of Nations Clause to the legitimacy of using foreign and international law in constitutional adjudication. The Supremacy Clause does not include the Law of Nations in the supreme law of the land and thus seems to exclude it as a legitimate basis for using international materials in American courts. However, the Law of Nations has played a role in American jurisprudence from the earliest days of the Republic. We therefore discuss the two competing formulations of the Law of Nations—as natural and positive law—and conclude that in neither case does it provide a valid basis for using foreign materials as a basis for decision in constitutional adjudication. Only in the few cases involving constitutional provisions that themselves refer to international law is reliance on foreign and international sources appropriate.

On its face, the Supremacy Clause appears to bar the Court from using foreign or international law as the legal basis for its decisions.

The Constitution, and the Laws of the United States which shall be made in Pursuance thereof; and all Treaties made, or which shall be made, under the Authority of the United States, shall be the supreme Law of the Land; and the Judges in every State shall be bound thereby, any Thing in the Constitution or Laws of any State to the contrary notwithstanding.[86]

The Clause identifies three, and only three, kinds of supreme law within the United States: (1) the Constitution itself; (2) Acts of Congress enacted in accordance with the procedures prescribed in Article I, Section 7; and (3) treaties ratified in

---

[81] International Covenant on Civil and Political Rights: Hearing before the Committee on Foreign Relations of the United States Senate, 102d Cong. 109 (1991) (Reservation Proposed by the Bush Administration).

[82] Roper, 543 U.S. at 567 ("This reservation at best provides only faint support for [the state] petitioner's argument").

[83] Id.

[84] Id. at 576–577.

[85] Id. at 622 (Scalia, J., dissenting).

[86] U.S. Const. art. VI, cl. 2.

accordance with the procedures prescribed in Article II, Section 2, Clause 2 together with treaties preexisting the Constitution that had been ratified "under the authority of the United States" during the period of the Articles of Confederation. Foreign and international laws, other than treaties ratified by the United States, are not included. They should not be treated as outcome-determinative in constitutional adjudication.

The purposes of the Supremacy Clause confirm this textual analysis. The Clause helped to cement together a federal union. The Framers were gravely concerned that claims of state sovereignty would undermine the nation's independence, threaten the survival of republican forms of government, and undo the achievements of the Revolution. In their view, the Articles of Confederation reinforced the unfortunate centrifugal tendencies of the postrevolutionary period. Article II of the Articles enshrined the principle that "[e]ach state retains its sovereignty, freedom, and independence, and every Power, Jurisdiction, and right, which is not by this confederation expressly delegated to the United States, in Congress assembled."[87] Thus, to some of the Framers, the Articles amounted to little more than a treaty among sovereign states that could be abrogated by any one of them. Given the sharp conflicts of interest between states and regions, the eventual dissolution of the union was a real possibility. And the Framers feared that the Union's dissolution would result in the emergence of an unstable, unrepublican, and war-prone international system in North America that would resemble Europe. They were convinced that a fragmented nation would inevitably be swept up in European power politics, just as statesmen on both sides of the Atlantic had predicted prior to the Revolution.[88]

James Madison recognized the danger:

The [con]federal system being devoid of both [sanction and coercion], wants the great vital principles of a Political Cons[ti]tution. Under the form of such a Constitution, it is in fact nothing more than a treaty of amity of commerce and alliance, between so many independent and Sovereign States. From what cause could so fatal an omission have happened in the articles of Confederation? from a mistaken confidence that the justice, the good faith, the honor, the sound policy, of the several legislatures would render superfluous any appeal to the ordinary motives by which the laws secure the obedience of individuals.[89]

The Supremacy Clause addressed these deficiencies by clearly subordinating state sovereignty to the authority of the federal government. The Clause operates, in

---

[87] ARTICLES OF CONFEDERATION, art. II.

[88] "[W]ith the growing importance of commerce and naval strength as elements of national power and their recognition in the theories of mercantilism, public opinion and leading men in France, England, and America realized, in the words of Franklin's opponent in the Canada-Guadeloupe controversy, William Burke, that 'there is a Balance of Power in America as well as in Europe.'" GERALD STOURZH, BENJAMIN FRANKLIN AND AMERICAN FOREIGN POLICY 113 (1954).

[89] James Madison, *Vices of the Political System of the United States*, in 9 THE PAPERS OF JAMES MADISON 348, 351 (Robert A. Rutland et al. eds., 1975).

effect, as a definitive conflict-of-laws rule, determining which of various laws is to be enforced in the event that a conflict arises. This rule has two aspects. It establishes the priority of the Constitution itself over all other law, whether federal or state, and the priority of federal law, whether in the form of the Constitution, an Act of Congress, or a treaty, over any form of state law.

The Supremacy Clause does *not* explicitly address the question of conflicts between domestic law and foreign and international law. This omission likely reflects the Framers' understanding that such laws could not serve as the basis for decisions by American courts, absent the consent of the American sovereign. As Chief Justice Marshall was later to explain in *The Schooner Exchange v. McFaddon*:

The jurisdiction of the nation within its own territory is necessarily exclusive and absolute. It is susceptible of no limitation not imposed by itself. Any restriction on it, deriving validity from an external source, would imply a diminution of its sovereignty to the extent of the restriction, and an investment of that sovereignty to the same extent in that power which could impose such restriction. All exceptions, therefore, to the full and complete power of a nation within its own territories, must be traced up to the consent of the nation itself. They can flow from no other legitimate source.[90]

The second purpose of the Supremacy Clause is to reinforce the democratic legitimacy of law within the United States. To stand as the "supreme Law of the Land," a measure must either be the Constitution itself, a federal law that represents the outcome of the constitutional processes prescribed in Articles I or II, or a treaty. The Supremacy Clause guarantees that laws will ultimately stem from the preferences of political majorities or supermajorities.

Both of the Supremacy Clause's purposes are undermined if foreign and international laws are treated as the law of the United States, and especially if such laws are deemed to limit or control the interpretation of the Constitution. The Framers sought to establish a federal union in large part to stave off "the imminent Europeanization of American politics" and used "modern Europe . . . as a conceptual antitype and foil for their energized, extended republic."[91] The Supremacy Clause furthered that purpose by guaranteeing "that the corporate interests of state governments would always be subordinate to the rights of the sovereign people . . . and that the states would not arbitrarily interfere with the free movement of trade and people across state boundaries."[92] The clause was integral to the creation and maintenance of a viable American nationhood, distinct from, but as strong as, that of any other nation

This reading of the Supremacy Clause is subject to challenge. Our analysis assumes that the clause's enumeration of the possible forms of "supreme Law" is exhaustive: international and foreign law, as such, cannot be "supreme Law" because they are nowhere mentioned in the clause. But long-standing historical practice could be

---

[90] 11 U.S. (7 Cranch) 116, 136 (1812).
[91] Onuf & Onuf, *supra* note 75, at 131.
[92] *Id.* at 132.

read to contradict that interpretation.[93] Though neither the "Law of Nations" nor common law is explicitly mentioned in the Supremacy Clause, American courts have long recognized and enforced such law in their decisions. Indeed, the Constitution itself, in Article I, Section 8, Clause 10, refers expressly to the "Law of Nations," thus suggesting that such law can provide a rule of decision for our courts. And if the Law of Nations can provide a rule of decision, it may be argued, it may legitimately provide a source of law in constitutional cases.

An assessment of this critique requires us to determine whether the early understanding of the "Law of Nations" provides any support for treating contemporary foreign and international law as a source of law in constitutional adjudication. We conclude that it does not. Some of the earliest commentators on the Constitution appear to have believed that the United States, merely by declaring its independence in 1776, assumed an obligation to comply with the Law of Nations. In *Chisholm v. Georgia*, Chief Justice John Jay stated that the United States "had, by taking a place among the nations of the earth, become amenable to the law of nations."[94] Likewise, in *Ware v. Hylton*, Justice James Wilson, an influential and prominent Founder from Pennsylvania, wrote that when "the United States declared their independence, they were bound to receive the law of nations, in its modern state of purity and refinement."[95] And Attorney General Edmund Randolph, another Framer from Virginia, opined in 1792 that the "law of nations, although not specifically adopted by the constitution or any municipal act, is essentially a part of the law of the land."[96] On this view, the constitutive act of founding the United States subjected the nation to the Law of Nations; and the change in the nation's constitutional arrangements in 1787 did nothing to alter that obligation.

Furthermore, elsewhere the Constitution authorizes federal courts to apply, as rules of decision, laws that are not the law of the United States under the Supremacy Clause. Article III, Section 2 of the Constitution states that the judicial power shall extend to "all Cases, in Law and Equity, arising under this Constitution, the Laws of the United States, and Treaties made, or which shall be made, under their Authority." That language corresponds closely to the categorization of laws found in the Supremacy Clause. In addition, however, Article III, Section 2 says that the federal judicial power shall extend to other matters, including, *for example,* "all Cases of admiralty and maritime Jurisdiction." In *American Insurance Co. v. Canter*, Chief Justice Marshall ruled that although a territorial court of Florida had been vested by an Act of Congress with such jurisdiction as arose under the Constitution and laws of the United States, it was not on that account also vested with the authority to

---

[93] See Stephen G. Calabresi & Stephanie Dotson Zimdahl, *The Supreme Court and Foreign Sources of Law: Two Hundred Years of Practice and the Juvenile Death Penalty Decision,* 47 WM. & MARY L. REV. 743 (2005) (extensive survey of Supreme Court constitutional case law relying on foreign law).

[94] 2 U.S. (2 Dall.) 419, 474 (1793).

[95] 3 U.S. (3 Dall.) 199, 281 (1796).

[96] 1 Op. Att'y Gen. 26, 27 (1792).

decide cases in admiralty.[97] "A case in admiralty does not, in fact, arise under the Constitution or the laws of the United States. These cases are as old as navigation itself; and the law of admiralty and maritime, as it has existed for ages, is applied by our courts to the cases as they arise."[98] The Constitution itself, therefore, appears to license the federal courts, sitting in admiralty, to apply a species of international law. If so, our argument that foreign and international law is not "law" as specified in the Supremacy Clause and thus cannot be applied to constitutional interpretation may seem to fail.

The existence of foreign and international law in the admiralty jurisdiction of the federal courts does not, however, lead to the conclusion that contemporary foreign and international law can be applied comprehensively to decide constitutional issues. Although the original meaning of "the Law of Nations" is uncertain and disputable, it does not appear to be equivalent to the later term, "international law" (which was first introduced in 1780 by Jeremy Bentham).[99] Still less did the eighteenth-century Law of Nations embrace anything resembling contemporary international human rights law.

There were at least two main points of view expressed by leading American statesmen and jurists during the Founding period. One view held that the Law of Nations was, at least primarily, an instance of the law of nature as applied to nations. On this approach, the Law of Nations (or such elements of it as were directly founded on the law of nature) was binding on all nations and could not be varied by local law, including domestic constitutional law. On the alternative view, the Law of Nations was primarily a matter of convention and derived its force from the consent of each nation, either through treaty or by practice, to be governed by that law. James Wilson, a proponent of the former view, explained that "the law of nature, when applied to states or political societies, receives a new name, that of the law of nations."[100] Wilson argued that the binding force of the Law of Nations does not depend on the consent of the nations subject to it:

I freely admit that there are laws of nations, which are founded altogether upon consent. National treaties are laws of nations, obligatory solely by consent. The customs of nations become laws solely by consent. Both kinds are certainly voluntary. But the municipal laws of a state are not more different from the law of nature, than those voluntary laws of nations are, in their source and power, different from the law of nations, properly so called. Indeed, those voluntary laws of nations are as much under the control of the law of nations, properly so called, as municipal laws are under the control of the law of nature. The law of nations, properly so called, is the law of nature applied to states and sovereigns. *The law of nations, properly so called, is the law of states*

---

[97] 26 U.S. (1 Pet.) 511, 545–46 (1828).

[98] *Id.* at 545.

[99] See Antonio Cassese, International Law in a Divided World 46 (1986).

[100] James Wilson, *Of the Law of Nations*, in 1 The Works of James Wilson 148 (Robert Green McCloskey ed., Belknap Press 1967).

and sovereigns, obligatory upon them in the same manner, and for the same reasons, as the
law of nature is obligatory upon individuals. Universal, indispensable, and unchangeable is
the obligation of both.[101]

Wilson's understanding of the Law of Nations as the "[u]niversal, indispensable, and unchangeable" law of nature underlies his opinion in *Ware v. Hylton* that the United States received the Law of Nations upon independence. Similar views persisted for decades afterward in American law. For instance, Justice Story's opinion (as a circuit judge) in *United States v. La Jeune Eugenie* held that the African slave trade was inconsistent with the Law of Nations because it was "founded in a violation of some of the first principles, which ought to govern nations."[102] He considered himself bound "in an American court of judicature" to hold that the slave trade was "an offence against the universal law of society" and to subject those who engaged in it to "the penalty of confiscation."[103]

In 1806, Secretary of State James Madison put forward an alternative, more positivistic view of the Law of Nations. Madison identified five sources of the Law of Nations, including the work of publicists and the evidence of treaties, but not the law of nature. The Law of Nations instead consisted of "those rules of conduct which reason deduces, as consonant to justice and common good, from the nature of the society existing among independent nations; with such definitions and modifications as may be established by general consent." Madison gave particular weight to the general treaty practice of nations: "Treaties can be sufficiently general, sufficiently uniform, and of sufficient duration, to attest that general and settled concurrence of nations in a principle or rule of conduct among themselves, which amounts to the establishment of a general law."[104]

Under Madison's approach, the Law of Nations does not depend on, and indeed may be inconsistent with, the law of nature. This was the view of Chief Justice Marshall, writing for the Court in *The Antelope*.[105] That the African slave trade was inconsistent with the law of nature, Marshall conceded, could "scarcely be denied," because it was "generally admitted" that "every man has a natural right to the fruits of his own labour."[106] But Marshall nonetheless ruled that the slave trade had been universally practiced by nations since antiquity. "This, which was the usage of all, could not be pronounced repugnant to the Law of Nations, which is certainly to be

---

[101] *Id.* at 150 (emphasis added). Wilson added that there was also a "voluntary" part of the Law of Nations, "founded on the principle of consent," which consisted mainly of the "publick compacts and customs received and observed by civilized states." *Id.* at 165.

[102] 26 F. Cas. 832, 846 (D. Mass. 1822) (No. 15,551).

[103] *Id.* at 847.

[104] James Madison, *An Examination of the British Doctrine, Which Subjects to Capture a Neutral Trade, Not Open in Time of Peace*, reprinted in 7 THE WRITINGS OF JAMES MADISON, 1803–1807, 204, 208, 238 (Gaillard Hunt ed., 1908). For a discussion of the circumstances of this writing, see ONUF & ONUF, *supra* note 75, at 201–11.

[105] 23 U.S. (10 Wheat.) 66 (1825).

[106] *Id.* at 120.

tried by the test of general usage. That which has received the assent of all, must be the law of all."[107] Although Madison and Marshall differ in their emphases—the former relying more heavily on treaty law, the latter on state practice—they appear to agree that the Law of Nations is ultimately founded on state consent, not on the law of nature.

Distinguishing between these two early understandings of the Law of Nations clarifies the question of the legitimacy of relying on international materials. As both Justice Wilson and Justice Story argued, all positive domestic law, including the Constitution, must be subordinated to the Law of Nations because it is a species of the law of nature. As Wilson wrote, the Law of Nations, considered as falling under the law of nature, is "of obligation indispensable" and "of origin divine."[108] From its decision nearly seventy years ago in *Erie Railroad Co. v. Tompkins*[109] through its decision last year in *Sosa v. Alvarez-Machain*,[110] however, the Supreme Court has rejected the idea of law "as a discoverable reflection of human reason," regarding it instead "in a positivistic way, as a product of human choice."[111] The Law-of-Nations-as-natural-law defense of the use of foreign and international law has long been rejected by the Court, including the current Court.

Nor is the Law of Nations relevant to constitutional interpretation even as a type of positive law. In eighteenth-century America as in eighteenth-century England, the Law of Nations was part of the "general common law" and was not the law of any particular national or local jurisdiction.[112] Like other kinds of common law, however, it could be overruled by statute.[113] The subordination of the Law of Nations

---

[107] *Id.* at 120–21.

[108] Wilson, *supra* note 100, at 149. Likewise, Sir William Blackstone, in a passage quoted by Alexander Hamilton, affirmed that the law of nature, "being co-eval with mankind and dictated by God himself, is of course superior in obligation to any other. It is binding over all the globe, in all countries, and at all times: No human laws are of any validity, if contrary to this." 1 BLACKSTONE, *supra* note 25, at *41, quoted in Alexander Hamilton, *The Farmer Refuted* (1775), reprinted in 1 THE WORKS OF ALEXANDER HAMILTON 53, 62 (Henry Cabot Lodge ed., 1904). See generally GERALD STOURZH, ALEXANDER HAMILTON AND THE IDEA OF REPUBLICAN GOVERNMENT 59–61 (1970) (exploring but not deciding the question whether Hamilton regarded the Constitution as subordinate to natural law).

[109] 304 U.S. 64 (1938).

[110] 542 U.S. 692 (2004).

[111] *Id.* at 729; see also *id.* at 744 (Scalia, J., concurring in part and concurring in the judgment) ("The Court recognizes that Erie was a 'watershed' decision heralding an avulsive change").

[112] *Id.* at 739–40 (Scalia, J., concurring in part and concurring in the judgment) ("The law of nations . . . at the time [of the Framing was] part of the so-called general common law" (citing Edward Young, *Sorting Out the Debate over Customary International Law*, 42 VA. J. INT'L L. 365, 374 (2002) and Curtis Bradley & Jack Goldsmith, *Customary International Law: A Critique of the Modern Position*, 110 HARV. L. REV. 815, 824 (1997))). For English law at the time, see 4 BLACKSTONE, *supra* note 25, at *67 ("[T]he law of nations (wherever any question arises which is properly the object of it's [*sic*] jurisdiction) is here adopted in it's [*sic*] full extent by the common law").

[113] See 1 BLACKSTONE, *supra* note 25, at *42–55 (doctrine of parliamentary sovereignty); see also FORREST MCDONALD, ALEXANDER HAMILTON: A BIOGRAPHY 58 (1980) (discussing Blackstone's views on parliamentary sovereignty in relation to the law of nature).

to national statutory law cuts against its use to decide constitutional questions. It would be incongruous if a court could invoke the Law of Nations to strike down an Act of Congress that sought to overrule a rule of the Law of Nations. Thus, Congress undoubtedly had the authority to ban the importation of African slaves (after 1808),[114] even if the African slave trade remained permissible under the Law of Nations at the time; and the legality of the slave traffic under international law could hardly have undermined the constitutionality of such a statute. To be sure, the Supreme Court held in *Murray v. The Schooner Charming Betsy*[115] that acts of Congress should be construed, if reasonably possible, to avoid conflicts with international law.[116] However, that international or foreign law is relevant when determining the intent of Congress does not mean that they are relevant to determining the constitutional validity of that statute.

Moreover, during John Marshall's lengthy tenure as Chief Justice, the Court appears to have relied on the Law of Nations only once to decide a question of constitutional interpretation.[117] That case, *Brown v. United States*,[118] addressed whether a congressional declaration of war in 1812 had authorized the President to seize enemy property, found on land at the commencement of hostilities, that U.S. citizens had purchased before the outbreak of the war. The Court held the seizure invalid on the grounds that further legislative authorization was needed before the President could seize enemy property. Relying on treatises by several noted European writers and publicists, the Court found that "the modern rule [of the Law of Nations] would then seem to be, that tangible property belonging to an enemy and found in the country at the commencement of war, ought not to be immediately confiscated. . . . It may be considered as the opinion of all who have written

---

[114] U.S. Const. art. I, § 9, cl. 1.

[115] 6 U.S. (2 Cranch) 64 (1804).

[116] Id at 118. For different views of The Charming Betsy canon, compare Curtis Bradley, *The Charming Betsy Canon and Separation of Powers: Rethinking the Interpretive Role of International Law*, 86 Geo. L. J. 479 (1998) (arguing that the canon is justified as a means to preserve the separation of powers, shift certain decision-making away from the courts to Congress and the President, and prevent Congress from unintentionally interfering with the diplomatic prerogatives of the President) with Ingrid Brunk Wuerth, *Authorizations for the Use of Force, International Law, and the Charming Betsy Canon*, 46 B.C. L. Rev. 293 (2005) (arguing that the canon not only shifts certain decision-making from the courts to Congress and the President but also prefers legislative over presidential decision-making).

[117] We rely here on the thorough and comprehensive survey of the Supreme Court's cases by Professor Stephen Calabresi and Stephanie Dotson Zimdahl. See Calabresi & Dotson Zimdahl, *supra* note 93. We exclude the Marshall Court's decisions in admiralty or maritime law, which did indeed frequently cite foreign or international law, but which did not implicate any constitutional questions (other than the scope of the Court's jurisdiction) to which that foreign law was relevant. As noted above, Article III, Section 2 seems to make express provision for the Court to employ foreign and international law in particular categories of cases, including admiralty and maritime law.

[118] 12 U.S. (8 Cranch) 110 (1814).

on *jus belli,* that war gives the right to confiscate, but does not itself confiscate the property of the enemy."[119] Further, the Court stated:

The constitution of the United States was framed at a time when this rule, introduced by commerce in favor of moderation and humanity, was received throughout the civilized world. *In expounding that constitution, a construction ought not lightly to be admitted which would give to a declaration of war an effect in this country it does not possess elsewhere,* and which would fetter that exercise of entire discretion respecting enemy property, which may enable the government to apply to the enemy the rule that he applies to us.[120]

Brown falls into a narrow and unusual category of cases in which, we concede, the use of international law to construe the Constitution is valid: cases in which the constitutional text itself refers to international law. The Declare War Clause is such a clause. It confers on Congress the authority to create and transform relationships existing in international law. Because an exercise of that power necessarily implicates international law, it is appropriate for a reviewing court to consult international law in reviewing the scope and effect of Congress's action. To that extent alone is the use of foreign and international law in deciding constitutional issues legitimated by early judicial practice.

Apart from the Declare War Clause, a few constitutional provisions may arguably permit a court to weigh foreign or international law. A court might properly consult foreign law in determining whether a federal officeholder had accepted a "title" of nobility from a foreign state within the meaning of Article I, Section 9, Clause 8. Or a court might examine the content of the "Law of Nations" in determining whether Congress had validly exercised its power under Article I, Sections 8 and 10 to "define and punish . . . Offences" against that law. But these provisions are isolated and are of marginal relevance to contemporary constitutional law.

To summarize: the Supremacy Clause makes no reference to foreign or international laws and thus is evidence against the argument that they form part of the "supreme Law" of the United States. Although the Constitution makes various references to foreign and international law, including the "Law of Nations," those references do not open the door to the general use of foreign and international law in interpreting the Constitution. International and foreign law had a constitutionally recognized place within early American jurisprudence, and provided rules of decision in admiralty and maritime law cases. International law might also be relevant to questions of statutory construction. It does not follow, however, that international or foreign law can be controlling in questions of constitutional interpretation. That consequence would be defensible if the Law of Nations was taken to be part of the law of nature; but such natural law thinking has long been eclipsed in American jurisprudence by *Erie*. The only place that remains for using foreign or

---

[119] *Id.* at 125.
[120] *Id.* (emphasis added).

international law to decide constitutional questions are those pockets of constitutional text that themselves refer to such law.

CONCLUSION

The Court's increasing use of foreign and international law in constitutional interpretation represents another way that globalization is affecting American public lawmaking. In doing so, the Court has embedded U.S. constitutional jurisprudence with certain foreign and international norms, and has done so without any input from the Congress and the President. What the Court may not realize, however, is that its tentative steps toward a globalized constitutional law threaten to undermine the principles upon which the Constitution was founded. Popular sovereignty requires that the Supreme Court and the other branches of government interpret the nation's founding law for themselves, free from the views of other nations or the international community. This is not to say that the United States cannot converge on policies similar to those that prevail in other parts of the world. The Constitution allows the political branches to look to the world for ideas—but it does not allow the courts to unilaterally compel changes in our fundamental law based on foreign or international law.

Conclusion

This book has explored the tensions between globalization and the U.S. Constitution. It does not deny the political, economic, and social transformations wrought by the acceleration of communication and transportation technologies. To the contrary: to us, these changes are astounding. Today, writers like us can post our thoughts on the Internet, and they are instantly accessible to anyone with a computer, laptop, or smartphone connected to a network, anywhere in the world. We can move money from accounts internationally with the touch of a button or a phone call. We can examine products on the web, order them, and have them arrive on our doorsteps within the week. We can drive to an airport in the United States and attend a meeting in Asia or Europe half a day later. The speed of communication and transportation has led to the rise of international markets and networks, where our actions in the United States can produce swift effects halfway around the globe.

Worldwide transportation and communications, of course, have been possible for centuries. But globalization has accelerated its pace. Knitting the world together into tighter transportation and communication networks creates both positives and negatives. Economies and markets are more closely integrated, which generally fosters competition, lowers prices, and moves capital to more efficient uses. But globalization also allows problems, such as pollution, disease, crime, and terrorism, to spread more easily beyond national borders.

It would be futile to attempt to stop these phenomena, even if one wanted to. Rather, the task at hand is to control globalization, in both its positive and negative dimensions. Activity that transcends nations requires regulation that reaches the international level. The nationalization of the American economy and society in the last half of the nineteenth century outstripped the capabilities of the states, leading ultimately to an expansion of regulatory responses by the federal government. Otherwise, the negative externalities generated by continent-spanning economic activity could not be controlled, nor positive externalities encouraged. Similarly, globalization has spurred activity at an international level that cannot be successfully regulated by individual nations acting alone. Pollution control is a good example. Because no supranational government has the independent authority to enforce legislation, global regulation requires cooperation between independent nation-states to succeed. Nations will have to overcome the usual transaction cost, free-rider, and prisoners' dilemma problems that beset collective action.

Our book addresses how the American constitutional system can embrace the intensive levels of cooperation required to tackle global problems. We take no position here about when the United States should engage in such cooperation. But when it chooses to do so, we believe that the United States must do so in line with the constitutional processes discussed in the preceding chapters. Treaties should generally take domestic effect only after implementation by Congress. International law should initially receive meaning through presidential, rather than judicial, interpretation. States should retain an important place in the development and conduct of foreign affairs that affect areas of traditional state control.

These devices stem from the traditional sources of constitutional interpretation— text, structure, and history. They have strong support in the historical practice of the three branches of government and in the substance of judicial precedent. Our claim, however, is that these doctrines go beyond formal legal arguments over legitimacy. We believe that they best allow the American legal system to adapt to the demands of international cooperation while maintaining the Constitution's commitment to popular sovereignty.

First, our approach keeps the basic processes of the American lawmaking system intact regardless of whether the government's action is domestic or foreign in scope. Congress will still make all rules with domestic legal effect, for example, when the nation's purpose is to enact new regulations for domestic reasons or to comply with an international agreement. Presidents will interpret international law, just as they are responsible for setting and carrying out foreign policy generally and for interpreting and enforcing administrative statutes. States will retain authority over certain core areas, such as criminal law, property, contract, and torts, subject, of course, to the Bill of Rights. Maintaining the same methods for making public law prevents the desire to engage in global regulation from distorting the constitutional system.

Second, our approach reserves decisions on whether and how America should cooperate internationally with the elected branches of the federal and state governments. These institutions have the greatest degree of accountability within the American political system and the most functional expertise in foreign affairs. By concentrating authority over international regulation in the political branches, accommodation of globalization can keep faith with the Constitution's fundamental norm of popular sovereignty. Devices such as non-self-execution, presidential interpretation of international law, and state participation in foreign policy combat any democracy deficit potentially created by the delegation—whether intentional or unconscious—of decision-making authority to international institutions and laws. Our approach ensures that as our government's reach extends upward, it does not lose touch with the people to which it is responsible.

Third, our approach takes into account the functional advantages and limitations of the different branches of government. As the current debate over the Supreme Court's use of foreign law shows, those who study international law reflexively look to the courts as the main engine for the incorporation of global norms into American society.[1] This is not surprising, as law schools focus on judicial decisions as the corpus of the law. The public law litigation model in constitutional law has also made courts the focus, for some scholars, of the articulation of public norms for the nation.[2] But in the context of foreign affairs, we believe that a broader, functional approach to the participation by the three branches of the national government and the states should be undertaken. Each of the branches has different abilities and limitations. The executive branch has the advantages of speed and decisiveness in unanticipated circumstances; Congress brings broader deliberation and a more open political process. The courts produce fairness, neutrality, and more rigorous error-correction. States, with the cooperation of the federal government's political branches, possess the experience and ability to manage the intersection of local affairs and international regulation in a more nuanced and flexible way. As the types of decisions facing the government move from unforeseen crisis situations to the routine enforcement of generally applicable rules, the costs of delay drop, and the benefits of shifting decisions from the President to Congress to the states and to the judiciary rise. The issue at hand should dictate which branch should take the lead in initially setting national policy. The President should not make every decision. Neither should the federal courts.

Critics might view our argument as an effort to strengthen the ability of American political institutions to filter the domestic impact of international agreements and institutions. They would see the requirement of consent from additional political actors as obstacles to the full integration of international law into the domestic legal system.[3] If the President and Senate can make a treaty, but domestic implementation must await legislation from Congress, the United States either will make fewer treaties or will be unable to live up to more of them. This would have the effect, critics might claim, of reducing the ability of the United States to engage in international cooperation at all.

We believe, however, that our approach might actually improve certain aspects of America's ability to cooperate at the international level. While our popular sovereignty–centered approach might slow American participation in efforts at

---

[1] For a criticism of this practice, see Robert J. Delahunty & John Yoo, *Against Foreign Law*, 29 HARV. J. L. PUB. POL'Y 291 (2005).

[2] See, e.g., Harold Hongju Koh, *Transnational Public Law Litigation*, 100 YALE L.J. 2347 (1991).

[3] See, e.g., Louis Henkin, *U.S. Ratification of Human Rights Conventions: The Ghost of Senator Bricker*, 89 AM. J. INT'L L. 341 (1995). But see Curtis Bradley & Jack Goldsmith, *Treaties, Human Rights, and Conditional Consent*, 149 U. PA. L. REV. 399 (2000).

international collaboration, it may well make United States commitment more consistent and sustainable. It does the United States, or the world, little good to make multifarious promises of international action, or to undertake broad pledges toward lofty, aspirational goals, without any deep commitment to follow through with resources and deeds. In our view, more serious American promises to work together can overcome the difficult obstacles that confront cooperation to combat global problems. Undertaking the implementation of international obligations through normal domestic lawmaking processes—whether by Congress, the President, or the states—will place global cooperation on firmer grounds in the domestic political system and will make it more difficult to undo.

To take one example, international trade agreements help coordinate national policies that produce benefits for global welfare. They allow nations to pledge to lower tariffs and eliminate discriminatory trade practices. While pro-trade policies will harm discrete interest groups in each country, David Ricardo's theory of comparative advantage teaches that reducing trade barriers will benefit consumers (and national welfare) in a greater amount. When the U.S. Congress enacts the agreements establishing the World Trade Organization or the North American Free Trade Area through statute, it makes it far more difficult for Washington to renege on its corresponding treaty obligations.[4] Breach of those agreements cannot arise just through the action of one branch of government, but must occur through a repealing statute—one that requires the concurrence of both Congress and the President, or two-thirds of the House and Senate if overriding an executive veto.

Our argument draws from the insights in international relations theory on bargaining and war. Political scientists James Fearon and Robert Powell ask why nations involved in a dispute go to war. Because the costs of armed conflict are so great and create a deadweight loss, nations in a dispute should prefer a negotiated agreement that avoids violence.[5] They act much like parties to a lawsuit who should settle rather than incur the expensive costs of discovery and adjudication in court. Negotiations will determine how the surplus is to be divided between the two parties, but both sides will come out ahead so long as their share is greater than the expected value of winning the war minus the expected costs of war. Nations can reveal private information to each other so as to reduce the chances of conflict. A few problems stand in the way of communication: nations might bluff—that is, feed misleading information in the hopes of exaggerating its probability of winning; moreover, there is so much public information in a democracy that it is too difficult to filter out the noise.

To reveal private information credibly, nations can send a costly signal. One way nations can do this is by escalating the conflict—in other words, taking military

---

[4] This point is further developed in John Yoo, *Rational Treaties: Article II, Congressional-Executive Agreements, and International Bargaining*, 97 Cornell L. Rev. (forthcoming 2011).

[5] See, e.g., Bruce Bueno de Mesquita, James D. Morrow & Ethan R. Zorick, *Capabilities, Perception, and Escalation*, 91 Am. Poli. Sci. Rev. 15 (1992); James Fearon, *Rationalist Explanations for War*, 49 Int'l Org. 379 (1995); Robert Powell, Nuclear Deterrence Theory: The Problem of Credibility (1990).

steps that heighten the possibility of war, as the United States did in the Cuban Missile Crisis—in order to show how much it is willing to risk, and thereby separate themselves from nations that are bluffing.[6] To put this in a non-war context, a nation seeking a global warming treaty might actually increase its pollution levels, or impose trade sanctions on polluting nations, until an agreement is reached. The mechanisms described here, by introducing new political players or further steps in implementation, can provide a way for a nation to send such costly signals. Congress or the states can provide additional credibility to messages already sent by other branches of the government, such as the President, the President and Senate or the courts.[7] The agreement of additional parts of the government provides more private information about the United States' overall preferences on following through on its promises (or threats). More information from competing institutional sources will be more reliable because it reduces the chances for manipulation or misrepresentation.[8] Further, if the President or the treatymakers must expend political resources to win the cooperation of Congress or the states, this will signal to other nations that their promise or threat is unlikely to be a bluff. The very process of convincing other governmental actors can produce private information about American resources and intentions that may reduce information asymmetries. This information is more credible in democracies such as the United States, where voters take into account the performance of their elected representatives in foreign affairs. Democratic leaders will be less likely to make promises or threats that they do not intend to live up to, because it will lead to higher political costs domestically.

Commitment problems pose a second, and perhaps greater, obstacle to nations seeking a bargain to resolve a dispute. Even if nations have full information about their opponent's probability of prevailing in conflict, for example, they still may be unable to reach a bargain to head off war. Full information allows each party to identify the acceptable range of outcomes for the other, and hence reach a resolution and a distribution of the surplus. Instead, the problem is that neither party has confidence that the other will perform its obligations in the absence of a supra-governmental enforcement mechanism.[9] A party to a global warming treaty may be less willing to make significant investments in pollution controls or spend to change manufacturing technologies if there is uncertainty whether other nations will live up to the agreement. Implementing changes unilaterally may place the nation's industries at a competitive disadvantage or involve heavy spending that cannot be easily undone. Without binding institutional enforcement, nations cannot rely on others not to cheat or take advantage of a relative shift in resources, even though they might have complete information about each other's costs and benefits from entering the treaty.

---

[6] See, e.g., THOMAS SCHELLING, THE STRATEGY OF CONFLICT (1960).

[7] Kenneth A. Schultz, *Domestic Opposition and Signaling in International Crises*, 92 AM. POL. SCI. REV. 829 (1998).

[8] KEITH KREHBIEL, INFORMATION AND LEGISLATIVE ORGANIZATION 84 (1991).

[9] See, e.g., Robert Powell, *War as a Commitment Problem*, 60 INT'L ORG. 169 (2006); Robert Powell, *The Inefficient Use of Power: Costly Conflict with Complete Information*, 98 AM. POLI. SCI. REV. 231 (2004).

Participation by other domestic actors (the political branches) may make American commitments to comply with international agreements more credible. The Constitution's division of foreign affairs and domestic lawmaking essentially divides authority over international agreements, in which the participation of other branches is required to begin or end international cooperation. The participation of more than one branch in the making of the agreement would signal a greater level of commitment by the political system. Requirement of approval by more than one branch in termination reveals commitment by showing that higher costs would accrue to end the agreement. Implementation of an agreement by congressional statute makes it that much more difficult to undo a commitment. If the United States, for example, were to undertake an international arms control agreement, like the New START Treaty, that reduces the nuclear arsenals of Russia and the United States, Congress would have to participate by authorizing the destruction of American weapons systems. Likewise, a treaty partner would have more confidence that the United States would not breach the agreement because Congress would have to authorize any construction of new weapons systems that might go beyond agreed-upon levels. To be sure, the Bush administration had little difficulty terminating the Anti-Ballistic Missile Treaty in 2001–02, though its path was eased by Congress's earlier efforts to force deployment of a national missile defense that was arguably inconsistent with the treaty already.[10] Implementation of the WTO and NAFTA by statute means that even if the executive branch attempted to withdraw from the agreements, the reduction in tariffs and trade barriers under domestic law would remain unchanged until Congress repealed them. State policy on matters such as the death penalty or family law rules would be even more difficult to change given the large number of governments involved.

Popular sovereignty and international cooperation, we suggest, do not suffer from irreconcilable differences. It seems undeniable that following the basic forms of domestic lawmaking—congressional control over legislation, presidential leadership in interpretation, or maintaining the interstitial nature of federal law against a background of state lawmaking—creates more arduous requirements for creating international law and organizations. But making commitments to other nations through the processes of popular sovereignty, as set out in the Constitution, may in fact lead to longer-lasting, more stable international agreements. The United States and other nations, we believe, will more effectively address globalization by avoiding more numerous, yet superficial, declarations of good intentions. With all of its consequences and rapid change, globalization presents challenges for the United States and the world that will demand more, rather than fewer, serious forms of international cooperation.

---

[10] See John Yoo, *Politics as Laws?: The ABM Treaty, the Separation of Powers, and Treaty Interpretation*, 89 Cal. L. Rev. 851 (2001) (discussing the conflict between Congress and President Clinton over national missile defense and the ABM Treaty).

Index

Accomodationist viewpoint, overview, 10–15
Accountability. *See* Political accountability
Ackerman, Bruce, 230
Administrative state. *See* New Deal era
Admiralty law. *See* Maritime and admiralty jurisdiction
Affirmative action programs, 175
Afghanistan war, 210, 215–16
Agency expertise, deference to, 134–38, 233, 236
Aggregation principle, 72
Agreement on Government Procurement (WTO), 168
Agreement on Trade-Related Aspects of Intellectual Property Rights (TRIPs), 74
Agricultural Adjustment Act (1938), 61, 67, 68
Alden v. Maine, 74
Alford, Roger P., 228*n*6
Alien Tort Statute (ATS), 17, 114, 119, 132, 179–88
Alito, Samuel, 217
al-Qaeda, 114, 210. *See also* *Hamdan v. Rumsfeld*
Alvarez-Machain, Humberto. *See* *Sosa v. Alvarez-Machain*
American Insurance Association v. Garamendi, 132, 155–56, 191–93, 195
American Insurance Co. v. Canter, 246–47
American Revolution, 26, 48, 54
Amnesty International, 3, 25–26
The Antelope case, 248–49
Anti-Ballistic Missile Treaty, 114, 258
Anti-commandeering doctrine, 157–60
Antitrust laws, 65

Appointments Clause, 59–60, 62, 75–76, 78, 102, 233–36
Arms control agreements, 12, 44, 137, 258. *See also* Chemical Weapons Convention (CWC)
Articles, constitutional. *See* U.S. Constitution
Articles of Confederation, 54, 180–81, 244
Articles of War, 214. *See also later* Uniform Code of Military Justice (UCMJ)
AT&T, 60
Atkins v. Virginia, 227–29, 232–33
ATS. *See* Alien Tort Statute (ATS)
Authorization to Use Military Force (AUMF), 211, 221
Avena decision (ICJ), 200–208

Baker v. Carr, 111
Banco Nacionale de Cuba v. Sabbatino, 185–87
Banking system, 61
Bell, Alexander Graham, 60
Bellia, A. J., 190
Bentham, Jeremy, 216
Bicameralism
  error correction, 135–36
  Framers on, 10
  international obligations and, 108, 121
  restrictions within, 58
  transparency and accountability, 75, 79
Bicultural exchange agreements, 166
Bill of Rights, 89, 90, 102, 165, 254. *See also specific Amendments*
bin Laden, Osama, 211
Black, Hugo, 90
Blackstone, William, 56–57, 249*n*108
Bolton, John, 78
Boumediene v. Bush, 17, 224–26

Bowsher v. Synar, 59, 76, 221
Bradley, Curtis A., 90, 115, 124, 134*n*84,
 188, 250*n*116
Brady Act (1993), 234
Breard v. Greene, 199–200
Brennan, William J., Jr., 111
Breyer, Stephen, 205, 222, 228–30
Bricker, John, 96
Brown v. United States, 250–51
Buckley v. Valeo, 59, 75–76, 234
Bush, George W. *See also*
 Boumediene v. Bush;
 Hamdan v. Rumsfeld
 on al Qaeda detainees, 215–16
 antiterrorism policies and laws of war,
 40, 114, 117–19, 193
 executive orders, 200–202, 206
 foreign affairs budgets under, 137
 MCA enactment, 224
 nonsignatory of Kyoto Protocol, 169
 termination of Anti-Ballistic Missile
 Treaty, 258
 use of force, 111, 117
Butler, United States v., 68

Calabresi, Stephen, 250*n*117
California, foreign affairs statutes, 155–56,
 166, 170*n*58, 191–92
Camarena-Salazar, Enrique. *See Sosa v.
 Alvarez-Machain*
Canada
 NAFTA and, 31, 46, 103
 state government reciprocal agreements
 with, 166–69
 treaties with U.S., 90
 treaty implementation system, 165
Canons of construction, 235–36
Capital markets, international, 23–24
Capital punishment. *See* Death penalty
Carter, Jimmy, 140, 174
Carter, Stephen, 83
Carter v. Carter Coal Co., 68, 69, 75
Chapter 19 Arbitral Panels (NAFTA), 32*f*,
 34, 77, 103
Charles de Montesquieu, 56, 57, 221
Chayes, Abram, 45–46
Chayes, Antonia, 45–46
Checks and balances, 4, 57–58, 221
Chemical Weapons Convention (CWC)
 delegation issues and, 74, 76, 83

 enforcement provisions, 43, 64–65
 impact on public/private conduct,
 72–73
 political accountability and, 81
 scope of, 52, 70
*Chevron U.S.A. Inc. v. Natural Resources
 Defense Council, Inc.*, 134–36,
 233–34, 236
Child labor, 65–66
China, currency valuation, 24
Chisholm v. Georgia, 246
Choper, Jesse, 134*n*83
CIL. *See* Customary international
 law (CIL)
Civil War, 60, 145–47
Claims settlements, 12
Clark, Bradford, 120, 190
Classified information, 138
Clayton Antitrust Act (1914), 61
Clear statement requirements/rules,
 205–8, 224
Clinton, Bill, 111, 114
Clinton v. New York, 58–59
Combatant Status Review Tribunal, 211
Commandeering of states, 157–60
Commerce Clause, 56, 65–73, 90–91, 165
Commerce Department, U.S., 31, 77
Communication networks, 60, 61
Compacts, 164, 167–68
Comparative advantage economic
 theory, 256
Comparative constitutional analysis, 230
Compound republic, use of term, 54–55
Congress, U.S. *See also* House of
 Representatives, U.S.; Senate, U.S.
 Commerce Clause powers, 65–66, 70–72
 compliance with WTO judgments, 208
 court application of ATS and, 187
 delegation authority, 141, 221
 ICJ jurisdiction and, 88–89
 import duties, 31
 Law of Nations, 231–32
 laws of war and, 17
 limitations of, 62
 military funding, 107
 NAFTA and, 256, 258
 nondelegation doctrine and, 66–68, 75,
 79–80
 non-self-execution doctrine and, 12,
 89–92, 109–12

passage of AUMF, 211, 221
potential delegation to international
  regimes, 75
private rights of action, 95
separation of powers, 54–60
treaty and foreign affairs power, 6, 9,
  100–101, 123, 196, 256–58
WTO and, 208, 256, 258
Constitution, U.S. *See* U.S. Constitution
Constitutional controversy and
  globalization, 177–226.
    See also Supreme Court, U.S.;
    U.S. Constitution
  Alien Tort Statute and *Sosa*, 179–88
  Boumediene v. Bush, 224–26
  CIL, states, executive branch and *Sosa*,
    188–97
  Hamdan v. Rumsfeld, 177–78, 209–26
  Medellín v. Texas, 177, 197–208, 226
  military commissions, 210–19
  non-self-execution doctrine and
    Medellín, 201–8
  Sosa v. Alvarez-Machain, 177–97,
    218, 226
  VCCR enforcement and *Medellín*,
    198–202
  war on terrorism and judicial role in
    Hamdan, 219–24
Constitutional Diplomacy (Glennon), 9
Constitutional scholarship
  internationalist approach, 4–6
  revisionist approach, 7–10
  transnationalist approach, 6–7
The Constitution's Text in Foreign Affairs
  (Ramsey), 9–10
Controlled Substances Act (1970), 73
Convention on the Form of an
  International Will, 170–73
Cooter, Robert D., 128n62
Corporations, 24, 60–61
Cosmopolitan law, 21, 22, 35
Council of Europe, 40, 241
Court of International Trade, 77
Court systems. *See* Federal courts, U.S.;
    State courts; Supreme Court, U.S.
Court-to-court communication, 3, 6–7,
  227–35
Criminal law
  ICJ decisions and, 17, 88–89
  lack of federal common law, 122

state governments and, 14, 17,
  56, 71–72
*Crosby v. National Foreign Trade
  Council*, 132
Cross-border activity, types of, 21, 23–24
Cuba. *See Banco Nacionale de
  Cuba v. Sabbatino*
Cuban Missile Crisis, 147–49, 256–57
Currency values, 24
Curtiss-Wright, United States v., 6, 49, 51,
  111, 137
Customary international law (CIL).
    See also Law of Nations; Presidents
    and customary international law;
    specific cases
  accomodationist approach, 13–14, 17
  ambiguous definitions of, 129–30
  binding of nonconsenting nations, 115
  Henkin on, 9
  internationalist approach, 5–6
  international organizations and, 39
  NGO influence on, 89
  non-self-execution doctrine, 89
  originalist approach, 9–10
  presidential interpretation of, 13,
    113–16
  state courts and, 188–97
  Supreme Court on, 36
  U.S. federal courts and, 13–14
CWC. *See* Chemical Weapons
  Convention (CWC)

Dahl, Robert, 82
Davis, Gray, 166
D.C. Circuit, 212
Death penalty, 80–81, 91, 154, 156–57,
  242–43. *See also specific cases*
Decision costs, 223
Declaration of Independence, 241
Declare War Clause, 251
Defense Department, U.S., 210–11
Democratic deficit, in international law
  making, 8, 82, 104–5
Detainee Treatment Act (2005), 224
Deterritorialism, use of term, 21
Developing countries, trade levels in, 23
Disaggregation of nation-states, 6–7, 8, 35,
  45–46
Dormant commerce clause doctrine, 165
Dotson Zimdahl, Stephanie, 250n117

Drug Enforcement Agency, U.S.
(DEA), 179. *See also*
Sosa v. Alvarez-Machain
Dual federalism, 65
Due Process Clause, 56, 66, 68, 78, 119,
180, 232

ECJ. *See* European Court of Justice (ECJ)
E.C. Knight, United States v., 65
Economic globalization, 23–25
Economy, U.S.
global economy and, 23–25
nationalization of, 60–63, 88
during New Deal era, 56
trade dependency, 1
Edmond v. United States, 234
Education, state governments and, 14, 72
Eighth Amendment, 229, 232
Eisenhower, Dwight, 96
Elections, as political accountability, 78, 79
Electricity networks, 60
Elkins, Stanley M., 106*n*74
Ellsworth, Oliver, 184
Ely, John Hart, 9, 134*n*83
Equal Protection Clause, 56
Erie Railroad Co. v. Tompkins, 124–25, 182,
185–86, 189, 249, 251
Eskridge, William N., Jr., 187*n*46, 224
European Convention on Human Rights
(ECHR), 241
European Court of Human Rights, 228, 241
European Court of Justice (ECJ), 30–31,
32*f*, 34–35
European Union
evolution of, 44
fiscal policy in Greece and, 24
political legitimacy deficit, 82
sovereign powers of, 32, 47
trade levels in, 23
Executive agreements, 12
Executive branches. *See headings under*
State government; Presidents
and presidency
Executive power. *See* Presidents
and presidency
Export Administration Act (1979), 139

Faithful Execution Clause, 121
Fallon, Richard H., Jr., 110*n*87
Family law, state governments and, 14, 72

Fearon, James, 256
Federal courts, U.S. *See also* Supreme
Court, U.S.
accomodationist approach, 11
agency expertise versus, 134–38
customary law and, 13–14
decentralization of system, 131–32
federal question jurisdiction, 94–95
foreign relations role, limitations of,
128–41
internationalist approach, 5–6, 9
judges as generalists, 131
lack of political accountability within,
134–35
legal transnationalism on, 6–7
non-self-execution doctrine, 108–12
political question doctrine, 110–11
process delays, 132–33
separation of powers, 54, 57–58, 59, 60
states' expertise versus, 162–65, 163*t*
transnationalist approach, 6–7
uniformity of decision-making, 164
use of legislative history, 130–31
Federal Elections Commission, 59, 75–76
Federal exclusivity, 154–57
Federalism
overview, 10–11, 16
definition of, 4
Henkin on, 6, 9
normative benefits of, 85–86
originalist approach, 9–10
Federalist Papers, 48, 53–55, 57, 85, 100,
105–6, 123–24, 137, 221–22,
237–38, 240
Federal question jurisdiction, 94–95
Federal Reserve Act (1913), 61
Federal Trade Commission, 59, 61
Field v. Clark, 66
Fifth Amendment, 66
Filartiga v. Pena-Irala, 186, 189
Finance minister coordination, 46
First Amendment, 91, 97, 152
Force, use of, 8, 52, 103, 117, 140–41, 148
Foreign affairs, Framers on, 9–10
Foreign Affairs and the U.S. Constitution
(Henkin), 9
Foreign law in constitutional
interpretation, 227–52
overview, 227–32
Appointments Clause, 233–36

judicial review, 232, 237–43
Law of Nations, 231–32, 243, 246–52
living constitution approach, 242
nondelegation doctrine, 232, 235–37
standards of deference potential, 232–35
Supremacy Clause, 232, 243–47
Foreign Sovereign Immunities Act
(1976), 195
Foster v. Neilson, 93, 158
Fourteenth Amendment, 66, 74, 228
Framers. *See also* U.S. Constitution;
specific individuals
on bicameralism, 10
concerns about Europeanization of
American politics, 241–42, 245
on foreign affairs, 9–10
formal structure, international
delegations' departure from, 83
on Law of Nations, 116*n*8, 246
on laws of war, 125–27
on popular sovereignty, 124, 237–38
on Senate's role with treaties, 106–7
on separation of powers, 60
on Supremacy Clause, 244–45
Framework Convention for Climate
Change (UN). *See*
Kyoto Protocol
France, 23, 114–15, 141–45
Franck, Thomas, 9, 103
Freedom of religion, 152
Free-riders, 52, 254
French Revolution, 114–15, 141–42
Frickey, Philip, 224
Friedman, Thomas, 20, 24
Frisbie v. Collins, 180

Gallatin, Albert, 98
Gender-motivated violence, 71
General Agreement on Tariffs and
Trade, 43
General Assembly (UN). *See* United
Nations (UN)
Genet, Edmund, 142, 143
Geneva Conventions and *Hamdan case*,
209–26
George III, King, 241
Germany, 155–56, 191, 199
Ginsburg, Ruth Bader, 175, 229
Glennon, Michael, 9
Global civil society movement, 6, 21

Global commons, international
cooperation and, 52
Global culture, use of term, 21
Global economy, 23–25
Global governance, 22–40. *See also specific
international institutions*
global economy, 23–25
globalization and, 3
nationalization during New Deal era,
comparison to, 63–65
popular sovereignty, comparison to, 50*t*
rise of international organizations,
25–40
Westphalian sovereignty, comparison
to, 42*t*, 50*t*
Globalization, definitions of, 2–4, 19, 20–22
Globalization and the Constitution, 1–18
accomodationist approach, 10–18
deference to presidential
interpretations of international law,
6, 11, 13–14, 17–18
globalization, defined, 2–4
internationalist approach, 4–6, 9
non-self-execution doctrine, 11–12,
16–17
revisionist approach, 7–10
states' autonomy in compliance with
international law, 14–15, 17
transnationalist approach, 6–7
Globalization system concept, 20
Global warming, 52, 63, 91, 168–69
Goldsmith, Jack L., 28, 115, 124, 188
Goldwater v. Carter, 111
Golove, David, 90
Gonzales v. Raich, 72, 73
Governmental structure and globalization,
51–86
constitutional accommodation,
70–78
federalism and separation of powers,
53–60
nationalization and, 60–65
regulation and, 65–70
sovereignty and, 78–84
Governors of states, 166–68
Graham v. Florida, 227–28, 232–33
Gray, Horace, 130
Great Britain, 56, 141–45
Great Lakes Charter, 167–68
Greece, 24

Guantánamo Bay, U.S. Naval Station, 111, 211, 224
Gun control, 71, 73, 157
Gunther, Gerald, 239

Habeas corpus, 119, 224–26
Hague Adoption Convention, 153
Hague Convention on the Civil Aspects of International Child Abduction, 5, 152–53
Hague Convention on the Conflicts of Laws Relating to the Form of Testamentary Dispositions, 173
Hague Convention on the Law Applicable to Trusts on Their Recognition, 173
Haiti, 138
Hamdan, Salem Ahmed. *See Hamdan v. Rumsfeld*
Hamdan v. Rumsfeld, 17, 177–78, 209–26
Hamilton, Alexander
  on executive power, 137
  on judicial role, 238
  on Law of Nations, 116*n*8
  Neutrality Proclamation and, 142–44
  Pacificus-Helvidius debates, 126–27
  on political accountability, 78–79
  on popular sovereignty, 123–24, 237
  on separation of powers, 54–55, 85
  on treaty power, 98–100, 105–6, 159, 184
  on wartime executive power, 222
Hammer v. Dagenhart, 65, 70
Hand, Learned, 190–91
Harlan, John Marshall, II, 156, 185
Hate speech, 91
Head Money Cases, 95
Helms, Jesse, 175
Helms-Burton Act (1996), 129
Henkin, Louis, 6, 9–10, 78, 91, 98, 117–18
Higgins, Roslyn, 22
Holmes, Oliver Wendell, 66, 89–90, 158
Holocaust Victim Insurance Relief Act (1999, California), 191–92
House of Representatives, U.S. *See also* Congress, U.S.; Senate, U.S.
  foreign policy, 107
  international delegation and, 207
  treaty approval and, 96–97, 98, 104, 105–6, 110
Howell, William, 222

Hudson & Goodwin, United States v., 122
Hughes, Charles Evans, 67, 69, 90–91
Human rights law, international
  as beyond reach of U.S. Constitution, 73
  cosmopolitan law and, 35
  First Amendment and, 91
  individual recourse under, 37
  jus cogens obligations and, 38–39
  non-self-execution doctrine, 183
  post-World War II rise of, 96
  presidential appeals to, 140
  responsibility to protect doctrine, 46–47
  RUDs associated with, 96–97, 173–75, 242–43
  state governments and, 153–54, 173–75
Humphrey's Executor v. United States, 59
Hussein, Saddam, 138

ICC. *See* International Criminal Court (ICC)
ICJ. *See* International Court of Justice (ICJ)
Imperial presidency, 137
Independent regulatory agencies, 59, 62–63, 67
Industrial chemical facilities, 64
In re. *See name of party*
Institutional competence in foreign affairs, comparative table, 163*t*
INS v. Chadha, 58
Intellectual ornamentation, 18, 228
Intellectual property rights, 74
Interest groups, 105
International Boundary Commission, 27
International capital markets, 23–24
International Committee for the Red Cross, 25–26
International Committee of the Red Cross, 220–21
International cooperation. *See* Global governance
International Court of Justice (ICJ). *See also* Vienna Convention on Consular Relations (VCCR)
  Avena decision, 200–208
  death penalty in U.S. and, 80–81
  interventionist expansion of, 42
  private parties and, 36
  selection of judges, 29

subsidiary means of identifying
CIL, 129
Supreme Court on jurisdiction of, 88
on UN as international person, 26
U.S. and consular relations cases, 17,
88–89, 198–208
U.S. withdrawal from mandatory
jurisdiction of, 43–44, 92
use of force, 140–41
International Covenant on Civil and
Political Rights (ICCPR)
allegations of voting rights violations
in U.S., 38
benefits of, 92
establishment of, 43
freedom of religion, 152
as non-self-executing by U.S., 38, 97
RUDs associated with, 97, 161, 173–75,
242–43
International Covenant on Economic,
Social, and Cultural Rights,
14, 38, 43
International Criminal Court (ICC)
authority of, 45, 52
complementarity principle, 45
Rabkin on, 45
U.S. withholding of membership in, 77
war crimes suspects, 77
International Economic Emergency Powers
Act (1977), 139
International institutions, overview, 3, 5,
63, 70–78. See also specific
international institutions
Internationalism, in constitutional
scholarship, 4–6, 9
International judicial cooperation, 3, 6–7,
227–35
International law, overview, 7–8, 36–37
International Monetary Fund, 24, 31, 42
International norms, transnationalist
approach, 6–7
International organizations (IOs)
definition of, 3, 25–26
global governance and rise of, 25–40, 63
independence of, 28–30
levels of threat to sovereignty from,
32–35
new international law and, 35–40
NGOs versus, 25–26
political accountability and, 81

political legitimacy and, 82–84
ratings of levels of threat from, 32f
sovereign powers of, 30–35
types of, 26–27
International person, use of term, 26
International Telecommunications
Union, 26
International trade, 23–24. See also specific
trade organizations
International Trade Commission, 77
International tribunals. See also specific
tribunals and cases
constitutional controversy of, 77–78, 85
international organizations and, 26
non-self-execution doctrine, 89, 102–3
rise of globalization and, 3
state government autonomy and,
160–61
U.S. federal court citation of, 46
International wills, 163–64, 170–73
Internet and global markets, 63
Interstate commerce, 65–73, 101, 165
Interstate Commerce Act (1887), 61, 62
IOs. See International organizations (IOs)
Iraq, 139
Iraq War, 111, 138, 141
Israel, 166

Jackson, Andrew, 61, 93, 239
Jackson, Vicki, 230
Janis, Mark, 41
Japan, 23
Jay, John, 107, 122, 246
Jay Treaty (1795), 26, 91, 97–98, 99,
101–2, 159
Jefferson, Thomas, 142, 143–45, 238–39
Johnson v. Eisentrager, 213–15, 225
Jones v. SEC, 68
Judges, as generalists, 131
Judicial review, 58, 237–43
Judiciary. See specific courts
Judiciary Act (1798), 94
Jus cogens obligations, 38–39
Juvenile death penalty. See
Roper v. Simmons

Kennedy, Anthony, 72, 217, 218, 228
Kennedy, John F., 147–49
Ker v. Illinois, 180
Keynes, John Maynard, 21–22

Knox, Henry, 143–44
Koh, Harold, 7, 9, 39, 137, 189, 230
Komesar, Neil K., 134
Korean War, 102–3
Kosovo, 33, 47, 138, 141
Kyoto Protocol, 52, 53, 63, 169

Labor law, 68–69
La Jeune Eugenie, United States v., 248
Last-in-time rule, 95, 165
Law of Nations, 116n8, 120, 122, 126,
    181, 231–32, 243, 246–52. *See also*
    Customary international law (CIL)
Lawrence v. Texas, 227–28, 232–33
Laws of war, 17, 114, 125–27, 145–47,
    250–51. *See also Hamdan v.*
    Rumsfeld; *The Paquete Habana case*
Lee, Thomas R., 108n82
Legal personality, use of term, 26
Legislative branch. *See* Congress, U.S.
Legislative branches. *See* Congress, U.S.
Legitimacy. *See* Political legitimacy
The Lexus and the Olive Tree
    (Friedman), 20
Lieber Code, 147
Limits of International Law
    (Goldsmith and Posner), 28
Lincoln, Abraham, 145–47
Line-item veto, 58–59
Lochner v. New York, 66
Locke, John, 56, 57
Lopez, United States v., 71–72, 73

Madison, James. *See also Federalist Papers*;
    Marbury v. Madison
  on Articles of Confederation
    deficiencies, 244
  on compound republic, 54–55
  on Law of Nations, 248–49
  Pacificus-Helvidius debates, 126–27
  on popular sovereignty, 48, 123, 237
  on separation of powers, 57, 221, 240
  on treaty power, 93, 98, 101–2, 159, 184
  on wartime executive power, 222
Marbury v. Madison, 58, 121, 199, 232,
    237–39, 240n71
Maritime and admiralty jurisdiction,
    231n25, 246–47, 250n117, 251
Marshall, John
  on executive power, 123n42

on judicial review, 232, 237–38
on non-self-execution doctrine, 92–96
on statutory implementation of
    treaties, 158
on Supremacy Clause implications, 245,
    246–49
on Westphalian sovereignty, 40–41
Massachusetts, foreign affairs statutes, 163,
    170n58
Massachusetts Constitution (1780), 48
McClellan, George, 145–46
McGinnis, John, 8, 10n, 88n5, 104–5, 108
McKitrick, Eric, 106n74
Medellín, Jose. *See Medellín v. Texas*
Medellín v. Texas, 17, 88–89, 92, 156–57,
    177, 197–208, 226
Medical marijuana, 72–73
Mexico, 31, 103. *See also Medellín v. Texas*;
    Sosa v. Alvarez-Machain
Mexico v. United States, 200–208
Military Commission Act (2006), 119, 210,
    211–12, 219, 224–26
Military tribunals, U.S., 76–77, 114,
    210–19, 225–26. *See also*
    specific cases
Milosevic, Slobodan, 139
Missouri v. Holland, 6, 89–90, 108, 158
Morehead v. Tipaldo, 68, 69
Morgan, J. P., 61
Morrison, United States v., 71–72, 73
Morrison v. Olson, 59, 75
Multinational banks, 24
Multinational corporations, 24
Murray v. The Schooner Charming
    Betsy, 250
Myers v. United States, 59, 62

National Conference of Commissioners for
    Uniform State Laws, 170–71
National emergency declarations, 139
National Governors Association
    report, 166
National Industrial Recovery Act (1933),
    66–67
Nationalization
  global governance, comparison to,
    63–65
  during New Deal era, 60–70
  during Progressive Era, 16
  of social regulation, 15, 88

National Labor Relations Act (1935), 67, 69
National Security Constitution (Koh), 9
National security crises, 115, 117, 139
National sovereignty. *See* Popular sovereignty; Sovereignty and globalization
National trusts, 60–61
NATO, Kosovo intervention, 47
Neutrality Proclamation, 121–22, 126–27, 141–45
New Deal era
    Commerce Clause, 56, 65–70
    constitutional law and, 65
    nationalization of economy, 60–63
    new international law, comparison to, 53
New international law
    international organizations and, 35–40
    use of term, 22
New sovereignty, use of term, 45–46
New START Treaty, 258
New York v. United States, 73–74, 80, 157–58
Nicaragua, 44
1977 Additional Protocols, Geneva Conventions, 217
Nixon, United States v., 209
NLRB v. Jones & Laughlin Steel Corp., 69
Nondelegation doctrine, 66–68, 75, 79–80, 232, 235–37
Nongovernmental organizations (NGOs).
    See also specific NGOs
    allegations of voting rights violations in U.S., 38
    definition of, 3
    influence on CIL, 89
    IOs versus, 25–26
    litigation in domestic courts, 35, 39–40
    opposition to U.S. capital punishment, 199
    state government compliance with ICJ decisions and, 17
Non-self-execution doctrine, 87–112.
    See also Medellín v. Texas
    overview, 11–12, 16–17, 87–92
    constitutional structure and, 99–104
    doctrinal history, 92–98
    executive agreements and, 12
    globalization and, 104–12

North American Free Trade Agreement (NAFTA)
    arbitral panels, 32*f*, 34, 77, 103
    broad impact on domestic economies, 81
    level of threat to sovereignty, 32*f*
    U.S. Congress and, 256, 258
    U.S. transfer of sovereign powers to, 31, 103
Nuremberg Trials, 219

Oaths Clause, 239
O'Connor, Sandra Day, 80, 157, 229
One voice argument, 164–65, 189
Optional Protocol (VCCR), 198–99, 201–5, 207. *See also* Vienna Convention on Consular Relations (VCCR)
Oregon, foreign affairs statutes, 155
Organization for the Prohibition of Chemical Weapons, 64–65
Organization of American States, 148
Originalism, on federalism and customary law, 9–10

Pacificus-Helvidius debates, 126–27
The Paquete Habana case, 36, 118–19, 123, 130, 141, 185–87, 189
Peace of Westphalia (1648), 41. *See also* Westphalian sovereignty, global governance and
Percheman, United States v., 94
The Perils of Global Legalism (Posner), 7
Permanent Court of International Justice (PCIJ), 35–36
Persian Gulf War, 103
Philadelphia Convention, 54–56
Physical territory, and culture, 21
Police power, 55, 65–66
Political accountability
    bicameralism and, 75, 79
    in constitutional democracy, 11
    elections as form of, 78, 79
    of executive branch versus judiciary, 134–35, 139–40
    Hamilton on, 78–79
    international regimes and, 78–81, 105
Political legitimacy, 81–84
Political question doctrine, 110–11, 190
Pollution control, 52, 63
Pope, John, 146*n*124

Popular sovereignty. *See also* Sovereignty
  and globalization
  constitutional structure and, 10–11
  definition of, 4, 20, 48
  Framers on, 124, 237–38
  international judicial cooperation and,
    227–35
  judicial review and, 237–39
  Westphalian sovereignty, comparison
    to, 47–50, 50*t*
Posner, Eric, 7–8, 28
Powell, Robert, 256
Presentment Clause, 58, 75, 108,
  121, 135
Presidents and customary international
  law, 113–49. *See also* Constitutional
  controversy and globalization
  overview, 113–16
  agency expertise and, 134–38
  federal courts and, 128–41
  functional advantages in interpretation,
    127–41
  Kennedy and Cuban Missile Crisis,
    147–49
  Lincoln and Civil War, 145–47
  political accountability of executive
    branch, 134–35, 139–40
  presidential violation of CIL, basis for,
    117–27
  Washington and Neutrality
    Proclamation, 122, 141–45
Presidents and presidency. *See also*
  specific presidents
  Appointments Clause, 59–60, 62, 75–76,
    78, 102
  Electoral College and, 54
  nondelegation doctrine, 66–68
  non-self-execution doctrine, 88–89,
    91–94, 97–98, 100, 106–12
  removal power, 59, 62, 75
  separation of powers, 52, 57–60
  treaty and foreign affairs power, 6, 11,
    13–14, 17–18, 100–101
  veto power, 58–59, 240*n*68
Principal-agent theory, 28
Printz v. United States, 73–74, 80,
  157–58, 234
The prisoners' dilemma, 63, 254
Private industry groups, political
  legitimacy and, 83

Private parties, international law and,
  36–38
Progressive Era, 16, 65. *See also*
  New Deal era
Public law model of litigation, 254
Public Utility Holding Company Act
  (1935), 67

Qui tam actions, 80

Rabkin, Jeremy, 8, 42–46, 78
Racial segregation, 96
Railroad networks, 60, 61
Ramsey, Michael, 9–10, 121, 155, 230*n*20
Randolph, Arthur Raymond, 212
Randolph, Edmund, 116*n*8, 142–44, 246
Raustiala, Kal, 3
Reagan, Ronald, 44, 98, 111, 125, 140
Reconstruction Amendments, 55, 89, 240
Rehnquist, William, 71, 72, 180, 183,
  229, 234
Reid v. Covert, 90
Removal power, 59, 62, 75
*Restatement (Second) of the Foreign
  Relations Law of the United States*
  (ALI), 37
*Restatement (Third) of the Foreign Relations
  Law of the United States* (ALI), 37,
  101, 115*n*5, 205
Ricardo, David, 256
Roberts, John, 197, 201
Roberts, Owen, 69
Rockefeller, John D., 61
Rome Statute (ICJ), 43, 45
Roosevelt, Franklin D. (FDR), 53, 66–69,
  211. *See also* New Deal era
Roosevelt, Theodore, 61
Roper v. Simmons, 227–28, 229*n*10, 230,
  232–33, 242–43
Rosenkranz, Nicholas, 159, 206*n*129
RUDs (reservations, understandings, and
  declarations), 92, 96–98, 160–61,
  242–43
Ryder v. United States, 234

Samantar v. Yousef, 194
Sanchez-Llamas v. Oregon, 199–200
Scalia, Antonin, 157, 183, 184–85, 188,
  229–30, 243
Schechter Poultry v. United States, 67–68, 70

Scholarship. *See* Constitutional scholarship

Scholte, Jan Aart, 21

The Schooner Exchange v. McFaddon, 245

Security Council (UN). *See* United Nations Security Council (UNSC)

Seminole Tribe v. Florida, 74

Senate, U.S. *See also* Congress, U.S.; House of Representatives, U.S.
  approval of treaties, 92, 106–7, 110
  Bricker amendment, 96
  constitutional powers, 55
  impeachment power, 235
  non-self-execution doctrine, 207–8
  RUDs associated with treaties, 97, 161, 173–75
  separation of powers, 59

Separation of powers. *See also* Non-self-execution doctrine; *specific governmental branches*
  overview, 10–11, 16, 51–58
  Blackstone on, 56–57
  definition of, 4
  Hamilton on, 54–55, 85
  Henkin on, 6
  judicial review and, 240
  Locke on, 56, 57
  Madison on, 57, 221, 240
  Montesquieu on, 56, 57
  normative benefits of, 85–86

Serbia, 33

Seventeenth Amendment, 107

Shapiro, Martin, 109n83

Sherman, William T., 145–48

Sherman Antitrust Act (1890), 61, 62

Slaughter, Anne-Marie, 3, 6, 46, 78, 230

Slave trade, 248–49, 250

Social Security Act (1935), 67

Somalia, 138

Somin, Ilya, 8, 10n20, 104–5

Sosa, Jose Francisco. *See Sosa v. Alvarez-Machain*

Sosa v. Alvarez-Machain, 17, 119, 132, 178–97, 218, 226, 249

Souter, David, 155–56, 180, 181–86

South Africa, 139

Sovereignty and globalization, 19–50. *See also* Popular sovereignty
  overview, 22–23
  global economy, 23–25
  global governance, 22–40

globalization, defined, 20–22
  international institutional impacts, 32f, 33–35
  legitimacy and, 81–84
  political accountability and, 78–81
  Rabkin on, 8
  rise of international organizations, 25–40
  Westphalian sovereignty comparison, 19–20, 25, 30, 31, 40–50, 42t, 49, 50t

Soviet Union, former, 148–49

Spanish-American War. *See The Paquete Habana case*

Spanish land grants, 93–94

Special Counsel, delegation to, 59, 75

Spending Clause, 56

Spiro, Peter, 7

Spying, defined, 211n140

S.S. Lotus decision (PCIJ), 35–36

Standard Oil, 61

State courts, 188–97, 200, 235

State Department, U.S., 5, 109n84, 137, 174–75, 195n81

State government and globalization, 151–76. *See also specific states*
  overview, 151–52
  alien criminality and, 197–208
  commandeering, 157–60
  federal exclusivity, Court retreat from, 154–57
  federal support for state autonomy, 160–61
  functional defense of state autonomy, 162–65, 163t
  implementation of national obligations, 170–75
  new international law and, 152–54, 164
  state autonomy in foreign affairs, 11, 14–15, 17, 154–61
  state international agreements, 166–70
  Supremacy Clause, 12
  Supreme Court on, 132
  Vienna Convention and, 15, 44

State governments, overview. *See also specific states*
  as laboratories of democracy, 85
  police power, 55, 65–66, 71–72
  political legitimacy, 83
  separation of powers, 51–60

Stephens, Beth, 188n47

Stevens, John Paul, 204–5, 208, 213–14,
    217–19, 224–25, 228–29
Stock markets, 63
Story, Joseph, 248, 249
Structural issues, constitutional. *See*
    Governmental structure
    and globalization
Subgovernmental networks, 3
Sunstein, Cass, 105, 134
Supranational law. *See* Cosmopolitan law
Supremacy Clause, 20, 93, 95, 99–100, 106,
    110, 113, 117–21, 232, 243–47
Supreme Court, U.S. *See also*
    Constitutional controversy and
    globalization; Foreign law in
    constitutional interpretation; *specific
    cases and justices*
    accomodationist approach to
        globalization, 17
    on adjudicatory authority in
        non–Article III courts, 77
    caseload, 131–32
    on customary law, 36
    on damages against states, 74
    on exclusion of aliens, 48–49
    on executive power, 6, 58, 137
    FDR and federal power expansion, 53,
        68–69
    foreign law and, 18
    on ICJ jurisdiction, 88
    international judicial cooperation and,
        227–35
    Law of Nations, 249–50
    on military commissions, 212–19
    New Deal era decisions, 56, 65–70
    on nondelegation doctrine, 75, 79–80
    political legitimacy of, 83
    on political question doctrine,
        110–11, 190
    preemption of state influence on
        foreign nations, 132
    on presidential violation of CIL,
        125–26*n*55
    refusal to interpret early treaties, 144–45
    on removal power, 62
    retreat from federal exclusivity in
        foreign affairs, 155–57
    on terrorism cases, 119
    on treaties and treaty power, 6, 95–96,
        144–45

Suspension Clause, 224
Sutherland, George, 51, 111
Swaine, Edward, 90
Swift v. Tyson, 124–25

Taft, William Howard, 59
Taliban, 210. *See also Hamdan v. Rumsfeld*
Tariffs, 23–24, 66
Taxation, state governments and, 14
Technical expertise, partisan politics vs.,
    62–63
Technology Assessment Office, U.S., 64
Telephone networks, 60
Tenth Amendment, 55, 89–90, 157–59,
    203–4
Texas. *See Lawrence v. Texas;
    Medellín v. Texas*
Thomas, Clarence, 183, 229–30
Torture ban, as jus cogens obligation, 39
Torture Convention (UN), 174
Total war strategy, in Civil War, 145–47
Trade, international, 23–24. *See also specific
    trade organizations*
Transaction costs, 62, 86, 107–8, 209,
    222, 254
Transnationalism, in constitutional
    scholarship, 6–7
Transnational legal process (Koh), 39
Transparency, in constitutional
    democracy, 11
Transportation networks, 60, 63
Treaties and treaty power. *See also*
    Non-self-execution doctrine;
    specific treaties
    executive power and, 6, 11, 13–14,
        17–18, 100–101
    Hamilton on, 98–100, 105–6, 159, 184
    internationalist approach, 5, 9
    last-in-time rule, 95, 165
    law of war and, 17
    Madison on, 93, 98, 101–2, 159, 184
    Marshall on, 92–94
    remedies for U.S. violations of, 92
    RUDs associated with, 92, 96–98,
        160–61
    self-executing types, 5, 91
    Supreme Court on, 6, 95–96, 144–45
    U.S. Congress and, 6, 9, 92, 96–98,
        100–101, 104–7, 110, 123, 196,
        256–58

Treaty of Alliance (1778), 127, 142, 143, 144

Treaty of Amity and Commerce (1778), 142, 144

Treaty of Paris (1783), 120

Treaty of Rome (1958), 45

Tribal authority, 80, 83

Tribunals. *See* International tribunals; Military tribunals, U.S.

Trimble, Philip, 115

Truman, Harry, 98, 102–3

Tushnet, Mark, 230

UCMJ. *See* Uniform Code of Military Justice (UCMJ)

UNIDROIT (International Institute for the Unification of Private Law), 170

Uniform Code of Military Justice (UCMJ), 17, 90, 119, 210–19, 225

Uniform Probate Code, 171–72

United Kingdom, currency valuation, 24

United Nations (UN)
  Bricker amendment and, 96
  Charter, 12, 26, 33, 34, 47, 52, 102, 140, 147–48, 202–3, 207
  General Assembly, 27, 29, 89, 104, 131
  international person status of, 26
  lack of authority to declare CIL, 131
  organization of, 27–28
  relations with WTO, 27

United Nations Convention against Torture and Other Cruel, Inhuman or Degrading Treatment or Punishment, 174

United Nations Convention against Transnational Organized Crime, 161

United Nations Convention for the Elimination of Discrimination against Women (CEDAW), 154, 175

United Nations Convention on the Rights of the Child, 14, 154, 228, 243

United Nations Genocide Convention, 98

United Nations Human Rights Committee (UNHRC)
  domestic courts and, 40
  domestic policy requirements of, 34
  level of threat to sovereignty, 32*f*, 34
  on U.S. presidential elections of 2000/2004, 38

United Nations International Children's Fund (UNICEF), 28

United Nations International Convention on the Elimination of All Forms of Racial Discrimination, 175

United Nations Law of the Sea Convention, 43, 206

United Nations Security Council (UNSC)
  authority of, 27, 29–30, 52
  Cuban Missile Crisis and, 148
  declarations of war, 102–3
  interventionist expansion of, 42
  level of threat to sovereignty, 32*f*, 33, 34
  NGO influence on, 105
  responsibility to protect doctrine, 46–47
  selection of judges, 29
  use of force, 52, 103
  veto power, 27, 33

United States
  early neutrality of, 115
  HVIRA challenge, 191
  ICCPR and, 38, 97
  lawmaking process, 105
  NAFTA and, 31, 46, 103, 256, 258
  RUDs associated with international treaties, 92, 96–98, 160–61, 242–43
  seat on Security Council, 33
  use of adjudicatory tribunals, 76–77
  withdrawal from mandatory jurisdiction of ICJ, 43–44, 92

United States v. *See name of opposing party*

Universalist law. *See* Cosmopolitan law

Universal Postal Union, 26

University of Michigan Law School, 175

Unlawful enemy combatant, defined, 225

U.S. Constitution. *See also* Constitutional controversy and globalization; Foreign law in constitutional interpretation; Globalization and the Constitution
  Appointments Clause, 59–60, 62, 75–76, 78, 102, 233–36
  Article I, 14, 31, 54, 55, 57, 58–59, 78, 91, 99, 102, 113, 120, 122, 175, 231, 240, 243, 245, 246, 251
  Article II, 57–58, 59, 91, 100, 102, 119, 121, 243–44, 245
  Article III, 57, 58, 77, 78, 93, 94, 102, 113, 128–29, 136, 203–4, 235, 239–41, 246

U.S. Constitution. (*cont.*)
Article IV, 93
Article VI, 99, 119–20
Commerce Clause, 56, 65–73,
90–91, 165
Declare War Clause, 251
Due Process Clause, 56, 66, 68, 78, 119,
180, 232
Equal Protection Clause, 56
Faithful Execution Clause, 121
foreign affairs and, 9
foreign law and, 18
Necessary and Proper Clause, 99,
122, 159
Oaths Clause, 239
political accountability, 78–81
political legitimacy and, 83
popular sovereignty, 10–11, 47–48
Presentment Clause, 58, 75, 108, 121, 135
Reconstruction Amendments, 55,
89, 240
Spending Clause, 56
Supremacy Clause, 20, 93, 95, 99–100,
106, 110, 113, 117–21, 232, 243–47
Suspension Clause, 224
transnationalist approach, 7
U.S.-Mexico Claims Commission,
30, 32*f*, 33
U.S. Steel, 61

Vattel, E. de, 184–85
Vazquez, Carlos M., 99, 110, 158
Vermeule, Adrian, 130, 134, 187*n*46
Veto power
of UNSC members, 27, 33
of U.S. president, 58–59, 240*n*68
Vienna Convention on Consular Relations
(VCCR). *See also* International
Court of Justice (ICJ); *Medellín v.
Texas*
alien arrest requirements, 15
benefits of, 91–92
ICJ decisions and impact on state
governments, 17, 44
neutral treatment, 77

Optional Protocol, 198–99, 201–5, 207
provisions, 198

War crimes, 77
War Crimes Act (1996), 225
Ware v. Hylton, 246, 248
War on terrorism (U.S.), 40, 117–19, 193,
219–24. *See also Boumediene v. Bush*;
Hamdan v. Rumsfeld
War powers. *See* Laws of war
Washington, George, 97–98, 106*n*74,
113–14, 121–22, 126–27, 141–45
Washington Convention (1973), 170–73
Washington Naval Treaty (1922), 45
Weisburd, Arthur, 115
West Coast Hotel v. Parrish, 69
Westphalian sovereignty, global
governance and, 19–20, 25, 30, 31,
40–47, 42*t*, 49, 50*t*
Weurth, Ingrid Brunk, 250*n*116
Wickard v. Filburn, 53, 72
Wills. *See* International wills
Wilson, James, 246, 247–48, 249
Wilson, Woodrow, 61
World Bank, 28–29, 31, 42
World constitutionalism, 230
World Customs Organization, 27
World Health Organization, 28
World law. *See* Cosmopolitan law
World Trade Organization (WTO)
Agreement on Government
Procurement, 168
development of, 42
dispute settlement, 25, 52
political accountability and, 81
relations with UN, 27
TRIPs, 74
U.S. Congress and, 208, 256, 258

Yamashita, In re, 218
Young, Ernest, 121
Youngstown Sheet & Tube v. Sawyer, 209
Yugoslavia, former, 139

Zschernig v. Miller, 155–57, 191–92